The Victorian Bookshelf

ALSO BY JESS NEVINS

*Pulp Magazine Holdings Directory:
Library Collections in North America
and Europe* (McFarland, 2007)

The Victorian Bookshelf

An Introduction to 61 Essential Novels

JESS NEVINS

McFarland & Company, Inc., Publishers
Jefferson, North Carolina

ISBN (print) 978-1-4766-6500-9
ISBN (ebook) 978-1-4766-2433-4

LIBRARY OF CONGRESS CATALOGUING DATA ARE AVAILABLE

BRITISH LIBRARY CATALOGUING DATA ARE AVAILABLE

© 2016 Jess Nevins. All rights reserved

No part of this book may be reproduced or transmitted in any form or by any means, electronic or mechanical, including photocopying or recording, or by any information storage and retrieval system, without permission in writing from the publisher.

Front cover image of books and magnifying glass © 2016 wragg/iStock

Printed in the United States of America

McFarland & Company, Inc., Publishers
Box 611, Jefferson, North Carolina 28640
www.mcfarlandpub.com

To my wife Alicia and my son Henry,
both of whose patience with me during the writing
of this book was extensive,

and to John Sutherland,
whose work on the Victorians has long been an inspiration

Table of Contents

Introduction 1

L'Assommoir	5
Barchester Towers	9
Barry Lyndon	13
Bleak House	15
The Charterhouse of Parma	21
Coningsby	24
The Count of Monte Cristo	28
Diana of the Crossways	32
Dr. Jekyll and Mr. Hyde	35
Dracula	39
East Lynne	43
The Egoist	47
Emma	51
Frankenstein	57
Great Expectations	61
Heavenly Twins	65
Huckleberry Finn	69
The Hunchback of Notre Dame	72
The Invisible Man	75
Jane Eyre	78
Jude the Obscure	84
Kidnapped	89
Kim	92
Lady Audley's Secret	96
The Last Days of Pompeii	100
The Last of the Mohicans	103
Little Women	108
Lorna Doone	114
Madame Bovary	119
Marius the Epicurean	122
Mary Barton	125
Middlemarch	128
Les Misérables	133
Miss Marjoribanks	137
Moby Dick	140
The Moonstone	143
Nana	148
New Grub Street	152
North and South	155
Pelham	159
Père Goriot	163
The Picture of Dorian Gray	168
The Portrait of a Lady	171
Pride and Prejudice	175
The Red and the Black	181
Salammbô	184
The Scarlet Letter	188
She	191
Silas Marner	195

Sister Carrie	198	*Under Two Flags*	218
The Sorrows of Satan	201	*Vanity Fair*	223
Tess of the d'Urbervilles	205	*Waverley*	227
The Three Musketeers	208	*The Way We Live Now*	230
The Time Machine	211	*The Woman in White*	234
Twenty Thousand Leagues Under the Sea	214	*Wuthering Heights*	238

Appendix: Concepts 245
Index 261

Introduction

The joys of the Victorian canon of great novels are, sadly, too often lost on readers. The length of those novels can be daunting. The sometimes difficult syntax and vocabulary can be off-putting. Readers often avoid the canon, or stick to reading study guides like *Cliff's Notes* or *SparkNotes* or *Masterplots* rather than reading the novels themselves. This, I think, is a shame, since there is a great deal of pleasure to be had in reading the Victorian canon—pleasure, and the benefits of being exposed to the great quality of work within those novels. *The Victorian Bookshelf* is my attempt to provide these wary readers with an introductory guide to the Victorian canon, explaining what the books are about, why they are a part of the canon, and why they are worth reading. But I hope that experienced readers will also find things of worth in this book as well.

Of course, using the word "Essential" in the subtitle raises the question about what the canon of Victorian novels is, and how that canon is determined. Rather than wade into the troubled waters of the debate over whether canons are a good thing or not—Harold Bloom and his interrogators handle the arguments far more articulately and knowledgeably than I'm capable of doing—I've fallen back on a more practical and defensible position: that the canon of Victorian novels and authors exists (legitimately or not), and that the canon can best be determined, for my purposes, through the lens of the syllabi of college courses for freshmen. The sixty-one novels in *The Victorian Bookshelf* were selected by going through a large number of college course syllabi and using the novels selected within them as the novels read for this book. I chose one additional constraint: a limit of two novels per author, so that, within the space provided, I would be able to include as many different canonical novelists as possible.

Naturally, this approach entailed restrictions which pinched on a number of occasions. Repeatedly, I had to leave out novels that in an ideal world would have been included, and that meant I had to make some uncomfortable choices:

of Trollope's Barchester novels, which to limit myself to? Of H.G. Wells' four great science fiction novels, which two to exclude? And so on. Making these decisions proved to be in some ways more difficult than writing the book itself was. To proponents of works and authors not included in this book, I can only apologize, and blame the space restrictions. I would have loved to include more Meredith, more Gaskell, more Dickens, and anything by Charles Kingsley or the New Woman novelists, but space simply didn't allow for it.

It might reasonably be asked, "Why the Victorian canon?" Apart from the inherent quality of many of these novels—and some, like George Eliot's *Middlemarch*, are of the very highest quality—there is the fact that so much of what was written and created in Victorian literature continues to influence us today, whether in literature itself or in the wider culture, whether in particular works or as cultural archetypes. One of the earliest books covered here, Mary Shelley's *Frankenstein* (1818), has not only provided us with the archetypal modern mad scientist and with a source material for numerous radio shows, television shows, movies, and comics, but also created the genre of science fiction. Earlier works mentioned in passing in the entry on the Gothic date to 1765 (Horace Walpole's *The Castle of Otranto*) and 1794 (*The Mysteries of Udolpho*), decades before Victoria's reign, but between the two of them they essentially created the Gothic, a cultural genre which flourishes in literature and film even today. The archetypal Victorian authors, from Charles Dickens to George Eliot to William Thackeray to Anthony Trollope, continue to provide models for modern books and movies, and the cultural assumptions and arguments in these novels continue, to a larger or smaller degree, to hold sway and be argued even today. To paraphrase William Faulkner, the Victorian era isn't dead. It's not even past.

As mentioned, some of the novels included in *The Victorian Bookshelf* appeared before Queen Victoria assumed the throne in 1837, and should probably be described as Georgian or Regency literature rather than as Victorian literature. The astute reader will also quickly notice that several of the novels included here are French or American, which traditionally aren't included in considerations of Victorian literature. But the argument can be made—and convincingly so, I think—that these works are Victorian in outlook and opinion, so that even if they appeared outside the strict limits of Victoria's reign or outside the geographic limits of the British Empire, they still can be considered Victorian. The Victorian cultural and literary outlook did not suddenly begin in 1837 (nor, for that matter, did it suddenly end in 1901, though none of the books included here appeared after Victoria's death). Well before 1837 Victorian ideas and events, arguments and tropes, made their appearance, and these ideas and events and arguments and tropes did not limit themselves only to the British Empire during Victoria's reign.

The Victorian era can be divided up into three rough time periods: the Early Victorian Period, from 1837 to 1850; the High Victorian Period, from 1850 to the 1870s; and the Late Victorian Period, from 1880 to Victoria's death in 1901. The Early Victorian Period embraced change while showing an obsession with maintaining stability and consensus in the face of calls for agitation and reform. The High Victorian period displayed the dominance of the middle class while also emphasizing the idea of the advancement of both individual and government and religion. The Late Victorian Period was a mixture of contradictions, between cultural confidence and self-doubt, between faith in the social and military strength of the Empire and a *fin de siècle* angst. The three periods are more or less equally represented here by books from those time periods.

The Victorian Bookshelf is written on the assumption that my readers will not have read the novels I describe—but I trust those who have read the novels described will find worthwhile commentary within each entry. The entry for each novel not only describes the plot of the novel, but contains critical commentary on the novel as well as personal reactions and reflections on the novel—in short, what the novel is about, why it's important, and whether or not it's worth reading. Each entry is written for an imagined interested reader who will follow up reading an entry with reading the novel itself. I occasionally use words and phrases that may be unfamiliar to this reader; having a dictionary at hand is recommended.

Because I have limited space in this book, I have not been able to write about each novel in the depth that it deserves. I gave myself roughly 1500 words per novel, where other writers have written entire monographs or books on each novel. So at the end of each entry, under the "For Further Research" heading, I have included citations of other works that readers will find useful regarding each novel, as I did in writing the entry for those novels. The works listed in the "For Further Research" heading are meant to be introductions to lead readers to further criticism—beginnings, not endings.

Additionally, in the appendix I have included four entries on common concepts in Victorian literature and the novels included in this book. The entries—on the Gothic, the New Woman, Romanticism, and the Sensation Novel—are not meant to be definitive on the concepts described in the entry, but include enough information to give the reader a background in the concept and why it is important to the Victorian era.

There are further some general resources that readers can consult on the Victorians that I relied on heavily—so heavily that rather than list them in every "For Further Research" heading I'm including them here, in the Introduction. All of them are worth consulting for readers interested in the subject, and I gratefully acknowledge their contributions here:

Baker, William, and Kenneth Womack, eds. *A Companion to the Victorian Novel* (Greenwood, 2002).
Bloom, Harold, ed. *The Victorian Novel* (Chelsea House, 2004).
Bloom's Literary Reference Online database.
David, Deirdre. *The Cambridge Companion to the Victorian Novel* (Cambridge University, 2001).
Levine, George Lewis. *How to Read the Victorian Novel* (Blackwell, 2008).
Literature Resource Center database.
Nevins, Jess. *The Encyclopedia of Fantastic Victoriana* (Monkeybrain Books, 2004).
Roberts, Adam. *Victorian Culture and Society: The Essential Glossary* (Oxford University Press, 2003).
Showalter, Elaine. *A Literature of Their Own* (Princeton University Press, 1999).
Sutherland, John. *The Stanford Companion to Victorian Fiction* (Stanford University Press, 1989).
Tucker, Herbert F., ed. *A Companion to Victorian Literature and Culture* (Blackwell, 1999).
The Victorian Web. http://www.victorianweb.org/index.html.

L'Assommoir

L'Assommoir was written by Emile Zola (**Nana**) and was published as a serial in 1876 and 1877 and as a novel in 1877. Zola (1840–1902) was the leading French practitioner of Naturalism and one of France's leading authors in the 19th century.

A young French woman, Gervaise, leads a hardscrabble life in one of Paris' slums. She has two children by her lover, Lantier, but he does not treat her well, and one day he deserts her. She receives this news at a laundry, where she is mocked by Virginie, the sister of the woman Lantier abandoned Gervaise for. Virginie's insults lead to a fight between her and Gervaise, which turns violent. Gervaise wins, and Virginie never forgives her.

The proprietress of the laundry gives Gervaise work there, and she earns just enough to support herself and her two children. She is wooed by Coupeau, a roofer, who first wants just to sleep with her (she refuses, as she's had enough of men) but then falls in love with her and proposes marriage to her, which she eventually accepts. The wedding day is riotous and drunken, including an outing to the Louvre. Slowly the pair start saving money, and they have a little girl, Nana.

Unfortunately, one day while working on a roof Coupeau is distracted by Nana and falls, badly injuring himself. His recovery is slow and has a bad effect on him: he is no longer ambitious or thoughtful of the family, he just wants to get drunk and spends all of his time at the local *assommoir* (roughly, dive bar). Gervaise wants to buy a shop of her own but is about to give up the dream thanks to Coupeau's drinking when Goujet, a neighbor in love with Gervaise, gives her enough money to open the shop.

But the money is never paid back. Coupeau drinks heavily, and Gervaise is not as thrifty as she once was. Virginie returns, then Lantier, and he cozies up to Coupeau and becomes his drinking buddy, eventually persuading him to let Lantier live with he and Gervaise. Lantier never pays his share of the expenses, and seduces Gervaise, and eventually she loses the shop (which Virginie buys). Nana, now a teenager, leaves home to live on the streets as a prostitute, and Gervaise becomes a full-time drunk like Coupeau, a state she maintains until she dies.

L'Assommoir is the seventh novel in Zola's "Rougon-Macquart" series, and the best known. It is the best known because of the controversy it aroused on publication, and it is the best known because of its use of Naturalism.

During the Victorian age American, English, and French literature went through three major phases: sentimental, influenced by the Cult of Sensibility; **Romanticism**; and Realism. Realism in fiction was a reaction to Romantic fiction, with Realistic authors like Flaubert (in ***Madame Bovary***) and Balzac (in ***Père Goriot***) emphasizing an accurate representation of reality in their novels, as opposed to a stylized reality full of artificial emotions, morals, and symbolism, as had been the case with Romantic literature. One reaction to Realism was Naturalism, which more or less began in France with the work of Zola and *L'Assommoir*—it was Zola who coined the term "Naturalism"—and spread to the United Kingdom and the United States. Like Realism, Naturalist novels reflected the reality which its authors observed, but unlike Realism Naturalism was written with an ideological, programmatic intent. Realistic novels simply reflected reality as an author saw it; Naturalist novels were written to promote a common point of view. Naturalist writers believed—a belief reflected in their work—that humanity was the product of circumstance and its environment, that Darwin's survival of the fittest affected humanity, rather than humanity being something that triumphed over both, as in Romantic literature. Naturalist novels like *L'Assommoir* and Gissing's ***New Grub Street*** emphasized the urbanization and capitalization of modern life, portrayed the poor, the uneducated, the mundane, and focused on the power of money and sex and humanity's baser instincts. Naturalist writers often wrote with an eye toward prompting reform of the ills they wrote about.

L'Assommoir, as the informal beginning of Naturalism, had to bear the brunt of the immensely negative critical and popular reaction to the movement. The only real upside to this reaction for Zola was that the controversy sold novels and catapulted Zola to fame. But otherwise Zola had to put up with a barrage of criticism, from the public (which resented Zola for not portraying the poor in romantic terms or through the lens of **Romanticism**, as was the literary tradition and as Hugo had done in ***Les Misérables***), from critics (who condemned *L'Assommoir* for its language, its deliberate crudities, its pessimism, and the general squalor of its characters' lives), and from activists (who felt that the novel's portrayal of the poor fed into stereotypes of the working class as lazy drunkards, or who felt that the novel was not political enough). Beneath much of this criticism was a bourgeois horror at the transgressive penetration of the proletariat into what was a bourgeois genre, the novel. As David McMurrey writes,

> Conservative critics clearly considered that Zola had transgressed the well defined limits of what could be written about. To focus entirely on urban workers was itself new and disturbing, and to make a working class woman a tragic heroine even more so. If the workers could take over the novel, perhaps they could also take over the government; the trauma of the Commune of 1871, when the people of Paris had repudiated their national government and set up their own, was still fresh in people's minds.

Zola dealt with the criticism well, of course, being confident in his work and its portrayal of the moral and physical degradation of the working classes saying all that needed to be said ("my novels refuse to come to any conclusions because I believe that it's not the business of the artist to do so"), and confident that the work brought attention to social classes hitherto neglected by writers. Time has borne out Zola's view of *L'Assommoir*. Similarly, Zola was aware that, as David McMurrey writes, "all levels of society in the Second Empire are marked by the same general egoism, corruption, greed, cruelty, and reckless extravagance." Lastly, as McMurrey writes, Zola was confident in his portrait of the people as an aesthetic statement rather than a political one:

> It constitutes an abrupt change in the narrative mode of portraying the working classes; it is a great protest against dreamy romantic visions of the sacred *peuple*. Zola's own working notes for *L'Assommoir* show him reminding himself not to fall into a romantic or sentimental mode of fictionalizing the people. Though he had in mind more popular literature such as Eugène Manuel's *L'ouvrière* which he actually mentions, he could have included the whole of "Romantic" literature, the archpriest of which he considered to he Victor Hugo.

The novel intensely focuses on the minute details of Gervaise's life, often at the expense of other aspects of the novel. Zola, like later Naturalist authors, wanted to treat Gervaise *et al.* like laboratory test subjects, with "narrative impartiality and objectivity" being of "paramount" importance. In this, *L'Assommoir* is a triumph; like other Naturalist novels *L'Assommoir* drops the reader into Gervaise's life in all its small details and shows us what her life is like. Zola said that *L'Assommoir* was the first novel about the poor which was not a populist romance, which "does not tell lies but has the authentic smell of the people," and it shows. But this is the central drawback to *L'Assommoir*, and to Naturalist novels as a whole. So much of the novel is naturalistic that while it presents a very detailed portrayal of life the novel also has a great deal of extraneous detail, chit-chat and small talk and descriptions of environments and things that are important to Naturalism but which take time and space away from other aspects of the novel that most writers and readers consider important, like characterization and character development, narrative style, and most especially the plot. Too, Zola's chosen approach results in what Harold Bloom calls a "certain chilliness in the relentless march to catastrophe."

Objectively speaking, the amount of plot in *L'Assommoir* is relatively small compared to contemporary novels; it's fair to say that not that much happens in *L'Assommoir* compared to, say, **Middlemarch**, to take one roughly contemporaneous novel. Nor is *L'Assommoir* told as well as Middlemarch and other contemporaneous novels; it is readable, of course, and the best current translations, which include all the slang and coarse language which Zola put in *L'Assommoir*, leave the novel with up-to-date language that students should find pleasant to read, but Zola didn't particularly care about literary style in telling his story, and it shows. Zola cared a great deal about themes and structures, and *L'Assommoir* is indeed carefully constructed—but the manner in which the story is told is of lesser concern, to the detriment of the novel. (To be clear, Zola cared a great deal about the language of the story, the inclusion of lower-class slang, obscenities, and puns, which he spent so much time researching and reproducing; he just didn't care about making the language pretty or artistic.)

Zola's authorial point of view in *L'Assommoir*, somewhat buried beneath his carefully objective writing, is another example of the *fin de siècle* unease so common to the late Victorians. Among the British, this pessimism about the British Empire and its inhabitants manifested itself during the last two decades of the 19th century and appeared in works as varied as **The Invisible Man**, *New Grub Street*, and **She**. For the British, the *fin de siècle* unease was caused by a variety of sources, including a distrust of and unease with the lower classes, the changing role of women in society, and a perceived degenerations in the physical fitness of the English people. For the French, the *fin de siècle* unease came earlier. To quote Angus Wilson in Bloom's *Emile Zola*,

> the optimistic, cocksure bourgeois world of the 'forties and 'fifties was giving way to fin-de-siècle, melancholy and ennui; all but the most obtuse felt the rotten boards creak beneath their feet, saw the scaffolding tremble above their heads. Zola ... drove the public to pile up his fortune as they queued to peer at the very hell they had spent most of their lives in avoiding. The peepshows were: cleverly labelled—the Sanctity of the Family, the Honour of the Army, the Virtues of the Poor, the Ideals of the Artist, the Traditions of the Peasantry, the Splendour of the Church, the Soundness of Finance—and in each there lay a putrescent corpse, far more terrible than the skeleton the poor reader had shut away so carefully in the cupboard of his own guarded conscience.

In *L'Assommoir* it is the Virtues of the Poor which produces the unease.

L'Assommoir is a triumph of the Naturalist approach, but Naturalism's concerns—Zola's concerns—result in a novel long on tedious detail and the squalor of the life of the poor and short on the more traditional literary pleasures.

Recommended Edition
Zola, Emile. *L'Assommoir* (Oxford University Press, 1995).

For Further Research

Bloom, Harold, ed. *Emile Zola* (Infobase Publishing, 2009).
Lethbridge, Robert. "Introduction." *L'Assommoir* (Oxford University Press, 1995).
McMurrey, David. "L'Assommoir and Germinal: Orpheus Among the Peuple." https://www.prismnet.com/~hcexres/dissertation/diss_zola.html.
Nelson, Brian. "The Politics of Style." *Meanjin* v64n4 (Dec. 2005).

Barchester Towers

Barchester Towers was written by Anthony Trollope (*The Way We Live Now*) and was published in 1857. Trollope (1815–1882) was one of the most successful and prolific of all Victorian authors. *Barchester Towers* is the second (and best) of Trollope's "Chronicles of Barsetshire."

Barchester Towers is about the scheming of two rival groups of clergymen in the English cathedral town of Barchester: one, led by Archdeacon Grantly, and one, led by Bishop Dr. Proudie, his formidable wife Mrs. Proudie, and the bishop's chaplain, Mr. Slope. Archdeacon Grantly is High Church, are followers of the old ways of the Anglican Church, while Dr. Proudie *et al.* are Low Church, favoring reform. After Mr. Slope preaches a sermon calling for the reformation of aspects of services, the war is on between Grantly and Proudie/Slope—a struggle which Grantly eventually wins.

In the meantime the position of warden of Hiram's Hospital becomes open, and two men are considered for it: the Reverend Septimus Harding, who formerly held the post but resigned, and Mr. Quiverful, who is poor, with fourteen children to support, and is willing to perform new duties in the role of Warden, duties the Reverend Harding is hesitant to perform. Eventually Mr. Quiverful is given the position, with the blessings of Reverend Harding.

While this is going on the Stanhope family, who have spent years in Italy, return to Barchester. Dr. Stanhope's eldest daughter, the disabled Signora Madeline Neroni, immediately quarrels with Mrs. Proudie and begins, in a leisurely way, to captivate and capture, spider-like, all the men of the district. "All the men" includes Mr. Slope, who becomes her pawn, and the Reverend Arabin, Dr. Grantly's friend and the new parson of St. Ewold's in Barsetshire. Reverend Arabin (who is High Church) and Mr. Slope also contend for the hand of

Eleanor Bold, Reverend Harding's widowed daughter—a hand Reverend Arabin eventually wins, thanks in part to Signora Neroni's machinations.

The preceding summary doesn't really do justice to *Barchester Towers*, which skillfully interweaves a number of plot lines and story arcs to accompany its satire. *Barchester Towers*, once described as not having enough plot, has more than enough of it, so that the novel almost feels short despite its length.

Barchester Towers is indeed a satire—of English society, of the "Young England" movement (see **Coningsby**), of the High Church-versus-Low Church struggle—but it is such a genial one that the modern reader can be forgiven for not seeing the satire. Trollope is so good at giving his characters three dimensions, of emphasizing that even the best of his characters has flaws and even the worst of his characters deserves charity and compassion, that modern readers may well see *Barchester Towers* purely as a mimetic, realistic novel, along the lines of **Middlemarch**. Certainly Trollope's contemporaries admired him as a realist, with Nathaniel Hawthorne (**The Scarlet Letter**) claiming that Trollope's novels were "just as real as if some giant had hewn a great lump out of the earth and put it under a glass case, with all its inhabitants going about their daily business, and not suspecting that they were being made a show of."

But satire *Barchester Towers* is, and some of the best satire of the century short of Jane Austen (see **Emma**, **Pride and Prejudice**). (Some prefer to put the novel into the comic category, but it seems clear to me that it is more accurately called a satire.) Henry James called Trollope "safe" and criticized him on the grounds that "he never played with a subject, never juggled with the sympathies or the credulity of his reader, was never in the least paradoxical or mystifying"—which is a peculiarly wrongheaded critical position to assume. As James Kincaid points out, *Barchester Towers* "quietly [subverted] many of the major tenets of traditional comedy," from its distrust of the young and admiration for the aged to its contempt for social groups *en masse* to the way in which the novel's "moral approval is directly proportionate to the decrease of power" of characters.

One of *Barchester Towers*' (admittedly minor) flaws is that the satire is predominant for roughly the first two hundred pages. Trollope is so busy shotgunblasting satire in every direction that his characters, real though they are, do not engage the readers' emotions. But if the modern reader sticks with Trollope and continues reading, to reach the Quiverful sections, that reader will find his or her sympathies suddenly engaged. *Barchester Towers* makes an almost *abrupt* change, from satire to drama, leaving the reader—not gasping, exactly—but suddenly hooked and flying across the pages, wanting to know what happens next.

Some readers find Trollope's authorial choices interfere with the reading experience, specifically, Trollope's decision to make his narrator intrusive and omniscient, a clear example of the influence of Thackeray (see **Barry Lyndon**,

Vanity Fair) (and before him Henry Fielding) on Trollope. Trollope's deployment of the narrator, and the narrator's tendency to reveal the endings of story arcs long before the text reaches them, can be off-putting to the reader, as it certainly was to Trollope's contemporaries. But Trollope uses his intrusive narrator voice more during the satire section of *Barchester Towers* than during the dramatic section, so that the intrusive narrator gradually becomes less distracting as the novel progresses.

A third flaw in the novel, and perhaps the most serious one as far as modern readers are concerned, is Trollope's assumption that all readers will be as familiar with the inner doings of the Anglican Church and religion as his contemporary readers were. (This is slightly unfair, as obviously Trollope was writing for his contemporaries rather than for posterity.) "Personal chaplain," prebendaries, deaconries—these are all details which the modern reader, in all likelihood, is unacquainted with. Trollope's creation of Barsetshire is detailed and living—Barsetshire is as alive in its way as Austen's Highbury (see *Emma*)—but the amount of detail can be off-putting for modern readers, who will need to have an encyclopedia (or a good set of annotations) on hand to comprehend the intricacies of the Anglican Church. Barsetshire is wonderfully vivid, but slightly alien as well, and this alienness can pose a barrier to modern readers.

These flaws are minor in comparison to the successes of the novel. *Barchester Towers* is the second of the six "Barsetshire Chronicles" series, but the reader does not need to have read the preceding novel, *The Warden*, to enjoy *Barchester Towers*; Trollope does such a splendid job of creating his world that the reader is barely ever reminded that Trollope is revisiting Barchester rather than creating it anew. *Barchester Towers*, though not a best-seller, was met with great critical acclaim on publication—understandably.

Barchester Towers has a multitude of virtues. Although a satire, its humor and indeed its general tenor are gentle, and although it is realist enough for any modern reader Trollope handles the realism gently, without the fury of a Dickens, much less the coarseness of a Naturalist (see **L'Assommoir, Nana**). Trollope's characters are mocked—note, for example, the comically inflated rhetoric that he uses to describe Mrs. Proudie or the conflicts between the clerics—but always with affection. Indeed, Trollope even describes the characters' flaws in a compassionate way. As James Kincaid writes,

> All his good characters have faults, but all his bad characters have their good points. Most of the time when a writer does this with his characters, he is excusing bad characters for doing, thinking, or being bad; he is excusing the badness. With Trollope, the impression is more that of a man trying to bring out the best in sinful people, without moral confusion. A good writer, I have heard it said, is one that can show you how to love the unloveable. Trollope has this gift—has it perhaps in greater quantities than any other author I've read. Even Mr. Slope is worthy of charity.

This particular book, even more so than *The Warden*, is a wonderful book about just that—charity, the Christian love of the unloveable. This kind of love is the kind of love which Christ said would be the hallmark of the true Church (John 13:35). This book, about divisive church politics in a town full of clergymen, records the triumph of charity over differences of opinion, doctrine, and temperament—as well as documenting the dangers that arise from a lack of charity.

Interestingly, *Barchester Towers* is a satire which ultimately has a conservative bent. Satirists and ironists are generally opposed to those in power—traditionally calling for liberal politics. But *Barchester Towers*, with its High Church leanings (Archbishop Grantly is notably the good guy in the Grantly-Proudie/Slope fight, and Slope is emphatically the bad guy), its traditional views of women (some might say misogynistic views, at least those voiced by the narrator), and its prudish sexual politics, is certainly a conservative work. But Trollope is too skilled a writer to let his politics guide his work, rather than flavor it; Trollope is interested in portraying the futility of human strivings, in carefully deploying irony, and in being a realist of the modern day, unlike Dickens and Thackeray. In fact, *Barchester Towers*, with its concerns about the role of religion, the Anglican Church, and the Catholic Church in modern England, is actually a "Condition of England" novel. During the 1840s English philosophers and legislators were forced to deal with the byproducts of the 18th century's economic growth. These problems, which included gross urban overpopulation, insufficient housing, bad sanitation, and high levels of unemployment, were described by the writer Thomas Carlyle as "the Condition of England." Writers from Benjamin Disraeli (in **Coningsby**) to Mrs. Gaskell (in **Mary Barton** and **North and South**) wrote novels, variously called "Condition of England novels," "industrial fiction," and "social problem novels," which examined the changes in the social classes and social structure and the current state of England. *Barchester Towers* focuses on the changes which modernity was forcing on the Anglican Church.

Barchester Towers is a gentle satire that rewards readers with constant quiet good humor and vividly-drawn characters. Its plot is complicated but is nicely resolved. It well deserves the designation "classic."

Recommended Edition

Trollope, Anthony. *Barchester Towers* (Oxford World's Classics, 2008).

For Further Research

Kincaid, James R. "Barchester Towers and the Nature of Conservative Comedy." *ELH* v37n4 (Dec. 1970).
Moore, Catherine E. "Barchester Towers." *Masterplots* Fourth Edition (Dec. 2010).
Sutherland, John. "Introduction." *Barchester Towers* (Oxford World's Classics, 2008).
Walker, Annalise K. "On Trollope's Barchester Series." http://www.victorianweb.org/authors/trollope/walker1.html.

Barry Lyndon

Barry Lyndon was written by William Makepeace Thackeray (***Vanity Fair***) and was published in serial form in 1844 and as a novel in 1856. Thackeray (1811–1863) was in his lifetime ranked second only to Charles Dickens, but today is known primarily for *Vanity Fair*.

Barry Lyndon is about the Irish rogue Redmond Barry, who is filled with pride despite his impoverished nobleman's upbringing but whose mother treats him well. As a teenager he is a brawler and bully. He falls in love with the older Nora Brady, who is in love with an Englishman. Infuriated that she should love someone else, Barry insults the Englishman and fights a duel with him, wounding him. Believing the man dead, Barry runs away and after an encounter with an adventuress joins up with the English Army, to fight in Europe during the Seven Years War. After a time he deserts to the Prussians, but after making his way up through the ranks and gaining a reputation as a scoundrel and bully he deserts from the Prussian service to become a professional gambler alongside his uncle. He is successful at this, but loses the hand of a wealthy heiress because of his involvement in a court intrigue.

Barry and his uncle gamble their way through Europe, but when he meets the Lyndons, who own the former Barry lands, Barry sets his mind to becoming the next Lord Lyndon. (The current Lord Lyndon is not in the greatest of health.) Through guile, blackmail, and intimidation Barry forces himself upon Lady Lyndon until he finally wears her down and becomes Barry Lyndon. As Lord Lyndon Barry lives a spendthrift life, browbeating (and physically beating) his wife and spending her money freely. He is elected to Parliament, and he and his wife even have a son, Bryan. But things go bad for Barry. Bryan is killed in a riding accident, aged nine, and Barry's unpopularity leads him to lose a second election. Then Lady Lyndon engineers an escape attempt from Barry's clutches, and Barry is cast out from the house. Eventually he is caught up for debt and sent to Fleet Prison, where he dies of delirium tremens after many years of imprisonment.

Like *Vanity Fair*, *Barry Lyndon* is a "novel without a hero," featuring instead an unlikable protagonist. *Barry Lyndon* is fact a fine representative of that genre of literature known as the rogue's novel, picaresque narratives about the lives, loves, and adventures of scapegraces, scoundrels, rogues and ne'er do wells. Thackeray quite deliberately and successfully imitated previous rogue's novel writers, 18th century authors like Daniel Defoe, Tobias Smollett, and Henry Fielding, especially Fielding's *The History of the Life of the Late Mr. Jonathan Wild the Great* (1743), in writing *Barry Lyndon*, while putting his own spin on the genre. (An excellent modern example of the rogue's novel—and, indeed, one undoubtedly influenced by *Barry Lyndon*—is George MacDonald Fraser's "Flashman" series of novels.)

Whether or not the reader actually enjoys *Barry Lyndon* is going to depend on their tolerance for rogue's novels and their deliberately unlikable protagonists. They are scoundrels and rogues, bullies and roarers, cowards and gamblers, mistreater of women and children, and many other traits designed to make them disliked by the reader, especially the modern reader, for whom likability has become a major part of whether or not a book is seen as good or not. Barry is a good example of these rogues, having all their traits to excess, and the modern reader can be forgiven for disliking him and preferring not to spend their time in his company. (Many protagonists of rogue's novels are somehow likable despite themselves; one finds oneself rooting for Fraser's Flashman, for example, despite his many despicable qualities.)

But there is more to *Barry Lyndon* than just a picaresque story. The novel is a comedy, first of all, albeit one in which the reader laughs at Barry Lyndon as much as it laughs with him. The comedy of the rogue's novel may not be one that the modern reader appreciates as funny; it is a sardonic kind of comedy, cynical and ironic, poking harsh fun at a wide variety of topics, and for readers accustomed to kinder, more modern comedy the humor of the rogue's novel and of *Barry Lyndon* can be hard to appreciate or see as funny. *Barry Lyndon* mocks not just its titular character and his appalling vices, but also many of the traits of Thackeray's contemporaries: egoism, materialism, pretense, opportunism, cowardly violence, and even imperialism. (This judgment, and the general harshness of the novel, were criticized when *Barry Lyndon* was first published, and were undoubtedly the cause of *Barry Lyndon* not being published as a collected novel for many years and being generally overshadowed by *Vanity Fair*.) Nor does Thackeray approve of Barry; the overt ironic condemnation of *Vanity Fair* is missing, but Thackeray lets the results of Barry's life speak for themselves, so that the reader spends his time in the company of a contemptible scoundrel, something Thackeray's contemporaries were loth to do, at least while reading.

Barry Lyndon is also a commentary on the Irish novel so popular with the Victorians. The Irish novel, written by Irish novelists, was usually a picaresque adventure in which the picaros adventured during the Napoleonic War, to successful (financial and moral) ends. Thackeray satirizes this genre, showing that it is what Thackeray portrays as Barry's stereotypically Irish traits that lead to what George O'Brien writes are Barry's failure to "integrate himself with the morality, decorum, laws of property, and codes of gentlemanliness that a responsible member of British society must observe."

Barry Lyndon has never been as popular as Vanity Fair, having among other things a much less appealing protagonist; in the words of John Sutherland, "the novel is a *tour de force* of ironic narration but so bitter in tone as to make even Thackeray wonder if it was worth writing." Nonetheless, Barry Lyndon is prime Thackeray. It has a very well constructed plot, an excellent first person voice, a suitably hard-edged satire, and a skillful application of the unreliable narrator. If the modern reader can swallow Lyndon himself they will be rewarded with an entertaining picaresque.

Recommended Edition
Thackeray, William Makepeace. *Barry Lyndon* (Oxford World's Classics, 2009).

For Further Research
Allingham, Philip V. "W.M. Thackeray's 'The Luck of Barry Lyndon' (1844)." http://victorianweb.org/authors/wmt/pva185.html.
Colby, Robert A. "Barry Lyndon and the Irish Hero." *Nineteenth-Century Fiction* v21n2 (Sept. 1966).
O'Brien, George. "Barry Lyndon." *Masterplots* Fourth Edition (Dec. 2010).

Bleak House

Bleak House was written by Charles Dickens (**Great Expectations**) and appeared in serial form from 1852 to 1853 and as a novel in 1853. Dickens (1812–1870) is arguably the most important and popular British writer of all time. *Bleak House* is a vastly entertaining work which has been called by at least one critic the greatest British novel of the 19th century.

Bleak House is about two things: "Jarndyce and Jarndyce," a never-ending lawsuit of several generations' standing, and Esther Summerson, a poor woman who endures a loveless childhood. When Esther is fourteen her cruel godmother dies, and Esther is taken into the care of John Jarndyce, a descendant of the original Jarndyces. Mr. Jarndyce brings Esther to his country mansion, Bleak House, to be the companion of his cousins Ada and Richard, who are Esther's age. All three become fast friends.

Meanwhile Sir Leicester and Lady Dedlock, a well-to-do couple in Lincolnshire, become involved in the Jarndyce and Jarndyce case when their lawyer, the formidable Mr. Tulkinghorn, shows Lady Dedlock a document whose handwriting causes Lady Dedlock to faint. Tulkinghorn is intrigued and traces the document, which reveals that Lady Dedlock had, years before, had a child out of wedlock: Esther herself.

Esther's friend Richard, who is part of the Jarndyce case, becomes obsessed with the suit. He abandons all efforts to establish a career and devotes himself to solving the case. Richard's obsession leads to a separation, but Ada marries Richard so that Richard can use her money to pay off the debts he incurs. Esther falls badly ill with smallpox, and when she recovers Lady Dedlock reveals herself to Esther as her mother. Mr. Jarndyce proposes marriage to Esther, and she happily accepts. Tulkinghorn, who is subtly blackmailing Lady Dedlock, is murdered, and the indomitable policeman Inspector Bucket begins pursuing his murderer, eventually catching her.

Finally Jarndyce's will is found. Richard and Ada are declared the heirs, but the suit has gone on so long that the entire fortune has been eaten up by the court costs. This shock destroys Richard's health, and he dies soon after the declaration, so that Mr. Jarndyce is left to take care of Ada and her son. Jarndyce realizes that Esther feels gratitude and great affection for him, not love, and that her true love is Allan Woodcourt, a doctor who had testified in the suit, and Jarndyce releases her from their agreement. She marries Allan, and they live happily ever after.

There are angry novels that are single-minded in their anger: *Nana*, for example, is angry at French society, and returns to that anger, over and over. But Dickens, in *Bleak House*, wanted to do something more. He wanted to panoramically create in fiction the world of Britain, circa 1852, from top to bottom, and *then* condemn it wholesale. And he succeeded, in a novel of sustained fury.

During the 1840s English philosophers and legislators were forced to deal with the byproducts of the 18th century's economic growth. These problems, which included gross urban overpopulation, insufficient housing, bad sanitation, and high levels of unemployment, were described by the writer Thomas Carlyle as "the Condition of England." Writers from Benjamin Disraeli (in **Coningsby**) to Mrs. Gaskell (in **Mary Barton** and **North and South**) wrote novels, variously called "Condition of England novels," "industrial fiction," and "social problem novels," which examined the changes in the social classes and social structure and the current state of England. *Bleak House* is a Condition of England novel in which the Condition of England is stagnant, diseased, and infuriating. Eighteen fifty-one was year of the Great Exhibition in London, an international exhibition meant to show the world that England was the world leader in industrial and social achievement. Dickens wrote *Bleak House* as a rebuke to the Great Exhibition—in the words of critical Daniel Burt, the novel is "a dissenting vision in which Dickens portrayed not an age of progress but a stagnated society, ruled by a crippling selfishness that refused to acknowledge social obligations or the inextricable link between the haves and the have-nots."

One of Dickens' specific intents in writing *Bleak House* was to savage the British legal system for its retarded backwardness, its almost malicious slowness, and its horrible, self-serving maze of laws which served the lawyers and their bank accounts far more than it served those unfortunate enough to become involved in a suit. Dickens succeeded; no modern reader of *Bleak House* can read its portrayal of Jarndyce and Jarndyce without feeling contempt for the legal system and some small measure of satisfaction that, even with their flaws, modern, civilized legal systems are not nearly so ghastly:

> Jarndyce and Jarndyce drones on. This scarecrow of a suit has, in course of time, become so complicated that no man alive knows what it means. The parties to it understand it least, but it has been observed that no two Chancery lawyers can talk about it for five minutes without coming to a total disagreement as to all the premises. Innumerable children have been born into the cause; innumerable young people have married into it; innumerable old people have died out of it. Scores of persons have deliriously found themselves made parties in Jarndyce and Jarndyce without knowing how or why; whole families have inherited legendary hatreds with the suit. The little plaintiff or defendant who was promised a new rocking horse when Jarndyce and Jarndyce should be settled has grown up, possessed himself of a real horse, and trotted away into the other world. Fair wards of court have faded into mothers and grandmothers; a long procession of Chancellors has come in and gone out; the legion of bills in the suit have been transformed into mere bills of mortality; there are not three Jarndyces left upon the earth perhaps since old Tom Jarndyce in despair blew his brains out at a coffee house in Chancery Lane; but Jarndyce and Jarndyce still drags its dreary length before the court, perennially hopeless....
>
> How many people out of the suit Jarndyce and Jarndyce has stretched forth its unwholesome hand to spoil and corrupt would be a very wide question. From the master upon whose impaling files reams of dusty warrants in Jarndyce and Jarndyce have grimly writhed into many shapes, down to the copying clerk in the Six Clerks' Office who has copied his tens of thousands of Chancery folio pages under that eternal heading, no man's nature has been made better by it. In trickery, evasion, procrastination, spoliation, botheration, under false pretences of all sorts, there are influences that can never come to good. The very solicitors' boys who have kept the wretched suitors at bay, by protesting time out of mind that Mr. Chizzle, Mizzle, or otherwise was particularly engaged and had appointments until dinner, may have got an extra moral twist and shuffle into themselves out of Jarndyce and Jarndyce. The receiver in the cause has acquired a goodly sum of money by it but has acquired too a distrust of his own mother and a contempt for his own kind. Chizzle, Mizzle, and otherwise have lapsed into a habit of vaguely promising themselves that they will look into that outstanding little matter and see what can be done for Drizzle who was not well used when Jarndyce and Jarndyce shall be got out of

the office. Shirking and sharking in all their many varieties have been sown broadcast by the ill-fated cause; and even those who have contemplated its history from the outermost circle of such evil have been insensibly tempted into a loose way of letting bad things alone to take their own bad course, and a loose belief that if the world go wrong it was in some off hand manner never meant to go right.

Secondarily, Dickens shows his fury at the state of the poor of London, whose plight is empathetically and at times harrowingly shown. Oscar Wilde (*The Picture of Dorian Gray*) reportedly said of Dickens' *The Old Curiosity Shop* that "one must have a heart of stone to read the death of Little Nell without laughing." Of *Bleak House*, only those readers without a heart altogether will read the death of Jo, a poor street sweeper boy, without feeling pity and sadness. (As Vladimir Nabokov points out, miserable children is one of the themes of *Bleak House*.) One of the usual criticisms of Dickens is that he is emotionally manipulative and too sentimental—that, as Aldous Huxley wrote, "whenever in writing he becomes emotional, he ceases instantly to use his intelligence." There are certainly moments in *Bleak House* when Dickens' gush of almost saccharine sweetness can be too much. But far more often he is "emotional" in writing about the desperation and crushingly difficult lives of his poor characters, of the hopelessness of the victims of the British legal system and the wasted lives of those entangled in Jarndyce and Jarndyce, of the damage done to children whose activist parents care far more about those who live far away than about their own families. The longer death scenes in *Bleak House* are blatantly manipulative attempts to wring tears from the reader, but there are many more moments when Dickens writes about those done wrong by society, and in those moments Dickens is more economical, much less didactic, extremely effective, and not at all lacking intelligence.

In one regard Dickens is not sentimental at all. There is comedy and laughter to be had from *Bleak House*, but there is a lot of sadness, as well. Dickens shows no hesitation in killing off characters, from significant ones, like Richard Carstone and Lady Dedlock, to minor ones, like the death of the baby of the homeless woman Jenny and the deaths of the parents of Charley, who becomes Esther's assistant. Dickens' purpose may have been to arouse emotions and manipulate the reader, but he also shows a fitting hardness. The world of *Bleak House* is a harsh one, and Dickens does not soften the blows, from the painful unhappiness of the Jellyby family and the Jellyby marriage to the gruesome spontaneous combustion scene of the junk dealer Krook to Esther's disfigurement. Some of the most damaging characters are, realistically, not villains but simply self-centered people, like the monstrously selfish Mr. Skimpole. And hypocritical and heartless activists like Mrs. Jellyby and Mrs. Pardiggle, and vain, empty evangelicals like Mr. Chadband, are given a well-deserved back-of-the-hand by Dickens.

Anger of course is not enough to create a great novel. To achieve greatness, enormous skill is required, and that Dickens has in abundance. The plot of *Bleak House* is intricate—the above summary does not do the plot justice in the slightest—and as a whole it is Dickens' most ambitious novel.

He is enormously entertaining in his language—as the long passage quoted above shows. The use of the *mot juste*, the memorable image heaped on top of memorable image, the wisdom regarding human character, the sometimes dark humor—they are all there. As Nabokov says, "all we have to do when reading *Bleak House* is to relax and let our spines take over." Dickens of course has a multitude of virtues as a novelist, so that it is clear, on reading *Bleak House*, why he is called the greatest of the Victorian novelists. His only fault, and this may not bother most readers, is that the book is very long, but the cast of *Bleak House* is large, and a great deal happens, and therefore Dickens needs the space to resolve all the many plots.

Dickens is splendid. He can make the modern reader laugh out loud, which is no small thing for a book a century and a half old. His descriptions are generally marvelous, so that places, like Chesney Wold and London, become characters. Dickens' names—"Caddy Jellyby," "Mrs. Pardiggle," "Mr. Turveydrop"—are so wonderfully idiosyncratic and singular that his very name has been adopted for use as a descriptive: "Dickensian" says as much as any adjective. He splendidly succeeds in creating an entire society, with members of the highest and lowest classes, so that the entire world of *Bleak House* feels real in a way that few other fictional worlds do. Dickens has vivid, colorful characterization, although his people can be exaggerated and caricatures. Dickens is particularly good with portraying women in a realistic fashion, so that Esther is three-dimensional as few other female characters from Victorian fiction are.

Most of the characters in *Bleak House* are well drawn and three-dimensional, but they are flawed as well, befitting the corrupt and unhappy society they live in. The two exceptions to this are Esther, narrator of much of the novel, and Mr. Jarndyce, Esther's guardian. Some critics and readers have found Esther sweet to the point of being insipid or unrealistic—critics disagree on whether or not she represents the "feminine ideal" or is meant to show how oppressive society was toward women—but I think her realistic, and simply good and kind. She is attractive: sensible, self-sacrificing, wise and modest, gentle and good-hearted. She is not insipid, and she is not stupid. She merely keeps her wit and emotion to herself. Jarndyce is Esther's match, the soul of generosity and kindness, although his romantic feelings for her—she is 16 or 17 to Jarndyce's late fifties—are much more potentially offensive to an audience which considers people children until they are 18, which the Victorians did not. It is Esther's attractiveness as a character that makes her half of the story more absorbing and compelling than the other half. Although the reader will be interested in how *Bleak House* turns out, what will be of greater concern is what happens to Esther, and if and how she lives happily ever after.

The single most significant character in *Bleak House* is neither Esther nor Mr. Jarndyce—it is Inspector Bucket. He is the first significant detective in English mystery fiction. (Edgar Allan Poe, who virtually created detective fiction and the fictional private detective with his C. Auguste Dupin, was American.) There were detectives in English literature before Bucket, including the casebook (proto-police procedural) characters of the 1850s, and Dickens did not create the police detective character. But just as Balzac, in **Père Goriot**, made Vautrin influential on later French detective characters, thanks to Balzac's stature and literary talent, so too did Dickens, through his position as much as the innate quality of Bucket, make Bucket the prototype for the fictional police detective until the time of Arthur Conan Doyle's Sherlock Holmes. Wilkie Collins' Sergeant Cuff, in **The Moonstone**, was memorable, but the larger influence on English mystery literature was Bucket's.

Similarly, *Bleak House* anticipates the **Sensation Novel**, and provides a model for it, in its complex plot and its portrayal of crime taking place in a realistic, contemporary setting, and helps to transform the **Gothic** novel in its use of a contemporary urban setting. As Allan Pritchard points out, "a major part of Dickens' solution to the problem of depicting the modern city was to turn to the conventions devised for Gothic horror fiction, which characteristically had an isolated rural setting at opposite poles to his crowded urban setting."

Later authors would emulate Dickens in setting their Gothics in urban settings, what Pritchard rightfully notes is a "fundamental reshaping of the tradition."

Bleak House may not be, in the words of critic Geoffrey Tillotson, "the finest literary work the nineteenth century produced in England," but it's definitely in the discussion of the great novels of the century.

Recommended Edition

Dickens, Charles. *Bleak House* (Modern Library, 2002).

For Further Research

Burt, Daniel S. "*Bleak House.*" *The Novel 100: A Ranking of the Most Influential Novels of All Time* (Checkmark
Books, 2010).
Gaitskill, Mary. "Introduction." *Bleak House* (Modern Library, 2002).
Nabokov, Vladimir. *Lectures on Literature* (Harcourt Brace Jovanovich, 1980).
Pritchard, Allan. "The Urban Gothic of Bleak House." *Nineteenth-Century Literature* v45n4 (Mar. 1991).

The Charterhouse of Parma

The *Charterhouse of Parma* was written by "Stendhal," the pen-name of Marie-Henri Beyle (***The Red and the Black***), and was published in 1839. Beyle (1783–1842) is best known as one of France's foremost writers of Naturalism, and *The Charterhouse of Parma* is, with *The Red and the Black*, his best work, albeit not one likely to overly appeal to modern readers.

In the age of Napoleon, Fabrizio is the son of the Marquese del Dongo and a French soldier. Fabrizio grows up in the del Dongo household, but he is happiest when he visits his aunt, Gina Pietranera, in Milan, and Gina views Fabrizio as if he were her son. When he is seventeen Fabrizio decides to run away and join Napoleon's forces. Despite some bad luck, including being imprisoned on suspicion of being a spy, Fabrizio eventually succeeds in joining up with Napoleon at the battle of Waterloo, although Fabrizio's own engagement in the battle is fragmentary and busier in retreat after the battle than during the battle itself.

Meanwhile at home Gina becomes the lover of Count Mosca, the prime minister of the city-state of Parma. At Mosca's connivance Gina marries the Duke of Sanseverina, and from that position uses her influence to help Fabrizio and to get him an appointment at a seminary. When his four years of study are up Fabrizio is a handsome monsignor, albeit not a chaste one, and he has mistresses while at the seminary. In Milan at the opera he is attracted to a young actress, Marietta, but she has a boyfriend, and Fabrizio ends up killing the boyfriend in a fight. Marietta flees the city with Fabrizio, while back in Parma the news of the fight becomes known and Fabrizio is condemned to death.

Fabrizio leaves Marietta and returns to Parma in pursuit of another woman, but is recognized and imprisoned. But Fabrizio is still happy, because the jailer's daughter, Clelia, is a woman who Fabrizio met years ago. The two become friends. Fabrizio escapes, and after the murder of the Prince of Parma Fabrizio is pardoned and returns to Parma. He becomes an archbishop and takes the now-married Clelia as his lover. But after she gives birth to his child, everything goes wrong: the child dies, then Clelia dies, and Fabrizio enters the monastery of the Charterhouse of Parma.

The Charterhouse of Parma, widely acknowledged as the second of Stendhal's masterpieces, is unlike *The Red and the Black* in most ways.

The Red and the Black had an acute focus on the psychology of one character, where *Charterhouse* is more of a mosaic novel focusing on a number of different characters. *The Red and the Black* was a savage societal critique, while *Charterhouse* is, in the words of Harold Bloom, a "mix of quixotic adventure and psychological analysis, tragedy and humor, romance and political satire." Love was a tool for Julien Sorel in *The Red and the Black*, while romance is the dominant subject matter of *Charterhouse*. *The Red and the Black* was a *Bildungsroman* (coming-of-age story), but a very male *Bildungsroman* (see **Marius the Epicurean**), about the education of a male character (Julian Sorel) in the big city. *Charterhouse* is a *Bildungsroman* but with what Daniel Burt calls a shifting focus, "compound narrative centers forming a collective novel of the social group, organized thematically by shared concerns of love and power." *The Red and the Black* was also a picture of the homey (and in many cases ugly) details of real life, while *Charterhouse* concentrates on the lives of the rich and powerful. (*The Red and the Black* was accurate in its minute details, while *Charterhouse* was not, creating an Italy that existed only in Stendhal's mind rather than in reality.)

The Red and the Black was not well-regarded in Stendhal's lifetime, while *Charterhouse* was the subject of a glowing review by Balzac (**Père Goriot**) in addition to the later praise of Henry James (**The Portrait of a Lady**), who found *The Red and the Black* "unreadable." (Stendhal thought that, like *The Red and the Black*, *Charterhouse* would only be appreciated after his death: "more natural and worthier to find favor in 1880.") *The Red and the Black* spent so much time on its psychological plumbing of Julian Sorel's depths and its portrayal of French society that the plot suffered for it, while *Charterhouse* has a great deal of immediacy and momentum in it, what Daniel Burt calls "an effect of breathless and artlessly improvised narrative movement."

What *Charterhouse* does have in common with *The Red and the Black* are strong female characters—no less than Simone de Beauvoir praised Stendhal's portrayal of women—as well as a feel for the texture of social interactions. Stendhal is as able at describing high society's interactions in *Charterhouse* as he was at describing middle society in *The Red and the Black*.

Charterhouse also has what *The Red and the Black* lacks: a sense of humor and even irony about itself, from its characters to its genre. (Daniel Burt goes so far as to call *Charterhouse* a "pastiche of romantic adventure.") Too, *Charterhouse* has the masterful depiction of the Battle of Waterloo as a patchwork of confused events, so that the cumulative effect of the Battle is one of chaos and disorganization, rather than the carefully-planned organization that history books describe. (*Charterhouse*'s portrayal of the Battle of Waterloo was influential on both Tolstoy and Hemingway.)

Sadly, what *Charterhouse* also shares with *The Red and the Black* is a certain uninterestingness to the prose style. What works in French does not always translate to English, despite the best efforts of translators (although the modern translations of *Charterhouse* are fine on a word-to-word and sentence-to-sentence level). Put simply, *Charterhouse* is dull reading, no doubt due in large part to its age. (By comparison, *Charterhouse* was written only eleven years after Bulwer-Lytton's **Pelham** and five years before Disraeli's **Coningsby**.) Modern translators render the text in modern English, but can do nothing about Stendhal's decision to spend time on descriptions of landscapes and on the minutiae of political maneuvering rather than on creating characters the reader might care about. Stendhal spends time on characters' psychologies, but does not succeed in arousing the readers' interest in what happens to them, and does not succeed in giving them any kind of vitality. The romances of the main characters do not arouse or engage; the ridicule of the minor characters' vices and follies do not amuse or penetrate; what Zola (**L'Assommoir, Nana**) called his "novel of adventure" is not adventurous. What was written in a rush does not translate into narrative movement. Balzac described it as "the novel Machiavelli would have written had he lived in the 19th century," but this is, in my view, completely wrong.

Naturally, many critics differ in their judgment of *Charterhouse*. Harold Bloom writes,

> The novel's unique blend of quixotic adventure and psychological analysis, tragedy and humor, romance and political satire, has continued to complicate its interpretation even as it has ensured its gradual emergence as an undisputed masterpiece.
>
> In this masterpiece of fiction, Stendhal's gift as a writer is at its height. The author's own passion for the glory of Napoleon, adventure, love, and love of Italy are all revealed in the character of Fabrice. Beyond Stendhal's signature clarity of style, the writing attains the quality of a Romantic poem while, at the same time, offering a series of philosophical and moral reflections. Stendhal reveals, too, his deftness at psychological analysis, reminding the reader of his admiration for Laclos.

The Charterhouse of Parma has some inherent qualities, without a doubt, but the modern reader can be forgiven for thinking that it is a difficult book to feel affection for.

Recommended Edition
Stendhal. *The Charterhouse of Parma* (Oxford World's Classics, 2009).

For Further Research
Ballard, Nancy G. "*The Charterhouse of Parma.*" *Masterplots* Fourth Edition (Dec. 2010).
Bloom, Harold. "Stendhal." *Novelists and Novels* (Chelsea House, 2005).

Burt, Daniel S. "*The Charterhouse of Parma.*" *The Novel 100: A Ranking of the Most Influential Novels of All Time* (Checkmark Books, 2010).

Coningsby

Coningsby was written by Benjamin Disraeli and was published in 1844. Disraeli (1804–1881) was a British Conservative politician (twice prime minister of the U.K.) and writer of Jewish birth (though his faith was Anglican). *Coningsby* is generally seen as his most important novel.

Young Harry Coningsby is the son of a nobleman who marries against his father's wishes. His father being the powerful Lord Monmouth, this means that Coningsby's parents are left in hard times. They die, and the orphaned Coningsby is brought up by school teachers. Eventually, however, he gains enough of Lord Monmouth's favor to be sent to Eton, which in *Coningsby* is an idyllic place. Coningsby makes a set of lifelong friends there, most importantly Oswald Millbank, the son of a rich industrialist. After graduation, Coningsby wanders around England, and quite by chance encounters the Jewish ubermensch Sidonia, whose omniscience and wealth of knowledge help mold Coningsby's mind and attitudes and inspire in him an idealism for Conservatism (the British political movement rather than the American cultural movement). Coningsby reunites with his friends at Cambridge, then falls in love with and marries Oswald Millbank's sister Edith. However, Coningsby becomes politically active for Conservatism, wanting a new movement (rather than the same old Tories and Whigs), which alienates his grandfather, and when he dies he leaves Coningsby nothing. Coningsby goes to work as a barrister, eventually wins the patronage of Oswald's father, and becomes a member of the House of Commons. When Monmouth's illegitimate daughter and heiress Flora dies, all of Monmouth's fortune devolves to Coningsby.

Modern readers will reasonably ask why they should read *Coningsby*, aside from being assigned to do so. Truthfully, *Coningsby* is a difficult novel to read, much less love. Fully half of the novel is virtually incomprehensible to modern readers. However, the other half of the novel is surprisingly entertaining, and the novel stands not only as one of Disraeli's best but as the first major "political novel." Unfortunately, the incomprehensible half of the novel is largely what makes up the "political" part of the "political novel," which means that modern readers will be forced to slog through tough, uninspiring terrain in order to successfully understand what makes *Coningsby* important.

The "political novel" can be defined as a novel dealing with contemporary politics, something which became common later in the century and in the twentieth century but which was still a relatively new concept when Disraeli wrote *Coningsby*. There were a few predecessors—Dickens' *Barnaby Rudge* among them—but these were only peripherally about contemporary politics, while Disraeli makes contemporary politics the most important element of *Coninsgby*. It was Disraeli who transformed politics into something that *could* be written about in novel form, and transformed the novel into something that could contain what John Richetti calls an "authoritative discourse" of politics.

Coningsby was the first in Disraeli's "Young England" trilogy (with *Sybil* [1845] and *Tancred* [1847]), which Disraeli intended to be a fictional voice for the Young England movement. That movement, which was informally led by Disraeli, consisted of a group of reactionary Tory aristocrats who were sickened by what they saw as the flaws and vices of modern England, including industrialization, centralized government, and middle class liberalism, and yearned for a return to what they saw as traditional English values, which included a return to feudalism, a predominant Church, and a commonly recognized *noblesse oblige* tying together the proletariat, the bourgeoisie, and the aristocracy. The Young England movement lasted little over twelve years, from its articulation in 1835 in one of Disraeli's books to its death in 1847 when Disraeli withdrew from the "Parliamentary coalition," but while it lived it gave birth to various novels, most notably *Coningsby*.

The problem for modern readers is that what made *Coningsby* notable on publication—its content dealing with contemporary politics—is what makes it virtually incomprehensible now. The novel is so thoroughly obsessed with the politics of the era, the Tories, Whigs, Reform Bill, anti Catholicism, and the like—so completely steeped in them—that it makes no effort to explain those politics to someone not already intimately familiar with them. *Coningsby* is, both literally and figuratively, dated; its concerns are of its time and place, and now that they have gone by what is left is near gibberish. The content of the numerous, long political and philosophical monologues and asides are as alien and unfamiliar to modern readers, American and British, as the politics of the Hohenzollerns, or of Northern Song dynasty China. Similarly, the *roman à clef* ("thinly veiled fiction" about real people) elements of *Coningsby*—who each person stands for, Sidonia being one of the Rothschilds, Lord Monmouth being Lord Hertford and so on—would be of great interest to Disraeli's contemporaries, but of no interest to modern audiences, who could not guess the real people behind the fictionalizations, much less be able to articulate their importance.

Besides being the first major political novel, *Coningsby* is also one of the canonical "Condition of England" novels. During the 1840s English philosophers and legislators were forced to deal with the byproducts of the 18th century's economic growth. These problems, which included gross urban overpopulation, insufficient housing, bad sanitation, and high levels of unemployment, were described by the writer Thomas Carlyle as "the Condition of England." Writers from Charles Dickens (in **Bleak House**) to Mrs. Gaskell (in **Mary Barton** and **North and South**) wrote novels, variously called "Condition of England novels," "industrial fiction," and "social problem novels," which examined the changes in the social classes and social structure and the current state of England. *Coningsby* is a Condition of England novel in which the government and the political parties are feckless, stagnant, or wrong-headed, the politicians useless, and the people under the sway of worse-than-useless ideologies. In *Coningsby* the Condition of England is dire, and it is only Sidonia and the Young Englanders who can rejuvenate it.

But the other half of the *Bildungsroman* (coming-of-age novel) of Henry Coningsby, turns out to be readable and even entertaining, for the most part. Disraeli writes in the stodgy mid-century style, and both Coningsbury and Edith are, to be kind, wooden. The plot lacks the entertaining complications of Dickens and Bulwer-Lytton, Disraeli's contemporaries, and the monologues and asides sit uncomfortably among relatively realistic dialogue and characterization. Most critically, both Coningsby and Sidonia are Gary Stus. In fiction written by amateurs or first time writers, whether published in fan magazines, vanity presses, or on the Internet as "fan fiction," stories written by fans featuring characters from their favorite books, television shows, or movies, a common phenomenon is the Mary Sue character—or the male equivalent, the Gary Stu. A Mary Sue/Gary Stu character is an idealized stand-in for the author, and is tougher, smarter, cooler, nicer, sweeter, more charming, more capable, and more skilled than the established characters, and becomes worshiped by them. Although Mary Sues appeared in 19th century magazine stories written by teenagers, as in stories where a teenaged girl saves a sleeping Indian chief from being mauled by a bear or is raised by Indians and becomes their leader, the traditional modern Mary Sue/Gary Stu appears in *Star Trek* fan fiction, where a new ensign on the starship *Enterprise* is a better pilot than Captain Kirk, smarter than Spock, and makes both fall in love with her. Harry Coningsby is Disraeli's Gary Stu as he saw himself; Sidonia, the *über*-Jew, the omnicompetent Semite who puts the Jew at the top of the racial scale, is Disraeli as he wished to be. (This literal racism leads to some distasteful passages in which people of color are defined as being, by their very essence, inferior to whites and Jews.)

But Disraeli is good at characterization, and his portraits of contemporary politicians have some bite. Even better, Disraeli enlivens the text with a fair amount of wit and even aphorisms, which keep the reader's interest and make the *Bildungsroman* sections of *Coningsby* entertaining and even amusing. These sections do not have humor in the same way that **Great Expectations** and *Pelham* do, but they have wit, which is the next best thing. Disraeli was noted as a wit, and it shows in the novel. A typical, enjoyably bitchy, passage from *Coningsbury*:

> He was just the animal that Lord Monmouth wanted, for Lord Monmouth always looked upon human nature with the callous eye of a jockey. He surveyed Rigby, and he determined to buy him. He bought him; with his clear head, his indefatigable industry, his audacious tongue, and his ready and unscrupulous pen; with all his dates, all his lampoons; all his private memoirs, and all his political intrigues. It was a good purchase.

Additionally, the picaresque elements of the work enliven the *Bildungsroman*, and the **Gothic** elements—Coningsby's obsession with the picture of his mother and the similarities between Edith and the picture—add surprising notes to what no one would have called a Gothic novel.

Lastly, there is a definite layer of homoerotics in the novel, as John Richetti points out in describing the attachment between Oswald and Coningsby, which begins as a passionate friendship at school and goes on to become something quite other: "Disraeli presents Coningsby's 'impassioned' advances to Oswald as a metaphorical seduction, advanced by a man made desperate by the frustration of his heterosexual desires."

Coningsby is a flawed work, to be sure, and even those knowledgeable about the politics and politicians of the era may find much of it heavy going. But Disraeli's wit redeems the half of the book that is about people rather than ideas.

Recommended Edition

Disraeli, Benjamin. *Benjamin Disraeli: Novels, Volume One, Including Coningsby, Sybil, Tancred and Endymion* (Benediction Classics, 2015).

For Further Research

Bradford, Sarah. *Disraeli* (Stein and Day, 1982).
Flavin, Michael. *Benjamin Disraeli: The Novel as Political Discourse* (Sussex Academic Press, 2005).
O'Kell, Robert P. *Disraeli: The Romance of Politics* (University of Toronto, 2013).
Richetti, John, ed. *The Columbia History of the British Novel* (Columbia University Press, 1994).

The Count of Monte Cristo

The Count of Monte Cristo was written by Alexandre Dumas *père* and appeared as a serial in 1844 and 1845 and as a novel in 1845. Dumas *père* (1802–1870) was a giant of 19th century French letters. He wrote a vast number of novels, plays, and poems, and is considered the greatest of the French romantic novelists. ***The Three Musketeers*** and *The Count of Monte Cristo* are regarded as Dumas' masterpieces, classics still read with pleasure today. *The Count of Monte Cristo* is not Art, is not flawless, and is too long, but nonetheless is a great read and a wonderful story.

In 1815 Edmond Dantès is a humble sailor with a bright future ahead of him. He has a loving father and a beautiful, innocent, and sweet fiancée, Mercédès, and he is going to be made the captain of his ship by the ship's owner. Unfortunately, Edmond is too good a man to realize that he has enemies: his shipmate Danglars, who hates Edmond for his favorable position, and Mondego, who loves Mercédès but who Mercédès cares for only as a brother. Danglars and Mondego collude and have Edmond framed as a sympathizer of Napoleon Bonaparte. Edmond is arrested, on his wedding night. Through the work of a crooked deputy Edmond is sent to the dreaded Château D'If, the prison from which none emerge.

Edmond languishes in the prison for fourteen years. In his early years he comes close to going mad, but he is fortunate enough to meet, quite by accident, another inmate, the Abbé Faria. (The Abbé thought he was digging a tunnel to the sea; instead he dug into Edmond's cell.) The Abbé and Edmond become friends, and the Abbé educates Edmond. Edmond also discusses with the Abbé his past and comes to the correct conclusion as to who had framed him and why. Edmond and the Abbé begin digging another escape tunnel. But the Abbé suffers from catalepsy, and after two attacks is partially paralyzed. The Abbé knows he is about to die and tells Edmond where to get an enormous treasure. The Abbé suffers another attack and dies from it. Edmond hides in the sack in which the Abbé's body was to be placed and is thrown into the sea in the Abbé's place. Edmond swims ashore and is picked up by a gang of smugglers, who he works with until he goes to the island of Monte Cristo, a small, rocky, uninhabited island on which the Abbé's treasure rests. Edmond unearths the treasure, which is as huge as the Abbé said it was, and then goes to the mainland. He discovers that his father had starved to death while Edmond was in prison and that Mercédès had married Ferdinand Mondego.

The rest of the novel is taken up with Edmond's lengthy revenge against those who wronged him, as well as his involvement in the lives of their friends and families. By the end of the novel the guilty have been punished and the good rewarded.

The Count of Monte Cristo was originally published as a *roman feuilleton*, a serialized novel appearing in newspapers. The *roman feuilleton* was the dominant mode of 19th century French literature in terms of sales, stature, and influence, and eventually became a sort of genre and literary mode on its own: action-adventure thrillers with a surfeit of incident and melodrama and an emphasis on plot complications over characterization or style.

The Count of Monte Cristo represents the apex of the *roman feuilleton*, both in terms of popularity and in terms of quality. *Monte Cristo* was enormously successful in its first incarnation as a *feuilleton*; it gave its reading audience both the thrills of Dumas' *The Three Musketeers* as well as the social humanitarianism of Dumas' *feuilletonist* rival Eugène Sue (author of the colossally successful and influential *The Mysteries of Paris* [1842–1843] and *The Wandering Jew* [1844–1845]). *Monte Cristo* has never been out of print in French or English, and remains one of most beloved books in the world.

However, perhaps inevitably—the novel is, after all, 170 years old—*Monte Cristo* has in some respects not aged well. The novel is undeniably melodramatic. Dumas never uses the light touch, in characterization, dialogue, or plot developments. *Monte Cristo* is not as over-the-top as Sue's *Wandering Jew* but it is hardly restrained. Even with the best modern translator, the dialogue remains dated, and has an awkward, stodgy, overly formal feel to it:

> "Where am I?" exclaimed she, when her first raptures at her son's recovery were past; "and to whom am I indebted for so happy a termination to my late dreadful alarm?"
>
> "Madame," answered the count, "you are under the roof of one who esteems himself most fortunate in having been able to save you from a further continuance of your sufferings."

Part of this can be ascribed to the differing expectations of French and English/American reading audiences of the era, of course—the inflated and grandiloquent style of rhetoric of that passage seems to be common among French popular writers of the 19th century and not so much among English and American writers of that period. But even taking into account changing styles and reader expectations, the style is still difficult and not particularly well-written.

Along with the melodrama and a certain straining for affect is the lack of depth to the characters. Edmond is the most complex of the cast of *Monte Cristo*, but everyone else is one-dimensional and does not change or grow. The novel's length is also a problem. *Monte Cristo* contains lengthy diversions which are almost irrelevant to the main plot. Dumas was trying to show the lives of those Edmond influenced, including the minor characters, but they are far less interesting or compelling than Edmond. Compared to his story, that of, for example, the daughter of Danglars is almost tedious, and yet Dumas spends more time on her than on Edmond.

So it is hard to call *The Count of Monte Cristo* well-written. It has too many flaws for that. But at the same time it is impossible to call it anything but a classic, because its virtues more than make up for its flaws. In the words of Umberto Eco:

> We would have to realize, as is only right, that from a stylistic point of view it is very badly written ... instead, the miracle of works like *The Count of Monte Cristo* is that, while being very badly written, they are still masterpieces of fiction. Consequently the second-level reader is not only he who recognizes that the novel is badly written but also the one who is aware that, despite this, its narrative structure is perfect, the archetypes are all in the right place, the *coups-de-scène* judged to perfection, its breadth (though at times stretched to breaking point) almost Homeric in scope—so much so that to criticize *The Count of Monte Cristo* because of its language would be like criticizing Verdi's operas because his librettists ... were not poets.

The Count of Monte Cristo is an exciting novel, with plot twists, clever maneuvering, thrilling escapes, intrigues, love affairs, duels, great riches, improbable yet emotionally fitting happy endings, poetic justice, and relentless vengeance. Even at its too great length the novel is a page turner, because the reader sympathizes with Edmond and wants to know what will happen next and how Edmond will achieve his vengeance. While the dialogue is dated in style and at times overheated, Dumas usually uses it to advance matters, rather than to provide endless reams of description, as Victor Hugo does in **Notre Dame de Paris**. The awkward introductory sections of other Victorian novels is lacking; Dumas gets things going immediately. Readers may wince at certain passages or grow annoyed with Dumas' style, but they will not be able to stop reading.

Too, there is more going on in *Monte Cristo* than just the virtues of a *roman feuilleton*. Although *Monte Cristo* was not written to rectify social ills the way that *The Mysteries of Paris* was, *Monte Cristo* still spends time and energy on the plight of the poor and the forgotten in French society—Edmond is a savior to them as well as to the better-off. *Monte Cristo* has been described as "the greatest revenger's tragedy in the history of the novel," a reference to the revenge tragedy, that genre of English plays popular in the 16th and 17th centuries which focused on the bloody revenge schemes of a murder victim's child or relative. *Monte Cristo* does indeed fit into the genre of revenge tragedy, albeit in prose form rather than as a play, and expresses a number of the revenge tragedy's themes at the same time that it expresses in wish-fulfillment form the dreams of ordinary Frenchmen and women for escape, wealth, and freedom. *Monte Cristo* is a novel of manners (a novel about the manners and customs of a particular group of people in a particular time and place) about Dumas' France. Although the early sections of the novel are historical, set in the last months of Napoleon's reign, the later sections of the novel are set less than ten years before the date of *Monte Cristo*'s publication, and much of what Dumas says about French society and manners is applicable to his contemporaries. *The Count of Monte Cristo* is a *roman feuilleton* first and a novel of manners second, and can hardly be compared to **Pride and Prejudice** and other more esteemed novels of manners, but it does serve the same purpose and make some of the same points.

Lastly, there is the character of Edmond Dantès. He begins as an innocent, almost a naïf, but after he is imprisoned and disillusioned he becomes another person entirely, the superior, alienated, morally ambiguous hero who was a staple of Dumas' work. Dumas loved the idea of the superior being who righted wrongs, helped the unfortunate and punished the wicked, and Edmond is the most prominent and best-defined of these characters. Edmond is also misanthropic, gaunt, and pale, consumed by vengeance more than compassion, compared to a Lord Ruthven (a famous fictional vampire of the early 19th century)—in other words, Edmond is the *feuilleton* version of the **Gothic** Hero-Villain.

Some critics interpret Dantès differently. Umberto Eco writes, of Dantès,

> And over everything towers the supreme topos of the serialization: the Superman. But unlike Sue and all the other craftsmen who have tried their hand at this classic instance of the popular novel, Dumas aims for a disconnected and breathless psychology of the superman, showing him to us as torn between a vertiginous omnipotence (by reason of money and knowledge) and a terror of his own privileged role, in short, tormented by doubt and lulled by the awareness that his omnipotence is born of suffering. Whereby, as a new archetype imbued with a superior strength, the Count of Monte Cristo is also a Christ, duly diabolic, who falls into the tomb of the Chateau d'If, a sacrificial victim of human malice and, in the thunderbolt of the treasure's rediscovery after centuries, rises again to judge the living and the dead, without once forgetting that he is the son of man.

In this interpretation, Dumas has created the transitional *übermensch* between the Hero-Villain of the Gothics and the supermen of story papers and dime novels.

The Count of Monte Cristo certainly has flaws. Its length, even in abridged form, can be daunting, and its language can be off-putting. But readers who persevere will be rewarded with a thrilling read, one of the classics of world adventure literature.

Recommended Edition
Dumas, Alexandre. *The Count of Monte Cristo* (Alfred A. Knopf, 2009).

For Further Research

Eco, Umberto. "Introduction." *The Count of Monte Cristo* (Alfred A. Knopf, 2009).
Hemmings, F.W.J. *Alexandre Dumas: The King of Romance* (Scribner's Sons, 1979).
Marinetti, Amelita. "Death, Resurrection, and Fall in Dumas' Comte de Monte-Cristo." *The French Review* v50n2 (Dec. 1976).
Stowe, Richard S. *Alexandre Dumas (Père)* (Twayne, 1976).

Diana of the Crossways

Diana of the Crossways was written by George Meredith (***The Egoist***) and was published in serial form in 1884 and as a novel in 1885. Meredith (1828–1909) was one of the major authors of the mid-to-late Victorian era, although he was never as popular with the public as he was with critics and his contemporary writers—the scholar John Sutherland calls him "the least read major novelist of the Victorian period." *Diana of the Crossways* was Meredith's most popular novel.

The beautiful and charming Diana Merion—"of the Crossways" because of her ownership of a house called "the Crossways"—surprises everyone, most of all her friend Emma Dunstane, when she agrees to marry a virtual stranger, Augustus Warwick. Diana is an orphan, but witty, healthy, and lovely, and she has her virtual pick of suitors, but she chooses Warwick because he offers her stability and protection from unwanted attention. Diana becomes popular in London and becomes particular friends with the elderly politician Lord Dannisburgh. He accompanies Diana on a visit to Emma, which gives rises to bitchy gossip about Dannisburgh and Diana and leads to Warwick filing a divorce suit against her on the grounds of adultery. Diana intends to leave England, feeling that fighting the suit isn't worth it, but Emma and Thomas convince Diana to stay behind and fight. She wins the suit, but feels—somewhat correctly—that in the eyes of the world she is guilty.

Diana writes a book which her friend Redworth, now wealthy from success investing in the railways, helps to make a bestseller. Lord Dannisburgh dies, leaving a sum of money behind for Diana. Diana meets a rising young politician, Percy Dacier, who falls in love with Diana. Diana is partially in love with him, but still married to Warwick (who is ailing and repeatedly tries to reconcile with Diana), so she can't be with Percy, even though he pursues her. Unfortunately for Diana, she lives extravagantly and has money problems, and when Percy entrusts her with an enormous political secret, Diana sells it to a newspaper editor for cash. The editor runs the secret, getting Percy in trouble. When he finds out that Diana was responsible for telling the editor, Percy breaks off the relationship and friendship with Diana, and it becomes publicly known that he was betrayed by Diana.

Warwick is struck by a cab and killed. Diana's response to her new freedom is a dangerous illness; she is saved from death by Emma. When she recovers, she returns to London and regains something of her old reputation as a wit and charmer. Eventually she comes to the conclusion that, despite her deep desire for freedom, she can be Redworth's wife (Redworth has loved her devotedly from the start) and the pair marry.

Diana of the Crossways was Meredith's most popularly successful book, as well as a critical favorite, and continues his streak of feminist work.

Diana is not, arguably, as good as *The Egoist*; in the latter work Meredith made his (eccentric but powerful) style paramount, so that the novel is both an expression of his comedic theories as well as a superlative performance of his narrative style. In *Diana*, conversely, Meredith subordinates his style to the exigencies of plot, so that the time spent in *The Egoist* in psychological exploration, and in comedy is spent, in *Diana*, in working out the intricacies of the story. But *Diana* is the more successful of the two novels as a novel because of this. At last Meredith successfully merges plot and characterization together, producing a novel of both deep characterization and a complicated story.

Meredith's style loses little power in being wedded to plot. His style is still as dense, poetic, rich and elliptical as ever, and despite losing the allusiveness it had in *The Egoist* it is as rewarding as ever. Meredith's penchant for narrative asides/*longueurs* is tamped down in *Diana*, though not extinguished, but the less of those is the better for the novel. Meredith remains one of the more difficult authors of the Canon to read: he makes you work for your understanding of what he says, and crafts his lines to be epigrammatic rather than understandable or readable. Meredith isn't approachable in the way that, say, George Eliot (**Middlemarch**) is, and his language is more difficult, though as carefully shaped, than Henry James' (**The Portrait of a Lady**). But Meredith remains great and *Diana of the Crossways* still has much to reward the reader with.

Diana is an 1880s version of a "Silver Fork" novel (see **Pelham**) crossed with a *roman à clef*, a novel about real life and real people. In the case of *Diana* the real person was Lady Caroline Norton (1808–1877), the feminist author who became notorious because of a lawsuit involving her estranged husband

and Norton's close friend Lord Melbourne, the Prime Minister. (The lawsuit and the conditions surrounding it were an obvious influence on the plot of *Diana*.) Meredith used the life of Norton and the unfortunate circumstances of her marriage and estrangement from her husband to lobby for the same causes that Norton did post estrangement: social justice for women and the expansion of rights for married and divorced women, whose position in British society was extremely unstable (like Diana's, post estrangement). *Diana* is, like *The Egoist*, an explicitly feminist work, but Meredith is too skilled a writer to make *Diana* a mere tract. Diana herself is a fully realized, three dimensional character, one of the finest fictional females of the century, and a sterling representation of the **New Woman** in fiction.

Of course, the novel's ending, with Diana's marriage to Redworth, seems like a betrayal of Diana and her long held desire for independence. It can be argued that Meredith was (as in *The Egoist*) making a concession to reality rather surrendering on Diana's part. But Meredith still seems to argue that marriage is the path to fulfillment, rather than success on one's own part.

Interestingly, *Diana* is not entirely positive about the changes to British society. While fully sympathetic to Diana and her friend Emma Dunstane, *Diana* is less sanguine about other changes in British society, viewing the breakdown in economic, educational, legal, and religious standards as a mixed blessing. Combined with the novel's remarks about Britain's inadequate responses to foreign provocation, this outlook is another example of the *fin de siècle* unease so common to the late Victorians. This pessimism about the British Empire and its inhabitants manifested itself during the last two decades of the 19th century and appeared in works as varied as **The Invisible Man, New Grub Street**, and **She**. The *fin de siècle* unease was caused by a variety of sources, including a distrust of and unease with the lower classes, the changing role of women in society, and a perceived degenerations in the physical fitness of the English people.

Diana of the Crossways, though not quite as artistic a triumph as *The Egoist*, is the better of the two novels, and is a strong feminist statement.

Recommended Edition

Meredith, George. *Diana of the Crossways* (Dodo Press, 2008).

For Further Research

Harman, Barbara Leah. *The Feminine Political Novel in Victorian England* (University of Virginia Press, 1998).
Hoskins, Katharine Bail. "Diana of the Crossways." *Masterplots* Fourth Edition (Dec. 2010).

Dr. Jekyll and Mr. Hyde

Dr. Jekyll and Mr. Hyde was written by Robert Louis Stevenson (**Kidnapped**) and was published in 1886. Although posterity, snobbery, and ignorance have relegated Stevenson (1850–1894) to the role of children's author, for *Kidnapped* and *Treasure Island*, in the second half of the 19th century Stevenson was a major writer, close friends with Henry James and H. Rider Haggard, producer of best-sellers and critically-acclaimed works, a writer who wrote for all age groups and whose work was read by both low- and high-brows. Discerning critics have (justifiably) called Stevenson the initiator of the "Age of Storytellers," the great flowering of high-quality popular fiction from the 1880s until 1914.

Dr. Jekyll and Mr. Hyde is about the dual life one man leads. As Dr. Jekyll, the man is known to a number of his friends as a good man. But as Mr. Hyde, the man commits various brutalities. The novel begins with the first of these, when Hyde, who is a small man, trampled a little girl and left her screaming on the ground. Enfield, a witness to the act, collared the man and forced him to pay the girl's family £100. Enfield tells the story to his friend Utterson, who is interested in the story, as the will of his friend Henry Jekyll entrusts his fortune to a Mister Edward Hyde if Jekyll should disappear for longer than three months. Utterson visits Jekyll, but their meeting goes badly. Jekyll will not discuss the matter with Utterson and insists that the terms of the will be followed. Utterson believes that Hyde is blackmailing Jekyll but is unable to take any further action.

Almost a year later a kind old man, Sir Danvers Carew, is brutally clubbed to death by Hyde. Utterson brings the police to Hyde's quarters, but he is not there. Utterson confronts Jekyll, who swears that he will have nothing further to do with Hyde. Some time later Doctor Lanyon falls deathly ill. Lanyon and Jekyll had formerly been close friends, but Lanyon refuses to see Jekyll or even discuss him, for reasons he will not tell Utterson of. Utterson and Enfield visit Jekyll, but he is ill and suffers from a paroxysm on seeing them. Soon after, Jekyll's servant Poole visits Utterson and tells him that he thinks Jekyll has been murdered. When Utterson tries to get into Jekyll's lab a voice which is clearly not Jekyll's tells Utterson to go away. Poole tells Utterson that for a week Jekyll has been shut up in his lab demanding a strange drug, and that recently Hyde has been seen in the lab rather than Jekyll. Utterson and Poole break into the lab and find Hyde's body, dead from suicide.

The novel then concludes with Jekyll's account of his life: how he became convinced that humans have dual personalities, and how he found a substance that could help separate his own two selves, one staying Jekyll and one, the evil side, becoming Hyde.

One of Stevenson's inspirations for *The Strange Case of Dr. Jekyll and Mr. Hyde* was the life of William Brodie (1741–1788), who was a respected member of Edinburgh society, a cabinet-maker, a member of the Town Council, and a deacon of the local Masons. By night Brodie led a gang of burglars; Brodie needed the money to support his mistresses, children, and gambling habits. Stevenson's father had owned furniture made by Brodie.

The premise of *Dr. Jekyll and Mr. Hyde* is commonly known. Despite its genre trappings the novel is now firmly in the literary canon, and no less than John Fowles wrote that "the fact that every Victorian had two minds … makes the best guidebook to the age possibly *Dr. Jekyll and Mr. Hyde*. Behind its latterday Gothick lies a very profound and epoch-revealing truth." The very phrase "Jekyll and Hyde" has become a cliché. But it is also true that most people have not read the novel as adults and are unfamiliar with some of its specifics.

Stevenson's first version of *Dr. Jekyll and Mr. Hyde* was criticized by his wife for being "merely a story—a magnificent bit of sensationalism—when it should have been a masterpiece." Stevenson responded to this by burning the original manuscript and rewriting it into its current form, making the allegory of the split personality more explicit. It is the allegory that is usually forgotten by those who have not read *Dr. Jekyll and Mr. Hyde* as adults, and it is the allegory that draws most of the attention from academics and critics. But what is often not mentioned in discussions of the novel is how readable the story is. Stevenson's style is slightly stiff, unlike his work in *Kidnapped*, but he has a deft hand at physical description, and his dialogue is at the least utilitarian, and more than occasionally apt. Stevenson never presents Hyde's perspective, but the wretched nature of Jekyll is fleshed out, giving the novel a psychological element that other similar stories of the time often lacked.

Dr. Jekyll also has the aforementioned allegory. The novel admits of many interpretations, some plausible and some outlandish. Four of the most common interpretations are Hyde as the Victorian underclass; Hyde as the repressed Id; Hyde as an evolutionary throwback; and, *pace* Elaine Showalter, Hyde as Jekyll's gay side, with Doctor Jekyll and Mr. Hyde being "a fable of *fin de siècle* homosexual panic, the discovery and resistance of the homosexual self." Interpreting the allegory is an almost irresistible game for the critic and an easy mark for a lazy student.

"Hyde represents the Victorian underclass" is an interesting interpretation but one not supported by the novel and wholly dependent on the political leanings of the critic—it is a possible interpretation but hardly a likely one. The "Hyde is the repressed Id" argument is not particularly compelling, either. What is commonly forgotten is that Hyde is not all rage or unchecked urges. In this Hyde is similar to the Creature in Mary Shelley's *Frankenstein*. Popular conceptions of both the Creature and Hyde spring from media portrayals rather than from their original, literary portrayals. The literary Creature is not mute and stupid, as he is in the movies, but rather articulate and literate. Nor is the literary Hyde all emotion or all anger. He is not unintelligent, is often civil, and he easily controls himself on a few occasions. He can certainly rage and be savage, but when confronted by a crowd or by one of Jekyll's friends, he is composed—hardly the behavior of raw Id.

Showalter's argument about Hyde's homosexuality is intriguing but ultimately not convincing. The novel lacks women entirely and every character is a bachelor, and Stevenson's contemporaries would have assumed that Hyde was blackmailing Jekyll over homosexuality, with the pair being from different social classes. But to interpret the horror caused by Hyde in a sexual manner is to make a leap in judgment that is not borne out by the text itself. If Hyde is in fact the repressed homosexual side of Jekyll, why is Jekyll so relieved when he stops becoming Hyde? Jekyll's relief is clearly not a guilty relief, as when the forbidden repressed disappears, but pure relief. Sometimes an all-male story has homosexual underpinnings. And sometimes a bunch of men is just a bunch of men.

The "*Jekyll and Hyde* is a parable about evolution" theory is perhaps the soundest. Jekyll's obsession is with something that his friend Lanyon calls "unscientific balderdash," and Lanyon and Jekyll have "differed at times on scientific questions." Evolution was only a little less controversial in 1885 than it was when Darwin introduced it, and the 1880s in particular were a time of vehement debate on the nature-vs-nurture question. *Jekyll and Hyde* is a response in fiction to this debate, coming down firmly on the nature side. The physical descriptions of Hyde seem to support this position. Hyde exhibits an "inexpressible deformity," his cry is one of "mere animal terror," and he walks in an "quick light way." Hyde is smaller than Jekyll, not bigger, which is another fact about *Jekyll and Hyde* which is commonly forgotten. Most symbolically, there is the "pious work" which Jekyll held in "great esteem" which Hyde "annotated, in his own hand, with startling blasphemies." Under the evolutionary-parable interpretation, Hyde is a brutal evolutionary throwback. Defacing Jekyll's "pious work" is a blow by evolution against religion. The "quick light way" in which Hyde walks is catlike, and the "scientific questions" which Lanyon and Jekyll differ on are not sexual questions, but scientific—i.e., evolutionary—ones. Hyde's "deformity" is the face of an earlier version of *Homo sapiens*. Hyde is smaller than Jekyll because most of the primates are smaller than humans.

Ultimately, however, even the evolutionary allegory is not satisfying or convincing, because it is clearly not what Stevenson meant. Jekyll specifically states that Hyde is smaller than he because Hyde's sins are "less robust and less developed" than his better side. Hyde's face is not just ugly or deformed, it inspires instant and vicious loathing to a supernatural degree. The revulsion Hyde causes is beyond reason; merely looking at him makes one "turn sick and white with the desire to kill him." *The Strange Case of Dr. Jekyll and Mr. Hyde* can be interpreted many ways, but ultimately it cannot be explained. The novel is close to being a **Gothic**, including its use of the *Doppelgänger* (double) and the motif of the Victor Frankenstein–like over-curious scientist. But the novel is a work of horror rather than of science fiction. Mr. Hyde is frightening because he is Wrong, in the same way that haunted houses are Wrong. Hyde cannot, finally, be explained by science, but by religion or magic. It may be that Stevenson never intended the allegory of *Jekyll and Hyde* to fully be plumbed, but rather to retain its mystery, and thereby its power.

Recommended Edition

Stevenson, Robert Louis. *The Strange Case of Dr. Jekyll and Mr. Hyde and Other Stories* (Barnes & Noble Classics Series, 2003).

For Further Research

Doane, Janice, and Devon Hodges. "Demonic Disturbances of Sexual Identity: The Strange Case of Dr. Jekyll and Mr/s Hyde." *NOVEL: A Forum on Fiction* v23n1 (Autumn 1989).
Gates, Barbara. "Robert Louis Stevenson's *The Strange Case of Dr. Jekyll and Mr. Hyde*." http://www.victorianweb.org/books/suicide/06e.html.
Punter, David. *The Literature of Terror: A History of Gothic Fictions from 1765 to the Present Day* (Longman, 1996).
Showalter, Elaine. "Dr. Jekyll's Closet." Smith, Elton, and Robert Haas, eds. *The Haunted Mind* (Scarecrow Press, 1999).
Williams, M. Kellen. "'Down with the Door, Poole': Designating Deviance in Stevenson's *Strange Case of Dr. Jekyll and Mr. Hyde*." *English Literature in Translation* v39n4 (1996).

Dracula

Dracula was written by Bram Stoker and was published in 1897. Bram Stoker (1847–1912) wrote a variety of novels, but remains best known, and will likely always be best known, for *Dracula*.

In 1893 Count Vlad Tepes Dracula, a Transylvanian nobleman, decides to move from his ancestral castle near the Borgo Pass, in Transylvania, to London. His British law firm sends one of its clerks, Jonathan Harker, to Castle Dracula to close the deal. Harker initially sees nothing unusual about the Count, but soon becomes alarmed at some of his more unusual behaviors. Harker eventually realizes that his life is in danger, but he is a prisoner in the Castle and can do nothing. After several frightening moments, including an attack by three vampire women, Harker watches Dracula depart for England and then makes his own escape attempt. Back in England Harker's fiancée Mina Murray visits her best friend Lucy Westenra and sees a ship run aground near them, its crew dead and the only living creature on board a gray wolf like dog, which soon escapes into the countryside.

Soon after that the bad things start. Lucy begins sleepwalking, and begins deteriorating physically, so much so that Mina is forced to ask for help from Doctor Seward, one of Lucy's rejected suitors. Lucy improves but then grows worse, and Doctor Seward asks for help from his old friend and tutor Doctor Abraham Van Helsing. Van Helsing discovers two bite marks on Lucy's neck and immediately recognizes Lucy's problem. He orders blood transfusions for her, first from her fiancé and later from the other men protecting her and hangs garlic around her. Her condition improves, but thanks eventually Dracula gets to her and she is drained so badly she dies. Harker returns to England, having escaped from the castle but becoming sick for some months and requiring lengthy care. She comes back as a vampire, and Van Helsing, Holmwood, Seward, Harker, and Quincey Morris, an American friend of the three, are forced to cut off her head and destroy her.

Dracula then preys on Mina, drinking her blood and, worse still, making her drink his blood. The men turn their sites on the Count. They first destroy the boxes of Transylvanian earth which he brought with him from home and which he needs to sleep in. Dracula decides that London is too much trouble and leaves by sea for Transylvania. The group follows him, using Mina as a spy—because she has fed on Dracula's blood, she has a link to him, and when put in a trance she sees and hears what he sees and hears. Van Helsing and the men pursue Dracula to Transylvania, and after a fight with his Romany followers they succeed in killing him.

Dracula is in those class of novels, with **The Count of Monte Cristo** and **Frankenstein**, which are powerful and enjoyable, even today, while also being flawed. *Dracula* is not Art or Literature, but it is a work of symbolism and terror whose potency has grown, not diminished, in the century since its inception. And, of course, it is a Victorian page-turner which keeps readers entranced even if they see Stoker's flaws. Stoker was not a particularly good writer. He was sloppy and hasty, his Victorian sensibilities overwhelmed his storytelling sensibilities, and he overindulged in the bathos common to the late Victorians. But even with its many flaws *Dracula* is still a work of great power, and a seminal one in the horror genre. Even readers jaded by horrors Stoker couldn't imagine can still glory in the horripilation *Dracula* is capable of. And Stoker is capable of some memorable lines as well as some surprisingly lyrical ones.

Dracula shares certain elements in common with the **Gothics**, including beautiful young women (Lucy and Mina) threatened with ravishment (both physical and spiritual) and pursued (through subterranean corridors or crumbling ruins in the Gothics, through more prosaic quarters in *Dracula*) by a dreadful, superhumanly evil being. And as in the Gothics, sexuality and its threat is a central, if submerged, theme. But the sexual symbolism is far more common and overt in *Dracula* than in any Gothic. Whether Stoker knew it or not—and there are moments, certainly in some of Van Helsing's speeches, that hint at a greater understanding on Stoker's part of what he was writing than is commonly assumed—*Dracula* is sodden with sexuality and with a commingling and equivalence of blood and sex. The "languorous ecstasy" which Jonathan Harker feels as he is about to be penetrated by the fangs of one of the vampire women and then sucked by her; the vampires' repeated use of "kiss" in the place of "bloodsucking"; the post-coital mood the single, flirtatious Lucy feels after Dracula's visit versus the guilt and depression the married Mina feels after a similar visit; the desire Mina feels for Dracula's "kiss"; the vampiric Lucy's aggressive and openly expressed desire ("my arms are hungry for you") for Arthur; the almost pornographic scene of Mina feeding on Dracula's blood, her face pressed against his naked breast; the open acknowledgment and articulation that Mina, having taken the bodily fluids (the blood) of several men (transfusions to replace the blood Dracula has taken), is the "bride," not just of Jonathan, her husband, but also of Dracula, Arthur, Quincy, Van Helsing, and

John Seward; the transformation in death of the proper (if flirtatious) Lucy to the carnal and "voluptuous" vampire; and the phallic weaponry—stakes and knives—of the men. *Dracula* was not the first vampire story to link vampirism with sexuality—French author Théophile Gautier managed that sixty years earlier with his "La Morte Amoureuse," and the linkage had become a tradition in vampire stories since—but *Dracula* achieved it more completely than any vampire story or novel before it.

The apex of the novel's eroticism comes in the first four chapters, with the appearance of the vampire brides and their near attack on Jonathan Harker. These chapters are also the novel's high point of horror. The frightening atmosphere is sustained with images like the creepy visual of Dracula crawling head first down the castle wall, and with atrocities like Dracula giving a baby to the vampire brides in the place of Harker. The shift to London changes the atmosphere, and while there are many moments of terror later in the novel they do not reach the peak of the first four chapters.

But while the transition to England and to the heavy use of documents—memos, diaries, letters—to narrate events does interrupt the novel's momentum, they are still effective, even if obtrusive, in establishing character and building suspense. (They also show the Modernist influence—more than in a Wilkie Collins-style epistolary novel, the many different scrapbook-style documents used anticipate the Modernism of T.S. Eliot's "The Wasteland" and John Dos Passos' U.S.A. Trilogy.) The novel could do with some tightening, the elision of superfluous detail, and the excision of the more bathetic and overindulgent prose. The surfeit of bathos, the "slough of feeling," can make Victorian novels such as *Dracula* a chore to read. Additionally, there are a few too many instances of Stoker's prejudices influencing the text. Class prejudices are common, with the English working classes figures which invite derision. Stoker's concerns for England's social purity appear in the novel's obsession with sex and with the invasion of England by a sexually dangerous foreigner; Dracula is a later version of the invasion novel genre. Similarly, Dracula's identity as a Transylvanian—an Asian rather than a European in the eyes of Stoker's audience—provides the novel with a Yellow Peril subtext. The novel is full of sexism, misogyny, and condescension to women, although it is Mina who is most often responsible for helping the men, and they who are responsible for her being victimized. Stoker has Mina mouth some contemptuous lines for the **New Woman**, although Mina is herself a New Woman in all but name. (She is independent, intelligent, and demurely assertive, as well as a working woman—she is an assistant schoolmistress at the beginning of the novel.)

And then there is Dracula. Curiously, for all his importance to the novel the reader sees relatively little of his personality. He is offstage for most of the novel, which heightens the suspense and increases the sense of danger but does not allow the reader the opportunity to get to know him. Dracula is malevolent and, as seen in the first few chapters, he is proud, not just of himself but of his land and his people. He is an ardent patriot and vocal about his people's achievements. But little else is seen of his personality. He speaks to Harker of his loneliness, but the reader cannot know how truthful he is being. Is the Count simply practicing his social skills on Harker? Mina asks the others to feel for Dracula, to sympathize with him, but are these her sentiments, or is Dracula speaking through her? Later in the novel the reader sees how contemptuous Dracula is of humans, but Stoker shows the reader little else about him. The film versions of *Dracula* change not just the novel's plot but also the Count's character, adding the romantic anti-hero characterization, adding restrictions to his powers (the literary Dracula can walk about during the day and assume the guise of another human, as he does in the novel's beginning, when he turns into the horseman who escorts Harker to Castle Dracula) that readers often project film representations of the Count on to the literary version.

Of course, thematically *Dracula* is particularly complex, being as Leslie Klinger puts it "a cottage industry for esteemed academics and serious scholars, who see the text as proof of virtually every wrong that may be blamed on the Victorians." There is the novel's aforementioned obsession with sexuality, and according to some scholars an attempt to repress and displace Stoker's own homosexuality. There is the novel's portrayal of masculinity, from Jonathan's passivity in the face of the vampire women to the phallic symbolism of each vampire-slayer's weapons, ranging from Dr. Seward's puny scalpel to van Helsing's enormous stake. There is the Christian allegory, with Dracula inverting aspects of Christ. There is the novel's obsession with modernity, in the aforementioned documentary Modernism as well as the use of up-to-the-moment technology and terminology and the New Woman status of Mina—all opposed to ancient Dracula from ancient Transylvania. There is Dracula himself, who can stand in for anything a critic wants, from Irish republicanism to reverse colonization by Eastern European immigrants to deviant sexuality. Lastly, there is the overall novel's *fin de siècle* unease, so common to the late Victorians. This pessimism about the British Empire and its inhabitants manifested itself during the last two decades of the 19th century and appeared in works as varied as **The Invisible Man, New Grub Street,** and **She.** The *fin de siècle* unease was caused by a variety of sources, including a distrust of and unease with the lower classes, the changing role of women in society, and a perceived degenerations in the physical fitness of the English people. In *Dracula*, the unease comes from Dracula himself and what he stands for.

Dracula is a classic. Not in the sense of the literary canon, but rather as a work which retains its power and is read for pleasure a century after its inception and will likely stay that way for at least another century. Those who have never read it should, because despite its flaws it still entertains and even at points frightens.

Recommended Edition
Stoker, Bram. *The New Annotated Dracula* (W.W. Norton, 2008).

For Further Research
Auerbach, Nina. *Our Vampires, Ourselves* (University of Chicago, 1995).
Burt, Daniel. "*Dracula.*" *The Novel 100: A Ranking of the Most Influential Novels of All Time* (Checkmark Books, 2010).
Johnson, Allan. "Modernity and Anxiety in Bram Stoker's *Dracula.*" *Critical Insights: Dracula* (Salem Press, 2009).
Marocchino, Kathryn Dorothy. "*Dracula.*" *Masterplots* Fourth Edition (Dec. 2010).
McCrum, Robert. "The 100 Best Novels: No. 31—*Dracula* by Bram Stoker." http://www.theguardian.com/books/2014/apr/21/100 best novels dracula bram stoker.
Stoker, Bram. *The New Annotated Dracula* (W.W. Norton, 2008).

East Lynne

East Lynne was written by Ellen Wood and appeared as a serial in 1860 and 1861 and as a novel in 1861. Wood (née Ellen Price) (1814–1887), under the name of "Mrs. Henry Wood," was one of the most successful and prolific writers of the second half of the 19th century. Her fame has receded considerably and today she is best known for *East Lynne*.

Lady Isabel Vane is the beautiful daughter of a poor, dissolute nobleman, the Earl of Mt. Severn. When he dies, he can leave her nothing, but fortunately for her Archibald Carlyle, a lawyer friend of her father, is in love with her, and proposes marriage to her, which she accepts. Unfortunately, not everyone is happy about the marriage; Archibald's sister Cornelia thinks he's a fool for marrying Isabel, and treats Isabel badly. Moreover, another of Archibald's clients is the Hare family, one of whose daughters, Barbara, is dreadfully in love with Archibald (for his part it is friendship only) and has her heart broken when he marries Isabel. However, he continues to help the Hares; their son Richard has been convicted in absentia of murder, though he swears he didn't do it, and Archibald helps investigate the case for the Hare family.

Prepared by the malicious words of a servant, Isabel misinterprets Archibald's attentions to Barbara and abandons Archibald and their three children, going to Europe with Francis Levison, a debauched rake who promises to marry her. He never does, and a year later, after Isabel's divorce from Archibald is made official, he abandons her and their child completely. There is a train accident, which kills Isabel's child by Levison and dreadfully injures and scars Isabel, ruining her health. Isabel is incorrectly reported to have died in the train wreck, thus freeing Archibald to marry Barbara Hare after all. At length Isabel becomes governess to her children, her new appearance and her carefully concealing mode of dress disguising her true identity, even from her own children.

Matters wend their melodramatic way. One of Isabel's children dies of consumption, and the other children add to Isabel's remorse by their constant remembrances of their true mamma. Francis Levison is revealed to have been the murderer, not Richard, and eventually Levison is convicted of the murder and Richard is freed. Isabel dies of a broken heart, but before she dies she reveals herself to Archibald and explains herself, gaining his forgiveness for her actions.

East Lynne, with **Lady Audley's Secret** and ***The Woman in White***, is generally held to be responsible for turning **Sensation Novels** from a successful subgenre of the 1850s into *the* successful subgenre of the 1860s. Like the latter two novels, *East Lynne* remains surprisingly entertaining, even 150-plus years after having been written.

Ellen Wood is an interesting case. She was an invalid mother whose husband Henry was a professional failure, leading Wood to begin writing professionally to support the family, something she continued to do through the rest of her life (Henry Wood died in 1865, leaving Ellen Wood to maintain herself and her four children through her writing). A clear-eyed professional, Wood set aside her usual conservative personality when it came to her writing and looked out for her own interests with a sharp eye.

East Lynne was only her second novel, and in some respects her inexperience shows in *East Lynne*. There are momentary infelicities, some adjectives are repeated too often, and at times Wood allows her religious feelings to impose themselves too overtly on the novel. And the novel has a surfeit of Sensation material. One can—sort of—understand why George Meredith (**Diana of the Crossways, The Egoist**) rejected the novel when he read it for publishers Chapman and Hall, and why so many contemporary critics condemned the work. But as events showed the rejection was a gross mistake on the part of Meredith and of Chapman and Hall; *East Lynne* was an immediate success, a runaway best-seller that sold more than a million copies by 1900 and was turned into smash hit plays.

The modern reader of *East Lynne* will be inclined to side with the Victorian public and not with Meredith *et al*. Even with its flaws, *East Lynne* is a professionally-told Sensation Novel with the usual pleasurably melodramatic Sensation Novel elements—murder, adultery, bigamy/divorce—wielded with a more-than-competent hand. In some respects *East Lynne* is written by the anti–Henry James. Care was not taken with the crafting of individual sentences, and characterization and narration-as-art were secondary concerns to Wood. The plot was all. Wood did not neglect characterization, exactly, and certainly made the narration as professional and competent as she could. But the plot was the most important aspect of the novel to Wood. She does not linger on scenes and wastes no time on preambles or material extraneous to the main plots. She rushes from chapter to chapter, making the plot become ever twistier and adding to the suffering of poor Isabel with every turn. As Stevie Davies writes, "It is written not with power but with immense gusto and relish; its hectic and most improbable plot is a triumph of the active enjoyment of storytelling."

Wood keeps her narrative voice to a minimum, and for the most part limits her moralizing to that of her characters—an important distinction in Sensation Novels, which would not be well-received by publishers or critics without the requisite moral tut-tutting over the sins of a Sensation Novel's characters, but which the reading audience was not necessarily interested in.

Of course, the degree to which a novel can be enjoyed has little relation to that novel's critical or historical importance—just witness the hot mess that is **Waverley**. *East Lynne* is now of interest for a number of reasons.

East Lynne is an intensely *feminine* novel, one that is, in Lyn Pickett's words, "a story of the feminine and a feminine story. The address is consistently woman-to woman. The way in which the story is unfolded replicates the rhythms of women's conversation … this apparently easy, gossipy address, full of trivia … positions the reader within a feminine discourse of a specific social register." The relationships between women, good and bad, are the core of the novel, with the men being off to the side, and more objects than subjects. Sensation Novels were often seen as women's novels, both due to the author and due to the presumed audience for them, but rarely were Sensation Novels as women-oriented as *East Lynne*. Indeed, *East Lynne* is far more of a domestic melodrama than most Sensation Novels—**Under Two Flags** is primarily adventure, while *Lady Audley's Secret* and *The Woman in White* are mysteries. *East Lynne* is focused on the home and a woman's place in it.

However, the message of *East Lynne*—such as it is—about the state of women is ambiguous. There is an emotional extravagance and a sadism in the lengthy exploration of Isabel's misery and too-late repentance of her sins, and her death and that of two of her children would seem to be a message by Wood about the morality of the book—that it is a particularly harsh application of Christian morality to the actions of a sinner. This has led critics like Stevie Davies to write,

> Personality is dangerous in Mrs Henry Wood's world, if you are a woman, and want to remain safely within orthodox society. Your nature is assimilated to your wifehood, and the duties of a wife are universal. Mrs Henry Wood's novel makes a classic statement of the Victorian sexual code for women. The wages of sin is death. For women, this means sexual "sin," the sin against the Holy Ghost being adultery, since the good man is God in his own household. The code is barbaric and primitive. Mrs Henry Wood shows no overt desire to criticize it. On the contrary she seems to relish it. She endorses its unforgiving judgment in a ringing authorial voice which urges the female reader to profit by the horrific fate of the gentle and aristocratic Lady Isabel, by sticking close to her own husband, putting up with her lot and avoiding jealousy, which, rather than lust, seems to be defined as woman's original sin.

But questions have been asked whether the novel subverts the preceding judgment or not—whether the amount of time spent with poor Isabel makes the reader sympathize with her to the point that the judgment of the novel is rendered incomprehensible and even loathsome. To contemporary readers—those not scandalized by the appearance of adultery and various sins in the novel—*East Lynne*'s appeal may well have been said to lie in its combination of the consequences of sin and a very conventional moral commentary. But readers may equally have responded to Isabel and rooted for her, as some or many undoubtedly did with M.E. Braddon's Lady Audley, and enjoyed the novel *despite* the ending rather than because of it.

Of equal interest is the novel's treatment of marriage. As Davies notes, Wood's view of marriage is a very realistic one—much more realistic than other novels, domestic or Sensational:

> The author does not pretend that love's first hectic raptures last. Woman's lot is likely—she gives it about two years at the most—to be less than idyllic, for your husband is in the course of things through familiarity liable to cool in ardour and set his mind on external matters, like business. The message is that you aim for a sensible and steady affection from your husband, fuelling this as far as possible by a stoic maintenance of his comforts and precedence, and aim for security and respectability rather than excitement.

At the same time, *East Lynne* was published only three years after the contentious passage of the Matrimonial Causes Act, which made divorce much more achievable for middle class men and women. As Andrew Maunder points out, *East Lynne* "probes many of the legal, financial, and emotional implications of the new Act."

Lastly, there is the class consciousness of the novel. Sensation novels were very much products of the middle classes, written by them and for them and about them. But *East Lynne* goes beyond that in its treatment of class. As Dinah Birch notes, not only would the Victorian middle classes recognize their virtues and aspirations in the book, but members of the aristocracy, from Sir Francis Levison to Isabel herself, are punished, and it is only the supposed work ethic of the middle classes, in the person of Archibald Carlyle, which will bring its bearer appropriate rewards.

East Lynne is usually dismissed as a classic Victorian potboiler, and the damning reviews of its worst critics are taken as considered judgments. But *East Lynne* is considerably more complex than those critics give it credit for, and despite occasional hiccups Wood wrote a work which holds up even today.

Recommended Edition
Wood, Ellen. *East Lynne* (Oxford University Press, 2005).

For Further Research
Birch, Dinah. "Fear Among the Teacups." *London Review of Books* v23n8 (8 Feb. 2001).
Davies, Stevie. "Mrs. Henry Wood's East Lynne—Introduction." http://www.steviedavies.com/henrywood.html.
Jaffe, Audrey. "Sympathy and Representation in Mrs. Henry Wood's *East Lynne*." http://victorianweb.org/authors/wood/1.html.
Maunder, Andrew. "Introduction." *East Lynne* (Oxford University Press, 2005).
Walker, Gail. "The 'Sin' of Isabel Vane: *East Lynne* and Victorian Sexuality." Browne, Pat, ed. *Heroines of Popular Culture* (Popular Press, 1987).

The Egoist

The Egoist was written by George Meredith (*Diana of the Crossways*) and was published in 1879. Meredith (1828–1909) was one of the major authors of the mid-to-late Victorian era, although he was never as popular with the public as he was with critics and his contemporary writers—the scholar John Sutherland calls him "the least read major novelist of the Victorian period." *The Egoist* is Meredith's best, and is an early work of feminist literature.

The titular character in *The Egoist* is Sir Willoughby Patterne, a genteel monster of vanity. On the day of his majority he announces his engagement of

Constantia Durham, but ten days before the wedding she elopes with a military officer, shocking everyone, especially Willoughby and his best friend, Laetitia Dale. (Laetitia loves Willoughby—secretly, she thinks, but everyone knows it.) Willoughby leaves the country for three years and returns home accompanied by his cousin Vernon and a young relative, Crossjay. Willoughby pursues and wins the hand of the beautiful and serene Clara Middleton, and Clara and her father come to Willoughby's mansion to live for a few weeks before the wedding.

Unfortunately for Willoughby, Clara notices the self-centered and selfish way in which he treats Crossjay, and then realizes that Willoughby is trying to completely control her thoughts about him, and Clara realizes that she has made a mistake in agreeing to marry him. Clara wants out, but unfortunately escaping from a betrothal in this time and place is not so. Constantia Durham did so, but she had a military officer to elope with, while Clara has nobody. Moreover, Willoughby simply refuses to break the engagement and Clara's father completely dismisses his own daughter's words and feelings, being more concerned with the quality of wines in Willoughby's cellar.

At length, Willoughby accepts that Clara is serious in refusing to marry him. To soothe his wounded pride he asks Laetitia to marry him, but she, surprisingly, refuses, having come to see his flaws (thanks to a conversation with Clara). Thanks to an unwitting bit of subterfuge on Crossjay's part, knowledge of Willoughby's proposal to Laetitia becomes public knowledge, and Clara's father changes his mind about Clara breaking the engagement. Willoughby, wishing to punish Clara, tries to manipulate matters so that Clara will marry Vernon, but Clara has gotten there before Willoughby did, and Vernon and Clara agree to be married in the Swiss Alps. Willoughby tries again with Clara and after a solid night of bothering her wears her down enough so that she will marry him, even though she no longer loves him and, admittedly, is marrying him for base and venal reasons.

The Egoist was a popular success, although critics loved it more than the public. Understandably so, as *The Egoist* is, if anything, rather too good for its contemporary audience.

The Egoist's popular success is on one level understandable. It is a kind of "Silver Fork" novel (see **Pelham**) of the 1870s, a long look at the lives and romances and gossiping of a set of upper class characters. The dialogue is epigrammatic to the point of being theatrical, there is only one setting (Willoughby's home) for the novel, the novel is deliberately comic—in sum, much of *The Egoist* feels like a stage play conveyed in novel form. Despite the many long narrative asides, which are often *longueurs*, the verbal exchanges crackle with wit and life. The characters come to life thanks to Meredith's emphasis on their psychology.

The novel is an effective expression of Meredith's theories of comedy. As entertainment much of *The Egoist* is superb.

But there is more to any novel than entertainment, of course, and on multiple other levels *The Egoist* stands out as a peculiarity, and arguably Meredith's most challenging novel.

There is Meredith's style, which one critic called "eccentric." Meredith writes intensely, anticipating Henry James in the quality and care with which every sentence is composed. As Max Beerbohm wrote, "Mr. Meredith, the only living novelist in England who rivals Ouida [*Under Two Flags*] in sheer vitality, packs tight all his pages with wit, philosophy, poetry, and psychological analysis." The richness of the novel, the endless witticisms—not to the level of an Oscar Wilde (***The Picture of Dorian Gray***), but at least that of a Bulwer-Lytton (*Pelham*) or a Disraeli (***Coningsby***)—and sprightly, tennis-match-like dialogue, the leisurely pace, all of these were challenging to Meredith's contemporaries, who were more used to the quickness of plot of the **Sensation Novels** and of Dickens (***Bleak House, Great Expectations***) and Thackeray (***Barry Lyndon, Vanity Fair***), and are no less so today. Moreover, *The Egoist* is a study of character and psychology rather than plot, again challenging to readers both past and present—and the prolonged exposure to Willoughby's ego can prove hard to take at novel length.

There is the self-lacerating feminism on George Meredith's part throughout *The Egoist*. Robert Louis Stevenson (***Dr. Jekyll and Mr. Hyde, Kidnapped***) conveyed the following anecdote: "A young friend of Mr. Meredith's … came to him in agony. 'This is too bad of you,' he cried. 'Willoughby is me!' 'No, my dear fellow,' said the author; 'he is all of us.'" Meredith wrote *The Egoist* in a fit of self-analysis, basing Willoughby in large part on himself as a younger man, and the result is the in-depth portrayal of a conceited ass and, more importantly, the effect of his self-centeredness on the women in his life.

The Egoist is a remarkably feminist novel—remarkable for its time period, a time when the movement for women's liberation was only just gaining momentum, and remarkable for its cutting analysis of the male ego. Constance Fulmer describes it as "a remarkable depiction of a sensitive and intelligent woman's mental, moral, and emotional agonies as she attempts to free herself from her engagement to an egotistical man," and if Meredith goes to some pains to establish egoism as a human failing rather than just a particularly male one, and if Sir Willoughby is himself an anachronism at the time of *The Egoist*'s publication, the reader is still left with the impression of a society that sees women as objects rather than subjects, and as adjuncts to male lives rather than independent possessors of their own lives. Of course, there is the question of the ending. Willoughby gets the girl, wearing her down so that she gives in—admittedly for base and venal reasons, but she gives in. Is this a defeatist message for women, or is it merely a realistic one? I tend to think it a realistic one, given Meredith's leanings, but the modern reader can be forgiven for feeling undercut by the ending and not a little betrayed by it.

Meredith certainly satirizes bourgeois stupidity through the satirizing of himself, and uses laughter—at Willoughby et al. rather than with them—as a corrective. Arguably his ultimate message is for common sense rather than ego to rule men's affairs. His intense concern with his characters' psychologies, with the problems of class, and with the form of *The Egoist* itself, is ahead of its time, anticipating Modernism, and looking forward to the 20th century rather to its contemporary 19th century. And Darwinism and natural selection emerge as central themes in the book, especially in the choosing of a wife and in the contradictory dynamic between Willoughby's desire for stasis and the evolving nature of Willoughby's world.

This being Meredith, there are further layers to *The Egoist*. As Margaret Harris writes,

> Willoughby's fantasizing about building up "the house" is generated in part by a fear of invasion or contamination; metaphorically, his fierce territoriality is aligned with an imperialist ideology. Like Sir Austin Feverel, he is self-authoring. When he is jilted he retreats to his domain and attempts to regulate it completely, in the belief that the principles of his laboratory science can be extended to ensure his control of all actions and reactions in his domain. But science is no match for the energies of the natural world, which are figured both in the familiar register of Home County rural beauty reinforced by the sublimity of imagery drawn from Alpine heights, and also in Darwinian terms (Meredith makes great play with monkeys who figuratively threaten devolution, or worse, revolution).

But the novel is a Condition of Women novel foremost. The women are shown to be as witty if not wittier than the gentlemen, smarter, more insightful, kinder, and less selfish, but they are all (with exception of the cutting Mrs. Montstuart, an aging widow who is friends with Willoughby) constrained by society's ties, repressed by male aggression, and caught in what Robert Adams calls "an inhuman system of commodity relationships." That there is much else to enjoy in *The Egoist* does not dull this message in the slightest.

Recommended Edition

Meredith, George. *The Egoist: A Comedy in Narrative* (HardPress Publishing, 2013).

For Further Research

Adams, Robert M. "Introduction." *The Egoist* (W.W. Norton, 1979).
Fulmer, Constance. "The Egoist." *Masterplots* Fourth Edition (Dec. 2010).
Harris, Margaret. "George Meredith at the Crossways." Baker, William, and Kenneth Womack, eds. *A Companion to the Victorian Novel* (Greenwood, 2002).
Stevenson, Richard C. "Introduction." *The Egoist* (Broadview, 2010).

Emma

Emma was written by Jane Austen (**Pride and Prejudice**) and was published in December 1815 (although it is usually dated to 1816). Austen (1775–1817) is generally regarded as one of the greatest of English novelists. Her best novels, like *Emma*, are a part of the canon of great literature, and she remains one of the most popular authors in the world.

Emma is a *Bildungsroman* (coming-of-age novel) about Emma Woodhouse, a young middle-class woman in the small village of Highbury. Emma is intelligent and spirited, but has little to do with herself and is vain and too self-assured about her own wisdom and perception, and she ventures to matchmake for her friend Harriet Smith—a venture that goes wrong when Emma discourages Smith (a bastard, or "natural child") from marrying a man, Robert Martin, who would be good for her. Emma instead encourages Smith to be with Mr. Elton, the local vicar—a further error, as Mr. Elton is attracted to and proposes to Emma, who turns him down. Mr. Elton later marries a gauche woman, and together the pair treat Harriet badly and attempt to replace Emma as the social leader of Highbury.

Into this situation arrives Frank Churchill, the son of the husband of Emma's former governess. Churchill is handsome, superficially charming and good-spirited, and he flirts with Emma enough that she considers him a possible mate and the village assumes that there is a budding relationship between them. The reality is that Churchill is secretly engaged to Jane Fairfax, the niece of Emma's neighbor—an engagement whose hiding requires a great deal of effort on both Churchill and Fairfax's part and which leads to a great deal of strain and misery for Jane Fairfax. Eventually the engagement comes to light and Emma sees Churchill for what he is: a cheerful young man of deeply flawed character. But the revelation of the secret engagement does allow for a friendship to grow between Fairfax and Emma, where earlier Emma's envy of Fairfax and the maintenance of the secret on Fairfax's part had led to cool relations between the two.

No longer considering Churchill as anything but a friend, Emma is at last clear to see who the man she should belong with is: Mr. Knightley, a close friend of Emma. Throughout the novel Knightley is critical of Emma, but the criticism comes from a place of affection, and after realizations on both sides—Knightley, that his disapproval of Churchill stems from jealousy of his possible relationship with Emma, and Emma, that she feels Mr. Knightley should only marry herself—a realization driven home after Harriet Smith declares her affection for Mr. Knightley—the two admit their affections for each other and marry. Frank Churchill and Jane Fairfax marry and Harriet Smith marries Robert Martin.

In the context of Austen's career *Emma* is an important novel. *Emma* was the last novel published in Austen's lifetime, and is generally seen in the critical community as Austen's best novel. It is not Austen's most *popular* novel—that title goes to *Pride and Prejudice*—and was not Austen's best-selling novel—indeed, *Emma* was not reprinted in her lifetime—but, most critics now agree, *Emma* is Austen's most accomplished novel. The moralizing of *Mansfield Park*, the romantic illusion of *Sense and Sensibility*, and the lightness and fairy tale setting of *Pride and Prejudice* are done away with, and in their place are Austen's greatest deployment of both realism and satire. *Emma* is hardly Austen's only comedy of manners, nor her only social critique, but it is the novel in which she best blends comedy, relationships, close description, dialogue, and romance.

Austen stands as perhaps *the* significant transitional writer between the writers of the Regency (1811–1820), and more broadly writers of the Georgian era (1714–1830), and Victorian writers. She is also an important author in the transition from the neo-classicism of the Georgian era to the **Romanticism** and realism of the 19th century. Neo-classicism was a phase in European literature in which the classical texts of the Greeks and Romans were held to be the highest forms of writing, so that the rules and principles of classical literature were dominant, and dialogic wit, narrative reason, and authorial control of fiction were privileged, as were rationality, order, and logic—the influence of the Enlightenment, that period during the 17th and 18th century when rationality, order, and logic were dominant virtues.

All of these principles were changed during the Romantic era (1780s-1830s), which put an emphasis on imagination and emotion, and during the Victorian era, which put an emphasis on realism. *Emma* still has classic elements, such as the traditional comic ending of multiple marriages, but *Emma* also prefigures the Victorian attention to realism in her minute creation of Highbury while also, in proper Enlightenment style, privileging the orderly logic of Mr. Knightley over the unreliable imagination of Emma. Moreover, *Emma* is arguably the first major novel which in the words of critic Mary Waldron "could not only enthral without seeking to astonish, but also enlighten without the need to preach." Before *Emma* and Austen, didacticism and instruction were portrayed as major purposes—perhaps *the* major purposes—of a novel. Austen and *Emma* began to change that.

As one of the great novels in English literary history, *Emma*, predictably, is a deep work which rewards critical thinking. A much more serious work than *Pride and Prejudice*, *Emma* is a serious work with comic highlights, where *Pride and Prejudice* is a comic work with serious undertones. Austen layers in numerous topics and themes of the sort that critics love to dissect—and which students will be expected to write about.

Austen portrays society in *Emma* as a merciless, all-controlling monster which forces people into disingenuity and forced politeness, a monster which Austen's heroine, like everyone else, is powerless to slay or change in any way. The deeply conservative ethics of the novel—much of *Emma* reinforces the class and socio-economic prejudices of its contemporary readers—are at war with the novel's nascent feminism and the way in which the reader is led to sympathize with Emma, a young woman for whom there is little to do but care for her self-involved, hypochondriacal father and socialize—a woman who does not have the advantages of modern readers' education or social mobility. Austen's fictional portrayal of life in a small village was without peer in her time and has few rivals even now; Highbury becomes remarkably real for readers.

In fact, Highbury and its inhabitants become so real that *Emma* achieves a kind of universality. *Emma* is a most English of novels, dealing as it does with a small English village, the English middle class, and the very English concerns of manners and class. But Austen's skill is such that contemporary readers don't need to be English to appreciate *Emma*, nor do they need a knowledge of England of the Regency era to understand the novel. The search for romance, the complications of family relations, the burdensome ties of society—these things are understood universally. The character foibles of Emma, Mr. Woodhouse, and all the rest of the cast of *Emma* are similarly common to all cultures, not just the English middle class of the Regency era.

Not as universal are the strictures of society which Austen satirizes in *Emma*. The rigid class boundaries, the severe limits in behavior and destiny which society placed upon young women, the near-brutal enforcement of social mores and the dominance of gossip and innuendox—which critic Peter Conrad describes as "genially malicious" in *Emma*—all these things were more present in Austen's England than in the modern era, so that the force of Austen's satire may be lost for modern readers, although it was not for Victorian readers and critics. While modern readers will need little effort to understand *Emma*'s prose, it may take significantly more effort on their part to understand the cultural associations and assumptions of *Emma*'s time and place.

Emma's greatness lies not just in the depth of the text but also its historical importance. During the early 18th century the novel was thought of as the province of men, but this began to change in the mid- and late 18th century, thanks in large part to the rise of the **Gothic** novel, so that by the time of *Emma* novels were seen essentially female, although "male novels" were still seen to exist (and seen as superior to the "female novel"). (The dominance of the "female novel" would change in the 1820s with the rise of the historical romance.) *Emma* is perhaps the high point of the "female novel," employing as it does the *Bildungsroman* structure of the female novel, a female author and a female protagonist, female concerns (such as a woman's place in society), and a male authority figure—in the case of *Emma*, Mr. Elton, the vicar of Highbury—as the story's villain.

Emma can be seen not just as a high point of the female novel of era, but also a significant reaction against the Cult of Sensibility and against the Gothic novel. The best example of the Sensibility and the sentimental genre is Henry Mackenzie's *The Man of Feeling* (1779), a novel of lachrymose excess whose titular character, Harley, is controlled by his emotions to the point that he is overwhelmed by the sufferings of other human beings and appears to die from joy alone. Harley's Sensibility is benevolence, compassion, and crying at the slightest opportunity taken to extremes. The heroes of Sensibility live in a society of injustice and evil and embody the feelings which others lack, but the heroes of Sensibility do not allow their emotions to be governed by self-interest. While *The Man of Feeling* contains an implicit critique of Sensibility—Harley's uncontrollable emotions lead him to defeats, unnecessary self-denial, and an early death—the English who adopted Sensibility overlooked or ignored this criticism and stressed the superiority of emotions and emotional responses to logic and rational thought. Those who easily blushed, cried, and fainted in response to sad or happy art or situations were therefore thought to be particularly virtuous. Sensibility was common in the Gothics, both in the heroine's personality and in the inability or unwillingness of the Gothic's primary villain, the Hero-Villain, to resist his passions.

Sensibility is absent in *Emma*. The closest a character comes to it is Harriet Smith, with her abundance of emotions and occasional fainting away, and her emotional abundance is seen as part of her immaturity and artlessness. In fact, *Emma* is not about the dominance of emotion, but the restraint of same. Maturity, in *Emma*, involves restraining emotions, hiding them behind manners and social courtesies, and deploying them in a restrained and proper fashion, as Mr. Knightley does when he finally declares his love for Emma. Mr. Knightley's restraint rather than some Sensibility-like excess is portrayed as the proper model. Likewise, emotions are in *Emma* shown to be best when limited, so that the intense friendship between Emma and Harriet, in the end, gives way to "a calmer sort of good-will."

Emma, like the rest of Austen's work, can be seen as a reaction against the

Gothic novel and an attempt to emplace an alternative mode of female novels. (Indeed, Austen went so far as to overtly satirize the Gothic mode in *Northanger Abbey* [1818]). The Gothic novel was the dominant popular form of novels in the 1790s, 1800s, and 1810s. Stories of terror and horror, about young women pursued through castles or young men in search of their heritage, the Gothic was thought of during Austen's lifetime in gendered terms, as "male" or "female." Many of the Gothics' writers were women, and the genre had a large female readership, and Gothics by women for women were often classified as female Gothics. The female Gothic is a *Bildungsroman*, a coming-of-age story for the female protagonist, with Sensibility as a dominant concern and with a male authority figure as the story's villain. *Emma*, like the female Gothic novels, is a *Bildungsroman*, but Sensibility of the Gothics is absent and the central male authority figure, Mr. Knightley, is an honorable hero rather than a flawed Gothic Hero-Villain.

Emma is also, put simply, a good read. Austen's style is notable; it is both elegant and precise, deploying its many words exactly with irony and wit. *Emma* has excellent characterization of its cast and a particularly strong narrative voice—the "free indirect" style which is third-person narrator while continuously giving us insight into Emma's motivations and thoughts. Austen's style is clean, in the Georgian manner, and requires relatively little adjustment on the modern reader's part—something which is not the case with many Victorian novels, especially those from the 1830s and 1840s. *Emma*'s realism is remarkable; her creation of Highbury stands as one of the best-imagined and best-described fictional locales. The characters, especially Emma, are three-dimensional and real enough that we can easily imagine their lives outside the confines of the novel. (This realism, and the depth of small, homey detail about Highbury and the lives of its inhabitants, was in fact disorienting to Victorian readers, accustomed as they were to dramatic spectacle rather than an examination of the mundane).

This is not to say that *Emma* is without faults. Austen famously declined to write about subjects outside her knowledge, claiming, "I must keep to my own style & go in my own Way; and though I may never succeed again in that, I am convinced I should totally fail in any other," and this is reflected in *Emma*, which is a deep slice of English rural life, but not a broad one. The world of Highbury, though exquisitely limned by Austen, is after all a small one, and in some ways a quite artificial one. Many of the realities of the era, whether the threat of Napoleon invading England, the loss of male relatives and friends in the Napoleonic wars, bank failures, food shortages, or the Irish question, are not allowed to intrude on the pastoral idyll that is Highbury. There is one intrusion, the scene in which the "gipsies" threaten Harriet, but it is dealt with quickly and the status quo rapidly reasserted. (This is an interesting contrast to *Pride and Prejudice*, which is a fundamentally comic rather than serious novel but which deals with the contemporary reality of the military intrusion into real life, which *Emma* never does.)

Austen's style is dialogue-heavy, which in some respects is good, as it makes the novel less dated. (Austen's dialogue itself shows only slight signs of aging and seems remarkably modern and contemporary in most respects.) But much of this dialogue is chit-chat—Miss Bates in particular is garrulous and can babble on for a page or a page and a half unchecked. Austen used her dialogue precisely—her dialogue is the equivalent of and does the job of action sequences in an action-adventure movie—and her dialogue often artfully conceals emotion and intention, but at the same time there is a great deal of inconsequential politeness and social niceties, and the modern reader's patience may at times be tested by just how much of the dialogue is truly meaningless.

Austen's pace is leisurely. Unlike many of the Victorians, who packed as much characterization and plot into the pages of their novels as they could, Austen prefers to take a more measured approach. With a stylist as exquisite as Austen, this is hardly a burden to the reader, but at the same time leisureliness can become repetitive and annoying. Too, *Emma* cannot be described as having a surfeit of plot. Austen does not cram plot twists into her novel; what plot there is is carefully examined and considered by her characters and discussed at length. Even during Austen's lifetime the relative lack of plot in *Emma* was criticized; this is even more true now, considering the length of *Emma*, and by comparison to the often over-stuffed quality of Victorian novels' plots.

Emma is after all a comedy of manners, and while we are invited to laugh with Emma we are likewise invited to laugh at the vulgar Mrs. Elton and at Mr. Woodhouse, Emma's father, the self-involved hypochondriac. And indeed there is much to laugh at there; he is one of Austen's most successful comic characters. But the question must be asked if *Emma* overdoes Mr. Woodhouse. He certainly functions well as a device to show how one of Emma's good sides, her devotion to her father and kindness in taking care of him, but his "comic" side—for this reader, at least—became annoying quickly. *Emma* in truth functions better as satire, at least in this regard, than as comedy; the number of people who smile in appreciation for its satirical qualities surely outweighs the number of people who laugh at its comic stylings.

Lastly, there is the case of Emma herself. Austen famously said of Emma that "I am going to take a heroine whom no one but myself will much like." As with her father, Emma is a character that may not appeal to readers. She is certainly flawed: self-assured, vain, unappreciative of her good fortune in life, jealous of anyone who might be a rival to her position as the queen of Highbury, and seemingly uninterested in anything but meddling in her friends' lives. These flaws are part of what endear Emma to many readers, but it can be fairly asked whether Austen asked too much of her readers to spend so much time so close to the thoughts and words of one flawed in such unpleasant ways, although admittedly the course of the novel teaches Emma the error of her ways, so that by the end of the novel many of Emma's flaws have been driven from her.

Nonetheless, even with these flaws—admittedly, flaws that not all readers will perceive as flaws—*Emma* remains a splendid work, the best novel by one of English literature's greatest writers and one which many modern readers thoroughly enjoy.

Recommended Edition:
Austen, Jane. *Emma* (W.W Norton, 2011).

For Further Research:
Conrad, Peter. "Introduction." *Emma* (Everyman's Library Edition, 1980).
Juhasz, Susanne. "Reading Austen Writing *Emma*." http://www.jasna.org/persuasions/on line/vol21no1/juhasz.html.
Kordich, Catherine. "Emma." *Bloom's How to Write About Jane Austen* (Chelsea House, 2008).
McCrum, Robert. "The 100 Best Novels: No. 7—*Emma*." http://www.theguardian.com/books/2013/nov/04/100 best novels jane austen emma.
Waldron, Mary. *Jane Austen in Context* (Cambridge University, 2006).

Frankenstein

Frankenstein was written by Mary Shelley and was published in 1818. Mary Wollstonecraft Shelley (1797–1851) was the daughter of William Godwin, the philosopher and author of *Caleb Williams*, and Mary Wollstonecraft, an early feminist and the author of *A Vindication of the Rights of Women*. Shelley was also the wife of the great poet and rotter Percy Bysshe Shelley. And, famously, Mary Shelley was a part of the story telling contest in Switzerland between herself, Percy Shelley, Lord Byron, and John Polidori. During the contest Shelley produced *Frankenstein*, one of the most influential science fiction novels of all time.

Victor Frankenstein is an Italian who as a bright young man is exposed to the likes of Cornelius Agrippa, Paracelsus, and Albertus Magnus. When Victor attends university at Ingolstadt he comes under the sway of more modern scientists and begins to develop intellectually as well as pursue his own area of interest: "whence ... did the principle of life proceed?" Victor eventually discovers this secret, and then, gripped by an obsession to put his new knowledge to use, spends months preparing to create life. He does, putting together a new man out of corpse parts, but when the Creature awakens Victor finds it so repulsive that he flees from it. The Creature, feeling rejected by Victor, takes this badly. Victor has a nervous breakdown and is gradually nursed back to health over the course of months. The Creature, meanwhile, wanders and encounters humanity on several occasions. He is rejected each time, even by the family he watched in secrecy and grew to love. The Creature feels alienated from and then hostile toward humanity and Victor in particular. The Creature goes in search of Victor, but finding Victor's younger brother William instead, kills him and then frames the Frankensteins' servant Justine. The Creature confronts Victor and explains himself. Victor rejects the Creature's affections but agrees to create a mate for the Creature as long as it stays away from "the neighborhood of man." The Creature agrees, and Victor then goes to the Orkneys to duplicate the creation of the Creature. At the last, however, Victor balks and destroys the mate for the Creature. The Creature is outraged by this and infuriated that Victor broke his word and promises misery and despair for him. The Creature then kills Victor's friend Henri and Victor's bride Elizabeth on their wedding night. A lengthy pursuit follows, ending in the Arctic, with Victor dying and the monster, wretched and sorry at the last, "borne away by the waves and lost in darkness and distance."

More than most novels, *Frankenstein* is grossly misunderstood by the public. This is mostly due to the movies, whose faithfulness to the book is at best casual and at worst capricious. The movie portrayal of the Creature is almost always of an inarticulate, childlike brute, rather than the sophisticated and thoughtful being of the book. But that is only one of several aspects of Shelley's creation which most people get wrong.

For one, the identity of the novel's monster is misunderstood. Whether Shelley intended this or not, for most modern readers it is a fact that Victor is the monster, not the Creature. The Creature is the product of cruelty and abuse, while Victor is a weak, immoral person.

Most people also assume that *Frankenstein* is a horror novel. This is part of the problem of classification which *Frankenstein* suffers from. The movie versions of the novel are horror movies, but the novel itself has different concerns. *Frankenstein* has famously been called "the first science fiction novel," but Shelley keeps the actual science to a minimum. The reader never learns just how Victor found the secret of life. Victor is simply a scientist, and that is meant to explain everything, in the way that scientists of the pulps were Scientists practicing Science. *Frankenstein* is actually a late period **Gothic** novel full of a didactic morality which earlier Gothics lack.

This morality is a third popular misunderstanding. The lesson of the novel is not to avoid meddling in things humans were not meant to know, but rather to embrace one's creation instead of rejecting it. It is Victor's rejection of the Creature and his cruelty toward it which produce the Fury-like monster of vengeance. The Creature wants to be accepted and loved by Victor, but he is too selfish to embrace his creation, which is what produces such misery later on. If Frankenstein is a Faust-like character, it is a Faust who does not dare too much but rather acts from cruelty rather than kindness.

The novel does not have a high level of quality. Shelley was only twenty-one when she wrote *Frankenstein*, and her inexperience as a writer shows in an immature and overwrought style. *Frankenstein* is dull in the beginning, and when Shelley pays attention to Victor rather than the Creature the novel drags. The Creature is the center of the novel. Without him, the reader's interest flags. There is only so much of Victor's emotional outbursts, his delicate, high-strung, neurasthenic, **Romantic** disposition, and his self-conscious breast beating and shrieking that the modern reader can take. The novel has other flaws as well. Harold Bloom unwittingly put it well when he said of the Creature that "he alone in Mary Shelley's novel possesses character." Minor characters appear and disappear as needed, the Creature always seems to find exactly what it needs, Shelley assumes there is wood for a funeral pyre in the Arctic, and the Creature seems to have an uncanny ability to track Victor no matter where he goes. Characters do not so much speak as declaim. But these flaws do not negate the power of the novel's ideas, nor render them, or the Creature, any less interesting.

One aspect of *Frankenstein* which is not so much misunderstood as unknown is the tie between the Creature and the myth of the Yellow Peril. The Creature is an early example of the Yellow Peril stereotype. The ethnic coding of the Creature was deliberate on Shelley's part, and Creature's role as a precursor to the Yellow Peril cannot be understated. The Creature was the first image of a Mongol in popular culture which portrayed an Asian not as a small figure but as a large one. The image of a large, dangerous Asian remained in British and American popular culture, becoming one of the motifs of the Yellow Peril.

I mentioned Victor's Romantic disposition. As Harold Bloom notes, there are substantial Romantic elements to the novel itself. Victor is a typically high-strung Romantic hero, but in its way so is the Creature, who like Victor is plagued by the Romantic disease of "excessive consciousness," so that the Creature "is racked by a consciousness in which every thought is a fresh disease," similar to Milton's Satan. The "Romantic mythology of the purgatorial self trapped in the isolation of a heightened self-consciousness" equally applies to Victor, who Ancient Mariner–style is forever trapped by his own guilt, and Wandering Jew–style is forced to eternal wandering. In reaction against the "rational-humanism of Godwin and Shelley" we have Victor's emotions—and the Creature's. In Bloom's words, "Frankenstein is the mind and emotions turned in upon themselves, and his creature is the mind and emotions turned imaginatively outward, seeking a greater humanization through a confrontation of other selves."

But *Frankenstein* is much more of a Gothic novel, and in fact is one of the outstanding male Gothics. It has a number of the traditional Gothic motifs, including the dysfunctional family, the Oedipal conflict between father (Victor) and son (the Creature), the *Doppelgänger* (the Creature), the hints of late night hauntings of graveyards and other forbidden places, and the confrontation between an innocent maiden (Elizabeth) and a monster (the Creature). *Frankenstein*, though appearing late in the Gothic genre's life, contributed two things to the Gothic: the mad scientist, in the figure of Victor, a more modern version of the over-ambitious (politically or sexually) villain of earlier Gothics, and the scientist's laboratory, which replaces the storm-swept castle as the location of evil acts. Too, a good deal of the novel's overblown rhetoric is straight from the Gothic tradition:

> These thoughts supported my spirits, while I pursued my undertaking with unremitted ardour. My cheek had grown pale with study, and my person had become emaciated with confinement. Sometimes, on the very brink of certainty, I failed; yet still I clung to the hope which the next day or the next hour might realize. One secret which I alone possessed was the hope to which I had dedicated myself; and the moon gazed on my midnight labours, while, with unrelaxed and breathless eagerness, I pursued nature to her hiding places. Who shall conceive the horrors of my secret toil, as I dabbled among the unhallowed damps of the grave, or tortured the living animal to animate the lifeless clay? My limbs now tremble, and my eyes swim with remembrance; but then a restless, and almost frantic impulse, urged me forward; I seemed to have lost all soul or sensation but for this one pursuit. It was indeed but a passing trance, that only made me feel with renewed acuteness so soon as, the unnatural stimulus ceasing to operate, I had returned to my old habits. I collected bones from charnel houses; and disturbed, with profane fingers, the tremendous secrets of the human frame. In a solitary chamber, or rather cell, at the top of the house, and separated from all the other apartments by a gallery and staircase, I kept my workshop of filthy creation; my eyeballs were starting from their sockets in attending to the details of my employment. The dissecting room and the slaughter house furnished many of my materials; and often did my human nature turn with loathing from my occupation, whilst, still urged on by an eagerness which perpetually increased, I brought my work near to a conclusion.

And:

> "You have destroyed the work which you began; what is it that you intend? Do you dare to break your promise? I have endured toil and misery; I left Switzerland with you; I crept along the shores of the Rhine, among its willow islands, and over the summits of

its hills. I have dwelt many months in the heaths of England, and among the deserts of Scotland. I have endured incalculable fatigue, and cold, and hunger; do you dare destroy my hopes?"

"Begone! I do break my promise; never will I create another like yourself, equal in deformity and wickedness."

"Slave, I before reasoned with you, but you have proved yourself unworthy of my condescension. Remember that I have power; you believe yourself miserable, but I can make you so wretched that the light of day will be hateful to you. You are my creator, but I am your master;—obey!"

Frankenstein begins the transition in the Gothic from a past-oriented genre to one capable of featuring more modern characters and embracing modern trends, like scientific experimentation. Although the past-oriented Gothic would continue to appear, *Frankenstein* prepared the genre for the future. Similarly, as the first science fiction novel, *Frankenstein* created the template for the science fiction of the 20th and 21st century (though not that of the 19th, which was more influenced by the work of Nathaniel Hawthorne [**The Scarlet Letter**] than that of Shelley). Though obviously the work of a novice, *Frankenstein* is a layered work and one of the most significant books of the 19th century.

Recommended Edition
Shelley, Mary. *Frankenstein: Ignatius Critical Editions* (Ignatius Press, 2008).

Great Expectations

Great Expectations was written by Charles Dickens (**Bleak House**) and was published in serial form in 1860 and 1861 and as a novel in 1861. Dickens (1812–1870) is arguably the most important and popular British writer of all time, and *Great Expectations* is generally regarded as his greatest work.

Great Expectations is a *Bildungsroman* (coming-of-age story) about Pip, a young orphan. He lives with his sister and her husband, Joe, a blacksmith. Pip is not happy with them because of his sister's physical and emotional abuse of him and of Joe, but he is happy with Joe, who loves Pip unconditionally. One day Pip helps Magwitch a convict (escaped from the nearby prison hulks), by giving him a file and some food, and although the convict is soon caught he does not forget Pip's kindness. Pip meanwhile becomes acquainted with Miss

Havisham, a local woman who was jilted by her lover on her wedding day and never got over it, and Estella, a beautiful girl (Pip's age) raised by Miss Havisham to be heartless and take revenge on men. Pip falls in love with Estella, who tries in her own cool way to discourage Pip.

Pip grows up, and as a teenager he is given a settlement of obscure origins: Pip will get enough money on a regular fashion to become a gentleman, but the source of the money is unknown to him. Pip moves to London and becomes a shallow young gentleman, spending money on useless pursuits and not treating Joe with any kindness. The only good that Pip does during this time is to use his money to help his friend Herbert gain a position at a shipping firm. Eventually the identity of Pip's benefactor is revealed: Magwitch, who repaid Pip's kindness by going overseas, working hard, and making enough money to fund Pip. But Magwitch returns to England—a crime for which the penalty is death—and after revealing himself to Pip and living with him for a time is caught by the police. Estella grows up and marries a brute, further breaking Pip's heart, and Miss Havisham dies. Eventually Pip, now broke, returns to Joe and asks for forgiveness, then takes a job as a shipping clerk with Herbert's firm. Years later he meets Estella, though the book ends with the relationship between the two of them left in ambiguous terms.

Great Expectations' critical reception—it was a popular smash—was muted, with a typical critical statement being that it is "not indeed his best work, but it is to be ranked among his happiest." Times have changed, and current critics are nearly universal in acclaiming *Great Expectations* as Dickens' greatest work. Not bad, for an autobiographical **Sensation Novel**. *Great Expectations*, unlike *Bleak House* and many other Dickens' novels, doesn't have an easily-accessible theme. Nor is *Great Expectations* ambitious in the way that *Bleak House* is—there is no attempt at creating an entire fictional world in *Great Expectations*. And *Great Expectations* has an overreliance on coincidence as a plot driver. But those are the novel's only real flaws.

What does the novel do well? Characterization, first of all: Pip, Estella, and the major and many minor characters become three-dimensional and real. Dickens had a real talent for sketching a person in a few lines and breathing life into them. The reader ends up caring, deeply, for Pip and wanting to know what happens to him, and what the final relationship between Pip and Estella will be. *Great Expectations* is also emotionally powerful—the sheer misery of an unhappy childhood is transmitted so well here (one of the autobiographical elements of the novel), as is the painful experience of personal disillusionment and professional disappointment. The novel is tautly plotted and moves quickly, especially at times when the tension is high as to what will happen. It is tautly told, readable and smooth. And the novel has insightful things to say about the causes of crime and the effects of childhood on adults; as Dickens powerfully demonstrates, the miserable child is father to the unhappy man. This is in addition to the typically Dickensian comedic characters, and the way in which a time and place are vividly described.

The novel's main theme is not something soaring or infuriated, as was the case with *Bleak House*. Here Dickens is simply telling the life story of one man and showing his mistakes. Autobiographical as it is, *Great Expectations* can seem to be a startling statement by Dickens about himself: here are some mistakes I've made, here are the types of hurt I've inflicted on other people, here is the price I paid for self-knowledge. The novel's ending is not a happy one—although the famous second ending of the novel lends itself to a happier reading than Dickens' initial ending for the novel—but it is a mature and adult one. Dickens thought of the novel as essentially comedic, but the comedy is dark and sad, and the hero of the story deeply flawed and unheroic (though sympathetic).

Other themes include the necessity of finding one's place in the world and being defined by work; the social and moral crimes parents commit against their children; the possibility of social mobility and the rise of the middle classes; the morality of self-reliance and self-help; affection, loyalty, and conscience are more important than social advancement, wealth, and class; and the Sensation Novel idea that society hides but is supported by a dark criminal underclass. The family as both fantasy and refuge, and as a nest of violence and lost illusions, with Magwitch as a criminal father and Miss Havisham as the insanely depressed mother. Money—its effects on people, good and bad, and the effects of the new capitalist machinery of the middle classes, with Joe, the pure one, being uncorrupted by desire for wealth but Drummle, the rich one, being wholly corrupted by it.

Great Expectations can be seen as the most Dickensian of Dickens' novels. Although it lacks the exuberant flair of some of his earlier novels—the passage quoted in the *Bleak House* entry is a verbal flight of fancy of the kind missing in *Great Expectations*—it has many of Dickens' other touches: the intricate plot, the melodrama, the sentimentalism, the comedy, the concise narration, the balanced structure, and the rich symbolism, and the grotesque (in the person of Miss Havisham). Likewise, *Great Expectations* uses some of Dickens' favorite themes: cruelty to children, the use of Dickens' own life in a novel, and crime and the law. But *Great Expectations* also has more modern elements. In the words of critic Jeff Ives, the novel has a modern sensibility: "it is more private, more individualistic, more concerned with the inner life than with outward events and issues than his other works, and it displays a greater all-around sense of uncertainty."

Likewise, *Great Expectations*, though a "first person confessional" novel, actually spans several sub-genres, in its critique/satire of society, its Newgate novel (see **Pelham**) elements, its **Gothic** elements (especially Satis House and Miss Havisham), its romance elements, its "novel-with-a-purpose," and its historical novel elements. And of course a *Bildungsroman*, though a *Bildungsroman* with a sense of humor (impossible without the example of *Pelham*)—and similar to *The Red and the Black* and *Père Goriot* in "dissecting the post–Napoleonic world and exposing its moral poverty," but different from them in its use of mystery and guilt.

In Harold Bloom's words, "Critics today tend not to share these views. Instead, they ignore Dickens's professed intentions and read the novel as an expression of pessimism occasioned by the novelist's personal estrangement from and disillusion with society. Social bankruptcy, non-communication, guilt, and confession number among the topics frequently explored in the current literature about the novel." G. K. Chesterton scores a direct hit when he describes *Great Expectations* as a book in which "for the first time the hero disappears." Chesterton sees the narrative as a whole as possessing "a quality of serene irony and even sadness" and he accredits this to the particular nature of Dickens's development as a novelist." Dickens' intention was to make *Great Expectations* different from David Copperfield, in making Pip a "hero who disappears," in Chesterton's phrase, and in making him lower-class and in lending the novel as a whole a sense of overriding guilt and final ambiguity. "Since Shaw's time, issues of social class have come to dominate the discussion of Great Expectations. Critics have all too often chosen to concentrate on ideas of class guilt or Marxist ideas of alienation and class betrayal, thereby distorting readings of the novel." "It does not seem to me that Dickens shaped Great Expectations as an apology for his earlier social aspirations, as Shaw insisted. Rather, he wanted to explore a new fictional idea. Pip is not of his own class, just as he is not of David's, but he will be given a series of false economic and social expectations that he will have to work out."

Chesterton deserves the final word on *Great Expectations*: "Art indeed copies life in not copying life, for life copies nothing. Dickens' art is like life because, like life, it is irresponsible, because, like life, it is incredible."

Recommended Edition

Dickens, Charles. *Great Expectations* (Penguin Classics, 2002).

For Further Research

Allingham, Philip V. "The Genres of Charles Dickens' *Great Expectations*—Positioning the Novel." http://victorianweb.org/authors/dickens/ge/pva101.html.
Burt, Daniel S. "*Great Expectations.*" *The Novel 100: A Ranking of the Most Influential Novels of All Time* (Checkmark Books, 2010).

Christiansen, Rupert. "Charles Dickens' Great Expectations."http://exec.typepad.com/greatexpectations/introduction.html.
Ives, Jeff. "Great Expectations." *Read* v61n7 (Feb. 2012).
Sanders, Andrew. "Great Expectations." *A Companion to Charles Dickens* (Blackwell, 2008).
Sweets, Sparky. "Great Expectations—Book Summary & Analysis."https://www.youtube.com/watch?v=mJsyzUgKGwY.

Heavenly Twins

The Heavenly Twins was written by Sarah Grand and was published in 1893 (although it was privately printed the year before). Grand, née Frances Elizabeth Bellenden Clarke (1854–1943), was perhaps the foremost New Woman writer of the 1890s and was responsible for popularizing the phrase, in a debate with Ouida (*Under Two Flags*). *The Heavenly Twins* was one of the most infamous of the New Woman novels.

The Heavenly Twins is the story of three women: Evadne Frayling, Edith Beale, and Angelica Hamilton-Wells. (Angelica and her brother Diavolo are the "heavenly twins" of the novel's title.) Evadne is a self-educated young woman of strong Views who has raised herself by reading numerous works of mathematics, history, and medicine. She meets a pleasant-looking man, Major George Colquhoun, and believes herself in love with him and agrees to marry him. Unfortunately, the Major not only led a scandalous previous life, he is also a syphilitic, and Evadne discovers this on the day after her wedding. Unwilling to risk her own health by being sexually involved with the Major, she leaves him, outraging her parents. At length Evadne changes her mind, and agrees to return to the Major, but only on the condition that they live together as celibate companions. The Major, wanting to avoid a public scandal, agrees to these conditions, and for a time all is well between them, but eventually Evadne begins to go mad, being stunted physically, emotionally, and romantically/sexually by the chaste marriage. Fortunately for Evadne, the Major dies of a heart attack, leaving her free to marry the doctor who has been caring for her. (He is a feminist of sorts, unlike the Major, and so is acceptable to Evadne.) She heals, has children, and lives happily ever after.

Edith Beale is not so lucky. She is raised as an innocent, unwilling and unable to look unpleasantnesses in the eye, and she makes the mistake of marrying Sir Mosley Menteith, a syphilitic womanizer. The marriage makes her miserable, and then her son is born with secondary syphilis, and her own syphilis (caught from her husband) leads her to insanity and death. Angelica Hamilton-Wells begins as a high-spirited/misbehaving child, but she insists on being taught everything that her brother is taught, so that when she is of marrying age she agrees to marry an older man who she calls "Daddy," but only on the condition that she be allowed to do what she wants. What she wants is to lead an independent life—even independent from her husband—but after an interlude in which she (disguised as a man) befriends a tenor, has a passionate friendship with him, is rescued by him when she nearly drowns, and then quarrels with him, only to have him die, she resolves to become a better wife to her husband.

One of the last of the triple-decker novels, *The Heavenly Twins* was one of the most controversial and best-selling novels of 1893, and was repeatedly reprinted over the next twenty years. Though not the first of the New Woman novels, *The Heavenly Twins* was the first best-seller, and (in the words of critic Carol Senf) it helped to establish the popularity of "the well-educated, middle-class woman who was openly critical of the traditional roles established for women, especially marriage and motherhood, and who was influenced by the feminist movement to speak out in favor of equal education for women and equal purity for men and women." Unlike many later New Woman novels, *The Heavenly Twins* does not strike a blow for sexual freedom—Grand did not agree with the free love proponents of the New Woman. Instead, Grand argues that, rather than woman being allowed to, as it were, sink down to the level of men when it comes to sex, what should happen instead is that men should rise up to the level of women. Grand's feminism in *The Heavenly Twins* is an unusual (for New Woman literature) combination of rights-oriented feminism—that woman should be given the same education as men, have the same legal rights, be able to take jobs, be granted legal protection, and all the other tenets of Victorian feminism—and duties-oriented feminism—that individuals must recognize that they are a part of a larger group, society, and that they have responsibilities toward that larger group, and act in accordance with those responsibilities.

Grand's feminism in *The Heavenly Twins* is of a kind that some modern readers may find objectionable. Grand argues not just that men and men's society have oppressed women and kept them from real opportunities for satisfaction and fulfillment, but that men are inherently inferior to women, and that men must reform themselves to make themselves the equal of women. This is not an argument that modern feminism often makes, but it was definitely a stream of Victorian feminism and the New Woman, and readers must accept it as one element of *The Heavenly Twins*'s Victorianism.

Grand's feminism, in fact, is the dominant element of the novel. Some students may find it objectionable—not Grand's men-are-inferior argument, but her feminism as a whole, and may argue (as some Victorian critics did) that Grand's feminism is of the shrill variety, and that the novel's ideology is allowed by Grand to overwhelm the novel's story-telling elements. Ultimately this is a matter of opinion, but those readers should ask themselves whether they made the same argument about Elizabeth Gaskell's **Mary Barton** and its inflammatory class-based politics, or Dickens' **Bleak House** and its position regarding the British legal system, or any of the other ideology-based Victorian novels covered here. If they did not—if, like me, they find those ideologies to be a feature of the novels and not a bug—then they must ask themselves if they are objecting to the effect of the feminism on *The Heavenly Twins*, or to the feminism itself?

Mark Twain said, of *The Heavenly Twins*, that "with the twins left out, this book is more than good: it is great, and packed full of hideous truths, powerfully stated." I suspect that this statement comes to close to most modern readers' positions on *The Heavenly Twins*. The adventures of the titular twins occupy a great deal of space in the novel, with decreasing returns to the reader. The British, especially in the late Victorian era, had a taste for stories and novels about misbehaving, prank-loving children—British readers found them humorous, and bought the novels in great numbers. This bit of Victorian humor, however, has not aged well, and most modern readers are likely to find the "humorous" moments involving the Twins to be tedious rather than funny, and the Twins themselves to be annoying rather than lovable.

Another unfortunate element in the novel is Grand's tendency toward speechifying. There are certainly ways to deliver ideology that do not involve long, impassioned monologues; Mary Barton did not lapse into them, but instead made its argument through actions and events. Grand does not take this approach, regrettably, but instead has her main characters lecture the other characters around them. Regardless of whether or not one agrees with the lectures, they are tedious to read *en masse* and at length.

Lastly, one element of *The Heavenly Twins* is a good reminder about how different Victorian morals were in some respects to ours: the novel's treatment of syphilis. Considered graphic for its time, the novel is now seen as elliptical in its portrayal of the characters with the disease. The word "syphilis" is never mentioned, and it is only through close scrutiny that readers will understand that Edith has a venereal disease which she caught from her husband. Much about *The Heavenly Twins* would have been implicitly understood by Victorian readers, like the reason why Evadne refuses to be a true wife to the Major, but these things are likely to be lost on modern readers unless they are paying close attention to the text.

But apart from the Twins and the speechifying, *The Heavenly Twins* is generally a good read. Grand is particularly strong on characterization, in giving her characters three dimensions and recognizable motivations. Even those characters she disapproves of are shown to be, if not respectable, at least understandable (if not agreeable) in their actions. Grand's style is of the 1880s, rather than the slicker, more magazine-based prose style of the 1890s, but for all that her style has aged only a little and remains readable and enjoyable to modern students. The plot has enough twists to keep the reader's attention engaged. *The Heavenly Twins'* format, with an interlude that seems to have little to do with the main plot and with a final volume—the only one—narrated in the first-person, was not agreeable to many Victorian critics but is now seen as an interesting piece of formal literary experimentation on Grand's part. The three plots are not incoherent, but are reflective of Grand's arguments about the effects of negative socialization on women. And Grand's feminism, though not as shocking or ground-breaking as it was in 1893, still has something to say to modern readers.

The Heavenly Twins is not a great work of fiction. Too long for its purposes and too given toward speechifying, the novel shows Grand's relative inexperience as a writer. But it remains a good read, realistic in its refusal to grant happy endings to all its characters, with particularly strong characterization and passionate arguments on behalf of Grand's feminist views.

Recommended Edition

Grand, Sarah. *The Heavenly Twins* (The Perfect Library, 2015).

For Further Research

Bonnell, Marilyn. "The Legacy of Sarah Grand's The Heavenly Twins: A Review Essay." *English Literature in Transition, 1880–1920* v36n4 (1993).
Jusova, Iveta. *The New Woman and the Empire* (Ohio State University Press, 2005). https://ohiostatepress.org/Books/Book%20PDFs/Jusova%20New.pdf.
Kennedy, Meagan. "Syphilis and the Hysterical Female: The Limits of Realism in Sarah Grand's The Heavenly Twins." *Women's Writing* v11n2 (July 2004).
Lowenstein, Adam Seth. "'Not a Novel, Nor Even a Well Ordered Story': Formal Experimentation and Psychological Innovation in Sarah Grand's "The Heavenly Twins." *Studies in the Novel* v39n4 (Winter 2007).

Huckleberry Finn

The Adventures of Huckleberry Finn was written by Mark Twain and was published in 1884 in the United Kingdom and in 1885 in the United States. Twain (1835–1910) was one of America's leading authors and humorists.

A sort-of sequel to *The Adventures of Tom Sawyer*, *Huckleberry Finn* begins where *Tom Sawyer* left off: dealing with the money that Tom and Huck had found in a robber's cave. Huck is taken home by the Widow Douglas and her sister, Miss Watson, who both try to reform him. Huck gradually becomes at ease with this, but the arrival of his monstrous father Pap disrupts Huck's life and drags him away in to the woods, keeping Huck a prisoner. Eventually Huck fakes his own murder and escapes from Pap, taking to an island on the Mississippi River. On the island he discovers Jim, Miss Watson's slave, who ran away because he overheard Miss Watson planning to sell him. Huck promises not to report Jim, and the two take to the river on a raft that they found.

A rambling life of adventure follows, with Huck and Jim sometimes being separated but always eventually reuniting. Huck becomes embroiled in the Grangerford-Shepherdson feud, staying with the Grangerfords and helping one of the Grangerford daughters elope with a Shepherdson son. (Unfortunately Huck's host and host's son die in the ambuscade that follows the elopement.) Huck and Jim meet the "Duke" and the "King," a pair of con men who swindle their way down the river. Eventually the King sells Jim for the reward money, leading Huck to agonize over whether to be a good Christian, civilized boy, and return Jim to his slave-master, or to help Jim escape and (Huck thinks) go to Hell. Huck decides to go to Hell and to help Jim escape.

Huck finds out where Jim is being held and goes there to rescue him, only to find out that it is the farm of Tom Sawyer's uncle and aunt who mistake Huck for Tom. Tom happens along, and joins in the foolery, pretending to be cousin Sid Sawyer. Tom agrees to help Huck free Jim, but wants to make the escape more complicated and romantic. Eventually they do help him escape, but in the ensuing chaos (Tom's scheme backfires) Tom is shot in the leg. Jim is recaptured, but Tom reveals that he has been keeping secret that Miss Watson died, giving Jim freedom in her will. Tom recovers, Jim reveals that Huck's father is dead, and Huck decides to light out for the frontier because Tom's Aunt Sally is going to try to adopt him and civilize him.

The Adventures of Huckleberry Finn is a novel that most students will have read (or at least skimmed) in high school. Approached years later, as either college students or adults, readers will find it a much different and more difficult book than they remember.

Historically, of course, *Huckleberry Finn* has won over both readers landmark works of American fiction. After an initially rough reception, with none other than Louisa May Alcott (**Little Women**) leading the charge to have it banned from her local library, *Huckleberry Finn* has won over both readers and critics, with no less than Ernest Hemingway writing that "all modern American literature comes from one book by Mark Twain called *Huckleberry Finn*." Hemingway is giving way to hyperbole, but one of his points is the inarguably true statement that Twain took vernacular American English and made poetry and literature with it in *Huckleberry Finn*, and that Twain, being the first to do so, liberated all following American writers to use properly American voices and properly American idioms to write literature in, rather than in imitation of English writers.

Huckleberry Finn is also perhaps the finest American attempt at the picaresque novel. Twain, in *Huckleberry Finn*, does an excellent job (despite the close focus on Huck's point of view) of establishing other characters' characters and voices. The dialects in which Twain tells the story are initially distracting and even bothersome, but the reader quickly becomes used to the dialects and eventually they become invisible to the reader. And there are enough lyrical passages and subtle characterization to satisfy those interested in High Art, and enough hairs-breadth escapes and picaresque adventures and low humor to satisfy those interested in entertainment and diversion. Twain has excellent control of his material and has created a compulsively readable novel.

And yet, and yet.... *Huckleberry Finn* is a deeply uncomfortable novel to read, in a number of respects. Foremost among them is the complex question of whether or not *Huckleberry Finn* is a racist novel—a question that quickly leads into tangled territory, indeed. Proponents of the yes-it-is-racist argument point to the novel's casual use of the word "nigger" and to the sometimes caricatured and stereotypical characterization of Jim and the other African Americans. Those who disagree with the argument point to the multivalent nature of Jim's characterization, of how he is often three-dimensional and a father figure to Huck without being a stereotype, of how the use of stereotypes is often undercut by the text itself. I tend to come down on the side of not-racist, but the fact that the is-racist argument has substantial ammunition for their argument is (or should be) troubling to the modern reader.

More broadly, *Huckleberry Finn* is an uncomfortable novel to read, as Toni Morrison cogently notes, because of the authorial choices Twain made. Important moments are told rather than shown—Huck's apology to Jim, for one. Scenes end abruptly, with none of the denouement readers expect, much less the lagniappe readers hope for. Characterization must be interpreted as much from elisions or allusions as from action and narration. There are what Morrison calls "entrances, crevices, gaps, seductive invitations flashing the possibility of meaning. Unarticulated eddies that encourage diving into the novel's undertow—the real place where writer captures reader."

Huckleberry Finn is an uncomfortable novel to read because of its darkness. The novel is not death-obsessed, but death is a dreadful constant for Huck, from the threats of Pap to the death of Buck Grangerford. Emotional and physical violence, too, is ever-present in Huck's world, again starting with Pap and extending throughout the novel, notably including the atrocious joke Tom Sawyer plays upon Jim at the end of the novel and the implicit physical violence to be enacted against Jim as a runaway slave, and Huck can very easily be seen as an abused child learning to adapt to his abused status by lying, misbehaving, and ultimately running away.

Huckleberry Finn is an uncomfortable novel to read because its themes—death and rebirth, freedom and bondage, the search for a father, the individual versus society, the flaws of "civilization" and its contrast with the purity of the frontier—are reified in harsh contrasts, with each opposing theme becoming unpleasant realities for Huck. Even his discovery of a father figure in Jim comes with troubling undercurrents: can Jim, a black slave, truly be a father to Huck, who holds the ultimate power of life and death over Jim?

And *Huckleberry Finn* is an uncomfortable novel to read because of its ending. Picaresque novels' endings are of course usually unsatisfying—one doesn't want the journey to end or the picaro/picara to have a happily-ever-after—but Twain complicated the issue by choosing such an abrupt and even disappointing ending for Huck and Jim's story. Set aside the vicious "joke" Tom plays on Jim, and set aside the penultimate happy ending for Jim that Hemingway called "cheating." Is Huck's setting out for the frontier Twain's way of having Huck refuse the responsibilities of adulthood, and prolonging his adolescence—or is it Twain's own refusal to impose adulthood on the ever-adolescent Huck? Is Twain making a statement about the preferability of clean, uncivilized life compared to the hypocritical, strait-laced civilization of Aunt Sally? Is Huck's flight from Jim an indication of Huck's inability to reconcile his relationship with Jim and the adventures they've had together with the strictures a racist society places on relationships between whites and blacks? Is Twain indulging in juvenile escapism with Huck's flight in a novel that confronts Huck and the reader with numerous harsh realities? Questions about the ending abound, with no resolution in sight.

As children and teenagers readers undoubtedly focus on the surface elements of the novel and find it satisfactory on that level. But as adults readers will find *Huckleberry Finn* a strange, uncomfortable reading experience, and all the more rewarding because of it.

Recommended Edition
Twain, Mark. *The Adventures of Huckleberry Finn* (Oxford University Press, 1996).

For Further Research
McCrum, Robert."The 100 Best Novels: No 23—The Adventures of Huckleberry Finn by Mark Twain." http://www.theguardian.com/books/2014/feb/24/100 best novels huckleberry finn twain.
Morrison, Toni. "This Amazing, Troubling Book." *The Adventures of Huckleberry Finn* (Oxford University Press, 1996).

The Hunchback of Notre Dame

The Hunchback of Notre Dame was written by Victor Hugo (*Les Misérables*) and was published in 1837. Victor-Marie Hugo (1802–1885) is seen as France's greatest lyric poet and the giant of 19th century French letters. He is best known for *Les Misérables* and *The Hunchback of Notre Dame*.

The Hunchback of Notre Dame is about Esmeralda, a beautiful Romany (Gypsy) girl. Esmeralda is loved by three men: Quasimodo, the brutish, hunchbacked ringer of the bells of the Cathedral of Notre Dame; Claude Frollo, a priest who changes, in the course of the novel, from severe and grave but essentially humane to diabolical; and Pierre Gringoire, an outcast writer and the most annoying character in the novel. Esmeralda, for her part, loves the handsome soldier Phoebus, who saves her life from a gang of thieves and from Quasimodo (in a case of mistaken motives) and in so doing wins her heart. Esmeralda holds Pierre Gringoire at arm's length, not seeing him as particularly worthy. Esmeralda dislikes Claude Frollo, and her dislike deepens into fear and hatred as Frollo increasingly succumbs to temptation. Esmeralda is initially afraid of Quasimodo, but after he rescues her from a mob and he hides her in the Cathedral and brings her food, she treats him a little kindly. But she is in love with Phoebus, and although Quasimodo is obviously smitten with her she is oblivious to this and is unconsciously cruel to Quasimodo about her love for Phoebus. Phoebus, for his part, wants Esmeralda only for sex and thinks little of her otherwise. It all ends badly, with Frollo betraying Esmeralda to the police and then watching and laughing as she is hanged. The outraged Quasimodo pushes Frollo off the Cathedral from a great height and watches him die. Quasimodo's body is found years later clutching Esmeralda's skeleton.

Critics usually count *Les Misérables* and the poetry collection *Les Contemplations* as Hugo's best work, but *The Hunchback of Notre Dame* was enormously popular in Hugo's lifetime, and was influential besides. Like many of the *romans feuilletons*, the serialized novels which were so popular with the public—**The Count of Monte Cristo** was a *feuilleton*—*Notre Dame* expressed Hugo's social humanitarianism and his sympathies for the poor and oppressed. The novel was one of the first to show commoners as playing an important role, and to have them speak in the vernacular—Hugo strove for authenticity even in the dialogue of his minor peasants.

As one of the first major novels of the French **Romantic** movement, *Notre Dame* has a fascination with medieval life and medieval Paris, and the novel took a nascent public interest in the Middle Ages and greatly amplified it. *Notre Dame* has been called by critics "the epitome of the **Gothic** Romantic novel," with the central edifice of the cathedral being an archetypal Gothic building, with Claude Frollo being a good example of the Gothic Hero-Villain, and with a variety of other Gothic elements.

Notre Dame remains an interesting read. It is a sprawling novel, almost overstuffed with information about life in Paris in the 15th century. *The Hunchback of Notre Dame* is a cornucopia of characters and places and vivid portrayals of both. Quasimodo is the character most often recalled from this novel, but he is not the main character in the novel. That is the Cathedral itself, with Paris being nearly as central a character to the story as the Cathedral. Although Hugo is interested in telling the story of Quasimodo, Esmeralda, Claude Frollo, and Phoebus, he is just as interested in relating the history of Paris and what it was like in the 12th century, in describing the Cathedral of Notre Dame de Paris at its height, in social commentary, in using characters as metaphors for different social classes, and in expressing the theme of decay, whether of the Cathedral, Paris, architecture, or the monarchy itself. Other themes include "an emphasis on fate, the contrast between beauty and the beast, the link between knowledge and power, the power, representation of change and development from monolithic opinion to individual ideas through the contrast between the cathedral and the printed word, and the types of repression that affect humankind and hint at future upheaval."

Hugo wrote *The Hunchback of Notre Dame* while under the influence of Sir Walter Scott (**Waverley**), but Hugo took a much different approach to his subject than Scott did and produced a substantially different novel than anything Scott wrote or was capable of writing. Scott's emphasis on a wide and shallow description of characters in the middle of history's procession has been replaced with a narrow but deep examination of both characters and landscape during one brief moment in time. Hugo did an enormous amount of research for *Notre Dame*, exhaustively searching through the available historical documentation, and the final result is a vivid recreation of Paris during the 15th century. Hugo's Paris is as alive as any city in fiction, from the beggars to the soldiers and from the alleys to the top of the Cathedral. If this recreation is not a completely historically accurate one—Hugo's research resources were of necessity limited themselves—Hugo does succeed in making his world *seem* real and accurate, and his characters sufficiently alien from the modern mind-set.

But this attention to Paris and the Cathedral is also the novel's largest flaw. *The Hunchback of Notre Dame* is almost too full of information. The pages seem to groan under the weight of all the facts and information about medieval Paris which Hugo has put into the novel. Hugo's purpose in writing *Notre Dame* seems to have been to combine a panoramic view of the history of the Cathedral and of Paris with a love story. But Hugo was clearly more interested in making Paris and the Cathedral into characters than in making Esmeralda and the rest of the cast come alive. Each of the main characters get their own chapters, and the novel tells a series of rotating stories about each character, but Hugo's characterization of each is much shallower than his characterization of the Cathedral, and the "fixed idea" that each is built around—Frollo as lust, Esmeralda as virgin beauty, Quasimodo as devotion—is not expanded upon beyond making the characters stereotypes. Hugo's digressions into the history and architecture of the Cathedral, into the way the Cathedral has developed a character over time, and the influence the Cathedral has on the personalities of those around it, are clearly far more interesting to him than the interactions of the human characters. And those not intimately familiar with Paris' layout will find the constant name-dropping of locations confusing and boring; the reader almost needs to have a map of Paris at hand in order to appreciate *The Hunchback of Notre Dame*.

Hugo does invest most of the novel with an acute consciousness not just of history but also of class. He focuses on the miseries of the poor and how the justice system of the time mistreated accused criminals, who had no rights under the law. But those socially-conscious moments are few compared to the *longueurs* featuring Esmeralda, Claude Frollo, and the other main characters. Quasimodo is compelling, in his way, but there are far too many dry infodumps, the sections devoted to the Cathedral hang together poorly with the sections involving the other characters, and Hugo's style does not create affection for most of the cast or even create much interest in their fates. The action sequences are few and far between, and whatever excitement the novel has is drowned in the wealth of detail.

Most readers will be happy to have read *The Hunchback of Notre Dame* once. Few will want to return to it.

Recommended Edition
Hugo, Victor. *The Hunchback of Notre Dame* (Signet Classics, 2010).

For Further Research
Ballard, Nancy G. "The Hunchback of Notre Dame." *Masterplots* Fourth Edition (Dec. 2010).
Cochran, Julie Lawrence. "The Gothic Revival in France, 1830–1845: Victor Hugo's *Notre-Dame de Paris*, Popular Imagery, and a National Patrimony Discovered." *International Congress of the History of Art: Memory & Oblivion* v29 (1999).
Marzials, Frank T. "Notre Dame de Paris." *The Harvard Classics Shelf of Fiction*. http://www.bartleby.com/312/2001.html.
Taylor, Karen L. "The Hunchback of Notre Dame." *Facts on File Companion to the French Novel* (Facts on File, 2007).

The Invisible Man

The Invisible Man was written by H.G. Wells (***The Time Machine***) and was published in 1897. Although Wells (1866–1946) is known today primarily for his science fiction, during his lifetime he was one the most prolific, versatile, and popular writers in the English language.

The Invisible Man is about Griffin, a scientist who discovers the key to invisibility. However, because the treatment only turns his body invisible, rather than both his body and his clothes, Griffin finds that invisibility is not only not the great boon he anticipated it to be, but a nuisance. So Griffin travels to a small village, hiding his invisibility beneath several layers of clothing, to work on an antidote. But he is continually bothered by the village's inhabitants, and when he is revealed to be invisible he is forced to flee the village. Griffin attempts to recruit a tramp to help him, but the tramp's assistance is minor, and he is afraid of Griffin and eventually runs from him. Griffin attempts to punish the tramp but is shot and takes refuge in the house of an old acquaintance, Doctor Kemp. Doctor Kemp betrays Griffin to the police, and after Griffin terrorizes the village of Burdock, where Kemp lives, and then attempts to kill Kemp, a crowd attacks Griffin and kills him.

The Invisible Man is a combination of the anarchy novel and the Condition of England novel. The last two decades of the 19th century were years of anxiety and distress for many Victorians, a pessimism about the British Empire and its inhabitants which appeared in works as varied as **Diana of the Crossways**, **New Grub Street**, and **She**. The *fin de siècle* unease was caused by a variety of sources, including a distrust of and unease with the lower classes, the changing role of women in society, and a perceived degenerations in the physical fitness of the English people. One of the largest reasons for this distress was the perceived threat—real enough by the late 1890s—of domestic and international anarchists. One way that many authors dealt with this threat was through the anarchist or terrorist novel, displacing the anxieties about anarchists into fiction where the threat could be defeated to the satisfaction of the audience. *The Invisible Man* is in this tradition of novels, with Griffin functioning as a personification of the anarchists, albeit one not motivated by real-life politics and grievances but rather through vanity and personal grievances, a combination of motives which would be more palatable for the English reading public to accept. The anarchic elements of the novel appear in its final section, when Griffin lays siege to the town of Burdock, declaring, "This is day one of year one of the new epoch,–the Epoch of the Invisible Man!" Although Griffin commits his attacks personally, rather than through the use of "infernal devices," his terrorism toward the town is similar to acts in other novels of anarchy. Some critics have seen the influence on Griffin of Sergei Nechaev (1847–1882), a Russian revolutionary. Nechaev's *Catechism of a Revolutionary*, however, is far more amoral and vicious than Griffin ever gets.

During the 1840s English philosophers and legislators were forced to deal with the byproducts of the 18th century's economic growth. These problems, which included gross urban overpopulation, insufficient housing, bad sanitation, and high levels of unemployment, were described by the writer Thomas Carlyle as "the Condition of England." Writers from Benjamin Disraeli (in **Coningsby**) to Mrs. Gaskell (in **Mary Barton** and **North and South**) wrote novels, variously called "Condition of England novels," "industrial fiction," and "social problem novels," which examined the changes in the social classes and social structure and the current state of England. One of the themes of *The Invisible Man* is the clash between modern science and the backwards culture and ideology of provincial England which Wells so disliked. Interestingly, however, and unlike many Condition of England novels, Wells and *The Invisible Man* are essentially in favor of industrialization and modern science. Ill-tempered though he is, Griffin is a brilliant scientist, and if not for the petty demands of the parochial villagers and of the capitalist society in which he lives, Griffin would have achieved great things. But the prying of the villagers and the need for money, to pay for rent and food as well as for materials for his experiments, goad Griffin and eventually drive him over the edge.

Another of the themes of *The Invisible Man* is Griffin's hubris and folly. Griffin values his discovery of invisibility above everything and is willing to sacrifice almost anything to gain his ends, even stealing from his father. Griffin does not care about the cost of his discovery, and he does not think about its effects. For Griffin invisibility is the means to an end, and because he is trying to gain the secret of invisibility, he is more important than other people, and they must be sacrificed in his favor. Despite Wells' approval of modern science, in the person of Griffin he is making a comment about the effect of unchecked power on scientists.

In this Griffin is the latest model of the mad scientist—a figure Wells had visited the year before in *The Island of Doctor Moreau* (1896). The mad scientist as a character type began in the 18th century, in works as varied as Jonathan Swift's *Gulliver's Travels* (1726), Christopher Smart's "The Temple of Dulness" (1745), and the Marquis de Sade's *La Nouvelle Justine* (1797), but achieved its early apotheosis in Mary Shelley's **Frankenstein**. But the mad scientist character type receded from view during the long 19th century, appearing only fitfully (primarily in stories by Nathaniel Hawthorne [**The Scarlet Letter**]) and reappearing only near the end of the 19th century, in works like *The Island of Doctor Moreau* and *The Invisible Man*. Griffin is not like other mad scientists, in that most of them are purely about the effect of unchecked power on scientists. Griffin stands for more than that. As an albino in London, and a poor albino at that—witness what critic Rosslyn Haynes calls his "bourgeois mania for financial gain"—Griffin represents the neglected underclass, the despised outsider, and his status as mad scientist is a message not only about the effect of unchecked power on scientists, but about the effect of sudden unchecked power on the poor in a capitalist society.

The book as a whole reads quickly and smoothly. Wells skillfully manipulates the dramatic tension, so that the final sequence arrives with a great deal of momentum. One of Wells' skills as a writer is the accumulation of small, believable details so that the more fantastic elements of the novel are more easily accepted by the reader. Wells' depiction of everyday life in provincial

England nicely grounds the novel, and the combination of basic scientific principles and the attention to detail, such as the food in the Invisible Man's body being visible until it is digested, creates a believable story. *The Invisible Man* has often been described as a comic novel, but the comedy seems to appeal more to the English than to Americans, who often find the comic elements lacking or nonexistent.

Lastly, there is an element of anti–Semitism in *The Invisible Man*. Those who are aware of Wells' anti–Semitic beliefs will not be surprised by this—a similar moment appears in *The War of the Worlds*—but many readers not aware of Wells' beliefs will be surprised and distressed by the remarks. Wells was a part of the pre–World War II strain of English anti–Semitism which can be seen in writers as various as Hillaire Belloc, G.K. Chesterton, Agatha Christie, and T.S. Eliot. English ambivalence about the price of modernity and progress, about politics, city values (as opposed to rural values), and the effects of unchecked Victorian capitalism manifested itself in a range of poems, stories, and novels with anti–Semitic comments and characters, from *The Invisible Man* to Chesterton's Father Brown detective stories.

Recommended Edition
Wells, H.G. *The Invisible Man* (Oxford University Press, 1996).

For Further Research
Sutherland, John. "Introduction." *The Invisible Man* (Oxford University Press, 1996).

Jane Eyre

Jane Eyre was written by Charlotte Brontë and was published in 1847. Brontë (1816–1855) is an English novelist and poet best known for *Jane Eyre*; she was also the sister of Emily Brontë (**Wuthering Heights**). Despite its age *Jane Eyre* remains one of the world's most popular novels. Additionally, it was one of the most important novels of the 19th century.

Jane Eyre is a *Bildungsroman* (a coming-of-age novel) about young Jane Eyre, an orphan. Her parents are dead, so she is forced to live, as a young child, with Mrs. Reed and her family, all of whom despise her and treat her awfully. When she goes to a boarding school for orphans, her luck does not initially improve, being underfed, exposed to typhus, and hectored by a religious zealot. She endures all of this, and eventually becomes an instructor at the school. Wanting more out of life than just her position at the school, she advertises for open positions, and accepts one as governess to a girl at a large mansion. Jane enjoys the position and the people, despite a series of strange occurrences at the mansion, but only slowly gets to know the mansion's master, Edward Rochester, who is haughty, proud, and treats her peremptorily.

However, Jane falls in love with Rochester, and after a time Rochester admits that he loves her as well. They are about to be married—literally at the altar—when a lawyer introduces an objection to the relationship: Rochester is already married. He admits this is true, but tells the whole story: that he married someone who turned out to be a crazy woman, and that she now lives in the attic of his mansion, cared for by a round-the-clock nurse. (The crazy woman was responsible for the strange occurrences.) He wants Jane to be his wife, still, but she refuses to be his mistress (which is what she would be) and leaves him. After three days of wandering and begging, she is taken in by a good family of Christians, a brother (a zealous pastor) and two sisters. They befriend and care for her, and she becomes schoolmistress of the local school. The brother proposes marriage to Jane—but it would be a chaste sort of marriage—he wants a companion to help him when he goes abroad to preach the Bible and convert heathens, and he refuses to go with her if she is not married to him. She is tempted, but she hears a phantom voice, Rochester's, calling her name, so she leaves the family and returns to Rochester's mansion.

She finds it a burned-out shell, and soon learns the truth: Rochester's crazy wife burned the house down, and while saving the servants Rochester was blinded and lost a hand. Jane goes in search of Rochester, finds him, and marries him anyhow.

Jane Eyre, like **Pride and Prejudice**, inspires a fervor among many of its readers. While I don't share that fervor for *Jane Eyre*, I do think it has a number of positive qualities. And, of course, it is hugely historically significant.

To start with *Jane Eyre*'s significance first … 1848 was a year of revolution in Europe, with the Austrian Empire, Denmark, France, Germany, Italy, and Poland most notably experiencing revolutions, and other countries experiencing significant unrest, both political and social. Great Britain did not experience a significant amount of unrest, but the upper classes feared it would, so that any novel that assaulted the upper classes and the status quo was strongly felt and reacted against. *Jane Eyre*, as loud a cry against the plight of the poor—specifically the mistreatment of governesses—and against callous religious zealotry as could be heard in that year, was bound to have an impact. That *Jane Eyre* also included a strong feminist message in its portrayal of its protagonist added to the novel's impact—what critic Daniel Burt calls "an assault on established social hierarchies, conventional morality, and the novel's accepted methods"— and led to criticisms like "altogether the autobiography of *Jane Eyre* is pre eminently an anti Christian composition" and that the book "might be written by a woman but not by a lady." Brontë intended *Jane Eyre* to be an attack on the hypocrisies of the era and of those who find it "convenient to make external show pass for sterling worth"—and she succeeds in that intention.

It is fair to say that some notable contemporary critics were not prepared to read, or fit to understand, as radical a book as *Jane Eyre*; its critical reception on publication was mixed, although it was a popular success. But in the 21st century readers and critics have the distance to properly appreciate the novel, and to understand its impact.

Arguably most importantly, Brontë was one of the first English novelists, and *Jane Eyre* one of the first novels in English, to write a *subjective* novel, one with first-person narration (which Brontë popularized in *Jane Eyre*) and which focused not on plot or dialogue-driven characterization but instead on the *inner* character of the protagonist, her thoughts and feelings and the path by which she develops psychologically. Such things had previously been poetry's preserve, not the novel's, and it was a revolutionary stroke on Brontë's part. To quote Mrs. Oliphant (**Miss Marjoribanks**) in 1855, "ten years ago we professed an orthodox system of novel-making … suddenly, without warning, *Jane Eyre* stole upon the scene."

Jane Eyre is no traditional *Bildungsroman*, no *Pride and Prejudice*-like quest for a husband and material comfort. Unusually, *Jane Eyre* is a coming-of-age novel but not the traditional form of the "female *Bildungsroman*," what is usually a quest for marriage and a stable place. *Jane Eyre* is a *Bildungsroman* about the quest for equality and autonomy, a quest to grow up into an adult rather than grow down into marriage. *Jane Eyre* is the first major female *Bildungsroman*, and one of the first major *Bildungsroman* about a member of the working classes, rather than a middle- or upper-class protagonist.

The portrayal of Jane Eyre herself was shocking to some of Brontë's contemporaries. Eyre herself is not a passive female or uneducated member of the working class. She is in many ways the antithesis of the Victorian female ideal, being neither docile, relenting, subservient to men, or even pretty. Jane Eyre is independent, assertive, stays in control of her destiny (at each point Eyre is the one to leave a job or position, rather than being discharged or cast out), and determines her own morality—it is Jane Eyre rather than Rochester who decides that living with Rochester as his mistress would be a sin, and it is Jane

Eyre who decides that a loveless (but secure) marriage to Rivers—a marriage that a secondary Austen character, like Charlotte Lucas in *Pride and Prejudice*, would quickly accept—is not for her. It is Jane Eyre who says, "I am no bird; and no net ensnares me; I am a free human being with an independent will" and behaves as such throughout the novel. As Elaine Showalter says, "The influence of *Jane Eyre* on Victorian heroines was felt to have been revolutionary. The post–Jane heroine, according to the periodicals, was plain, rebellious, and passionate; she was likely to be a governess, and she usually was the narrator of her own story."

Brontë violates conventional class prejudices by giving Jane schooling and making her both literate and intellectually curious—she possesses a life of the mind, something many Victorian males would not admit to women having. Jane Eyre is a woman of both intellectual ability and substantial passion, both emotional and sexual—this, at a time when proper women were considered to be cool and passionless, or at least were supposed to be. Jane Eyre is rebellious against authority, whether Mrs. Reed's, the teachers at Lowood Institution, or even Rochester's. Even as a child Jane speaks out against the heartless treatment shown to her by Mrs. Reed. Jane is in control of her feelings and her relationships with her men—she is the one who decides that she will marry Rochester and not marry Rivers (the pastor), not they. The famous quote, "Reader, I married him," deserves emphasis: *Jane* married *Rochester*, not vice-versa.

Little wonder that some contemporary reviewers found her appalling, and that modern readers see in *Jane Eyre* a feminist classic. (If **Emma** and *Pride and Prejudice* are early feminist works, than *Jane Eyre* is of the next generation, arguably written in reaction to them and others of the earlier generation.)

Jane Eyre is also, in the words of Daniel Burt, "the literary fountainhead of the modern gothic suspense novel that has inspired such imitators as Daphne du Maurier's best selling *Rebecca* as well as countless sentimental romance novels featuring an unassuming though plucky heroine and a dark, Byronic bad boy ultimately redeemed by love." In 1847 the **Gothic** was essentially dead as a genre. The historical novel and changing literary tastes were responsible for its demise, and despite temporary revivals in the mid–1830s (following Harrison Ainsworth's imitation Gothic *Rookwood* [1834]) and in the penny bloods of the mid- and late-1840s (following James Malcolm Rymer's *Varney the Vampyre; or, The Feast of Blood* [1845–1847]) the traditional Gothic was not returning. Brontë and *Jane Eyre* created a new Gothic (or what some critics have called an "anti–Gothic"). *Jane Eyre* has Gothic trappings, a Gothic atmosphere, and Gothic suspense, but the novel does not follow the Gothic conventions. (*Jane Eyre* is in fact at core a **Romantic** novel.) Although *Jane Eyre* has a haunted mansion and a young woman pursued by elements of the past, the novel ends with the domestication of the Hero-Villain, not his death, and with the female protagonist fully in control of her self-hood, rather than an object of the novel's plot, to be manipulated and married off. *Jane Eyre* ended up creating a new set of novelistic conventions to accompany the Gothic atmosphere and suspense.

One of the objections contemporary reviewers had was the novel's "murmuring against the comforts of the rich and against the privations of the poor, which, as far as each individual is concerned, is a murmuring against God's appointment"; for reviewers and critics like that one, the poor were meant by God to be poor, and objecting against the treatment of the poor was objecting to God's plan. Interestingly, the two groups that treat the poor, orphaned, young Jane Eyre—the Reed family and the charity school, Lowood Institution—are both homosocial or nearly entirely so, both the sphere of and controlled by women. So far, no different from the fictional worlds created by Jane Austen or other female writers. But unlike Austen, whose female worlds are for the most part positive, Brontë makes both the Reed family and the Lowood Institution greatly flawed, and the women in both a mixture of good and evil. Brontë was a feminist, of that there can be no doubt, but she was too deeply observant of human character, and had too much experience with bad people (much of *Jane Eyre* is autobiographical), to believe that female separatism was the answer.

As the foremost female practitioner of the *Bildungsroman* before Brontë, Jane Austen would in fact seem to be the natural comparison for Charlotte Brontë. But Brontë famously didn't like Austen, writing,

> Anything like warmth or enthusiasm, anything energetic, poignant, heartfelt, is utterly out of place in commending these works: all such demonstrations the authoress would have met with a well bred sneer, would have calmly scorned as outré or extravagant. She does her business of delineating the surface of the lives of genteel English people curiously well. There is a Chinese fidelity, a miniature delicacy, in the painting. She ruffles her reader by nothing vehement, disturbs him with nothing profound. The passions are perfectly unknown to her: she rejects even a speaking acquaintance with that stormy sisterhood.... What sees keenly, speaks aptly, moves flexibly, it suits her to study: but what throbs fast and full, though hidden, what the blood rushes through, what is the unseen seat of life and the sentient target of death—this Miss Austen ignores.... Jane Austen was a complete and most sensible lady, but a very incomplete and rather insensible (not *senseless* woman), if this is heresy—I cannot help it.

This criticism, that Austen lacks anything approaching the passion that *Jane Eyre* is full of, may lie at the heart of why some readers take to *Jane Eyre* with a fervor and others, like myself, react somewhat coolly to it. Some readers are thinkers, others are feelers, and the former take to Austen as the latter take to Brontë.

No reader can deny *Jane Eyre*'s innate qualities. The book is well-written, the prose the product of great thought and careful crafting, the phrasing far less dated than, for example, Dickens' later **Bleak House**. The imagery is fine, the prose often poetic and full of potent symbolism. (T.S. Eliot's "objective correlative," the external objects which provide insight to a character's internal thoughts and emotions, is in full play in *Jane Eyre*.) Although *Jane Eyre* was a rebellion against fashionable realism (see **Vanity Fair**) in its use of the uncanny and the supernatural and the Gothic elements, the novel's tracing of Jane Eyre's development and maturation is realistic; Jane becomes fully three-dimensional. (As well as a pleasingly different heroine from much Victorian fiction.) Mr. Rochester does not quite approach that, but he remains one of the most memorable of the Gothic Hero-Villains, as well as a model for countless modern romance heroes. For those not exposed to any of the numerous film or TV versions of *Jane Eyre*, the plot is pleasingly twisted—the revelation of Rochester's wife comes as a genuine surprise, if one doesn't already know about it—and Brontë always plays fair with the reader about the consequences of characters' actions.

Jane Eyre's references and homages—to Shakespeare, to Bunyan's *Pilgrim's Progress*, to Cinderella, Bluebeard, Samson, Cupid and Psyche—work to strengthen *Jane Eyre*, to reinforce its familiarity, rather than reduce the novel to a mere set of allusions. And the central theme of repression—emotional, sexual, and political—and what critic Lucy Hughes-Hallett calls "the hideous but ultimately salutary consequences of confronting the repressed" are played out strongly.

Still, *Jane Eyre*, at least for this reader, inspires respect rather than affection. I freely acknowledge its historical importance and am happy to admit it into the literary Canon, and I will gladly argue for its finer points as a novel. But.... Jane and Rochester are not exactly *likable*. One cares for what happens to them, and is glad for the happy ending, but one doesn't wish for them to step out of the pages of the novel and into reality, the way one does with Elizabeth Bennet or **Lorna Doone**'s John Ridd. If the reader is not naturally inclined to extreme passions, the inflamed hearts and swirling emotions of *Jane Eyre* will not touch them, at least not in the deep and lasting way that *Jane Eyre* does with its devotees. It's said that the right age to read science fiction is twelve; perhaps the best age for reading *Jane Eyre* is sixteen?

Moreover, the novel has a troubled relationship with issues of race—Rochester's first wife, Bertha Mason, is a mixed-race Creole, and described in animalistic terms—and imperialism—the role of Rivers as converter of foreign heathens, a role applauded by Jane Eyre, is a purely imperialistic one. The work of Jane Austen can be seen, arguably, as an argument for whiteness, with non-whites notable by their absence; non-whites, conversely, are present in *Jane Eyre*, and portrayed in racist terms. Brontë, in *Jane Eyre*, was agitating for the oppressed of the 1848 revolutions—hence the famous quote that "millions are condemned to a stiller doom than mine, and millions are in silent revolt against their lot. Nobody knows how many rebellions besides political rebellions ferment in the masses of life which people earth." But Brontë was purely of her time when it comes to race and imperialism.

Jane Eyre is worth reading—once—for its prose, and to understand its historical significance. More than that I cannot say.

Recommended Edition
Brontë, Charlotte. *Jane Eyre* (Penguin Classics, 2006).

For Further Research
Brackett, Virginia. "Jane Eyre." *Facts on File Companion to the British Novel: Beginnings through the 19th Century, vol. 1* (Facts on File, 2006).
Burt, Daniel S. "Jane Eyre." *The Novel 100: A Ranking of the Most Influential Novels of All Time* (CheckmarkBooks, 2010).
Gilbert, Sandra M. *The Madwoman in the Attic: The Woman Writer and the Nineteenth Century LiteraryImagination* (Yale University Press, 2000).
Hughes-Hallett, Lucy. "Introduction." *Jane Eyre* (Everyman's Library, 1991). "Jane Eyre." *The Victorian Web*. http://www.victorianweb.org/authors/bronte/cbronte/eyreov.html.
McCrum, Robert. "The 100 Best Novels: No. 12—*Jane Eyre*." http://www.theguardian.com/books/2013/dec/09/100 best novels jane eyre.
Oates, Joyce Carol. "Jane Eyre: An Introduction." *Jane Eyre* (Bantam Classic, 1988).
Shuttleworth, Sally. "Introduction." *Jane Eyre* (Oxford University Press, 2000).
Sweets, Sparky. "Jane Eyre—Book Summary & Analysis." https://www.youtube.com/watch?v=lPlN_HIU55U.

Jude the Obscure

Jude the Obscure was created by Thomas Hardy (**Tess of the d'Urbervilles**) and was published as a serial in 1894 and 1895 and as a novel in 1895. Hardy (1840–1928) was an English novelist and poet regarded as one of the greatest of his generation. *Jude the Obscure* was his last published novel.

Jude Fawley is a poor stonemason in the small English village of Marygreen. As a boy he hungers for learning and wants to go to the Oxford-like city of Christminster to study for a degree, but he is too poor and has to stay in Marygreen and help his great-aunt Drusilla at her bakery. He teaches himself the classics with the help of his former schoolmaster Phillotson. At the age of nineteen Jude apprentices himself to a stonemason, and while walking home he catches the attention of a local girl, Arabella, who seduces him and tricks him into marriage by telling him she is pregnant. But the marriage quickly goes bad, and he tries to commit suicide. Arabella leaves him for Australia, although they remain married.

Jude moves to Christminster, and there meets his cousin, Sue Bridehead. Jude tries to view her simply as a cousin, but he falls in love with her. She becomes Phillotson's asssistant, and Phillotson, too falls in love with her, which hurts Jude, and he takes to drink, having also been disappointed in his academic hopes at Christminser, and loses his job. He returns to Marygreen. Sue enters a teacher's college at Melchester, but is kicked out of the college after an innocent night out with Jude. She goes ahead and marries Phillotson, but married life—specifically the sexual aspect of it—is not for Sue, and she lets Jude know how unhappy she is. He lets her know he is in love with her, and Phillotson, out of the goodness of his heart, lets Sue go to be with Jude. Jude and Sue move to another city where they live together unknown to the public. Phillotson grants Sue a divorce and loses his teaching position, and Jude grants Arabella a divorce so she can remarry.

Sue and Jude never quite get around to being married, largely due to Sue's dislike for a binding contract. Arabella sends the pair her son by Jude, the pathetic Little Father Time, but when people find out about Jude living with an a woman but not marrying her they decline to give him business, and he is forced into a wandering lifestyle. Two and a half years later Jude and Sue have two children and a third on the way, but poverty has them in its grip, and when Sue complains to the gloomy Little Father Time that children should not be brought into the world, Little Father Time hangs the two babies and himself, on the grounds that "we are too menny."

Believing herself a sinner, Sue leaves Jude and returns to Phillotston, who she remarries, to punish herself. Jude begins drinking heavily, and is tricked into remarrying Arabella. Jude's health declines and he dies after hearing that Sue has completely become Phillotston's wife.

Jude the Obscure is Hardy's bleakest, most despairing novel. That it is quite readable, and Hardy's best novel, does not salve the pain of Jude's fate.

The story is ultimately what critic Harold Bloom calls "the reverse of theodicy, being Hardy's ultimate declaration that the ways of the Immanent Will towards man are unjustifiable," and many contemporary readers and critics found *Jude* variously depressing, infuriating, obscene, and even blasphemous. The modern reader is likely to agree in part with Hardy's contemporaries, as *Jude* is one extra-long buzz-kill. Nothing works out for Jude, ever. What little joy there is in his life is soon crushed from him, and what happiness he achieves soon expires. In J. Hillis Miller's phrase, "in Hardy's world what you want you cannot have, and what you have you do not want." Even if he brings some of his own misery on himself, through his own foolishness, life still deals him nothing but defeat after defeat. Those modern readers who manage to identify with him will find *Jude* extremely depressing. (One critical argument *contra* this approach is to credit Jude with an innate dignity, and to point out that Jude continues to struggle against uncaring fate to the end—that as Sue Bridehead says, "if you have failed, it is to your credit rather than your blame," in that he continued trying. A second critical argument is that *Jude the Obscure* is actually full of black humor, although this argument is likely to be seen as improbable by many readers.)

However, modern readers will find a number of the concerns of Hardy's contemporaries alien or extreme. The supposed vulgarity of the novel, in the attention it pays to the sexual aspect of relationships, is minor compared to the vulgarities that modern readers have routinely become exposed to in modern life; many Young Adult novels are more explicit and vulgar than *Jude*, which—explicit though it was for a Victorian audience—is now relatively illusive and eliptical in dealing with its more earthy material. Only an educated reader will be able to understand that Arabella, to catch Jude's attention, throws a pig's penis at him; the text merely calls it the "characteristic" part of the pig.

Similarly, what contemporary readers found to be the most obscene and grotesque moment in the novel, Little Father Time's murder of himself and the other children, retains its power to shock and dismay, but as obscenity it falls short compared to the many other obscenities of our fallen world that students have been exposed to. Students today will, again, find *Jude* depressing and perhaps even shocking, but will in all likelihood not react with the same venom that some of Hardy's contemporaries did, a venom that ultimately drove Hardy away from writing novel-length fiction ever again. (This venom did not stop the novel from becoming a best-seller and, in its way, helping to put an end to the influence of the moralistic lending libraries over publishers.)

Hardy is one of the most acclaimed novelists of the 19th century, and is seen as a key bridge between the world of George Eliot (**Middlemarch**) and the realist, Naturalist world of 20th century authors like D.H. Lawrence. Certainly Hardy has much of the trappings of Victoriana while establishing the more earthy, and earthly, style of Lawrence and later authors. His style is in the very readable, little-dated mode of the 1890s (albeit there are moments when he lapses into regional dialect, which can make for trying reading). But where Hardy is *sui generis*, neither of the more religious 19th century nor the more agnostic/atheistic 20th century, is his insistence that God exists, but is inimical to humanity—that, in Harold Bloom's words, *Jude* is "the triumph of life over human integrity." (In this, as in his use of a Schopenhauerian will in relation to his fictional geography, Hardy prefigures the work of horror writer H.P. Lovecraft.)

Other themes of the novel include Hardy's attack on the few societal choices available to the working poor; the "deadly war waged between flesh and spirit," in Hardy's own words; an attack on conventional morality and a small-minded society; and attacks on the higher education's exclusion of the poor, on the social class structure, and especially on the restrictions of contemporary marriage laws.

Of interest to the modern reader is Sue Bridehead's role as an example of the **New Woman**. Bridehead has been called one of the first feminists in Victorian literature, and she certainly represents the New Woman in her dissatisfaction with the strictures of marriage and society. But where Jude is a particularly hapless Everyman, someone unable to resist his passionate impulses nor drink, Bridehead is an unappealing New Woman, and one that is not constructed to represent the New Woman in a positive way. She fulfills the stereotype of the undersexed female intellectual, the feminist who hates sex (or at the least has no sex drive), while also being a tease toward poor Jude and someone ultimately without the courage of her own convictions. Hardy can be criticized for going beyond a despairing and bleak outlook in Bridehead's depiction and into making her a negative stereotype, albeit a complicated one. (Bridehead, like Jude, has three dimensions and is more than just a stereotype, though stereotype she is.) To quote J. Hillis Miller, Bridehead can be interpreted in Freudian terms, as "a certain kind of hysteric who punishes men by arousing their desire and then holding them off."

As mentioned, Hardy's style is eminently readable and has aged only a very little. *Jude*, though, is not plot-heavy, despite its length. It is a study of character and environment rather than of a novel of ideas or plot. In that respect it is quite successful. The depressing stuff aside, *Jude* creates three-dimensional, humanly complicated characters in Jude and Sue, and aptly creates an entire world in Christminster and Marygreen—not to the degree he does in *Tess of the D'Urbervilles*, with that novel's magical recreation of rural life, but skillfully done nonetheless. Regardless of what one might think of his choices as an author, Hardy is enormously talented in creating both character and environment. Likewise, in creating an anti- *Bildungsroman* (coming-of-age novel) Hardy exquisitely limns the maturation and destruction of Jude—it is not a pleasant limning, but it is a very skillfully-wrought one.

Jude the Obscure can also be seen as a late-19th century **Gothic** novel. Although it lacks the flash and sizzle of other late century **Gothics**, such as ***Dracula*** and ***Dr. Jekyll and Mr. Hyde***, *Jude* has Gothic architecture and geography, in the decaying city of Christminster, has the Gothic "trauma of the past's eruption into the present," in Patrick O'Malley's phrase, in the Fawley family curse, and the Gothic sexual and religious deviance—this time not as a foreign element, but as an intrinsic part of modern English society.

Hardy's focus on rural life, and the old ways of Christminster, sits somewhat oddly with a tone of *fin de siècle* unease that he strikes. Hardy does not present rural life or Christminster's ways as being in danger—they seem to be as strong as ever, much stronger than poor Jude or any of the poor can master. But Hardy does have a *fin de siècle* unease, that pessimism about the British Empire and its inhabitants that was common among writers and thinkers during the last two decades of the 19th century—an unease that manifests itself in works as varied as **New Grub Street**, **She**, and **The Invisible Man**. The unease was caused by a variety of sources, including a distrust of and unease with the lower classes, the changing role of women in society, and a perceived degenerations in the physical fitness of the English people. In *Jude the Obscure* it manifests itself in Little Father Time and his mentality when he kills himself and the other children:

> The doctor says there are such boys springing up amongst us—boys of a sort unknown in the last generation—the outcome of new views of life. They seem to see all its terrors before they are old enough to have staying power to resist them. He says it is the beginning of the coming universal wish not to live.

Recommended Edition

Hardy, Thomas. *Jude the Obscure* (Everyman's Library, 1992).

For Further Research

Bolch, Judith. *Masterplots* Fourth Edition (Nov. 2010).
Kramer, Dale, ed. *The Cambridge Companion to Thomas Hardy* (Cambridge University Press, 1999).
"The Literary Works of Thomas Hardy." http://victorianweb.org/authors/hardy/works.html.
McCrum, Robert. "The 100 Best Novels: No. 29—*Jude the Obscure*." http://www.theguardian.com/books/2014/apr/07/100 best novels jude obscure thomas hardy.
Miller, J. Hillis. "Introduction." *Jude the Obscure* (Everyman's Library, 1992).
O'Malley, Patrick. "Oxford's Ghosts: Jude the Obscure and the End of Gothic." *MFS Modern Fiction Studies* v46n3 (Fall 2000).

Kidnapped

Kidnapped was written by Robert Louis Stevenson (**Dr. Jekyll and Mr. Hyde**) and was published as a magazine serial in 1886 and as a novel later that year. Although posterity, snobbery, and ignorance have relegated Stevenson (1850–1894) to the role of children's author, for *Kidnapped* and *Treasure Island*, in the second half of the 19th century Stevenson was a major writer, close friends with Henry James and H. Rider Haggard, producer of best-sellers and critically-acclaimed works, a writer who wrote for all age groups and whose work was read by both low- and high-brows. Discerning critics have (justifiably) called Stevenson the initiator of the "Age of Storytellers," the great flowering of high-quality popular fiction from the 1880s until 1914.

Kidnapped is about David Balfour, a teenaged Scotsman. David's father dies and leaves David only a letter which will introduce David to his Uncle Ebenezer. David happily travels to the house of Shaw, his ancestral home. But Uncle Ebenezer does not welcome David's presence, and after a short, uneasy stay Ebenezer arranges for David to be kidnapped, taken on board the *Covenant* by its captain, Hoseason and its crew, and held there. The *Covenant* is bound for the Carolinas, where David is to be sold into indentured slavery. David initially has a hard time on the *Covenant*, but the longer he is on board the ship the kinder the crew is to him. But one day, off the coast of England, the *Covenant* runs down a small boat and cuts it in two. Only one of the boat's crew, Alan Breck Stewart, a Scottish Jacobite and soldier of fortune, is saved. Captain Hoseason pretends to agree to put Alan ashore, but this is a ruse—Hoseason and the crew plan to rob Alan and kill him—and David, on hearing the Captain plan Alan's death, reveals the plot to Alan. Alan and David fight off the Captain and crew, killing several, and when the *Covenant* runs ashore (the crew, decimated by Alan and David, is not sufficient to pilot the ship) Alan and David are cast ashore. Unfortunately an enemy of Alan's is murdered in front of David, and Alan and David are blamed for the murder. Through the course of the novel Alan and David are hunted across Scotland, usually through areas controlled by the enemies of David's clan. The pair suffer privation and misery before reaching safety. They manage to contact Mr. Rankeillor, a lawyer friendly to David's family friend, the Reverend Campbell, and with Rankeillor's help they confront Ebenezer and force him (through a neat trick) to give David the share of his inheritance he is rightly due.

It is highly regrettable that the vagaries of librarianship and publishing have put *Kidnapped* in the category of Young Adult fiction and so convinced generations of readers that *Kidnapped* is therefore not to be considered as seriously as, for example, *Dr. Jekyll and Mr. Hyde*. This is in part the result of Stevenson's dedication, that he "has in this new avatar no more desperate purpose than to steal some young gentleman's attention from his Ovid, carry him awhile into the Highlands and the last century, and pack him to bed with some engaging images to mingle with his dreams."

Stevenson certainly considered the novel seriously, and the modern reader can only conclude, after reading it, that *Kidnapped* is a novel for adults as well as, or perhaps rather than, children.

There are, certainly, fine novels for children and young adults. But *Kidnapped* addresses more serious matters, in a more serious manner, than most 19th century novels for children and young adults did. *Kidnapped* has a high level of realism, of characterization, description, and action, which young adult novels often lack, and there is a real harshness, even brutality, to *Kidnapped* which authors of novels for young adults usually refrain from describing.

The realism of *Kidnapped* is well done. All of the characters, from David and Alan to more minor ones, are recognizable and human, neither unrealistically perfect nor cartoonishly vile. David has his pettiness, Alan his vanity, while the villainous Captain Hoseason is good to his men and the avaricious Uncle Ebenezer is as generous a host as his neuroses about money allows him to be. The dialogue is conversational and recognizable, and while Stevenson, a vigorous Scottish patriot, puts in a large amount of Scottish dialect and slang, in almost every case the meaning of the Scottish word is understandable from its context. Similarly, while Scottish history is important to the story, modern readers do not need to know any of it to enjoy *Kidnapped*; Stevenson does a good job of providing context for the novel's backdrop and characters. However, a good set of annotations will substantially add to the modern reader's enjoyment of the novel.

The fights and escapes have a realistic feel, so that they seem like events that might actually happen rather than the fun but essentially unrealistic exploits of **The Three Musketeers**. Even more authentic are the hardships which David and Alan endure. There is little of the picaresque in *Kidnapped* or the romanticization and idealization of a Sir Walter Scott (**Waverley**) novel, and the novel might well be read as a rebuke to them. David and Alan suffer from starvation, are usually cold and wet, fall sick, and endure the many other anti-romantic but realistic things that men hunted across the Scottish highlands during the winter would have to endure. Their lives are hard, not easy, which is as it should be.

The tone and pace of the novel are perfect. There is a near-constant pressure on David and Alan, and Stevenson never lets up nor gives the characters or the reader much time to pause and reflect on the situation. The reader feels the danger threatening David and Alan. Likewise, Stevenson's use of emotion is understated, rather than overblown, with the result that its appearance is more keenly felt. The argument between David and Alan, which almost breaks their friendship, is painful to read. Theirs is a more sophisticated portrayal of the heroic figure than was common among Stevenson's contemporaries. Indeed, *Kidnapped* might even be a reaction to Romanticism's idealization of the innocence of childhood.

Stevenson's use of language is precise; there is a sparseness to it which suits the story. In a novel in which most of the text is spent on characters being hunted, over-done descriptions of the environment or prolix dialogues, would not only be out of place but would hurt the tone of the novel. Instead, the language is stripped-down, to better service the story. People often come away from *Kidnapped* with vivid memories of the Scottish landscape, but the truth is that Stevenson spends relatively little time actually describing the landscape, instead relying on impressionistic descriptions which convey the meaning he intended. And the humor of the novel is witty and ironic rather than awkward jokes or slapstick scenes. In a novel like *Kidnapped*, this is a wise and welcome choice, for it enhances the tone of the novel rather than spoiling it.

The novel does have its share of brutality, and appropriately so. We see the very real and sad effects of violence and drunkenness. Stevenson does not understate the effects of either or downplay their consequences. And with certain characters, like the ship's boy Ransome, the brutality leads to a sad end.

Recommended Edition

Stevenson, Robert Louis. *Kidnapped* (Oxford Worlds Classics, 2014).

For Further Research

"Kidnapped." *Masterplots* Fourth Edition (Dec. 2010).
McCrum, Robert. "The 100 Best Novels: No 24—Kidnapped by Robert Louis Stevenson." http://www.theguardian.com/books/2014/mar/03/100 best novels kidnapped robert louis stevenson.

Kim

Kim was written by Rudyard Kipling and appeared as a serial in 1900 and 1901 and as a novel in 1901. Kipling (1865–1936) was one of the dominant British popular writers of the late 19th and early 20th century. Kim is his best novel-length work.

Kim is about Kimball O'Hara, the son of a British soldier in India. Kim is orphaned as a child and grows up on the streets of Lahore, where he is cared for only by an Indian woman who lets him run wild and do as he wishes. One day Kim meets Teshoo Lama, a Tibetan lama, and escorts him to a local museum. The two strike up a friendship and Kim decides to accompany the lama on his quest for the river of enlightenment. Kim begs for the lama and acts as his "chela," or disciple. At the same time Kim is carrying a message from an agent of the British Secret Service to a British Colonel. This message, when delivered, helps avert a local rebellion. Kim finds the British regiment his father belonged to and is sent to a British school, where he is educated. Meanwhile Kim is recruited by the British Secret Service, and after three years he leaves school and carries out missions for the Secret Service. Eventually Kim rejoins his beloved Teshoo Lama and treks with him through the Himalayas. During the trip Kim helps foil a Russian spy mission. During the trip the lama is injured, and after a harrowing journey across the mountains Kim carries the lama back to safety and civilization. Kim and the lama heal, and the lama finds enlightenment.

As one of the best-known works of Victorian popular literature Kim has a well-earned reputation for entertainment. As time has passed Kim's more problematic aspects have been cast into starker relief.

Purely as entertainment, and leaving aside its political and moral flaws, Kim is superb. Its charms are many. Kim is Kipling's most successful novel-length work, and is the product of a craftsman with both heart and substantial skill. Kipling was better known in his lifetime for his work about India than any of his other work, and his portrayal of the post–Mutiny, pre–Gandhi India is sure-handed and utterly convincing—as much so, in its way, as Gustave Flaubert's Carthage in **Salammbô**. Kipling spent his first six years in India and viewed it as almost a paradise, a feeling he amply conveys in Kim. The level of local color and detail is perfectly done, neither too scanty nor overwhelming, and Kipling's use of Anglo-Indian dialect is sure-handed and wonderful. Some critics and some Indians have criticized the portrayal of India in *Kim* as inaccurate, and there is an undeniable element of sentimentality to Kipling's depiction of the land and its people. But if Kipling got India wrong, his portrayal is the way India—not the Indians and the British, but the country itself—should have been, and Kipling's affection for India and the Indians should forgive any factual inaccuracies. If Kipling erred, he did so out of the best of intentions.

The novel has a high level of craft about it. Though obviously influenced by Twain's **Huckleberry Finn** in its portrayal of Kim as a free-but-lonely wanderer in a picaresque adventure, *Kim* goes in much different directions than Twain did. The style is smooth and polished and has none of the torpid prolixity that can damage the modern reader's enjoyment of other Victorian novels. The narrative voice is strong, distinctive, and unique, although it may take some readers some time to adjust to it. Kipling maintains the tone and characterization flawlessly. Kipling does not linger over matters the way Victor Hugo (**Hunchback of Notre Dame**) or James Fenimore Cooper (**Last of the Mohicans**) do. Where they are long-winded, Kipling is precise; where they prolong scenes, he ends them quickly and possibly even too soon. Where they are overblown, he is understated.

The cast of characters is wonderful: Mahbub Ali, the wise, cynical Pathan horse dealer and British agent; Colonel Creighton, the British Secret Service commander in India; Teshoo Lama, the dotty and suitably unearthly lama in search of enlightenment; Lurgan Sahib, the healer of sick pearls; and Hurree Chunder Mookerjee, the irrepressible Bengali spy. These characters are all human and recognizable. Those who might be stereotypes, like Teshoo Lama or the Pathan horse dealer Mahbub Ali, are given depth and are characters rather than stereotypes. Kipling's humor is good-natured and lacking in mockery or cruelty; character traits rather than ethnicity are the source of humor. Nor does Kipling have a brief for Christianity over Buddhism, Islam, or Hinduism. He is in fact much friendlier to the Buddhism of Teshoo Lama than he is to Catholicism and Christianity, neither of which come off particularly well in *Kim*.

Too, the novel has real feeling to it. The sentiment in Hugo and Cooper, among others, is overblown and will leave most modern readers unmoved. But the understated but nonetheless very real love between Kim and Teshoo Lama is genuinely affecting.

But of course entertainment is not the beginning and end of a work of fiction. There is the question of its artistic value—and Edward Said, in his invaluable analysis of *Kim*, called the novel "a work of great aesthetic merit," and Kipling clearly spent as much time crafting each sentence as Henry James did in *The Portrait of a Lady*—and the question of its moral and political aspects, and this is where an understanding and judgment of *Kim* becomes less kind. Like Kipling himself *Kim* is controversial. Kipling is seen as the poet laureate of British Imperialism and Empire, a proponent of racism and bigotry, a water-carrier for virtues best forgotten, and so on, and *Kim* is viewed as, again in Said's words, "the racist imagining of one fairly disturbed and ultra-reactionary imperialist."

A close reading of *Kim* does show that Kipling was not an ignorant, unthinking mouthpiece for Empire, and that his treatment of race and race relations is, if not nuanced, at least more thoughtful than his severest critics allege. Kipling's views on race are certainly those of a conservative member of and believer in Empire, circa 1901. Which is to say, he is not enlightened or progressive in modern terms. But Kipling is a believer in essentialism: the "Oriental" is essentially one way (albeit, like H. Rider Haggard [*She*], made up of individual races and groups with their individual racial or group traits), and the Englishman is essentially another way—a view expressed strongly in *Kim*. Kipling, and *Kim*, believe that India is best governed not by Indians but by a small group of experienced and knowledgeable Englishman (Kipling was hostile to democracy for both Indians and English). Colonialism, for Kipling, is what is best for India, and the English are, on balance, superior to the Indians.

The reader, in other words, is forced to grapple with the age-old conundrum of politically/morally flawed art written by a politically/morally flawed author. Is *Kim* racist, colonialist, imperialist, paternalistic, stereotypical, and unrealistic? Or is it rich, sympathetic, colorful, and sensitive? Is Kim himself a proponent of colonialism, or someone caught within it and struggling the best he can to survive in it?

The answer is "yes." A work of art can be many things at once, and a work's good qualities do not cancel or justify its bad ones—nor does a work's bad qualities negate the work's good qualities. *Kim* is all of these things.

Of note is *Kim's* role in the history of espionage fiction. Espionage was not well-respected in England during the 19th century, being seen with contempt, as the tawdry, sordid work of immoral, mercenary men. The popular fiction of the time reflected this attitude toward espionage. The story papers and dime novels of the mid- and late 19th century occasionally featured heroes who spied. But the authors of these stories always portrayed the hero as a gentleman who performed espionage out of noble patriotism, thus redeeming otherwise sordid behavior. The rise in cultural and political anxieties at the end of the century—the *fin de siècle* unease mentioned in other novels (see **New Grub Street**, *The Portrait of a Lady*, *The Invisible Man*)—began to change approach to spying. *Kim* started a trend toward the amateur spy, a trend which would culminate in Erskine Childers' *The Riddle of the Sands* (1903), the most popular espionage story of the era. Despite being an early novel about espionage *Kim* handles the subject more interestingly than many later novels. The spy subplot is straightforward, but Kipling's treatment of it consistently holds the reader's interest. Because it is only a subplot, and not the main point of the novel—*Kim* is what Kipling called "a naked picaresque"—the espionage aspects are not overdone or given undue attention. They are referred to enough to whet the reader's appetite but never to sate it.

Equally interesting is *Kim*'s status as an anomalous work of English frontier fiction. One of the core conflicts of traditional (read: American) frontier fiction (read: the Western) is this: the frontier is inhabited by barbarians; barbarians can only be defeated by the gun; but all those who pick up the gun are barbarians; therefore those who defeat the barbarians cannot inhabit the newly-civilized frontier. In American frontier fiction, and especially in Western films (see, for example, John Ford's *The Searchers* and Ford's *The Man Who Shot Liberty Valence*) this means that after the hero has defeated the barbarians he must leave the newly civilized frontier. In English frontier fiction the hero who picks up the gun is not a barbarian and is allowed to return to civilization even after committing barbarous violence. (One reason for this is that in English frontier fiction barbarians are an irruption of evil into an ordinarily civilized status quo, the status quo that the protagonist comes from, and once the status quo is reinstated by the defeat of the barbarians, civilization reigns supreme and the gun-slinging hero can return to his home. In American frontier fiction barbarians—and the gun-slinging hero—are a part of a fallen, barbaric frontier world, and when the new, civilized status quo is imposed, the gun-slinging hero has no place in it.) This was the case for **Lorna Doone**, and for other novels set in English frontier settings, such as Scotland, Ireland, and Australia. But India is different, and Colonel Creighton, that would-be member of the Royal Geographical Society, is far closer to the traditional American taker-up-of-the-gun than he is to most English frontier heroes.

For all its many flaws *Kim* remains a strong work of Victorian popular fiction, what Edward Said called "large in perspective and strangely sensitive" and which Harold Bloom said "is one of the great instances in the language of a popular adventure story that is also exalted literature."

Recommended Edition
Kipling, Rudyard. *Kim* (Penguin, 1987).

For Further Research
Jussawalla, Feroza. "(Re)reading *Kim*: Defining Kipling's Masterpiece as Postcolonial." *Journal of Commonwealth and Postcolonial Studies* v5n2 (Fall 1998).

McCrum, Robert. "The 100 Best Novels: Nov 34—Kim by Rudyard Kipling (1901)." http://www.theguardian.com/books/2014/may/12/100-best-novels-kim-rudyard-kipling
Said, Edward. "Introduction." *Kim* (Penguin, 1987).
Wegner, Phillip E. "'Life as He Would Have It': The Invention of India in Kipling's 'Kim.'" *Cultural Critique* v26 (Winter 1993–1994).

Lady Audley's Secret

Lady Audley's Secret was created by Mary Elizabeth Braddon and was published as a serial in 1861 and 1862 and as a novel in 1862. Braddon (1835–1915) was a popular novelist. *Lady Audley's Secret* is her best known novel.

Sixty-year-old widower Sir Michael Audley marries the beautiful, enchanting, doll-like blonde Lucy Graham, about whom little is known beyond that she was a governess before Audley married her. Meanwhile Audley's cousin Robert welcomes his old friend, George Talboys, back to England. George has just returned from Australia, where he became rich, and is anxious to hear word of his wife, whom he abandoned three years before. Tallboys is heartbroken when he discovers that his wife died just before he returned to England. To comfort Tallboys, Robert takes him to meet Sir Michael, where they do not meet Lady Audley, but they see a portrait of her, which causes George to act strangely. And then he disappears, something that upsets Robert enough that he devotes his life to searching for George. While doing so he begins taking notes and begins suspecting Lady Audley of having been involved in George's disappearance. Circumstantial evidence leads him to believe that Lady Audley is actually George's supposedly dead wife. Robert meets and begins to fall in love with George's sister Clara, who looks like a female version of George.

Investigating further, Robert discovers the truth: Lady Audley was George's wife, and faked her own death as a way to escape poverty and begin a new life elsewhere. (She also abandoned her son and left him with her father.) Lady Audley tries to kill Richard off by burning down an inn he is sleeping in, but she fails, and he confronts her, forcing her to confess all to Sir Michael. Sir Michael, heartbroken (he truly loved his wife, and she, for her part, loved him to the best of her ability), leaves for Europe, and Robert has Lady Audley committed to a European insane asylum. George Tallboys turns up alive—even though Lady Audley had tried to kill him on the night of his disappearance—Richard marries George's sister, and Lady Audley eventually dies.

Lady Audley's Secret is an infuriating work, for the modern reader can't help but conclude that *the bad guys won and the heroine lost.*

This conclusion would not have been reached by Braddon's contemporary audience—who read *Lady Audley's Secret* in droves—as they would have viewed the novel as being about a bigamist and child abandoner who married a man under false pretenses and ultimately got her comeuppance. The contemporary view of *Lady Audley's Secret* was that the plot was conventional—though of course written enthrallingly, virtually forcing the reader to turn the page—with the only exceptional aspect being Lady Audley herself. The contemporary view of *Lady Audley's Secret* was that Lady Audley was the villain, Richard Audley the hero, and so Richard's triumph is that of the hero.

But modern readers will likely feel differently. Braddon does an excellent job of characterizing Lady Audley, of describing her hopes and her many fears and the torment she lives with. Poor Lady Audley—product of a broken home and an insane mother, and taught from a young age that her mother's madness is hereditary and that she may well be subject to it, and living her whole life in poverty, suffering through a first marriage to a man who abandoned her. Modern readers, unless they have a heart of stone, will empathize with Lady Audley, whose treatment of Sir Michael (apart from the deception of her background) is flawless, and will come to conclude that Richard is a monomaniacal prig whose merciless hounding of Lady Audley is unjustified under the circumstances, and that she, despite her desperate attempts at violence, is the victim and he the persecutor.

Those, of course, are the emotional reactions of a reader to what is a very well-told story, one readable, suspenseful, and involving. There are other aspects of *Lady Audley's Secret* which are to be considered, however, and these aspects lead critics to view the novel as an outstanding example of the **Sensation Novel**.

Most significant is Lady Audley herself. The traditional trope in English popular literature was to identify sin with dark hair and innocence and purity with blonde hair. Heroines were blonde and villainesses, or at least complex women, had black hair. This was the case in *Jane Eyre*, among others. Braddon's reversal of this trope, which is thought to have been written as a kind of direct rebuke to Wilkie Collins' **The Woman in White**, with Lady Audley being a villainous replay of Laura Fairlie, proved to be immensely influential, and created a new kind of character in English Sensation, crime, and popular fiction: what Mrs. Oliphant (**Miss Marjoribanks**) said was "that gentle and amiable heroine, fair haired, blue eyed, and capable of every crime, who has been so often repeated since."

There is also the relationship between Richard Audley and George Tallboys. Few novels, Sensation or otherwise, come as close as *Lady Audley's Secret* to describing a homosexual relationship. Richard's obsession with finding George, his constant dwelling on him, his interest in Clara only when discovering that she has her brother's looks—even the moment when he should be thinking of Clara but George's image floats before him—they all contribute to a novel in which, quite deliberately, a homosexual (or bisexual) protagonist is described, in a way that was obvious, but rarely so in Victorian literature.

And "quite deliberately" it was, on Braddon's part, it seems clear. As later critics have concluded, *Lady Audley Secret* was intentionally written as an inversion of traditional Victorian literary cliches, and deliberately written to play on Victorian gender and class anxieties—Braddon *intentionally* wrote the archetypal Sensation Novel. If the Victorians would think of crime and murder as something that happens outside the home, *Lady Audley's Secret* would have the murder of George Tallboys attempted at Lady Audley's home. If the Victorians would think of blonde women and mothers as vehicles of domestic bliss, Braddon's novel would give them Lady Audley, a bad mother who abandoned her child and twice attempted to commit murder. If the Victorians would tink of women as authentic, passive and pure, Braddon would give the reading audience a pro-active woman who assumes femininity as an act rather than as part of her innate nature. If the Victorians would think of heroes as being dashing, hardworking, and resolute, Braddon would give them a passive, irresolute lounger and reader of French novels as her novel's putative hero. If the Victorians would consider criminals to be inherently sinful, Braddon would write a novel in which readers were compelled not only to sympathize with the villain but to conclude that poverty, and not Lady Audley's supposed hereditary madness, was to blame for crime. If the Victorians would view the class system as a comforting constant, Braddon would tell a story about how easily someone could rise from the servant class to the ruling class. If the Victorians wanted novels in which good triumphed and evil was punished, Braddon would give them *Lady Audley's Secret*, in which Lady Audley's punishment is only (!) being committed to an insane asylum, rather than dying as a male villain would. If the Victorians took their novels seriously, Braddon would introduce them to irony.

Braddon's readers loved *Lady Audley's Secret*, which John Sutherland calls "the most sensationally successful of all sensation novels." Braddon's contemporary critics were not so sympathetic, finding its popularity shocking and a sign of moral decay in the reading audience. Of particular note and alarm to these critics was *Lady Audley*'s popularity with female readers, something modern feminist critics ascribe to the novel's expression of female emotions—rage and desire for social betterment among them—that men desired to see suppressed, and to the novel's expression of specifically female fantasies of social movement, escape, and rebellion.

As a side-note, *Lady Audley's Secret* is of interest for its approach to crime-solving. *Lady Audley's Secret* is a Sensation Novel, written near the beginning of that genre's ascendance but in the wake of *The Woman in White*, so *Lady Audley's Secret*'s crime and mystery elements are part of the genre in which the novel was written, rather than being something new. But what is new in *Lady Audley's Secret*, besides the notion of the audience solving the mystery at the same time that the detective does, is the identity of the detective: Richard Audley. The tradition in British mystery up to the time *Lady Audley's Secret* was written was for the detective to be a professional—most notably Inspector Bucket in **Bleak House** and the crime-solvers in the casebook mysteries (proto-police procedurals) of the 1850s. Braddon's crime-solver is an amateur, rather than a detective, and while the amateur uncoverer of mysteries was not new—uncovering a mystery is largely what the **Gothics** and the Newgate novels (see **Pelham**) were about—the idea of the amateur *detective* was. Audley anticipates—and thanks to the popularity of *Lady Audley's Secret*, is an influence on the amateur detectives of the 20th century. Audley is a departure from previous detectives, neither an aristocratic recluse, like Edgar Allan Poe's C. Auguste Dupin, a hard-boiled policeman of the streets, like the casebook detectives, or a cheerful, working class policeman, like Dickens' Inspector Bucket.

Lady Audley's Secret was one of the most financially successful of all Sensation Novels and was one of the most aesthetically successful. It is a match for the more heralded *The Woman in White* and can be credited with jump-starting the Sensation genre. It is a shame that the era's expectations led Braddon to conclude the book wrongly.

Recommended Edition

Braddon, Mary Elizabeth. *Lady Audley's Secret* (Oxford University Press, 1987).

For Further Research

Skilton, David. "Introduction." *Lady Audley's Secret* (Oxford University Press, 1987).
Tomaiuolo, Saverio. *In Lady Audley's Shadow: Mary Elizabeth Braddon and Victorian Literary Genres* (Edinburgh University Press, 2010).
Voskuil, Lynn M. "Acts of Madness: Lady Audley and the Meanings of Victorian Femininity." *Feminist Studies* v27n3 (Autumn 2001).
Woolston, Jennifer M. "Lady Audley as the Cunning 'Other': An Economic, Sexual, and Criminal Attack on the Victorian Patriarchal Mindset." *EAPSU* v5 (2008).

The Last Days of Pompeii

The Last Days of Pompeii was created by Lord Bulwer-Lytton and was published in 1834. Edward George Earle Bulwer-Lytton (*Pelham*), 1st Baron of Knebworth (1803–1873) was a popular, productive, and influential writer for over 40 years. His reputation has unjustly suffered for many decades. *The Last Days of Pompeii* was an enormous hit when it was first published.

The Last Days of Pompeii is about the lives of several characters in Pompeii in the final days before Mt. Vesuvius erupted: Glaucus, a popular Greek; Arbaces, the wicked Egyptian priest of Isis; Ione, a beautiful Greek woman; and Nydia, a blind slave girl. Against the colorful backdrop of Pompeii a love quadrangle plays out. Glaucus and Arbaces both love Ione; Ione falls in love with Glaucus, much to Arbaces' dismay; and Nydia falls in love with Glaucus.

Arbaces is the guardian of Ione and her brother Apaecides, although he is not their friend—he has no friends among the Romans and Greeks, who he despises as having fed on Egypt's corpse. (Besides being an Egyptian patriot, the wealthy Arbaces is also man of depraved tastes who holds orgies of great debauchery.) Arbaces plans to make Apaecides a priest of Isis as a way to get Ione to marry him, but Glaucus warns Ione against Arbaces, and when he declares his love for her she turns him down.

Knowing that Glaucus is his rival, Arbaces goes to a local witch and has her prepare for him a drug which Arbaces engineers Glaucus into drinking. The drug drives him temporarily made, and he runs, raving, into the streets of Pompeii. Arbaces murders Apaecides (who has threatened to tell all of Pompeii about Arbaces' wickedness) and frames Glaucus for it. Glaucus is arrested and condemned to fight wild animals in a gladiatorial show. But when Glaucus is thrown to a lion, it refuses to eat him. A friend of Glaucus, having been convinced of his innocence thanks to a note from Nydia, turns the crowd against Arbaces, but then Vesuvius erupts, and the city begins to riot and flee. Nydia gets to Glaucus and the pair go to Arbaces' palace, where they rescue Ione. They flee the city for the coast and go out to sea in a small boat. Arbaces is killed in the earthquake. Glaucus, Ione, and Nydia spend the night in the boat, but before Glaucus and Ione awaken, Nydia, heartbroken over Glaucus, drowns herself.

Lord Bulwer-Lytton is now mostly a forgotten author, and is primarily remembered as the author of the sentence "It was a dark and stormy night" (from *Paul Clifford*), which was the inspiration of San Jose State University's bad writing competition, the Bulwer Lytton Fiction Contest. This is unfortunate, as Bulwer-Lytton was a highly successful author, with a number of good qualities, who was a major Victorian author. One of his talents—which he had to a greater degree than any other 19th century novelist—was for publishing a novel at the precise time in which it was guaranteed to be most popular. Few novelists had Bulwer-Lytton's nose for the *Zeitgeist*.

The Last Days of Pompeii is a prime example of this. From the 1820s through the 1840s a number of artists, authors and playwrights created paintings, poems, plays, and novels depicting enormous disasters. These works were popular with the British and American public and were given the name "the school of catastrophe." *The Last Days of Pompeii* was by no means the first novel from the school of catastrophe, but it appeared a time when none of those other works did: a month after the 1834 eruption of Mount Vesuvius and a week after news of the eruption reached the English newspapers. Thanks to this serendipitous coincidence, *The Last Days of Pompeii* became not only the most successful novel from the school of catastrophe but a sensation—the most successful novel since Sir Walter Scott's **Waverley**. *The Last Days of Pompeii* was one of the most acclaimed historical novels of the 1830s, was responsible for Bulwer-Lytton being seen as the best of the post–Scott historical novelists, and was largely responsible for the genre of novels about late Rome, including Lewis Wallace's *Ben Hur* (1880) and Walter Pater's **Marius the Epicurean** (1885). *The Last Days of Pompeii* is (unjustly) the one novel that Bulwer-Lytton is remembered for.

That doesn't mean *The Last Days of Pompeii* is enjoyable, though. Like most of Bulwer-Lytton's work the novel is badly dated. Bulwer-Lytton tells the story in an inflated style which makes much of the book slow reading. Bulwer-Lytton does not stint at bombast, straining after effects, fustian, naked melodrama, exclamatory speeches, and loquaciousness taken to the point of excess. The style is poor even compared to other 1830s historical novels, which is to say quite dated, quite unlike Bulwer-Lytton's "Silver Fork" novels (see *Pelham*), and a universe away from the sprightliness of someone like Austen in **Pride and Prejudice**.

The first three quarters of the book have a tediousness in the unfolding of the plots. The concerns of the characters, such as Arbaces' obsession with Ione's chastity and the repulsion the Romans feel toward pagan ceremonies, are those of Bulwer-Lytton rather than historically accurate. The Christian apologetics are a bore. With a few exceptions his characterization is flat and it is only his villains—Arbaces, the Roman Julia (who lusts after Glaucus), and Arbaces' corrupt ally Calenus—who show vigor and life. The heroes of Bulwer-Lytton's fiction are often insipid, stiff, and unlikeable, and with the exception of the sweet, noble, and sad Nydia none of the nominal "good guys" of *Pompeii* particularly endear themselves to the reader. *Pompeii* is in some ways a recasting of *Pelham* in Roman times, but the likable characteristics of Glanville and Pelham are missing from Glaucus, Clodius, and Apaecides.

However, being unenjoyable does not mean that *The Last Days of Pompeii* is without virtues. Bulwer-Lytton spent nearly a year in Pompeii doing research for the novel, and the result of his efforts is a painstaking and almost completely accurate recreation of daily life in Pompeii, down to the eating utensils and construction methods of the buildings. Pompeii comes colorfully alive—much more so, unfortunately, than Glaucus and Ione do. Bulwer-Lytton practices full immersion of the reader into the past, similar to what Flaubert would later perform with **Salammbô**, and if Bulwer-Lytton never learned that he didn't need to include everything he learned about Pompeii in his novel, there is nonetheless a remarkable amount of detail about the city.

As mentioned, Bulwer-Lytton's villains are memorable and even enjoyable, and Nydia's bitterness at her blindness and her futile love for Glaucus lend her dimensions the other heroic characters lack. Arbaces is a post–**Gothic** example of the Gothic Hero-Villain, and in his great passions and inability to resist his weaknesses and impulses anticipates heroes of many later historical romances, and arguably even **Wuthering Heights**' Heathcliff. And Arbaces' neo-Rosicrucian philosophy, of the esoteric truths of ancient Egypt, is an interesting forecast of the themes Bulwer-Lytton would later return to in *A Strange Story* and *Zanoni*, two occult novels largely responsible for the creation of the occult fantasy genre.

Most of all, Bulwer-Lytton is good at heightening the tension of the tale. The reader knows from the novel's title that Pompeii is soon to be destroyed, and the novel's momentum and pressure do not falter before the end. The best section of the novel is the final one, with Vesuvius' eruption and the reaction of the Pompeiians, and Bulwer-Lytton almost achieves eloquence in his description of the fire and ash raining down on the city and the resulting hysteria and terror of the Romans.

The Last Days of Pompeii is, to be honest, a hard slog for the modern reader, but it remains a historically important novel and is not without its virtues.

Recommended Edition

Bulwer-Lytton, Edward George. *The Last Days of Pompeii* (CreateSpace, 2014).

For Further Research

Brackett, Virginia. "The Last Days of Pompeii." *Facts on File Companion to the British Novel: Beginnings through the 19th Century*, vol. 1 (Facts on File, 2006).

Dahl, Curtis. "Bulwer-Lytton and the School of Catastrophe." *Philological Quarterly* v32 (Jan. 1, 1953).

Daly, Nicholas. "The Volcanic Disaster Narrative: From Pleasure Garden to Canvas, Page, and Stage." *Victorian Studies* v53n2 (Winter 2011).

The Last of the Mohicans

The Last of the Mohicans was written by James Fenimore Cooper and was published in 1826. Cooper (1789–1851) was one of the major early American writers, although he is known today primarily for *Last of the Mohicans*.

Set in northern New York in 1757, during the French and Indian Wars (1756–1763), *Last of the Mohicans* is about Natty Bumppo, a.k.a. "Hawkeye," and his adventures alongside his friends Chingachgook, a Delaware Mohican, and Uncas, Chingachgook's son. Half-sisters Cora and Alice Munro are traveling through the wilderness to Fort William Henry, where their father, the Colonel, is the commanding officer. They are accompanied by Major Duncan Heyward. They are convinced to take a shortcut through the wilderness by Magua, a native scout who unbeknownst to them is an outcast Huron and ally of the French. Magua leads the group astray, but they are found by Hawkeye *et al.*, who agrees to lead them to the fort. That night they are attacked by Hurons, and Heyward and the sisters are initially captured, with Magua unsuccessfully proposing to free them if Cora will marry him, before Hawkeye and the Mohicans rescue them. They all make it to the fort and fight in the siege until the Colonel Munro is forced to surrender. The British are granted safe passage from the fort, but as they are leaving they are attacked and slaughtered by the Hurons. During the attack Magua kidnaps Alice, and Cora goes after them, only to be taken in by a Delaware tribe.

Hawkeye *et al.* follow Magua and Alice and rescue her, then go to the Delawares, but when Magua and his group of warriors arrive at the Delaware camp the Delaware chief says that Magua's wish to marry Cora gives him a claim on her. Magua and Cora leave, but Hawkeye *et al.* pursue them. In the final battle Magua kills Uncas and is killed by Hawkeye. Cora also dies. Heyward and Alice plan to marry, and Hawkeye goes with Chingachgook, who is now the last of the Mohicans.

The modern reader of Cooper faces something of a dilemma. Any discussion of this novel must deal with two aspects: its style, and its accomplishments. More than any other work covered in this book, those two aspects are at odds with each other.

To begin with the positive: the accomplishments of *The Last of the Mohicans* and James Fenimore Cooper are numerous and large. It was the first American best-seller, and enabled Cooper to become the first American professional writer. *The Last of the Mohicans* was also the first major American novel and the most influential American work of fiction in the 19th century, and one of the most influential works in the world.

The Last of the Mohicans is so full of firsts and so influential, in fact, that Cooper is reasonably called "the American Homer." The novel became iconic, and its portrayal of the frontier and the people in it archetypal, and part of American myth. *Mohicans* did more to shape the foreign views of Americans, America, and Native Americans than any other novel. *Mohicans* was the first novel to portray the conflict between the British and the French and Indians. *Mohicans* was the first novel to portray Native Americans as humans, with individual motivations and psychologies. It was *Mohicans* which, in the person of Hawkeye, created the archetypal fictional frontier hero. And it was *Mohicans* which popularized the idea of the wilderness as a place of renewal and rebirth. Through the 17th and 18th century the Puritan view of the wilderness, as a place of evil which must be vanquished by inhabitants of the shining "city on the hill," was the dominant one, but *Mohicans* changed that, and made the American frontier a place of innocence and purity, and a place in which myths were created.

Mohicans created the quintessentially American genre of frontier fiction. Cooper imitated Sir Walter Scott's approach in **Waverley** of using historical details and elements in fiction, but made use of specifically American forms of fiction—the captivity narrative (American women being kidnaped by Native Americans) and frontiersmen stories among them—to create a genre of fiction about the taming of a frontier. *Mohicans* created the idea of the frontier hero helping to settle the frontier but then being forced to flee civilization for the new frontier. *Mohicans* created the idea of the white hero being paired with a non-white companion. *Mohicans* was the first to portray Native Americans in a relatively progressive way, not as unredeemable savages but as human beings, good and bad.

In the words of Richard Slotkin,

Cooper's mythologization of frontier history and his representations of frontier characters also influenced the writing of historians who in effect read Cooper's fiction into the historical record...

The image of the American hero as a man armed and solitary, plebeian but worthy somehow of nobility, fronting a native wilderness and seeking in action his heart's desire....

Cooper makes two contributions to the mythologization of American history: he puts the Indian and the matter of racial character at the center of his consideration of moral questions, and he represents the historical process as essentially a violent one.

Using terms codified by Cooper, succeeding generations of historical romance writers, historians, and dime novelisits elaborated the Myth of the Frontier into a myth-ideological language system, rich in symbols and types that could be deployed as political or literary occasion seemed to require. In its essence, the Cooperian mythology centered on the repreesentation of the history of American development as the confrontation between warring races, Indian and white. In the triumph of the white and the vanishing of the red, the progress of civilization is achieved, in both moral and material terms. From this characteristic historic action of race war, we can gather symbols of value which allow us to interpret conflicts within the white society which succeeds the Frontier. Racial imaginary provides a key to interpreting the moral standing of individuals and classes: the Indian represents the primitive natural extreme of human possibilities, and the moral standing of characters can be measured by the extent to which they resemble or "transcend" the qualities of Indians.

Mohicans was the foremost propagator of American **Romanticism** during the 19th century—the notions of feelings over reason, faith in imagination, the shunning of civilization and the seeking out of nature, the preference of innocence to sophistication, the fight for individualism against authority, the idea that nature gives spiritual wisdom, the intense private sentiment experienced by the characters. *Mohicans* was the foremost fictional propagator in the 19th century of the American fear of miscegenation (in its abhorrence toward the idea of Magua marrying Cora and its killing off, rather than marrying off, Uncas and Cora). *Mohicans* was the foremost 19th century novel which justified the genocide-like killing of Native Americans while simultaneously mourning it. And *Mohicans* was the foremost 19th century novel to propagate the Wilderness **Gothic**, with nature standing in for the house or castle and the landscape assuming the functions of the house or castle.

So there is all that to be said for *The Last of the Mohicans* and James Fenimore Cooper: he created a piece of literature uniquely American, containing a uniquely American character (in Hawkeye) and conveying a uniquely American message (freedom from the old ways and a celebration of the new). Quite a series of accomplishments, and critics are unanimous in celebrating them. But then there is the question of his style, which critics are, if not unanimous, then mostly united in viewing critically. And it is on Cooper's style that Mark Twain was most damning in "Fenimore Cooper's Literary Offenses":

"Cooper is the greatest artist in the domain of romantic fiction in America."
Wilkie Collins.

> It seems to me far from right for.... Wilkie Collins to deliver opinions on Cooper's literature without having read some of it. It would have been much more decorous to keep silent and let persons talk who have read Cooper. Cooper's art has some defects. In one place in "Deerslayer," and in the restricted space of two thirds of a page, Cooper has scored 114 offenses against literary art out of a possible 115. It breaks the record.

Brilliantly funny as it is, Twain's savaging of Cooper has become a cliché in discussions of Cooper or *The Last of the Mohicans*. And Twain's deservedly celebrated essay, as much abuse as it is argument, is hardly the final world on *Mohicans*, and in fact is not, really, a fair evaluation of the novel. But those readers who manage to finish the novel will nonetheless likely agree with Twain. "Stupefying" is in fact not too strong a word to describe the novel.

Cooper is prolix. He has the penny-a-word-writer's inability to get to the point. His descriptions are circumlocutious. His declamatory, speechifying dialogue style lacks all verisimilitude. The story is plot-heavy and obsessed with violence. The characters have no internal life, and the only characterization comes through heavy-handed, obtrusive dialogue. The pace of the novel, which was once thought to be almost too fast—this is definitely a novel of incident rather than a novel of ideas—is hampered by the endless flood of atrocious dialogue. Many of the conventions of the novel, including the Noble Savage and the pure, innocent heroines in need of rescuing, are dated, and while earlier generations found *Last of the Mohicans* to be exciting, current readers, with generations of better writers behind them, are more discerning.

Even more damning is the primitive view of race presented in *Mohicans*. Biology is destiny, for Cooper: any Mingo (Iroquois) is automatically bad and untrustworthy. Miscegenation is evil: Cora (Alice's step-sister and the descendant of a slave) admires (and fears) Magua's "swarthy lineaments," and Uncas is attracted to Cora, but they cannot marry outside their own "race," so they are killed, leaving Alice to marry Duncan and Hawkeye to flee from civilization. The Mingos are vile and deserve eradication, while the Mohicans are noble but doomed by destiny, so their mutual destruction at the end of the novel, and by extension the destruction of the American First Nations by the whites, is shown by Cooper to be ultimately a good thing. In John McWilliams' words, "Uncas and Magua perfectly embody the white reader's split view of a Natural Man who is 'other' than the civilized self." Hawkeye repeatedly calls himself a "man without a cross," meaning that there is no crossing of races in his blood (and also that he is, in Richard Slotkin's words, "a man without a cross of sin to bear, a man exempted from the fall, a new Adam. Yet he is also, implicitly, a man beyond the pale of Christianity, a man without the Cross to guide him").

Cooper wrote that he intended to create a story rather than something more true to life: "the reader who takes up this volume in expectation of finding an imaginary and romantic picture of things which never had an existence, will probably lay it aside disappointed. The work is exactly what it professes to be in its titlepage—a narrative." He wanted to create a romance (in the old sense, meaning a heroic adventure story) about American myth, not duplicate the historical record. But the novel is programmatic in a number of ways. Besides its treatment of race and miscegenation, and besides the creation of an American Romantic hero in Hawkeye (in his predilection for nature, his intuitive understanding of other people, and his freedom from authority), there are the set of oppositions, obvious on reading *Mohicans*: good/bad, light/dark, country/city, Alice/Cora, Hawkeye/Heyward, feminine/unfeminine, pure/tainted, etc. These oppositions do not feel organic in origin, but like part of a plan on Cooper's part, and the narrative suffers for it.

As a reading experience the novel is wretched, but it does have some notable elements. The descriptions of nature can be compelling. Although Cooper's biological essentialism is simplistic, he does not descend to the sort of racism which later writers propagated. Cooper's treatment of race has a certain ambiguity: he approves of the triumph of the white colonists but also mourns the passing of the noble Mohicans. This message appears intermittently not just throughout *The Last of the Mohicans* but also in several of Cooper's other novels, especially the five Leatherstocking novels. Genocide becomes destiny, but since it has already taken place it can conveniently be both celebrated and mourned. Several concepts which would later become traditions and clichés in frontier fiction appeared for the first time in Cooper's work, particularly that of the frontier hero, who has the skills of both the civilized and the savage and who can help tame the wilderness but who is out of place among civilized people. Another concept is the clash between the worldly-wise frontiersman and the hapless, incompetent city dude. Cooper was primarily responsible for the spread of these concepts. His work was internationally popular, and readers as far away as Turkey, the Middle East, North Africa and Russia devoured his work and believed that Cooper was accurately portraying the American frontier, and wrote imitations.

Cooper's style is indeed wretched, and *The Last of the Mohicans* is a tedious reading experience. But students should note that it was extremely influential and accomplished a great deal more than its author ever dreamed of.

Recommended Edition
Cooper, James Fenimore. *The Last of the Mohicans* (Signet, 2014).

For Further Research
Burt, Daniel S. "*The Last of the Mohicans.*" *The Novel 100: A Ranking of the Most Influential Novels of All Time* (Checkmark Books, 2010).
McWilliams, John. "Introduction." *The Last of the Mohicans* (Oxford University Press, 2008).

Scalia, Bill. "*The Last of the Mohicans.*" *Facts on File Companion to the American Novel* (Facts on File, 2006).

Slotkin, Richard. *The Fatal Environment: The Myth of the Frontier in the Age of Industrialization, 1800–1890* (University of Oklahoma Press, 1998).

Twain, Mark. "Fenimore Cooper's Literary Offenses." http://twain.lib.virginia.edu/projects/rissetto/offense.html.

Wardrop, Stephanie. "Last of the Red Hot Mohicans." *MELUS* v2n22 (Summer 1997).

Little Women

Little Women was written by Louisa May Alcott and was published in two volumes in 1868 and 1869. Alcott (1832–1888), an American, was a professional novelist. *Little Women* is her best-known novel; it has never been out of print and has been a cherished classic of girls' literature for generations.

Little Women is a *Bildungsroman* (a coming-of-age novel) about the four March sisters: Meg, Jo, Beth, and Amy, and their lives growing up during and after the American Civil War. As teenagers, they suffer through poverty but are never as desperately poor as their neighbors, and usually have enough to give to their poorer neighbors, the Hummels. Jo befriends the neighbor's boy, Laurie, and he becomes one of the family; Jo later befriends Laurie's intimidating grandfather and warden, Mr. Laurence, and he becomes a steadfast friend to the family, although his favorite is the music-playing Beth, who Mr. Laurence gives a piano to.

The girls have various adventures—Amy nearly dies while skating on thin ice, Meg attends a party and learns that appearances are not everything, and Jo begins writing stories for the local newspaper. These relatively innocent times end when the Marches receive a telegram informing them that their father, who is serving in the Army as a chaplain, has been injured, and that Mrs. March has to go to Washington to take care of him. With Mrs. March being absent, the girls neglect their chores, with the result that Beth is exposed to scarlet fever and only partially recovers from it. Laurie's tutor falls in love with Meg, and she reciprocates his feelings, much to Jo's dismay.

In the second volume, three years have passed, and Laurie is nearly done with college. Meg marries Mr. Brooke and moves into a house with him. Jo becomes a successful writer and Amy goes to Paris with the Marches' Aunt

Carrol. Jo moves away from home in an attempt to try to prevent Laurie from loving her, and while away from home meets Professor Bhaer, a poor German language instructor. A deep friendship grows up between them. When Jo returns home, Laurie proposes to her, but she declines him, temporarily rupturing their friendship. Beth dies from complications of her disease. Laurie, who has gone to Europe to recover from her heartbreak, meets up with Amy, and they fall in love and marry. Professor Bhaer comes to visit Jo and they fall in love, marry, and found a boarding school for boys.

Like **Kidnapped**, *Little Women* has been ill-served by its relegation—driven by librarians and book-sellers—to the category of Young Adult literature. *Little Women* is justly beloved by the girls who read it, but the novel is considerably more complex than traditional 19th century children's literature, and has content which should appeal to adult readers as well. Historically, *Little Women* is important as a transitional novel between traditional Romantic children's literature and Sentimental literature and more modern children's literature.

It is true that *Little Women* is Young Adult literature. As mentioned, it is a coming-of-age story, covering the childhood, adolescence, and young adulthood of the four March sisters, and in that respect the novel is apposite reading for young adults. Compared to other Victorian *Bildungsroman*, such as **Emma** or **Père Goriot**, *Little Women* lacks sophistication and is considerably simpler in style. *Little Women* is not a simple text—Alcott intermixes a great deal of moral and religious instruction with the story of Jo and the other sisters, and repeatedly chooses to make unpredictable and even uncomfortable authorial choices—but it is told in a simpler manner than Austen or Balzac would have chosen. Alcott was not the equal of those two authors, of course, but she deliberately chose to tell *Little Women* in a direct, simple style: "never use a long word, when a short one will do as well," in her own words. The content of the novel often becomes quite serious and even verges on tragedy—Beth's decline and death due to scarlet fever and Jo's turning down Laurie's marriage proposal would be fitting material for an adult novel, and Alcott does not turn away from the more sobering aspects of poverty—but the plot proceeds without the complications of adult fiction, or the more mature narrative description of it.

That said, *Little Women* is surprisingly complicated for Young Adult literature. It's not that the plot is complicated (although it is modeled on John Bunyan's *The Pilgrim's Progress*) but that Alcott's world is complicated and complex—and realistic. Good people like Beth and innocents like the Hummels' baby grow ill, waste away and die from disease. Soldiers at war, like Mr. March, get injured, leading to frightening telegrams home to their family. Young men impassioned by love find that the objects of their desire don't love them back, despite plot momentum and the laws of narration seeming to indicate that they should. These are not matters for children, but for young adults, and *Little Women* treats and portrays them in a sober and unblinking fashion, albeit one colored by Alcott's religious faith.

This complication is part of the evolution of children's literature in the 19th century. Before the 1860s stories written specifically for children had a moralistic and didactic element to them: they were intended to reach children proper morals and behavior. Authors wrote fairy tales of various stripes as well as adventure stories for children, but through all of these ran a heavy strain of moralizing, and the notion that what the children read must be morally instructive was never far from authors' minds, especially in domestic novels for children, whose characters were portrayed in flat, pious, one-dimensional terms. This began to change in the 1860s, first with the Reverend Charles Kingsley's *The Water Babies* (1863), which brought a realism to the genre of children's fiction in its treatment of the plight of child chimney sweeps and established that it was possible to write a story for children that was both popular and at least partially rooted in the real world. Next came Lewis Carroll's *Alice's Adventures in Wonderland* (1865), which lacked any moralizing or didactic aspect, and is a nonsense satire which lampoons adults but makes no attempt to instruct children and is nearly absent of sentimentality. Then came *Little Women*, which did contain a significant moralizing element but which used autobiographical elements from Alcott's own life to create three-dimensional human beings in the children and to portray family life in realistic (though still unobjectionable) terms. These three works allowed children's literature as a genre to begin to evolve.

Alcott also made something new in *Little Women*. The sentimental novel—the modified, 19th century version of novels of **Sensibility**—led to the creation of a type of domestic fiction (the most dominant fictional type in the middle of the 19th century, domestic fiction is about the story of a young women winning her way in the world) called the "conduct novel." In these novels female characters endure hardship to triumph while also instructing the reader about the proper conduct of women, with emotion (Sensibility) being used as an argumentative tool to convince readers. Alcott took elements of the conduct novel and undertook, in her words, "to write a little story about Young America, for Young America." As critic Sarah Elbert notes, Alcott created the first fictional portrayal of the specifically American adolescent female (as opposed to English or European), essentially creating the market for American Young Adult fiction that was about America rather than England.

This Americanism in the novel expressed itself in other ways. One of the major themes of the novel was the portrayal of the American self-reliance promoted by Ralph Waldo Emerson; another was the tension between individualism and community, of the desire to go one's own way versus the necessity to be a part of a family and greater social organism—again, a very American dilemma, especially during the time in which *Little Women* was written.

Little Women has numerous other themes: the glorification of domesticity and the family life; marriage as the proper fate for women; the necessity to grow up and set aside childish things. All traditional, conservative themes, which have led some critics to see the novel as inherently repressive, teaching women how to become submissive and domesticated—to become "little" women. But much of *Little Women* is not conservative, but radical, and part of the tension in *Little Women* is a novel at war with itself—Alcott working out her own issues through the writing of the novel.

Alcott's childhood, adolescence, and young adulthood were deeply unhappy—her family was often desperately poor, forcing Alcott to work to support them from an early age, one of Alcott's sisters died and another married. Alcott funneled these unpleasantnesses into *Little Women* but transformed them into something more genial, turning oppressive poverty into a more romanticized, mere wanting of better things (Alcott went hungry as a child, but the March children never did), the loss of hair due to disease into Jo voluntarily cutting and selling her hair, the death of Elizabeth Alcott into the gentle departure of Beth and the destruction of the family unit by Anna Alcott's marriage into Meg's marriage, which only gently strains the sisterhood of the March sisters.

There is also the matter of anger—Jo's anger, Marmee's anger, and Alcott's anger. This anger, what critic Ann Murphy calls "unending rage against the cultural limitations imposed on female developments," is a recurring theme through the novel, but how Alcott has the novel deal with the anger has led to numerous critical debates. Is the novel conservative in teaching Jo and Marmee to suppress their anger, or is the novel radical in acknowledging the anger and at times letting it vent? The novel remains ambiguous and admits of multiple interpretations on this issue, and many others.

Also interesting to modern critics is the question of gender and sexuality in *Little Women*. Alcott's own sexuality remains a matter of much debate; she seems to have been attracted to much older or younger men, and apart from a two week trip in Europe with a younger Polish man—a trip that seems to have been a brief romance—Alcott never had a relationship with a man. Of herself she even said that "I am more than half persuaded that I am a man's soul put by some freak of nature into a woman's body … because I have fallen in love with so many pretty girls and never once the least bit with any man." This, and the portrayal of Jo—Alcott's fictional substitute—as someone who for most of the novel is not interested in men or romance, have led many to suppose to Alcott was a lesbian or bisexual.

The issue of the erotics of Alcott extend to *Little Women* as well. Rebellious, tomboyish Jo, who turns down Laurie's marriage proposal, and who repeatedly says she has no use for romance, is ultimately married to Professor Bhaer, a much different kind of man than Laurie—a patriarch fifteen years her senior and her instructor in German and in morality. Under the influence of Bhaer, Jo gives up her sensationalist writing and writes more morally acceptable fare (in much the same way that Alcott herself gave up writing sensationalist fiction to write the "moral pap," in her own words, of children's literature). Does this constitute Alcott's sacrifice of Jo, forcing her to submit to the limitations of marriage to Bhaer? Or does the fact that Jo maintains her self-sufficiency as a writer and person mean that Alcott was actually subverting Victorian ideals of domesticity and womanhood? The usual critical assessment is that Jo's marriage to Professor Bhaer rather than Laurie was Alcott's way of frustrating readerly desires for a conventional fate for Jo (marrying Laurie) and instead urging readers to keep an open mind in matters of love (by marrying the elderly, German Bhaer, as different from Laurie as it possible to be). But a good argument can be made that the resolution of Jo's life is as unconvincing as the ending of Dostoevsky's *Crime and Punishment*, and that Alcott essentially bowed to market pressure by marrying her off rather than letting her live life independently, as Alcott herself did, and perhaps finding another woman to form an "intense friendship" with, as a number of Victorian women did.

There is certainly, in *Little Women*, a substantial amount of 19th century feminism: one of the themes of the book is of women seeking satisfaction on their own terms, rather than through husbands and family. And in the character of rebellious, tomboyish Jo, who supports herself and her family through writing, who turns down Laurie's marriage proposal, and who repeatedly says she has no use for romance, women readers of *Little Women* found a new fictional role model to emulate. More broadly, there is a kind of gender instability in the novel, with the adolescent Jo—more of the protagonist of *Little Women* than any other character—being relatively mannish (at one point going so far as to describe herself as the man of the household) and adolescent Laurie having various feminine qualities and essentially becoming one of the March sisters.

Will modern readers find *Little Women* worth reading? Yes, both adolescents and adults. Alcott's documentary approach to the lives of the March family gives modern readers a detailed glimpse into the lives of New England villagers during the Civil War (although in volume one of *Little Women* Alcott's focus on the March family is so tight that life outside the household is only vaguely described). Alcott's documentary style also lets readers see how children and adolescents of the 1860s really spoke—again, Alcott was trying to write "a little story about Young America, for Young America," rather than emulating traditional English children's literature and making the children's diction and grammar as perfect as their characters would be.

Despite the dating of the novel *Little Women* still provides adolescent readers with material to laugh and to cry at. The adolescent mindset of the March sisters still rings true to adolescent readers today. Adult readers will find that the characters are realistically good and realistically flawed, so that the characters are generally good but make mistakes, some of which are critical, such as Jo's obsessive focus on writing leading to Beth catching scarlet fever and ultimately dying from it. Despite Alcott's portrayal of the March family being a loving and positive one, Alcott does not sentimentalize their life or flaws.

Adults will find the portrayal of the March family as an interesting homosocial female paradise, where Mr. March is absent through the first volume and essentially absent through the second, and in which the only male to enter the family—Laurie—feminizes himself and even goes so far as to take on a feminine nickname.

Too, although Alcott took the material of her own life and romanticized it to a certain degree, there remains much unsentimental material, and Alcott does not shy away from showing unpleasant events: the telegram from the front informing the Marches that their father has been injured, saintly Beth catching a disease and eventually dying, and the emotional distress, on both sides, caused by Jo not loving Laurie and turning down his marriage proposal.

Finally, although there is a definite moralistic streak in *Little Women*, Alcott tends to keep the homilies and moralizing short. The novel keeps to the right side of being saccharine, and does not pretend that the hardships of life are not difficult to deal with.

Although *Little Women* lacks the sophisticated style of similar Victorian coming-of-age stories, the content of the novel is as mature and complex as any other Young Adult novel of the era, and readers will find themselves caring about the characters.

Recommended Edition

Alcott, Louisa May. *Little Women: An Annotated Edition* (Belknap Press, 2013).

For Further Research

Alberghene, Janice M, and Beverly Lyon Clark, eds. *Little Women and the Feminist Imagination* (Routledge, 1998).
Elbert, Sarah. *A Hunger for Home: Louisa May Alcott's Place in American Culture* (Rutgers University Press, 1987).
McCrum, Robert. "The 100 Best Novels: No. 20—*Little Women*." http://www.theguardian.com/books/2014/feb/03/100 best novels little women louisa may alcott.
Murphy, Ann B. "The Borders of Ethical, Erotic, and Artistic Possibilities in *Little Women*." *Signs* v15n3 (Spring 1990).

Stern, Madeleine."Louisa May Alcott: Overview." *Twentieth-Century Children's Writers* (St. James' Press, 1995).

Thompson, Stella. "Little Women." *Facts on File Companion to the American Novel* (Facts on File, 2006).

— · —

Lorna Doone

John Ridd was created by R. D. Blackmore and appeared in *Lorna Doone* (1869). Blackmore (1825–1900) was an English novelist. His fame, during and after his lifetime, is the result of *Lorna Doone*, one of the most entertaining historical romances of the 19th century and a work which has deservedly never been out of print.

Lorna Doone is set in the latter half of the 17th century, in the area of western England known as Exmoor. John Ridd is a young boy when his father is killed by the Doones of Badgery, a villainous clan of thieves and murderers. But John has a solid, loving family, and with the help of his mother and his sisters Annie and Eliza the family survives. One day John is out exploring when he sees a young girl, at the edge of Doone Valley, who identifies herself as "Lorna Doone." John is taken with her and remembers her. Years pass, and as a young man John returns to Doone Valley, meets up with Lorna again, and falls in love with her. She is not in love with John, not to the same degree that he is with her, but she likes him, and she hates the Doones. But she is destined to be the wife of Carver Doone, the monstrous son of Sir Ensor Doone, the leader of the Doones, and freeing her from them is no small thing. After months of waiting the worst frost and snow of the century arrive in west England, and under cover of the snow John succeeds in freeing Lorna from the Doones. But the course of love never did run smooth, and before John and Lorna can live happily ever after they must endure separation (Lorna goes to London to assume her role as a lady of a noble family), danger (John goes in search of his sister's roguish husband and gets arrested and nearly hanged as a rebel during the collapse of Monmouth's rebellion), more danger (an attack on Doone Valley), and near-heartbreak (Lorna is shot on the altar by Carver Doone, who John then kills in hand-to-hand combat). But there is, finally, a happily ever after, and all's well that end's well.

Lorna Doone is one of those massive Victorian novels known as a "triple-decker" due to its publication in three volumes. Because of its length and age, modern readers may approach it with some trepidation. In the case of *Lorna Doone* they needn't, since it well deserves the title of "classic." *Lorna Doone* is a classic because it is both well-written and emotionally involving.

Lorna Doone is also a classic because of its importance: it was one of the works most responsible for the rise in popularity of the adventure novel in 19th century English letters, and it spawned a new trend in regional historical romances.

Lorna Doone is one of those popular novels which critics and academics tend to slight because of its popularity. *Lorna Doone* was, after all, the most popular, best-selling regional historical novel (see below) of the century, and has never been out of print—it's no surprise that academics would view it as too popular to be worth studying. This is unfortunate, since *Lorna Doone* deserves recognition as a historically important novel. In the 1860s, when *Lorna Doone* was written and published, the historical novel—also known as the "historical romance"—had already gone through several changes. Sir Walter Scott's **Waverley** novels had established the form in the 1820s, with its initial wave of popularity lasting through the 1830s; the 1850s saw a revival of the form, with the novels being written more seriously, more historically accurately, and with more serious aims, than previously; and the 1860s saw a return to more popular novels less concerned with strict historical accuracy. *Lorna Doone*, with its tight focus on the English West Country (the counties in the southwest corner of England), sparked a craze for historical novels set in particular regions as well as for historical romances which deviated from strict realism.

But *Lorna Doone* was considerably more carefully written than most other historical romances of the time, as we'll see, and achieved greater things—quite deliberately, on Blackmore's part—than merely creating an enthusiasm among readers and writers for regional historical romances. *Lorna Doone* is a vocal advocate for the pastoral tradition (that literature which compares and contrasts the rural lifestyle with that of the urban lifestyle); in the words of critic Sally Shuttleworth, *Lorna Doone* "carefully [delineates] the relationship between inner feeling and the outward cycle of the seasons, in ways which anticipate the later work of Hardy (who was himself a strong admirer of Blackmore)." *Lorna Doone*, in its portrayal of West Country life and of the lives of yeomen, like John Ridd, who work there, brought a new, pastoral patriotism to the historical romance, celebrating the values of pastorialism while also promoting the Victorian values of hard work and family.

Again quoting Shuttleworth, "the strength of *Lorna Doone* lies in the fact that it refuses to fall within the narrow perimeters of any one defined category."

A historical novel written at a time when strict historical accuracy was the vogue among historical novel writers, *Lorna Doone* is instead full of elements from **Romanticism**, including larger-than-life characters, a highly Romantic heroine, what Shuttleworth calls "elemental conflicts," and an epic landscape. A historical romance, *Lorna Doone* so carefully observes and records the life of West Country yeoman that it almost becomes documentary in style. A historical novel written at a time when historical novels were written by male authors for male audiences, *Lorna Doone* proved to be fabulously popular not only with men but with women, and over a long period of time. (Writers as diverse and modern as Angela Carter and Anita Desai invoke *Lorna Doone* in their novels.)

Most interestingly, *Lorna Doone* is frontier fiction, but it is English frontier fiction rather than American, and that leads it to violate one of the core conflicts of traditional (read: American) frontier fiction (read: the Western) is this: the frontier is inhabited by barbarians; barbarians can only be defeated by the gun; but all those who pick up the gun are barbarians; therefore those who defeat the barbarians cannot inhabit the newly-civilized frontier. In American frontier fiction, and especially in Western films (see, for example, John Ford's *The Searchers* and Ford's *The Man Who Shot Liberty Valence*) this means that after the hero has defeated the barbarians he must leave the newly civilized frontier. In English frontier fiction the hero who picks up the gun is not a barbarian and is allowed to return to civilization even after committing barbarous violence. (One reason for this is that in English frontier fiction barbarians are an irruption of evil into an ordinarily civilized status quo, the status quo that the protagonist comes from, and once the status quo is reinstated by the defeat of the barbarians, civilization reigns supreme and the gun-slinging hero can return to his home. In American frontier fiction barbarians—and the gun-slinging hero—are a part of a fallen, barbaric frontier world, and when the new, civilized status quo is imposed, the gun-slinging hero has no place in it.)

One further way that *Lorna Doone* eludes pat categorization is its challenge to the expectations and formulas of historical fiction in the areas of masculinity and class. John Ridd is by nature conservative and seems to agree with the traditional placement of the aristocracy as being above the yeomanry—the traditional and preferred relationship of the classes in historical fiction of the time—but his marriage to Lorna Doone and the way in which the middle and lower classes vie with the aristocracy for power in the novel are a blow not for the traditional relationship of the classes, but for the triumph of the middle classes over the aristocracy. And John Ridd is, though heroic, quite different from the typical hero of Victorian historical romances. Bashful and self-deprecating where they are proud, compassionate where they are merciless, quiet where they are loud, unwilling to kill where they are brutal, and unsure of his own masculinity where the typical Victorian male hero takes Victorian masculine virtues for granted—soft where they are hard—John Ridd is continually negotiating with those masculine virtues.

Is *Lorna Doone* worth reading? Heavens, yes.

Admittedly, the language of the novel is stylized and mannered, and takes some adjusting to. Part of Blackmore's remarkable attention to the novel's West Country accuracy is the use of West Country dialect in dialogue as well as older rhetorical constructions, such as the use of "thou." Despite being written in the late 1860s, *Lorna Doone* is set two hundred years earlier, and the language of the novel reflects that. Blackmore's contemporaries, like Wilkie Collins (see: **The Woman in White**) were writing prose that has not aged particularly badly and can easily be read and enjoyed by modern readers, but Blackmore was too devoted to accuracy to tell a historical novel in modern language. Too, *Lorna Doone* is not the fastest-paced of books; it is slow to get going but picks up momentum when it finally does.

Those are the only two flaws in the novel, however. *Lorna Doone* is a particularly well-crafted novel, with Blackmore having paid close attention to the spoken cadences of prose. The novel is intelligently written, with memorable, carefully-chosen words—much more carefully chosen than the average historical romance of the time.

Blackmore is quite good at descriptions of environment. Whether those descriptions are "lyrical," as critics have traditionally described them, is a matter of taste, but the descriptions are at the least well-written. Blackmore effectively portrays the pastoral life as an idyllic one and one much superior to urban life; there is never any doubt where Blackmore thinks the better life is. If Blackmore is long-winded in his descriptions the cumulative weight of the descriptions is effective in portraying the life of a rural farmer as an enviable one. Interestingly, however, Blackmore does not portray that life as an easy one. Much of *Lorna Doone* is taken up with the specifics of farm life, the necessities of day-to-day work and the real life concerns of farmers: frost, drought, livestock lost to disease, theft, scavengers, the price of crops, and getting farm workers to earn their pay. This is an unusual theme for a historical novel, most of which are not, at heart, concerned with the exigencies of real life. Matters of economics—making money, doing one's job, putting a roof over one's head and food on one's table—these are not inherently exciting and are not usually a part of most adventure novels. Characters in Historical Romances are often gentlemen of leisure or nobility and already have money, or go off sailing to be pirates and take booty. Novels with these characters are fun, of course, but they lack a certain grounding in reality. This is why novels like *Lorna Doone* and Robert Louis Stevenson's **Kidnapped** are unusual, and welcome. The characters in these novels are recognizable and even familiar in a way that characters from the historical romances of the 1890s are not. Most readers will be able to both identify with and empathize with John Ridd's daily struggles with his farm, where they cannot identify with and empathize with, for example, the struggles of the French aristocracy against the forces of the French Revolution.

Blackmore is similarly realistic in his characterization. John Ridd, his family, Lorna Doone—even Carver Doone, vile though he is, has an exchange with John Ridd late in the novel which provides a glimpse of Carver's massively deluded and hypocritical personality. Delusion and hypocrisy are bad character traits, to be sure, but they are recognizable ones, and they make Carver Doone more than just one-dimensional villain. Beyond the realism of the characters is the skillful way with which Blackmore portrays emotions. Blackmore keeps emotions real and understated, saying much more by implication or hidden tears than shrieks and too-strenuous attempts at affect. Blackmore also shows a sure touch at making Ridd, as a child, neither overly simple nor absurdly precocious. Ridd's interior life is likewise well done; he becomes a real person, so that the reader knows, or thinks they do, what Ridd would say and do in situations removed from the novel. The novel's pace is comfortable, if not leisurely, so that the relationship between John and Lorna is naturally developed and is not rushed. The naturalistic and unhurried way in which *Lorna Doone* proceeds is one of its greatest strengths. The reader feels the passage of time along with the characters, and the reader identifies as much with John as farmer as much as with John as maturing adult. Blackmore also has a light touch with the humor of the novel.

The novel's only negative is its West Country dialect, which is bothersome. But it is also a part of *Lorna Doone*'s greatest strength: its completely convincing depiction of a departed time and place. Blackmore did a great deal of research to get the dialect and vocabulary of John Ridd and his family accurate, and it shows. The vocabulary and cadence, the rural lifestyle and practices, the concerns of those living in a lawless and wild land, they all feel very real. The reader is completely convinced that they are hearing a voice from the past.

Although *Lorna Doone* is a historical romance, it is not really an adventure novel. It is a romance, in the modern sense of the word. There are certainly elements of adventure in the novel, but it is much more concerned with the love story of John Ridd and Lorna Doone than with the violent destruction of the Doones. And because the characters are emotionally real (John more than Lorna, but Lorna as well as John) and the lives portrayed are recognizable to the reader, and because the characters are likable, the reader cares about what happens to John and Lorna and wants a happy ending for them. The plot may be conventional, but the novel is emotionally involving.

Lorna Doone is involving reading of surprising depth and well worth the effort it takes to come to grips with the language. As critic Pamela Knights writes, "it contains humour and high adventure, romance and history, lyricism and violence, in settings ranging from the domestic to the demonic—often … within a single chapter." Readers are advised to seek it out.

Recommended Edition
Blackmore, R.D. *Lorna Doone* (Oxford University Press, 1989).

For Further Research
Byer, James E. "Lorna Doone." *Reference Guide to English Literature* (St. James Press, 1991).
Knights, Pamela. "Introduction." *Lorna Doone* (Wordsworth, 2004).
Merchant, Peter. "Rehabilitating *Lorna Doone*: Prospects and Problems." *Children's Literature in Education* v18n4 (1987).
Shuttleworth, Sally. "Introduction." *Lorna Doone* (Oxford University Press, 1989).
Sutton, Max Keith. "The Mythic Appeal of *Lorna Doone*." *Nineteenth Century Fiction* v28n4 (Mar. 1974).

Madame Bovary

Madame Bovary was written by Gustave Flaubert (***Salammbô***) and appeared as a serial and as a novel in 1856. Flaubert (1821–1880) is one of the major writers of the 19th century. Although he is best known for *Madame Bovary* he has a respectable body of work, from short stories to dramas. His work is generally placed in the realist genre, but his skill as a stylist and technician is far above most of the other realists.

Charles Bovary is a medical student. One day he is called in to tend to a farmer, and while there meets the farmer's daughter, Emma. She is attractive, charming and graceful, and he finds excuses to visit the farmer. Bovary's older wife suspects him of cheating on her, but she dies following a quarrel, and Bovary returns to the farmer's house. Eventually the farmer persuades him to marry Emma, which he does. Unfortunately, Emma quickly finds that marriage is a lifetime jail sentence—she is completely disillusioned with her husband. She has read many books which have given her an idea about romance and marriage which is finding unrealistic, something she finds insupportable. Then she meets one of Charles' noble patients, who is attracted to her and invites her to a ball at his chateau. The ball only makes Emma more and more discontented with her own life, and eventually she falls ill. To give her a change of air Charles moves to the village of Yonville, where Charles' and Emma's daughter Berthe is born.

In Yonville she meets a law clerk, Leon, and he falls in love with her, although their relationship does not become physical, and he goes to Paris. Again she becomes ill from sheer boredom and misery, but then she meets a handsome stranger, Rodolphe. He, too, is attracted to her, and he succeeds in seducing her. They carry on a long affair, but Rodolphe tires of her. She makes him promise to run away with her, but on the night that they are supposed to go he sends her a letter telling her that it is over between them. She falls ill for several months and slowly recovers. She again meets Leon, and this time their relationship becomes physical. She spends recklessly, living only for pleasure, but eventually the bills come due and she is unable to pay them. Leon can't give her enough money, Rodolphe won't, and she cannot prevent her house's furniture from being seized. Knowing that Charles is about to discover the secret life she led, Emma takes poison and dies.

Few works of importance in the 19th century are so tedious as *Madame Bovary*. But in that tedium lies its importance.

Madame Bovary is the first major work of realism in 19th century literature—indeed, it is regularly called "the first modern novel"—as well as the first truly aesthetically and intellectually serious novel of the century. Before *Madame Bovary* the novel was not taken seriously, by critics or by writers, as an art form. It was there to entertain and to divert, but it was not to be taken seriously, not like poetry. Flaubert, with *Madame Bovary*, changed that. Flaubert took infinite pains with every word of *Madame Bovary*'s manuscript, and it shows.

The student who has just finished *Madame Bovary* and is reading this will be forgiven for rolling their eyes at the preceding sentence. The novel is a monotonous account of the lives of Charles and Emma Bovary, totally lacking in the narratorial asides or stylistic flourishes of many other Victorian novels, like George Eliot's **Middlemarch** or Flaubert's own *Salammbô*. *Madame Bovary* is so lacking in authorial presence, in fact, that it might as well be a shopping list. (Of course, the novel is not without metaphor and simile; Flaubert is a realist, not a Naturalist like Zola [*L'Assommoir*, *Nana*].) The idea that Flaubert labored five years over the manuscript to the novel (which he did) might seem ludicrous.

It's not, though. The point of *Madame Bovary* was to write an ordinary life, in Flaubert's own words, "as one writes history or epic": as Art, with painstaking attention to material detail and an abundance of information about characters' motivations and emotions and actions. But, unlike previous novels, there are no great actions and events, just ordinary lives being lived by ordinary people. That these characters were small, vulgar, and mundane, and their actions ignoble and tawdry—ordinary, in other words, and not idealized or fantasy characters—was part of what was revolutionary about the novel. Novels, in 1856, simply didn't write about housewives having affairs, being bored with their stultifying lives, and committing suicide—not, at least, without a great deal of authorial tsk-tsking. That Flaubert refused to take the time and space in *Madame Bovary* to condemn Emma, and instead calmly related the facts of her actions and her motivations, shocked and appalled many readers, even leading the French government to charge Flaubert with immorality. (He was ultimately acquitted of the charge.)

So it was both *Madame Bovary*'s style *and* subject matter which were revolutionary: a completely authentic depiction of a little person's life, told with great attention to detail, and describing her sordid behavior, but flatly and without condemnation. In this, Flaubert essentially created novelistic realism, and even anticipated Modernism in its demands on the reader—Flaubert goes in depth in his exploration of Emma's psyche, but leaves it up to the reader to find an indictment of her behavior and that of Leon and Rodolphe.

Madame Bovary's themes are numerous: how shallow material and physical satisfaction is; how society suffocates young women; how middle-class values are crass and the middle class self-righteous and without depth; the ludicrousness of faith in science and progress, the pointlessness of religious beliefs, and the ridiculousness of the idea that romance and passion are ennobling. The novel satirizes provincial life and the notion—common among readers then as now—that vulgar behavior does not somehow undercut romance. And through the lack of authorial condemnation of the behavior depicted in the novel, Flaubert succeeds in his ambition to create "pure art," separate from morality—another Modernist notion.

Flaubert's success, however—his achievement in writing, in his own words, "a book about nothing, a book with no exterior attachment ... a book that would have almost no subject"—and his skill in portraying Emma's life do not translate into entertainment for the modern reader. In the 21st century the idea of adultery is no longer shocking, nor will a portrayal of tawdry behavior without condemnation raise an eyebrow among readers. There is an obvious skill behind the writing of the novel, but that skill has nothing to do with readerly pleasure. Bloom's statement that "Emma has no Sublime, but the inverted Romantic vision of Flaubert persuades us that the strongest writing can represent ennui with a life-enhancing power" will not ring true for most readers—*Madame Bovary*'s ennui is infectious rather than life-enhancing. Byatt's statement that "there is no greater study of boredom than Madame Bovary—which is nevertheless never boring, but always both terrifying and simultaneously gleeful over its own accuracy" overlooks that the terror and glee do not communicate themselves to the reader.

Madame Bovary is a book, in other words, that academics can appreciate but which most readers will not enjoy.

Recommended Edition
Flaubert, Gustave. *Madame Bovary* (Penguin, 2010).

For Further Research
Bloom, Harold. "Gustave Flaubert." *Novelists and Novels* (Chelsea House, 2005).
Byatt, A.S. "Scenes From a Provincial Life." http://www.theguardian.com/books/2002/jul/27/classics.asbyatt.
Davis, Lydia. "Introduction." *Madame Bovary* (Penguin, 2010).
Nabokov, Vladimir. *Lectures on Literature* (Harcourt Brace Jovanovich, 1980).
Wall, Geoffrey. "Introduction." *Madame Bovary* (Penguin, 2003).

Marius the Epicurean

Marius the Epicurean was written by Walter Pater and was published in 1885. Pater (1839–1894) was an English essayist and critic. *Marius the Epicurean* was his only completed novel.

Marius is a young Roman in the time of Marcus Aurelius. He lives in rural northern Rome, on the family estate, following the pagan gods and sharing their beliefs. He is a contemplative boy rather than an active one, and he is full of idealism and religiosity. Unfortunately, on returning from the temple of Aesculapius, Marius finds his mother dying, and her death makes him a skeptic, one who questions every aspect of life. Afterwards, Marius is sent to school in Pisa, where he decides to become a poet and he meets the older boy Flavian. The two become close, reading all the literature they can, but Flavian sickens and dies of the plague. Marius, needing comfort, becomes attracted to mysticism and begins reading the early Greek philosophers to find out what happens to the soul after death.

Marius reads Heraclitus and Aristippus and decides that, because knowledge is limited to experience, he owes it to himself to experience as much sensual pleasure as possible—life as the primary purpose of life, or Epicureanism. Marius becomes a writer of prose. He goes to Rome and becomes secretary to the Emperor, helping him put together his memoir and his meditations. On the way to Rome Marius befriends Cornelius, a young army officer, and Cornelius tutors Marius in the ways of Rome. But Cornelius is happier than Marius, something which mystifies Marius until he finds the answer: Cornelius is a Christian, a member of the strange new religion that is sweeping the empire.

Months later Cornelius and Marius are traveling when the town they are in is hit by an earthquake. Marius joins Cornelius and other Christians in thanking God for not dying, but the local pagans feel that the Christians caused the earthquake and attack them. Marius and Cornelius are arrested by the pagans and sent to Rome, but Marius identifies himself as a Christian and Cornelius as a non-Christian, leading to Cornelius' release by the pagans. Marius becomes mortally ill and dies.

Despite the proceeding summary, *Marius the Epicurean* is about anything but plot. It is a long philosophical treatise in which plot is not just secondary but tertiary.

Marius the Epicurean is not the easiest of reads, to be sure. Pater spent a great deal of time crafting *Marius*, in much the same way that Henry James took infinite pains with **The Portrait of a Lady**, and the result is described as a prose poem, albeit one that is leisurely and almost equivocal. The substantial amount of untranslated Latin puts the modern reader in a difficult position, and Pater's style, which can be described as Latinate, or difficult, allusive, and dense, is often seen as off-putting by students and requires a relatively sophisticated level of reading by the students in order to be fully comprehended. And as mentioned the subordination of plot to the contemplation of philosophy means that students who are expecting a story to accompany Pater's deep thoughts will be disappointed.

But what's going on in *Marius* is much like what takes place in Victor Hugo's **The Hunchback of Notre Dame** and Gustave Flaubert's *Salammbô*: a deep immersion in the past, with such depth of detail that the author is perforce led to subordinate the novel's plot to the recreation of the past. Unlike Hugo and Flaubert, however, Pater is not interested in material details or the sweep of history—critics have charged that Pater's grasp of the material details of Roman life is shaky—but in the details of long-dead philosophies and religions, of Numa and the Epicureans and the Cynics and Stoics—the "intellectual and philosophical timbre of ancient Rome," and it is in those details which he excels. (Whether those details will be interesting to freshmen readers is another question, of course...)

Similarly, Pater is writing a novel of "sensation and ideas," in the words of *Marius'* subtitle, rather than a historical romance, so that the end result is not a novel about distinctive characters or well-wrought, accurate history, but instead what Harold Bloom calls "a unified reverie or aesthetic meditation upon history, through a history as idealized and foreshortened as in Yeats' *A Vision*." *Marius* is not a cracking good read, and does not have stand-out moments, but instead tries to leave impressions on the reader rather than memories. As Osbert Burdett wrote in 1926, "a good criticism will warn the reader … not to be disappointed if incidents, passages, or chapters alone linger with him, but to remark that certain effects … are none the less real because they seem to be contradictory."

Marius, though not of interest purely as a story, is of interest for a few other things.

Pater in *Marius* goes against the then-contemporary trend of historical romances—the 1850s and 1860s had been the peak decades of production for the historical romance, but by the 1870s the historical romance was shifting toward adventure writers and writers of boys' fiction, as with **Lorna Doone**, so that by the time *Marius* was written the historical romance was the province of popular rather than serious novelists. Pater wasn't attempting to change this trend, but was defying it in the writing of this "philosophical romance."

What Pater succeeded in doing, in fact, was in creating a work of Modernism *avant la lettre*, something which surprised Pater's contemporaries almost to the point of shock. (Not so shocking to modern audiences, of course, accustomed as we are to Modernism.) The intertextuality of *Marius*, its incorporation of other genres into a historical romance and its interpolation of quotes and non-novelistic elements, such as the inclusion of the long Cupid-Psyche story, is Modernist in its breaking down of conventional novelistic formulae, and anticipates (and was influential on) the English *fin de siècle* and the Aesthetic and Decadent movements, and especially on Oscar Wilde (**The Picture of Dorian Grey**).

Too, *Marius* is a *Bildungsroman* (coming-of-age story), but a male *Bildungsroman*—almost prototypically so. The female *Bildungsroman* is a quest for marriage and stability, while the male *Bildungsroman*, in the words of Jerome Buckley, is about a "child of some sensibility [who] grows up in the country or in a provincial town, where he finds constraints, social and intellectual, placed upon the free imagination," but later is educated, formally and informally, in the big city. *Marius* certainly fits this definition, but interestingly *Marius* is seen as Pater's own statement of his philosophical development, with Marius' personality being that of Pater himself, and Marius' philosophical questing being that of Marius. (Too, *Marius* draws explicit comparisons between Imperial Rome and Victorian Britain—more biographical fodder.)

Marius the Epicurean is not an easy read, and most students will undoubtedly not find it worth their while to read or to finish it. Those who persevere will be rewarded with a contemplative work of historical imagination.

Recommended Edition
Pater, Walter. *Marius the Epicurean* (Cosimo Classics, 2005).

For Further Research
Bloom, Harold, ed. *Walter Pater* (Chelsea House, 1985).
Burdett, Osbert. "Introduction." *Marius the Epicurean* (Everyman's Library, 1934).
Delaura, David J. "Marius and the Necessity of Religion." http://victorianweb.org/books/delaura/19.html.
"Marius the Epicurean." *Masterplots* Fourth Edition (Dec. 2010).
Potolsky, Walter. "Fear of Falling: Walter Pater's Marius the Epicurean as a Dangerous Influence." *ELH* v65n3 (Fall 1998).

Mary Barton

Mary Barton was written by Elizabeth Gaskell (*North and South*) and was published in 1848. Gaskell (1810–1865) was in her time a noted writer. She produced a wide range of stories and novels and was well-known for her "social problem" novels.

John Barton's life is an affliction of misery. Work in Manchester in the late 1820s is uncertain, his wife's sister Esther disappears, and his wife goes into labor and dies during childbirth, leaving him alone with only his teenaged daughter Mary. Meanwhile Mary becomes an apprentice to a dressmaker. She has two possible *beaux*: Harry Carson, the handsome son of the local mill owner, and Jem Wilson, a poor-but-good working man who is a family friend. The Carson's mill catches on fire, and Jem saves the lives of his father and another mill worker. Unfortunately, the insurance pays more than keeping the mill open would, so Mr. Carson keeps the mill closed, putting many of the locals out of work and leading to widespread starvation and death. Worse, Mary rejects a marriage proposal from Jem but then rejects Harry. A meeting of trade unionists leads to an avowal to murder one of the mill owners, to make them pay. John is chosen to be the murderer, and soon afterwards Harry Carson is shot and killed. Jem is arrested for the crime—he and Harry had recently quarreled in public over Mary—but Mary realizes that her father is the murderer, and goes to great lengths to find the one witness, Jem's foster brother Will, who can exonerate Jem. At the trial Will testifies and Jem is acquitted. However, he loses his job and decides to go to Canada. John, who is dying, calls for Mr. Carson, admits that he murdered Harry, and asks for forgiveness. At first Mr. Carson refuses, but a change of heart returns him to the Bartons' house, where John dies in his arms. The novel ends with Mary and Jem emigrating to Canada and starting anew in the New World.

Mary Barton is a "Condition of England" novel. During the 1840s—the "troubled Forties"—English philosophers and legislators were forced to deal with the byproducts of the 18th century's economic growth. These problems, which included gross urban overpopulation, insufficient housing, bad sanitation, and high levels of unemployment, were described by the writer Thomas Carlyle as "the Condition of England." Writers from Benjamin Disraeli (in **Coningsby**) to Charles Dickens (**Bleak House**) wrote novels, variously called "Condition of England novels," "industrial fiction," and "social problem novels," which examined the changes in the social classes and social structure and the current state of England. Mary Barton is a Condition of England novel in which the England, as represented by Manchester, is starving, poor, oppressed, and infuriated with the wealthy. Mary Barton was written by Gaskell to expose and illuminate the appalling conditions in which the working class lived and labored. In this it succeeded; Mary Barton was, in critic John Sutherland's phrase, "the most directly influential of the social problem genre." Mary Barton did not directly lead to public legislation—the collapse of the Chartism movement in 1848, the same year that Mary Barton was published, put an end to both the Condition of England genre and to legislative activity designed to support Chartism and reform—but Mary Barton did help to prod the national conscience. (Such was her purpose. In her own words: "I believe that there is much to be discovered yet as to the right position and mutual duties of employer, and employed.") The novel was very successful, although a number of critics felt that it was too one-sided, too inflammatory, and too slanderous toward manufacturers, and even supporters thought that the novel was too heartbreaking.

As a Condition of England novel Mary Barton is hugely successful. The plight of the poor is harrowingly shown, with hunger and disease everywhere and death by starvation ("clemming") an ever-present fate. The grim conditions in which they lived, the horrifying uncertainty which economic depression inflicted on them—rarely has being out of work been shown to be this terrible—and the sheer inequality and unjustness of life in a ruthlessly capitalist society are graphically described. Gaskell wrote from a place of familiarity—

not graspingly poor herself, she was nonetheless familiar with the poor—she lived in Manchester and was the wife of a minister who served the poor—and knowledgeable about the horrible conditions in which they lived—and it shows. In the words of critic Kathleen Tillotson, *Mary Barton* has "a wider impartiality, a tendrer humanity, and it may be a greater artistic integrity" than other, less successful Condition of England novels.

But as fiction *Mary Barton* is only passably successful. The novel has several flaws and few things to recommend it.

Gaskell's style—*Mary Barton* was her first novel—is, to say the last, unsubtle. Her prose style is dated, being a bit thick and description-heavy and with a very 1840s style of dialogue. Worse, *Mary Barton* is a "thesis novel" —that is, in critic Edward Quinn's words, "a novel in which the focus is less on character and action than on philosophical questions that are debated and discussed at length. Although most novels contain abstract ideas in one form or another, in the "novel of ideas" they play a central role." Gaskell has a point to make and an axe to grind, and goes about it quickly and forcefully (to say the least). And obviously—the themes of the novel, the comparisons between the rich and the poor, the influence of family (and lack of same) on individuals, the helplessness of the poor in the grip of heartless capitalism, and the need for Christian redemption—are repeatedly hammered home and openly stated. Gaskell both shows *and* tells her themes, at length.

Endlessly, the hopelessness of the lives of the Bartons and Wilsons is shown, and things like characterization and complexity are sacrificed to drive the point home that the life of the poor is misery reified. It is no surprise that manufacturers and their allies in literary criticism were outraged by *Mary Barton*; the novel (before its unconvincing call for mutual forgiveness and compassion) all but calls out for class warfare.

The novel has two plots: John's story, the industrial plot, and Mary's story, the romance plot. The two mesh poorly. To this reader, at least, John's story seems to be where Gaskell's heart truly was—her initial intent was to name the novel "John Barton"—and Mary's story seems almost tacked on, or added from a different novel. Too, Mary's story is rife with melodrama and frankly predictable plot complications; Gaskell's lack of subtlety (again, this was her first novel—she became more skilled in later years) and writerly sophistication is apparent in those sections. (Critic Kamilla Elliott intriguingly argues the opposite, that *Mary Barton*'s "generic boundaries break down as the political plot turns to romantic melodrama for its resolution and the romance plot turns to legal and political action for its resolution" and that "it is the romance plot, not the political plot, that contains the most radical political critique in the novel.")

The novel isn't dire by any means. The most obvious aspect of the novel, its constant descriptions of the lives of the desperate poor, is clearly written by someone familiar with them, and is full of observations and descriptions which have the ring of veracity. One character, for example, complains that the laws against child labor only turn the children out on to the street, and at one point John notes that most industrial accidents occur in the final hours of a shift, when the workers are exhausted.

Gaskell is successful in making the poor individuals rather than an undifferentiated mass of figures. John Barton is her most successful creation; she is entirely convincing in showing how this good man falls spiritually until murder seems a logical activity to him. (His desire for Carson's forgiveness is less convincing but still well-written.) The poor are given positive attributes—one is an entomologist, another resourceful enough to overcome her blindness, a third (Jem) is a skillful inventor—without being portrayed in romanticized terms. There are scenes in which crowds of people are portrayed as passive, but individuals rarely are, even if they are helpless.

Mary Barton was enormously successful in making its point, and modern readers will agree with its arguments, but will probably lament Gaskell's lack of skill in making them.

Recommended Edition
Gaskell, Elizabeth. *Mary Barton* (Penguin Classics, 1997).

For Further Research
Brackett, Virginia. "Mary Barton." *Facts on File Companion to the British Novel: Beginnings through the 19th Century*, vol. 1 (Facts on File, 2006).
Elliott, Kamilla. "The Romance of Politics and the Politics of Romance in Elizabeth Gaskell's Mary Barton." *The Gaskell Society Journal* v21 (2007).
Malcolm, Elizabeth. "Mary Barton." http://victorianweb.org/authors/gaskell/malcolm/2.html.
Tillotson, Kathleen. *Novels of the Eighteen-Forties* (Oxford University Press, 1985).
Tredennick, Bianca. *Victorian Transformations: Genre, Nationalism and Desire in Nineteenth Century Literature* (Ashgate, 2011).

Middlemarch

Middlemarch was written by George Eliot (**Silas Marner**) and was published as a serial in 1871 and 1872 and as a novel in 1874. Eliot, the pseudonym of Mary Anne Evans (1819–1880), was regarded in her lifetime (especially after the death of Dickens and Thackeray) as perhaps the greatest living English novelist, and *Middlemarch* is usually seen as her supreme achievement.

Middlemarch is about the small provincial county of Middlemarch and of six people within it. Dorothea Brooke is an idealistic woman full of a yearning to help the less fortunate and to dedicate herself to some life long task. Her initial decision on how to achieve this is to marry Edward Casaubon, an aging, pedantic, emotionally stunted scholar who is obsessed with writing a masterwork, The Key to All Mythologies. She seeks fulfillment by serving her husband in writing this work, but he acts coldly toward her ambitions, and gradually their marriage becomes strained. She becomes friends with Casaubon's cousin, Will Ladislaw, who Casaubon dislikes. Casaubon dies of poor health, but in his will he includes a codicil that if Dorothea ever marry Ladislaw she will lose Casaubon's inheritance. Ladislaw and Dorothea are both attracted to each other and after various misunderstandings and distancings marry.

Tertius Lydgate is an idealistic doctor who moves to Middlemarch in order to carry out his ideas for medical research and reform. He meets and falls in love with Rosamond Vincy, the loveliest woman in Middlemarch, and she falls in love with her perception of him. But their marriage, too, goes bad, thanks to his profligacy with money and her monstrous narcissism, and they endure painful days together. Dorothea helps Lydgate pay off his debts, but Rosamond allows her idea of friendship with Ladislaw to become a fantasy of love, a fantasy he is forced to harshly dispel. Eventually the pair overcome their troubles as Rosamond wears Lydgate down, and their marriage ends unhappily.

The third couple is Rosamond's brother, Fred, and Mary Garth. Fred is university educated but irresponsible and unwilling to enter service with the Church. He loves Mary, and she loves him, but he is too flighty and irresponsible for her to seriously consider marrying, and she tells him so. Worse, Fred is forced to turn to Mary's father, Caleb, to pay off a serious debt, which darkens the Garths' view of him and make them even more unwilling to have Fred marry Mary. Eventually, after much emotional and even spiritual struggle, Fred takes seriously to work, serving as an assistant to Caleb. He proves himself to all of the Garths, Mary included, and they become a happy couple and live happily ever after.

Middlemarch has been described by critics like Martin Amis and Julian Barnes as the greatest novel in the English language. Those are high words indeed, and it is hard for any novel to live up to them, but if any novel can, it is *Middlemarch*. The novel is a magnificent fictional achievement, one immediately acclaimed by Eliot's contemporaries (though there were of course some critics who caviled at its minor flaws) as well as by later critics and readers.

Middlemarch's achievement is one of style, substance, and historical importance. If it cannot be said to have singlehandedly destroyed the **Sensation Novel**, its appearance at least had a great deal to do with the fall of the genre from its place of popular prominence, to be replaced by the realism which *Middlemarch* so splendidly represents.

Eliot was and is one of the most respected of the Victorian writers of the second half of the 19th century. (The venerable critic Harold Bloom goes so far as to call her one of the greatest Western writers of all time.) Her first three novels—*Adam Bede* (1859), *The Mill on the Floss* (1860), and *Silas Marner* (1861)—were regional novels. Her 1866 novel, *Felix Holt*, was a social novel in the mode of *Middlemarch* but was more overtly political. In all of these novels—published at the height of the Sensation Novel craze—Eliot wrote in the realist mode, emphasizing ordinary characters and commonplace events. Eliot did not entirely separate herself from the Sensation Novel—even in *Middlemarch* there are Sensation elements, such as blackmail and a hidden, scandalous past coming back to haunt the present—but she presented an alternative literary mode for readers to consume. William Thackeray died in 1863 and Charles Dickens died in 1870, and when *Middlemarch* began appearing, in 1871, the field was clear for a new Greatest Living English Writer, which status Eliot was duly awarded. Eliot's influence, and the greatness of *Middlemarch* and *Daniel Deronda* (1876), established and popularized the realist mode of novel-writing, replacing the Sensation Novel and lasting until the advent of Modernism early in the twentieth century.

Middlemarch has often been compared with Tolstoy's *War and Peace*. Similarly epic in scope, *Middlemarch* is broad rather than deep, creating an entire world in the county of Middlemarch and its inhabitants. *Middlemarch* is as ambitious as *War and Peace*, encompassing not only the ordinary doings and romances of the inhabitants but also topics as various as the Reform Act of 1832 (which changed the electoral system in England), spirituality, sex, corruption, the railway, the clergy, the electoral process, the medical profession, and the world of provincial England forty years before the novel was written. But where *War and Peace* is about the sweep of history, *Middlemarch* is an incisive portrayal of individual characters and their place in society as well as the relationship of those individuals to their groups and to society as a whole. Eliot is comparable to Balzac (**Père Goriot**) in her examination of the relationship between individuals and the "wider historical scene" and is comparable to Thackeray (**Vanity Fair**) in her close observation of "society in depth."

To compare her to those other writers, however, is to do her a disservice, as it somehow implies she was laboring under their influence and that *Middlemarch* would not have been written without them. *Middlemarch* is rather the exemplar of the realist movement, working roughly in the same mode as Balzac, Dickens, and Thackeray, but evolved beyond them. *Middlemarch* is more panoramic in scope than Balzac, lacks the sentimentality, coincidences, and eccentrics of Dickens, and was written with far more empathy than Thackeray. *Middlemarch*'s attention to human psychology, to both the actions as well as the thoughts and feelings of its characters, were unique to that point in English literary history, and created a new model for the novel

Too, *Middlemarch* is supremely *orderly*, and the product of enormous narrative control. Fate and destiny, for Eliot, are the products of behavior, and the events of the novel spring entirely from each character's behavior. Although Eliot's narrator—which, though distinctive in voice, she was always at pains to stress was not Eliot herself, but a separate character—often interjects itself into the text, both as philosopher and as commentator on the characters, the reader never gets the sense that the narrator or Eliot is controlling what the characters do. Instead, what controls them is their own behavior and the consequences of that behavior. In this, too, *Middlemarch* is an advance over Dickens *et al*.: contrary to their plots, which often showed the influence of the author's hand, *Middlemarch* is entirely the result of characters' behavior.

Lest you think that *Middlemarch* is somehow a joyless clockwork machine, let me say that it is in many ways an exhilarating read. Eliot writes beautifully, albeit at length—*Middlemarch* is an expansive book in many ways, physical length not least among them—and in a style that is light but not quite at the level of lightness of the 1880s and 1890s. Her narration includes substantial genuine wit—the book is endlessly quotable. Much of *Middlemarch* is concerned with serious matters, from the dissolution of marriages to the mean pettiness of provincial English ways, but there are numerous light moments as well, and enjoyable, well-meaning characters to accompany the deeply flawed Bulstrodes and the odious Rosamond Vincys. *Middlemarch* is, along with everything else, a comedy of manners, and Eliot does not stint on the comic elements.

Too, Eliot is famously sympathetic to her characters. Her approach to characterization is delve deep enough into each character's interstices that the reader understands why they act the way they do at all times—and in the words of the French writer Mme. de Staël, "to understand all is to forgive all." Eliot is *generous* with her characters. With one exception—John Raffles, the emotionally and verbally sadistic predator who brings ruin to Mr. Bulstrode, the banker and uncle of Fred and Rosamond Vincy—there are no villains in *Middlemarch*, and no heroes, just individuals, and even those like Rosamond and Casaubon whose behavior hurts others are shown to be acting out of understandable and even relatable motives.

As several critics have pointed out—Rebecca Mead and Adele Waldman among them—one of the brilliant aspects of *Middlemarch* is that it means something different to each reader based on their age. The younger reader is likely to identify with Dorothea, whose struggles to find romantic and spiritual fulfillment will be recognizable to the young. An older reader, conversely, is likely to look at Tertius Lydgate and empathize with his failing marriage or his attempts to achieve something greater than himself via his research and professional work. (As critic Robin Gilmour wrote, "there is perhaps nothing in Victorian fiction—or English fiction for that matter—to match the slow deterioration of Lydgates' marriage under the pressure of debt and the growing sense of incompatibility between two people.") And an elderly reader will undoubtedly see something in Mr. Bulstrode, whose lifetime of good works (in his own eyes) is ruined by John Raffles, or Casaubon, or in the waspish Peter Featherstone. Like a cut jewel, *Middlemarch* has many facets for its viewers to enjoy.

Some modern readers—and freshmen—will undoubtedly hold *Middlemarch*'s length against it. Some critics have. But Eliot's attempt to encompass the entirety of life in Middlemarch county, from the lowest farm-worker to the richest man in the county, and to address the topics listed above, and to juggle multiple plotlines and resolve them all, could only be achieved at length—at *Middlemarch*'s length. Readers who quail at reading something so long should instead look at the novel in musical terms. If most novels are pop hits of varying lengths, *Middlemarch* is a full-length symphony, and to give yourself up to it is to yield yourself into the hands of a master. Such an experience is rare, and to be treasured.

Naturally, not every critic has been unremittingly positive about the novel. Some contemporary critics assailed what critic Daniel Burt calls "the perceived chilly behaviorism and analytical dissection"—an odd charge to lodge against a novel noted for its compassionate treatment of even the most unlikable of characters. Henry James, among others, found Will Ladislaw too slight a character, or too improbable, or simply too thinly sketched. (A charge which is ultimately a matter of opinion.) Another critic alleges that the novel's chief flaw is the "day-dreaming self-indulgence of her idealizing portrait of yearning spirituality" in the person of Dorothea—again, a matter of opinion. (This writer didn't find it idealized, only an attempt to understand and appreciate it. Idealization would imply that Eliot was not critical, in her own subtle way, of Dorothea's yearning—something not borne out by the novel.) Eliot's unusual narrative voice, which not only narrates the novel but provides a running commentary on plot and characters, has been called "narrative bullying"—a peculiar criticism, to say the least. Harold Bloom strangely (and erroneously) says "Eliot was not a great stylist, and was far more immersed in philosophical than in narrative tradition" and charges her with "frequent clumsiness in authorial asides" and "hesitations in storytelling."

And so on. These criticisms are generally minor in scale and minor in conception, and are easily dismissed. As Daniel Burt wrote, "*Middlemarch* remains, like Tolstoy's *War and Peace*, an exemplary novel because it both risked and achieved so much in pursuit of a comprehensive vision of human nature and experience."

The last words here are left to Harold Bloom, who wrote "the novel compels aesthetic awe in me, if only because it alone, among novels, raises moral reflection to the level of high art," and to Henry James, who wrote of *Middlemarch* that it is "a very splendid performance. It sets a limit, we think, to the development of the old fashioned English novel. Its diffuseness, on which we have touched, makes it too copious a dose of pure fiction. If we write novels so, how shall we write History? But it is nevertheless a contribution of the first importance to the rich imaginative department of our literature."

Recommended Edition
Eliot, George. *Middlemarch* (Penguin Classics, 2003).

For Further Research
Bloom, Harold. "Bloom on *Middlemarch*." *George Eliot's Middlemarch* (Chelsea House, 1987).
Burt, Daniel S. "*Middlemarch*." *The Novel 100: A Ranking of the Most Influential Novels of All Time* (Checkmark Books, 2010).
Byatt, A.S. "Rereading: Middlemarch by George Eliot." http://www.theguardian.com/books/2007/aug/04/fiction.asbyatt.
"George Eliot's Middlemarch." http://victorianweb.org/authors/eliot/middlemarch/middlemarchov.html.
James, Henry. "Henry James on *Middlemarch*." http://www.complete review.com/quarterly/vol3/issue2/jameshmm.htm.
McCrum, Robert. "The 100 Best Novels: No. 21—*Middlemarch*." http://www.theguardian.com/books/2014/feb/10/100 best novels middlemarch george eliot.
Mead, Rebecca. *My Life in Middlemarch* (Crown, 2014).
Waldman, Adele. "A Year in Reading." http://www.themillions.com/2013/12/a year in reading adelle waldman.html.

Les Misérables

Les Misérables was written by Victor Hugo (*The Hunchback of Notre Dame*) and was published as a serial and as a novel in 1862. Victor-Marie Hugo

(1802–1885) is seen as France's greatest lyric poet and the giant of 19th century French letters. He is best known for *Les Misérables* and *The Hunchback of Notre Dame*.

In France in 1815 Jean Valjean is released from prison after nineteen years inside for having stolen bread. But once on the outside, he immediately tries to steal the silverware of the bishop who puts him up for the night. Valjean is caught by the police, but the priest pretends that he had given Valjean the silverware, causing the police to release Valjean. Privately the priest requests that Valjean use the silver to earn an honest life. Two years later, in Paris, a woman named Fantine gives birth to an illegitimate child, Cosette, who is given to neighbors to be raised while Fantine goes to a town nearby to work in a glass factory which is run by the mysterious but kindly Father Madeleine. Everyone loves Madeleine except police inspector Javert, who views him with suspicion and eventually discovers that Madeleine is actually Jean Valjean.

Fantine is forced to become a prostitute to pay for her child's care, and Javert arrests her. Father Madeleine tries to help her, but Javert tells Valjean that the "real" Jean Valjean has been arrested and is to be tried in Arras. Valjean, unwilling to let an innocent man be jailed, reveals himself at the trial and is jailed, but promptly escapes. Fantine dies. Javert takes Cosette, now eight years old, away from the cruel couple raising her, and they live together happily. Javert pursues them, but they elude him, and Cosette grows up in a convent school. After school Valjean and Cosette live in Paris, where one of their neighbors, the young lawyer Marius, falls in love with Cosette. Javert discovers Valjean, forcing he and Cosette to flee. This takes place during a minor insurrection, and Marius, Javert, and Valjean become entangled in the events of the rebellion. Valjean saves Javert's life, but Javert later arrests him—but, reluctant to return Valjean to prison but also feeling the call of duty, Javert drowns himself. Marius marries Cosette, and at length Valjean dies, happy.

Students are likely to have one of two reactions to *Les Misérables*: the love that many readers have historically had for it, or the contempt that Hugo's contemporary critics had for the novel. "Contempt" is perhaps too strong a phrase, but Hugo's contemporaries really didn't like *Les Misérables*, calling it "infantile" (Gustave Flaubert [*Madame Bovary*]) and "tasteless and inept" (poet Charles Baudelaire). Those modern readers who dislike *Les Misérables*, however, are likely to do so for entirely different reasons that Flaubert and Baudelaire had.

Les Misérables was an immediate best-seller, both domestically and internationally, on a level never seen before, and ever since its first appearance it has held sway over huge numbers of readers, who use phrases like "an epic," "more an anthem than a novel," "not just a novel; it is a monument" and "magnificent" to describe it. It is a vast, sprawling, expansive work, bursting at the seams with side-stories and narrative musings and asides. The summary above does *Les Misérables*' story scant justice, for the novel is about much more than just Jean Valjean, Cosette, Marius, and Inspector Javert; Hugo spends fifty pages just telling the story of the bishop whose silverware Jean Valjean steals. Like Dickens, Hugo is aiming to create an entire world, and like Dickens, Hugo attempts to do so through the sheer, crowded, over-stuffed bulk of the text. Hugo's narrative approach is to obey the dictum that "too much is too much, but *way* too much is just enough."

And that's the problem, for those (like me) who are not fans of *Les Misérables*. Taken on a micro level, Hugo's writing is fine. Modern translators have succeeded in making his prose readable and entertaining on a line-by-line basis. Hugo has an eye for the small, telling detail as well as the momentous scene, and many of the small moments and scenes are memorable. Jean Valjean and Inspector Javert are, in effective ways, larger-than-life.

And yet, and yet … the cumulative effect of so much prose is exhausting. Even if the reader is not inclined to repeatedly scream "GET TO THE POINT" at *Les Misérables*, Hugo is not good enough as a writer to make us care for all the characters and stories he throws at the reader. Like Dickens, Hugo indulges himself as a writer to the point of gross excess. But unlike Dickens, Hugo's taste for sentimentality, melodrama, and coincidence is accompanied by narrative bombast and overstatement, an unwillingness (or inability) to cut *anything* from the text, and an inability (or unwillingness) to recognize when a detour in the story should be ignored. (Based on *Les Misérables* Hugo seemingly believed that the detour *was* the story, or at least that the main plot should be subservient to detours in it.) Too, the characterization is flat and one-note, as in *Hunchback of Notre Dame*: Javert is obsessed with the law, Marius with his love, Jean Valjean with charity towards others.

Of course, much of the preceding is a matter of taste; what I find deadening about Hugo, many readers find exhilarating. But even Hugo's greatest fans must admit that he is prone to excess as a writer—and that excess is what will repel some or many readers. Sometimes a freshman is right to object that a work is too long to be read; sometimes length itself is not a virtue. Sometimes a complex work really is what Kathryn Grossman calls a "chaotic, disjointed, multidimensional hodgepodge."

What did Hugo intend with *Les Misérables*? His intention was a noble one. As he wrote in the book's preface,

> So long as there shall exist, by reason of law and custom, a social condemnation, which, in the face of civilization, artificially creates hells on earth, and complicates a destiny that is divine, with human fatality; so long as the three problems of the age—the degradation of man by poverty, the ruin of woman by starvation, and the dwarfing of childhood by physical and spiritual night—are not solved; so long as, in certain regions, social

asphyxia shall be possible; in other words, and from a yet more extended point of view, so long as ignorance and misery remain on earth, books like this cannot be useless.

Written partly in reaction to Eugène Sue's immensely popular *roman feuilleton* (serial novel) *The Mysteries of Paris* (1842–1843), *Les Misérables* shares *The Mysteries of Paris*' intention to change how the reader viewed the subject of the novel. *The Mysteries of Paris* helped change how the public saw Paris and what Paris could ultimately become. Hugo, in *Les Misérables*, wanted to write a modern myth that would lead to a social and spiritual reform, that would force people to see that the law and justice were not equivalent, nor were crime and evil. *Les Misérables* is in large part a detective novel, but the tradition in French detective novels, going back to the late 1820s and the fictionalized memoirs of Parisian policeman Eugène François Vidocq (1775–1857), was of inscrutable, infallible detectives and wicked criminals. Hugo changed this, making the criminal Valjean *Les Misérables*' protagonist and the policeman Javert the novel's antagonist.

Hugo was a serious artist, and his intention with *Les Misérables* was to produce society-changing art that would be read on every level, from the intelligentsia to the common man and woman. Hugo's themes—the battle between will and destiny, the possibility of salvation through good works, the question of justice and (and versus) the law—are universal enough but were particularly apposite to Hugo's French readers. And Hugo threw every mode and approach into the novel, from the lyrical to the dramatic, from the tragic to the comic, from **Romantic** grandiloquence to near Naturalist realism. These, combined with Hugo's positive qualities as a writer, are enough for many critics. But not for this reader, and perhaps not for many readers.

Recommended Edition

Hugo, Victor. *Les Misérables* (The Modern Library, 2008).

For Further Research

Burt, Daniel S. "*Les Misérables.*" *The Novel 100: A Ranking of the Most Influential Novels of All Time* (Checkmark Books, 2010).
Gopnik, Adam. "Introduction." *Les Misérables* (The Modern Library, 2008).
Langness, David. "Les Miserables by Victor Hugo." *Paste Magazine* (Dec. 18, 2012). http://www.pastemagazine.com/articles/2012/12/les miserables by victor hugo.html
McMurrey, David. "Les Misérables: A Populist Hagiography." https://www.prismnet.com/~hcexres/dissertation/diss_hugo.html
Reeves, Bruce D. "*Les Misérables.*" *Masterplots* Fourth Edition (Dec. 2010).

Miss Marjoribanks

Miss Marjoribanks was written by Margaret Oliphant and was published in serial form in 1865 and 1866 and as a novel in 1866. Margaret Oliphant (1828–1897) was one of the most formidable writers of the Victorian age. She wrote widely, on a number of subjects, was well-respected in her time, and is seen now as one of the best writers of the supernatural of the century. In John Sutherland's phrase, "*Miss Marjoribanks* is thought by some to be Oliphant's masterwork."

Lucilla Marjoribanks is only fifteen years old when her mother dies, and she decides at that point that she will, after leaving school, spend at least the next ten years of her life to caring for her widowed father. But Lucilla has too much energy and drive to settle for being her father's pendant, or for being a mere wife, and Lucilla decides that she will reorganize the entire society of Carlingford, the town in which she lives. She does so by organizing a series of evening get-togethers—not parties, but Evenings—made up of the best men and women in town. Toward this end she recruits a nobody, Barbara Lake, the mere daughter of the town drawing-master, to sing at the Evenings. Lake and Lucilla sing beautifully together, but Lake is brimming with class resentment toward Lucilla, and when the town favorite, Mr. Cavendish, gets in trouble—his somewhat scandalous background is in danger of being revealed, a situation that Lucilla cleverly prevents from happening—Lake tries to draw Cavendish's affections away from Lucilla and toward herself.

That's the second of Lucilla's major triumphs. (The first was adroitly taking control of her father's household.) The third involves engineering the election of the town's Member of Parliament so that her favorite, Mr. Ashburton, is elected. However, by novel's end ten years have gone by and Lucilla has not married. Mr. Cavendish, who flirted with her and seemed ready to propose, has showed himself not to be the thing. The Archdeacon, who seemed a suitable match, married instead a much lesser women. And Lucilla, at age twenty-nine, is beginning to feel old and less than she once was—that she was "gone off." Fortunately for Lucilla, following the election (and the death of her father), her cousin Tom (who Lucilla long ago dismissed as being only a man and beneath her serious attention) returns from India and proposes marriage to her—he has loved her for many years. She accepts, and then begins to dream of a new campaign, one in which she organizes a new village and then gets her husband elected to Parliament.

Miss Marjoribanks is undoubtedly the most obscure work covered in this book. Despite her many accomplishments during her lifetime, Oliphant was if anything too prolific, and despite being the "queen of popular fiction" and Queen Elizabeth's favorite, Oliphant has been relegated to the second or perhaps even the third tier of Victorian novelists in the minds of academics. This is a shame, since in her lifetime she was one of the leaders of the domestic genre, along with Anthony Trollope (**Barchester Towers, The Way We Live Now**) and George Eliot (**Middlemarch**), and her stupendous output was usually at a high level of quality.

Miss Marjoribanks (pronounced "Marchbanks") is the book of Oliphant's that is usually assigned to freshmen. Understandably so, as it is (despite its mid–Victorian heft and thickness) full of humor, wry irony, and wit—not quotable, but fun to read aloud. *Miss Marjoribanks* has been described by Q.D. Leavis as bridging the gap between Jane Austen (**Emma, Pride and Prejudice**) and George Eliot, and this is indeed the case. *Miss Marjoribanks* lacks Austen's light touch, and does not have Eliot's level of Art of moral reflection, but is as enjoyable as either author's work, and in its more superficial way is the middle ground between Austen and Eliot.

"Superficial" is perhaps too harsh a pejorative to lob at *Miss Marjoribanks*. Certainly Oliphant, via Lucilla, has something to say about a society in which someone with as much intelligence, organizational skills, and drive as Lucilla is wasted hosting Evenings and being forced to act as the power behind the throne of an M.P. rather than being the M.P. herself. Oliphant is generally seen as an anti-feminist—she was highly critical of the idea of women getting the vote—but from a 21st century perspective there is an undeniable feminist message to be found in *Miss Marjoribanks*. Oliphant may be mocking Lucilla at times, and uses comedic overstatement to good effect in comparing social occasions to battles, but most readers will take away the message that Lucilla's talents, and by extension those of many women, are wasted by the restrictions placed upon her by society, and that women of talents, like Lucilla, are capable of much. (Not for Oliphant the idea of a repressed, hapless, hopeless woman—Lucilla is formidable even within the limits imposed on her.) In Joseph O'Mealy's words, Lucilla "can subvert convention and have things her own way by appearing to personify conventionality itself … she serves up revolution with a smile, founded as it is on a paradoxical adherence to the hoariest Victorian standards of decorum."

Miss Marjoribanks is in fact very much a woman's novel about women's world. The male characters receive much less attention than do Austen's and Eliot's men, and the emphasis of the characterization is on the women and their hopes and dreams and concerns rather than on the men. Men don't come off particularly well in *Miss Marjoribanks*, to be frank, being dismissed as unimportant (or simply means to an end) by Lucilla, and generally behaving unintelligently, immaturely, or simply in a weak fashion. There is no Mr. Knightley in *Miss Marjoribanks*, nor even a Will Ladislaw or Fred Vincy, and the closest thing to an admirable male is Lucilla's father. (As Q.D. Leavis points out, this is a recurring theme in Oliphant's work, as in her life: "this history was inevitably reflected in her writings in a preponderance of male characters who disappoint or let down their womenfolk … a general disillusionment with that sex that is too realistic to run to cynical characterizations but has a saddening effect.") Romance is of much less concern to Lucilla, even near the end of the novel, than other matters, including society and the affairs of other women. Lucilla has her own concerns, and men are mostly irrelevant to them except as tools to be used to further her goals.

Of course, Oliphant was too skilled a writer to make her main character an angel compared to the characters around her. Lucilla is in large part a figure of fun in the novel. Whether or not Oliphant has affection for Lucilla has been a subject of some critical debate, but to this writer, at least, it seems clear that Oliphant's opinion of Lucilla is exasperated affection. Q.D. Leavis perhaps overstates the case when she writes that Lucilla is "more entertaining, more impressive, and more likable than either" Austen's Emma Woodhouse or Eliot's Dorothea Brooke—to this writer Lucilla is in fact hard to like in much the same way that Emma is (famously, Austen said that "no one but myself will much like" Emma; one wonders if Oliphant thought the same of Lucilla) and is much less likable than Dorothea.

As Anne Scriven notes, Lucilla is neither a madwoman nor an angel, two of the dominant archetypes of female characters in the Victorian era. "Oliphant, I argue, is one of the few exceptions, as her young women are constructed as very intelligent, practical, and astute; attractive without being doll-like; wiser than many around them and, most important of all, they foreground objectives in life other than the marriage prospect." Lucilla is, in her way—as Scriven notes—a forerunner of the **New Woman**, in addition to (per Leavis) a possible/likely influence on Eliot and *Middlemarch*.

Miss Marjoribanks is a bridge between *Emma* and *Middlemarch*, and deserves to be mentioned in conversation with both works, which is high praise, indeed.

Recommended Edition

Oliphant, Margaret. *Miss Marjoribanks* (Penguin Classics, 1999).

For Further Research

Leavis, Q.D. "Mrs. Oliphant: *Miss Marjoribanks* (Introduction)." *Q.D. Leavis: Collected Essays: Volume 3* (Cambridge University Press, 1989).
O'Mealy, Joseph H. "Mrs. Oliphant, Miss Marjoribanks, and the Victorian Canon." *The Victorian Newsletter* 82 (Fall 1992).
Robinson, Amy J. "Margaret Oliphant's Miss Marjoribanks: a Victorian Emma." *Persuasions: The Jane Austen Journal* 30 (2008).
Scriven, Anne. "Oliphant's Heroines as Catalysts for the New Woman." http://www.strath.ac.uk/media/faculties/hass/knowledgeexchange/ecloga/media_134987_en.pdf.

Moby Dick

Moby Dick was written by Herman Melville and published in 1851. Melville (1819–1891) was an American novelist best known in his lifetime for his nautical adventures. Now he is best known for the titanic *Moby Dick*, a competitor (and favorite) for the title of The Great American Novel.

Ishmael is an American schoolmaster who feels the need to go to sea to rid himself of the November of his soul. On arriving in New Bedford, he finds the only bed available to be shared by a tattooed Polynesian harpooner, Queequeg. After an initial fright, Ishmael discovers that Queequeg is actually a nice guy, and the two become intimate friends and decide to ship out together. They sign on to the *Pequod*, despite warnings against doing so and despite not meeting the captain, Ahab. Eventually they do see him—he has a wooden leg, having lost his flesh one to the cursed white whale, Moby Dick, and Ahab is furthermore scarred on one side of his face.

Eventually Ahab summons the crew and tells them that the purpose of the voyage is to hunt down and kill Moby Dick, who is Ahab's nemesis. Through personal magnetism, and despite the misgivings of first mate Starbuck, Ahab leads the crew to agree to focus especially on Moby Dick rather than on hunting sperm whales in general. From then on, whenever the *Pequod* runs into another ship, Ahab always asks that ship's captain if he has any news of Moby Dick. (They also kill some sperm whales and drain them of their sperm, but the goal of the voyage is always to hunt down Moby Dick.) The answer is usually negative, but when they reach the Indian Ocean they meet a ship whose captain lost his arm to the white whale, and who tells Ahab where he encountered Moby Dick. Ahab takes off after the whale and pursues it, ignoring various bad omens and the strange prophecies of one of his crew. Eventually they spot Moby Dick, and for three days the chase is on. Despite the crew landing three harpoons in him, Moby Dick keeps shattering the whaling boats. On the third day of the chase, Moby Dick goes after the *Pequod* itself and sinks it. Ahab is caught in the rope of one of his own harpoons and dragged into the sea, the crew of the *Pequod* drowns, and Ishmael is the only survivor.

Moby Dick is a great novel, according to some critics the greatest novel that America has yet produced. It wasn't always seen that way, however. It was a critical and popular failure on initial publication, and it wasn't until the 1920s and 1930s, when the Melville Revival began, that *Moby Dick* gained its due reputation, which it has retained ever since. The average student assigned to read *Moby Dick* may question this reputation, but it is an accurate one.

Part of the problem with appreciating *Moby Dick* is that it isn't just one thing, as a novel. Some of the greatest novels of the century—**Bleak House**, **Middlemarch**—can be easily described in one phrase, as a "mystery" or "romance" or what have you. But *Moby Dick* is not one thing, it is many, and describing it as a "whaling novel" is to do it a grave injustice. *Moby Dick* is a novel of many parts: part sea story, part picaresque, part psychological novel, part epic quest, part romance (in the old sense, meaning a heroic adventure story), part tragic drama, part travel book, part essay on cetology (the study of whales)—*Moby Dick* is many things at once, and is far too complicated to be easily summarized as the other great Victorian novels are.

A large part of its complexity is due to the layers of meaning and symbolism Melville incorporated into the book. As Kenneth Atchity puts it,

> Many of those themes are characteristic of American **Romanticism**: the "isolated self" and the pain of self-discovery, the insufficiency of conventional practical knowledge in the face of the "power of blackness," the demoniac center to the world, the confrontation of evil and innocence, the fundamental imperfection of humans, Faustian heroism, the search for the ultimate truth, the inadequacy of human perception.

And the symbolism is rich and constant. Nearly everything in the novel has at least one meaning beyond its surface, from Ishmael's famous opening sentence, "Call me Ishmael," to the very ending, when Ishmael is found floating on Queequeg's buoyant coffin. An entire industry has developed around Melville and *Moby Dick*, so that nearly any interpretation of the novel, from Marxist to New Historical to postmodernist, can be found.

Moby Dick is, in other words, an immensely rich novel, and moreover was deliberately written so by Melville. Some of the novels covered I've covered—***Kim, Les Misérables, The Moonstone***—were written because the author wanted to be paid, and whatever symbolism and deeper meaning there is to be found in these novels is coincidental or unintentional. But *Moby Dick* is different. Melville intended it to be a complex masterpiece from the beginning.

In truth, no one essay or book entry can encompass the novel. *Moby Dick* is many things—anything a reader or critic wants it to be:

Moby Dick is an epic, as Kenneth Atchity points out, "replete with the characteristic elements of that genre," from the "piling up of classical, biblical, historical allusions to provide innumerable parallels and tangents that have the effect of universalizing the scope of the action" to the "alienated, sulking hero" to the novel's "didactic purpose…to inspire the reader to become an epic hero."

Moby Dick is, as Chris Cook points out, "protean formalism as American allegory—the people comprised of all peoples, flowing into the government improving upon all others. It was, after all, the avowed intention of Melville's New York circle to create a conspicuously American literature."

Harold Bloom writes, "Money, finance, buying, and selling permeate *Moby-Dick*. The novel makes it quite clear that whaling is an industry and that whales are products with great commercial value. How might you read *Moby-Dick* as a commentary on economics and the process of commodification?" Bloom, in another book, writes at length about the Gnosticism in the novel.

Daniel Burt writes, "Ishmael's attempt to make sense of his experiences and the speculative testing of everything he encounters give the novel its peculiarly modern tone of indeterminacy as open-ended questions of free will and determinism, the source of human identity, purpose, and destiny, and what with any certainty can be known are debated," and "With his massive, destructive ego, 'a crucifixion in his face,' and a tendency toward iambic pentameter, Ahab is one of fiction's most oversized, suggestive characters, derived from Attic and Shakespearean tragedy and the brooding, romantic questers of Byron and Shelley."

There are **Gothic** elements, from the flashing eyes of Captain Ahab to its "pervading Gothic unspeakability the whale suggests" (Chris Cook's phrase) to its ascendance when, as Kris Lackey writes, "Melville wishes to develop sympathy for a character's gloomy or paranoid cast of thought." There are the aforementioned Romantic themes. There are a continuing series of homoerotic moments, most especially during the early sections of the novel, with Ishmael and Queegqueg's relationship. There is "presentational duality," as Chris Cook writes, "Ishmael is and is not the narrator … *Moby-Dick* (the book) as both chronicle and allegory; Moby-Dick (the whale) as both meaning and nothingness; and Captain Ahab as both hero and villain are only a few central ones."

These are just a few of the aspects and interpretations of *Moby Dick*, which gives you an indication of how complex the novel is and how open to interpretation it is, and what a rich read it is.

There is more to the novel than symbolism and themes, of course. Relatively speaking, there's not a lot of plot. Melville does love his digressions. But Melville is so skilled at altering his narrative voice, going from circumlocutious and long-winded to bombastic to wry to written in dialect to parodic, that the digressions become of interest to the reader, in addition to the main plot. Those readers who skim the digressions can be forgiven for doing so, but miss out on some interesting writing. Most interesting will be Ahab's monologues, which contain some great quotes.

Moby Dick is a masterpiece, one of the greatest novels in the English language. Its complexity is such that no one critic or criticism can encompass it. In Harold Bloom's words, "it remains the darker half of our national epic, complementing *Leaves of Grass* and **Huckleberry Finn**, works of more balance certainly, but they do not surpass or eclipse Melville's version of darkness visible."

Recommended Edition
Melville, Herman. *Moby Dick: or, the Whale* (Modern Library, 1992).

For Further Research
Atchity, Kenneth. "Moby Dick." *Masterplots* Fourth Edition (Dec. 2010).
Dowling, David Oakey. *Chasing the White Whale: The Moby-Dick Marathon, or, What Melville Means Roday* (University of Iowa, 2010).
McCrum, Robert. "The 100 Best Novels: No 17—Moby Dick by Herman Melville (1851)." http://www.theguardian.com/books/2014/jan/13/100-best-novels-observer-moby-dick
Philbrick, Nathaniel. *Why Read Moby-Dick?* (Viking Adult, Oct. 2011).
Sweets, Sparky. "Moby Dick—Book Summary & Analysis." https://www.youtube.com/watch?v=XIoAYq9iD4A.

The Moonstone

The Moonstone was written by Wilkie Collins (*The Woman in White*) and was published as a serial in 1868 and later that year as a novel. Collins (1824–1889), an English novelist and opium addict, wrote both mysteries and Gothic novels. Unlike most mid-level novelists of his era, Collins is still well thought of today; although, most readers are only familiar with *The Moonstone* and *The Woman in White*. His good reputation is well-deserved, because both are enjoyable novels. *The Moonstone* is more than that: it is historically significant within the mystery genre.

The Moonstone is about a sacred gem known as "the Moonstone." Stolen from India in 1799, the thief, John Herncastle, passes the stone on to his niece, Rachel Verinder. She receives it on her 18th birthday, at the same time being reunited with her cousin, Franklin Blake. The two hit it off very well. Unfortunately, on the night of her birthday party, the Moonstone is stolen. The local police are summoned, but their methods only upset the staff. Eventually the famous Sergeant Cuff of Scotland Yard is sent for. He immediately analyzes a vital clue, some smeared paint on a door frame, in such a way that the local police are shown to be fools, and his questions clearly unnerve one of the servant girls, Rosanna Spearman, who has a hopeless crush on Franklin. Rachel is markedly uncooperative, going so far as to stymie Cuff's investigations by not allowing her wardrobe to be searched. Cuff is forced to drop the investigation, although he makes it clear to everyone that he suspects Rachel of having stolen the Moonstone and used poor Rosanna as her patsy. Rosanna then commits suicide, throwing herself into quicksand. She leaves a letter for Franklin with a friend, but Franklin, heartbroken at Rachel's ongoing and mysteriously frigid treatment of him, leaves the country before the letter is found.

Rachel leaves for London, her reputation sullied due to Sergeant Cuff's suspicions. When Franklin Blake returns to England later that year, he finds out about Rosanna's letter. In it, Rosanna wrote that she was sure that Franklin was guilty and that she had hid his nightgown, which was smeared with the paint from Rachel's doorframe. When Franklin and Rachel meet up again, she displays her love for Franklin but she tearfully confesses that she actually saw him steal the gem. Franklin is shocked at this, and returns to the Verinder estate to try to reconstruct what might have happened. There he meets Ezra Jennings, assistant to the local doctor, who eventually tells Franklin that on the night of the party the doctor had played a joking revenge on Franklin by giving him a dose of opium to cure his insomnia. This, as it turns out, was the cause of the theft of the Moonstone: Franklin, suffering from the effects of the opium, stole the gem in his sleep.

After various plot complications the Moonstone is returned to its rightful place and Franklin and Rachel get married and have a child.

The Moonstone was the last major **Sensation Novel** and Collins' last major novel. (And an exceedingly popular one it was, with contemporary readers.) As a reading experience, it is excellent, with a number of inherent qualities. *The Moonstone* is also significant to the history of the mystery genre.

T.S. Eliot said, famously for his time, that "*The Moonstone* is the first, longest, and best of English detective novels." Eliot, however, does not have it quite right. *The Moonstone* lies in the same position as *The Woman in White* and numerous other novels of the 1850s and 1860s: *The Moonstone* is a mystery with a detective character. One of the basic features of the detective novel is the detective as protagonist, rather than as a secondary character, which is how Sergeant Cuff appears in *The Moonstone*. There is certainly a crime at the heart of *The Moonstone*, which is another of the basic features of the detective novel, but Rachel Verinder and Franklin Blake, not Sergeant Cuff, are the main characters.

The importance of *The Moonstone* to the mystery genre lies in its quality, in the figure of Cuff himself, and in what *The Moonstone* gave to the genre. *The Moonstone* is far and away the best-written mystery novel to appear to that time, and is the best-written mystery novel of the 19th century. Purely as a mystery it has some flaws, but its quality as a novel is high. This was significant because it demonstrated that mystery novels could be well written and successful. It established credibility, to some small degree, for the genre, so that writers like T.S. Eliot and Henry James would not completely snub the genre and its writers. *The Moonstone* was very popular, almost as much as *The Woman in White*, and brought positive attention, from both the public and other writers, to the still-nascent genre of the mystery novel. As Dickens did earlier in **Bleak House**, Collins made the setting of *The Moonstone* recognizable to the middle class, which was a change from the casebook (proto-police procedurals) mystery fiction of the 1850s, and which made the novel more palatable to respectable middle-class households.

The Moonstone also contributed to the development of the Great Detective figure. The "Great Detective" is how Sherlock Holmes is known, and the Great Detective character type was for many years the dominant one in detective and mystery fiction, just as Sherlock Holmes was for many years the most imitated character in the world. *The Moonstone*'s Sergeant Cuff contributed to the evolution of the Great Detective character, although Cuff is similar to his Great Detective predecessors. Cuff has an omniscient manner, like Edgar Allan Poe's C. Auguste Dupin, and Cuff is both cryptic and identifiably human, like Dickens' Inspector Bucket (from *Bleak House*). What Cuff contributed to the Great Detective character type is the humanizing quirk, in Cuff's case a great affection for the cultivation of roses. Dupin's eccentricities are aristocratic and **Romantic**; Cuff's simply make him human and identifiable. Because of the popularity of *The Moonstone*, and in particular Collins' influence on Arthur Conan Doyle and Sherlock Holmes, Cuff is more significant as a character, even with his similarity to Dupin and Bucket, than some of his lesser-known Great Detective predecessors.

Collins created or helped to popularize several tropes of detective fiction, including: what John Sutherland calls "the uncovering of a crime [becoming] a pseudo-scientific exercise crime involving the application of superior powers of intellect and deduction"; a rural setting (not, *contra* traditional Victorian fiction, an urban one); the clever city detective confronting hapless country police; the notion of multiple, plausible suspects; the idea that the detective should know only as much as the reader does—the "Fair Play" so beloved of mystery readers and writers; the summary of the crime before the gathered suspects; the use of real cases to provide fodder for fiction (popularized by Collins, although Edgar Allan Poe had done it decades before); the use of multiple accounts to piece together the truth; the amateur who finds a clue that the professional misses; amateur sleuths solving a case when the professional does not; the "locked room" mystery; the "inside job" mystery; the least-likely-suspect; and the re-enactment of a crime to solve the mystery.

Readers who are not particularly interested in the development of the mystery genre will still enjoy *The Moonstone* because of its excellence as a novel. Like *The Woman in White*, *The Moonstone* makes for a splendid reading experience. Collins starts the novel much faster than he did in *The Woman in White* and does not let up. Collins does a superb job of balancing the basic elements of mystery fiction—motive, means, and opportunity, the detective and the solving of the crime—with the elements of mainstream fiction—characterization, dialogue, plot, and attention to social issues—with the end result being a novel that excels both as fiction and as mystery. The plot is suitably complex, and as he does in *The Woman in White* Collins injects a certain arch humor and wit into *The Moonstone*. Gothic elements, including opium dreams and sleepwalking, enliven the novel, and the addition of unreliable narrators add to the pleasing complexity of the plot.

The character of Gabriel Betteridge, the servant to the Verinders who narrates the first quarter of the story, is idiosyncratic and amusing, especially in his *I Ching*-like consultation of *Robinson Crusoe*, and Miss Clack, the religious fanatic who narrates another section of the story, has struck many over the decades as funny, although some modern readers may not find her so, religious fanaticism being perhaps less humorous in the 21st century than in the 19th. Rosanna's description of the Shivering Sands brings an unexpected and pleasing moment of fright to the novel. Collins' characterization is excellent, both of the major characters—Franklin is far more vital than Walter, in *The Woman in White*—and of the minor ones—the woeful, soulful Ezra Jennings, whose bodily agonies, necessitating ever increasing doses of opium, were taken from Collins' personal experiences with gout. And Collins manages to portray and evoke emotion without belaboring moments or through the use of over-obvious rhetoric. A typical criticism of Collins—one voiced by T.S. Eliot among others—is that he is strong on plot construction but weak on character. This may be true of Collins' work as a whole, since he often makes use of certain character types, but taken novel by novel this is not true, and certainly does not apply to *The Moonstone*.

As much or more than any of his novels, *The Moonstone* demonstrates Collins' sympathies with outsiders and the dispossessed. Regardless of the results, Collins' intention was clearly to show the underclass members—the servants—of the novel in a sympathetic light, as human beings rather than caricatures, and to stress the difficulty of their lives. Similarly, Collins' attempt to portray Indians in a somewhat sympathetic light may not have been entirely successful, but the attempt is clearly there, just as his views on Hinduism versus Christianity lean considerably more toward the former than the latter. Too, Collins' views toward British imperialism in India were considerably more nuanced and progressive than many of his contemporaries, and he put his views on this into *The Moonstone*, making clear that he equated Britain's presence in India with the theft of the Moonstone. Lastly, Collins' sympathies for women are on display in *The Moonstone*, from poor Rosanna Spearman, the object of most readers' great sympathy, to Rachel Verinder, who is intelligent, articulate, independent, and self-willed—a comparative rarity in Victorian fiction. (Although it is true that Rachel is comparatively pallid next to the sublime Marian Holcombe, in *The Woman in White*.)

The Moonstone is not entirely without flaws. The sexual subtext, with the theft of the Moonstone standing in for Rachel's loss of virginity and subsequent high-strung behavior, is hardly subtle. The view of India and the Hindus is dated, and might be uncharitably described as racist, but it is not mean-spirited, and certainly nowhere near the poison of other Victorian novels. Collins' treatment of the class system, of the assumptions of the Verinders about social status and position and the proper place of servants and the lower classes, is unreconstructed. One couldn't expect more out of Collins, for he was a product of his time and place, but in other respects he was socially progressive, especially in his portrayal of the helplessness of married women. But in terms of class Collins was conservative, if benign. Lastly, Collins does not play fair with the reader. All of the suspects are presented to the reader, true, and Collins takes pains to include clues to the solution, but the actual solution (opium-induced sleepwalking?) strains credulity. Most readers might not mind, since the mystery is properly mystifying and the solution and the guilty party are hard to guess, but from an objective standpoint some of Collins' moves seem like cheating.

Still, even with its flaws, *The Moonstone* makes for a cracking good read, and is important historically besides.

Recommended Edition

Collins, Wilkie. *The Moonstone* (Penguin, 1998).

For Further Research

Allingham, Philip. "*The Moonstone* and British India." www.victorianweb.org/authors/collins/pva30.html.
Ashley, Jr., Robert P. "Wilkie Collins Reconsidered." *Nineteenth-Century Fiction*, v4n4 (Mar. 1950).
Farmer, Steve. "Introduction." *The Moonstone* (Broadview, 1999).
Kemp, Sandra. "Introduction." *The Moonstone* (Penguin, 1998).
McCrum, Robert. "The 100 Best Novels: No. 19—*The Moonstone*." http://www.theguardian.com/books/2014/jan/27/100 best novels moonstone wilkie collins.

Nana

Nana was written by Emile Zola (*L'Assommoir*) and was published as a serial in 1879 and 1880 and as a novel in 1880. Zola (1840–1902) was the leading French practitioner of Naturalism and one of France's leading authors in the 19th century.

Nana is a young French actress in Paris in the late 1860s. She plays the lead in *The Blonde Venus*, a scandalous farce about the life of the Olympian gods in which she appears nearly nude. The play is dull and Nana does not sing well, but she is so attractive and saucy that the mostly male audience falls in lust with her, making the show a success.

The role is the making of Nana, who begins sleeping her way to success in the city. She becomes the mistress of many men. Steiner, a banker, buys her a house in the country. She becomes the older lover of young George, a seventeen year old smitten with Nana from her debut. Nana leads on the aristocrat Count Muffat, a middle aged Roman Catholic who has never known the pleasures of sex before becoming entranced with Nana; at length Nana becomes Muffat's mistress for financial reasons. But Nana becomes bored with Muffat and drives him away.

She goes to live with the actor Fontan, but he treats her badly, and she turns to streetwalking to pickup easy money. She returns to acting and does badly at it, and takes back Muffat, then adds the aristocrat Count Xavier de Vandeuvres and the prostitute Satin to her stable of lovers. (It is with Satin that Nana is truly tender; with men she merely plays the role.) De Vaneuvres loses his money through crooked betting and commits suicide. Nana picks up with George again, but when she refuses to marry him he kills himself in front of her. She ruins many, but she does not escape the corruption that she brings to everyone. Eventually she catches smallpox from her dying son and dies a long, slow, painful death in a hospital.

Nana, ninth in Zola's "Rougon-Macquart" series and an informal sequel to *L'Assommoir*, is arguably Zola's best-known novel. An immediate best-seller, it was not nearly as popular with contemporary critics.

As with *L'Assommoir* and the rest of the Rougon-Macquart novels, *Nana* was written with an eye toward Naturalism. During the Victorian age American, English, and French literature went through three major phases: sentimental, influenced by the Cult of Sensibility; **Romanticism**; and Realism. Realism in fiction was a reaction to Romantic fiction, with Realistic authors like Flaubert (in **Madame Bovary**) and Balzac (in **Père Goriot**) emphasizing an accurate representation of reality in their novels, as opposed to a stylized reality full of artificial emotions, morals, and symbolism, as had been the case with Romantic literature. One reaction to Realism was Naturalism, which more or less began in France with the work of Zola and *L'Assommoir*—it was Zola who coined the term—and spread to the United Kingdom and the United States. Like Realism, Naturalist novels reflected the reality which its authors observed, but unlike Realism Naturalism was written with an ideological, programmatic intent. Realistic novels simply reflected reality as an author saw it; Naturalist novels were written to promote a common point of view. Naturalist writers believed—a belief reflected in their work—that humanity was the product of circumstance and its environment, that Darwin's survival of the fittest affected humanity, rather than humanity being something that triumphed over both, as in Romantic literature. Naturalist novels like *L'Assommoir* and **New Grub Street** emphasized the urbanization and capitalization of modern life, portrayed the poor, the uneducated, the mundane, and focused on the power of money and sex and humanity's baser instincts. Naturalist writers often wrote with an eye toward prompting reform of the ills they wrote about.

But *Nana* was not nearly in the grip of Naturalism as *L'Assommoir* was. Zola's goal was "to see everything, to know everything, to say everything," to tell a novel in a *scientific* way, combining scientific determinism, Darwin's laws of the survival of the fittest, and a mechanistic view of human behavior, but *Nana* is a much more traditional novel, despite its Naturalism, than *L'Assommoir*. Symbolism is at a minimum in *L'Assommoir*, which is a relentless, detailed view of a character's downward spiral without any seeming influence from the author—it's a story that reads like a newsreel, absent of the controlling hand of a creator. *Nana*, conversely, trucks in metaphor, near-lyrical prose, and allegory to a degree unimaginable with *L'Assommoir*. The smallpox that destroys Nana is an allegory for the disease that is in Zola's view destroying French upper class society. Nana herself functions as a symbolic means for Zola to critique the French Second Empire. Nana is not the traditional prostitute as object-of-pity, the stereotypical prostitute of French literature; she is a *femme fatale* whose purpose in the novel is to strip away the romantic lies about the world of prostitution. Nana stands in for the proletariat. Nana stands for the "apotheosis of the female body," in Jonathan Krell's words. Nana is nearly or overtly mythic in her allure, her performances, and what she represents (the Scarlet Woman, the personification of sex, etc). And so on.

In other words, Zola does not engage in pure reportorialism in *Nana*, as he did in *L'Assommoir*. He is making use of Naturalism as a means to an end, rather than as the end itself. He is still Naturalistic in his objective observation of society, but as Douglas Parmee writes "Zola's naturalism never excluded poetic license ... through Nana, not only do male chauvinists receive their just deserts but the poor get their revenge on the inhuman bourgeoisie, men and women, held responsible for social justice." Zola was not necessarily happy about this deviation from pure Naturalism; in the words of Joanna Kashdan, "Zola was quite distressed over his romantic tendencies, seeing them as flaws in the naturalistic scheme of things; however, he seemed blind to the flaws of naturalism systematically applied, especially its morbidity, its monotony, and its fundamental mediocrity."

"Monotony" seems to be a fairly accurate charge, leveled against *Nana*. Nana certainly has life, but the constant affairs and doings of her cast become boring in ways that *L'Assommoir* didn't suffer from. The modern reader is not likely to be disgusted by *Nana*'s content; Henry James' description of *Nana* as bearing "monstrous uncleanness" is likely to strike the modern reader as amusingly prissy hyperbole. Not so, however, James' statement that "the obstacles to interest in *Nana* constitute a formidable body, and the most comprehensive way to express them, is to say that the book is inconceivably and inordinately dull," which is uncomfortably apposite in describing the final feeling the reader will take away from *Nana*.

Too, Zola was not nearly as successful as he would have liked or as he would have assumed he was in depicting prostitution (in the person of Nana) in an objective way. Zola's objectivity gives way to more problematic viewpoints. Again quoting Jonathan Krell,

> Through metaphors characterizing Nana as a sex-crazed beast or a filthy insect, Zola perpetuates contemporary "myths" on hysteria and prostitution, reinforcing some of the very prejudices he desires to overturn. He "underwrites," in the words of Charles Bern-

heimer, a "conservative patriarchal ideology" which "defines the working class's functions within the social organism as libidinal sexuality, primitive instinct, and excremental release."

Krell goes on to quote Peter Brooks about "the equation, typical in Zola, between a strong female sexuality and the lower classes: the body as a source of class confusion, of potential revolution, as an object of fear." Valerie Minogue says, "some critics have seen Nana, and in particular the horror of Nana's death, as an expression of patriarchal misogyny on Zola's part, punishing Nana for her seeming revolt against male domination, her narcissism, her lesbianism, and the sexual supremacy by which she remains, to borrow Brian Nelson's useful term, a 'virgin/whore.'" Without a doubt, Nana is a kind of *femme fatale*, aimed by Zola at the Second Empire he so loathed and which he saw as a dictatorial alliance of police state and Roman Catholic church—but a *femme fatale* of very problematic symbolism.

Zola's authorial point of view in *L'Assommoir*, somewhat buried beneath his carefully objective writing, is another example of the *fin de siècle* unease so common to the late Victorians. Among the British, this pessimism about the British Empire and its inhabitants manifested itself during the last two decades of the 19th century and appeared in works as varied as **The Invisible Man**, **New Grub Street**, and **She**. For the British, the *fin de siècle* unease was caused by a variety of sources, including a distrust of and unease with the lower classes, the changing role of women in society, and a perceived degenerations in the physical fitness of the English people. For the French, the unease came earlier. To quote Angus Wilson in Bloom's *Emile Zola*,

> the optimistic, cocksure bourgeois world of the 'forties and 'fifties was giving way to fin de siècle, melancholy and ennui; all but the most obtuse felt the rotten boards creak beneath their feet, saw the scaffolding tremble above their heads. Zola ... drove the public to pile up his fortune as they queued to peer at the very hell they had spent most of their lives in avoiding. The peepshows were: cleverly labelled—the Sanctity of the Family, the Honour of the Army, the Virtues of the Poor, the Ideals of the Artist, the Traditions of the Peasantry, the Splendour of the Church, the Soundness of Finance—and in each there lay a putrescent corpse, far more terrible than the skeleton the poor reader had shut away so carefully in the cupboard of his own guarded conscience.

In *Nana* it is the Virtues of Women which produces the sense of unease.

Nana is problematic in ways that *L'Assommoir* was not. Readable, certainly; of a good level of quality, without a doubt; flawed, inarguably; and of low entertainment value, without question. To Oscar Wilde I leave the final statement on *Nana*: "if Zola has not got genius, he can at least be dull."

Recommended Edition

Zola, Emile. *Nana* (Oxford University Press, 1992).

For Further Research

James, Henry. "A Review of Zola's Novel *Nana*." *The Parisian* (Feb. 26 1880).
Kashdan, Joanna G. "Nana." *Masterplots* Fourth Edition (Dec. 2010).
Krell, Jonathan F. "Nana: Still Life, *Nature Morte*." Bloom, Harold, ed. *Emile Zola* (Infobase, 2009).
Minogue, Valerie. "*Nana*: The World, the Flesh, and the Devil." *The Cambridge Companion to Zola* (Cambridge University Press, 2007).
Parmee, Douglas. "Introduction." *Nana* (Oxford University Press, 1992).

New Grub Street

New Grub Street was created by George Gissing and was published as a novel in 1891. Gissing (1857–1903) was in his later lifetime regarded as one of England's top three novelists. *New Grub Street* is generally seen as his best and most important work.

Edwin Reardon is a young writer struggling with writing. His previous books each brought in decreasing amounts of money, and his current novel even less so. His marriage hinges upon his success or failure as a writer, because his wife, Amy, has no tolerance for life in poverty. Her uncle John Yule is prosperous, but her uncle Alfred Yule is an embittered and unsuccessful writer. Unfortunately for Edwin, he is friends with Jasper Milvain, a hustling journalist who writes solely for money and who orients his life around being financially successful. Jasper's positivity and energy are a stark contrast to Edwin, who is too sensitive for the cruel vicissitudes of fate and the compromises needed to survive in a capitalist society.

Jasper becomes interested in Marian Yule, Alfred's daughter, who serves as her father's amanuensis and researcher, but Jasper is interested in marrying for money, and Marian has none. Edwin's newest novel fails, and when he writes something he considers beneath himself aesthetically, it fails as well, and he refuses to write something commercial, leading to quarrels with Amy. When he accepts a job as a clerk, Amy leaves him. Then Amy's uncle John dies, leaving her ten thousand pounds, but Edwin is too proud to take any of his wife's money, and following the death of their son Willie Edwin dies.

John Yule also left Marian Yule money, leading to Jasper proposing marriage to her, but when the money turns out to be much less than expected, and

Marian's father Alfred begins going blind, Jasper forces Marian to break off the engagement, and she becomes a librarian to support her father and mother. Jasper writes a glowing review of Edwin Reardon's novels, which gets him in Amy's good graces, and the two realize they are well-matched: she is wealthy, and he is socially respectable (which she has always longed for). The novel ends with Jasper successful and happy in his marriage to Amy.

New Grub Street is a vicious satire of the contemporary publishing scene, and a standout work of Naturalism. Unfortunately for Gissing, his protagonist is too weak to be heroic and his villain is too positive to be villainous.

New Grub Street succeeds on a number of levels. Its portrayal of modern publishing is both accurate and incisive. Gissing shows no mercy for publishers, editors, writers, reviewers, or readers, but strafes them all in his depiction of a world in which only works written for the lowest common denominator, the "quarter educated," are successful—everything else is doomed to failure, both because of the constant flood of new books and because of the weaknesses and pettiness of those who edit, publish, and review them. The only financially successful character in the novel, Jasper Milvain, is a social climber and opportunist who sees his work as having all the value of toilet paper. Any writer with higher ideals is doomed to a life of misery and starvation.

New Grub Street's Naturalism is of a particularly harsh variety. During the Victorian age American and English literature went through three major phases: sentimental, influenced by the Cult of Sensibility; **Romanticism**; and Realism. Realism in fiction was a reaction to Romantic fiction, with Realistic authors like Balzac in **Père Goriot** (Balzac is praised in New Grub Street) emphasizing an accurate representation of reality in their novels, as opposed to a stylized reality full of artificial emotions, morals, and symbolism, as had been the case with Romantic literature. One reaction to Realism was Naturalism, which more or less began in France with the work of Emile Zola (**L'Assomoir, Nana**)—he was the one who coined the term—and spread to the United Kingdom and the United States. Like Realism, Naturalist novels reflected the reality which its authors observed, but unlike Realism Naturalism was written with an ideological, programmatic intent. Realistic novels simply reflected reality as an author saw it; Naturalist novels were written to promote a common point of view. Naturalist writers believed—a belief reflected in their work—that humanity was the product of circumstance and its environment, rather than being something that triumphed over both, as in Romantic literature. Naturalist novels like New Grub Street emphasized the urbanization and capitalization of modern life, portrayed the poor, the uneducated, the mundane, and focused on the power of money and sex and humanity's baser instincts. Naturalist writers often wrote with an eye toward prompting reform of the ills they wrote about.

Not in Gissing's case, however. *New Grub Street* is certainly a work of Naturalism, like much of Gissing's work, but a brutal variety of it. The novel is full of, in George Orwell's words, "grime, the stupidity, the ugliness, the sex starvation, the furtive debauchery, the vulgarity, the bad manners, the censoriousness," but it lacks the programmatic intent of much Naturalism. For Gissing, there is no cure or reform possible for the literary world—or, indeed, for the world in general. Gissing's life was largely a miserable one, and he communicates, in *New Grub Street*, his feeling that life is a catastrophe, that the market triumphs over all, and that in critic Virginia Brackett's words, social ills are "immutable forces not to be challenged." Gissing (inaccurately) looks back to the publishing world of a century before, in the era of Dr. Johnson, where (Gissing believes) an artist could prosper writing high art books—unlike the present era, where writing is a profession subject to market forces. Gissing contrasts the older, supposedly more idealistic era with the modern age, and shows the reader that in the modern era writers are screwed, and hopelessly so.

In fact, this view of the modern age compared to the previous leads Gissing to strike a note of *fin de siècle* unease, that pessimism about the British Empire and its inhabitants that was common among writers and thinkers during the last two decades of the 19th century—an unease that manifests itself in works as varied as *New Grub Street*, *She*, and *The Invisible Man*. The *fin de siècle* unease was caused by a variety of sources, including a distrust of and unease with the lower classes, the changing role of women in society, and a perceived degenerations in the physical fitness of the English people. At one point in *New Grub Street* John Yule rants about modern English civilization and the effect of the publishing industry on it:

> "Civilization!" exclaimed John, scornfully. "What do you mean by civilization? Do you call it civilising men to make them weak, flabby creatures, with ruined eyes and dyspeptic stomachs? Who is it that reads most of the stuff that's poured out daily by the ton from the printing-press? Just the men and women who ought to spend their leisure hours in open-air exercise; the people who earn their bread by sedentary pursuits, and who need to *live* as soon as they are free from the desk or the counter, not to moon over small print. Your Board schools, your popular press, your spread of education! Machinery for ruining the country, that's what I call it."

As well, *New Grub Street*, in the person of Edwin Reardon, anticipates the alienated, sensitive, despairing anti-hero of 20th century fiction. But Reardon is the problem with *New Grub Street*—Reardon, and Milvain. Reardon, Gissing's Me character, his stand-in, is ultimately a proud weakling who hides his weakness behind artistic ideals. The reader is supposed to view Reardon as a tragic figure because of his inability to write for the market and because of the way he is treated by his wife, and the reader is supposed to view Milvain as a villainous figure, or at least the novel's antagonist, because of his lack of artistic ideals and ambitions. But Gissing succeeds too well in showing the reader Reardon's flaws, so that the feeling the reader is ultimately left with is not sympathy but contempt—contempt for a character who is too proud to adjust, as a writer, to the realities of a capitalist market society, and who is too weak and feckless to assume the duties and responsibilities a writer must to survive in a capitalist market society. Similarly, Gissing succeeds too well in showing Milvain's positive attributes—his work ethic, his clear-eyed view of reality and the market, and his willingness to admit his own limitations and work within them. Reardon is too sensitive and weak for real life, and should have spared his wife and son the agonies of grinding poverty, rather than forcing them to endure it with him.

Gissing's characterization is strong, and he skillfully describes a time and a place now foreign to readers. But he succeeds too well in limning his hero's weaknesses, and in making the villain admirable.

Recommended Edition
Gissing, George. *New Grub Street* (Penguin Classics, 1976).

For Further Research
Ahuja, Akshay. "New Grub Street, by George Gissing." http://occasionalreview.blogspot.com/2008/04/new grub street by george gissing.html.
McCrum, Robert. "The 100 Best Novels: No. 28—New Grub Street." http://www.theguardian.com/books/2014/mar/31/100 best novels new grub street gissing.
"New Grub Street by George Gissing." http://swiftlytiltingplanet.wordpress.com/2012/08/07/new grub street by george gissing/
Orwell, George. "George Gissing." *London Magazine* (June 1960).
Taft, Joshua. "'New Grub Street' and the Survival of Realism." *English Literature in Transition, 1880–1920* v54n3 (July 2011).
University of Iowa Department of English. "George Gissing, *New Grub Street*, 1891." http://www.uiowa.edu/~boosf/questions/gissinggrub.htm.

North and South

North and South was written by Elizabeth Gaskell (*Mary Barton*) and was published as a serial in 1854 and 1855 and as a novel in 1855. Gaskell (1810–1865) was in her time a noted writer. She produced a wide range of stories and novels and was well-known for her "social problem" novels.

Margaret Hale is in her late teens and lives in the small pastoral village of Helstone in southern England. She loves it there. Unfortunately, two things spoil her idyllic life: the proposal of marriage by Henry Lennox, brother of her cousin's fiancé, and the resignation by her father from his vicarage with the Church of England. The proposal she rejects coldly (she only considers him a friend). The resignation means the family must move, something she is heartbroken over. Margaret's father takes a tutoring job in Milton (a stand-in for Manchester), in northern England, and the family moves there.

Milton takes Margaret some getting used to. It is smoky, dirty, and filled with busy people, quite a change from the pleasant, slow life of southern England. In Milton she meets John Thornton, who is to be her father's student and who is a factory owner. Margaret and John don't hit it off, initially. Margaret also gets to know the Higgins, a working class family. Unfortunately, Bessie Higgins is dying of an industrial disease, and just as she and Margaret are becoming friends she dies. Then Margaret's mother dies, leaving Margaret's father prostrate with grief.

Margaret meets John Thornton's family, and saves John's life during an industrial strike. John proposes marriage, which Margaret angrily rejects. John continues to love her, and mistakenly takes Margaret's brother, a sailor wanted by the law for taking part in a mutiny, for her lover, leading to further misunderstandings between Margaret and John. Margaret's father suddenly dies, and she revisits Helstone, finding it disturbingly changed and backward compared to Milton. Then her father's best friend dies, leaving her his fortune. She finds out that John Thornton has come upon hard times, and she refinances him and they both finally admit that they love each other.

North and South is a "Condition of England" novel. During the 1840s—the "troubled Forties"—English philosophers and legislators were forced to deal with the byproducts of the 18th century's economic growth. These problems, which included gross urban overpopulation, insufficient housing, bad sanitation, and high levels of unemployment, were described by the writer Thomas Carlyle as "the Condition of England." Writers from Benjamin Disraeli (in **Coningsby**) to Charles Dickens (**Bleak House**) wrote novels, variously called "Condition of England novels," "industrial fiction," and "social problem novels," which examined the changes in the social classes and social structure and the current state of England. By the mid–1850s much of the energy was going or had already left the Condition of England novel, as the labor problems which had wracked the 1840s were subsiding (the 1850s ended up being called the "age of equipoise"), and the Condition of England novel was on its way into splintering into the novel of ideas and the novel of social conscience. *North and South* is the last great Condition of England novel. (As well as a "provincial novel," that is, a novel that explores the ways of life and beliefs of rural areas of England rather than London itself.)

A major difference between *North and South* and Gaskell's *Mary Barton*, as Condition of England novels, is that *Mary Barton*'s sympathies are wholly with the workers, while *North and South*'s lie equally (and programmatically) between the workers and management. *Mary Barton* portrays working life in Manchester as unrelentingly horrible, with the only true hope for a worker being in flight to Canada. *North and South* sees hope for both sides lying in reconciliation and mutual understanding between the two classes. Gaskell stresses this enough that some critics describe *North and South* as a "national *Bildungsroman*," a coming-of-age novel, but for England as a whole rather than just Margaret Hale and John Thornton.

Gaskell faced substantial criticism following the publication of *Mary Barton* on the grounds that she had been unfair to the manufacturing class. *North and South* was her response to this, a novel in which she gave equal space to both sides. Unfortunately, *North and South* reads as if written to explore a thesis, not because the characters cried out to be created and explored, much less that the characters took control of the novel. *North and South* reads as if written to make an argument, with the characters being mere voice-boxes for each side. Both *Mary Barton* and *North and South* are "thesis novels"—in critic Edward Quinn's words, "a novel in which the focus is less on character and action than on philosophical questions that are debated and discussed at length. Although most novels contain abstract ideas in one form or another, in the 'novel of ideas' they play a central role." In *Mary Barton* Gaskell used her skill as a writer to invest John Barton with a level of characterization above that of normal thesis novels. She does not succeed in doing so in *North and South*, where the characters obviously move about because Gaskell needed them to take certain actions to make the plot go (or to make an argument), rather than because it is what a real person would do. The final marriage between Margaret and John Thornton functions as, in Sally Shuttleworth's words, "metonymically for the union of the classes they have come to represent: class issues have been displaced into those of gender," but it does not spring from real emotion or story-telling logic.

North and South is, to put it bluntly, historically important but a great disappointment for readers. *Mary Barton*, for all its flaws, had real passion in its portrayal of the miseries of the working class of Manchester and in its arguments on their behalf. *North and South* wants to make those same arguments and expand on them, but does so without the same fire and heat as in the previous novel. (Perhaps the criticism she had endured made Gaskell slightly gunshy?) *Mary Barton* is a novel written by a woman who is desperately trying to get the world's attention through her fiction. *North and South* is that same woman trying to make an argument rather than write a novel, using Margaret, in Sally Shuttleworth's words, "as a vehicle, both directly and indirectly, to comment on the limitations of each society, whether it be the harshness of the northern masters or the shallowness of London gentility."

Gaskell makes her themes overt: the pastoral South versus the energetic North; marriages of convenience versus marriages of romance; the need for justice, both at sea and in the factory; the need for Christian compassion between groups of people separated by economics and class; and how far individual freedom should be sacrificed in obedience to authority. However, she is less persuasive in writing about these themes than she was in *Mary Barton*, and (again) more programmatic in her doing so. Similarly, what Sally Shuttleworth calls "one of the most intricately structured industrial novels of the Victorian age" falls down not in the novel's structure but in its execution.

The novel's greatest attribute is in its descriptions of its settings, both Helstone and Milton. The former is convincingly portrayed in idyllic terms, although Gaskell takes pains to describe how hard rural life can be on those who live it. The latter is not shown in inviting terms, but it is vividly portrayed nonetheless, as a vitally *alive* city.

The novel's most critical flaw is its characterization, especially of Margaret Hale and John Thornton. Gaskell is not without skill as a writer, and was definitely a better stylist in *North and South* than she was in *Mary Barton*—the book is at all times readable, if not enjoyable—but her characterization of these characters is a woeful error on her part. The only likable character, poor diseased Bessie Higgins, dies early on, leaving a repugnant group in her stead. Critic Janine Barchas argues that *North and South* was a reprise of Jane Austen's **Pride and Prejudice**; the reader of *North and South* can be forgiven for thinking this is true, if everyone in *Pride and Prejudice* were hateful, two-dimensional, and unconvincing, and the plot itself more melodramatic (though, it must be said, less so than in *Mary Barton*).

North and South has its place in literary history as the last major Condition of England novel. But students will not be thankful that they read it.

Recommended Edition

Gaskell, Elizabeth. *North and South* (Oxford University Press, 1998).

For Further Research

Barchas, Janine. "Mrs. Gaskell's North and South: Austen's Early Legacy." *Persuasions: The Jane Austen Journal* n30 (2008).
Barratt, David. "North and South." *Masterplots* Fourth Edition (Nov. 2010).
Johnson, Patricia E. "Elizabeth Gaskell's North and South: A National Bildungsroman." *The Victorian Newsletter* 85 (Spring 1994).

"North and South." http://victorianweb.org/authors/gaskell/n_sov.html.
Shuttleworth, Sally. "Introduction." *North and South* (Oxford University Press, 1998).

Pelham

Pelham was written by Lord Bulwer-Lytton (**The Last Days of Pompeii**) and was published in 1828. Edward George Earle Bulwer-Lytton, 1st Baron of Knebworth (1803–1873) was a popular, productive, and influential writer for over 40 years. His reputation has unjustly suffered for many decades.

Henry Pelham is a young English dandy of great talent and ability. His best friend at school is Sir Richard Glanville, although as Pelham grows older the pair drift apart. After school Pelham goes to Paris for a time and enjoys himself and the ladies of the city. After Paris, Pelham returns to England and becomes involved in politics, being of great service to his party but denied rewards because of jealousies and intrigues.

As this is happening Pelham reunites with Glanville and falls in love with Glanville's sister Ellen. Unfortunately, Glanville becomes a suspect in the murder of Sir John Tyrrell, whom Glanville had threatened because Tyrrell had behaved atrociously toward a lady who was under Glanville's protection. More unfortunately, the circumstantial evidence seems to point at Glanville's guilt, leading Pelham to act coldly toward Glanville. But he tells Pelham the long story of his life and of his involvement with Tyrrell, and Pelham changes his mind about Glanville's guilt. Then Glanville is threatened with blackmail by the true murderer, Tom Thornton, and refuses to submit to it, leading Thornton to accuse Glanville of the crime and Glanville to be arrested.

Pelham knows the one man, Dawson, who can testify that it was Thornton who killed Tyrrell. But Dawson has disappeared and is being held by Thornton somewhere in London. However, Pelham knows a London thief, Job Johnson, who once stole from Pelham but who Pelham retains a fond impression of. Pelham decides to hire Johnson to find Dawson. Johnson does so—Dawson is in a house inhabited by some of the most desperate criminals in the city—and hatches a plan. Johnson disguises Pelham as a thief and teaches him the patois that the thieves use, and the two steal into the house and at some danger to themselves spirit Dawson out of the house.

Dawson's testimony convicts Thornton, and Glanville is exonerated. Glanville dies of consumption, but knowing that the world now believes him innocent. Pelham gets the political rewards due him and marries Ellen.

In the middle of the 19th century Lord Bulwer-Lytton was seen as Great Britain's most important novelist, and later he was regarded as Dickens' main rival, but due to the vagaries of critics and changing tastes in literature Bulwer-Lytton has become a mostly forgotten man. This is unfortunate, as Bulwer-Lytton was a very successful author with a number of good qualities who was also more influential, in different ways, than any other Victorian author. In the words of John Sutherland, the dean of Victorian criticism, Bulwer-Lytton "can plausibly claim to be the father of the English detective novel, science fiction, the fantasy novel, the thriller, and the domestic realistic novel."

Pelham is an excellent example of Bulwer-Lytton's influence and ability. Bulwer-Lytton currently has a bad name as a stylist—he is known primarily as the author of the sentence "It was a dark and stormy night" (from *Paul Clifford*), which was the inspiration of San Jose State University's bad writing competition, the Bulwer Lytton Fiction Contest. *Pelham* stands as a rebuke to this reputation. Bulwer-Lytton was capable of writing in a number of different modes, from the stiff, bombastic style of *The Last Days of Pompeii* to the stripped-down prose of *The Coming Race* (1871) to the society novel style of *Pelham*. *Pelham*, told in first-person by Pelham himself, is narrated in a wry, languid, dandified and snarky way. Seen by Bulwer-Lytton's contemporaries as comedic, *Pelham* does not achieve true wit, but it makes a reasonable attempt at it, and what results is prose that is generally quite readable and only slightly dated. It strongly draws characters—its portrayal of the dandy *à la mode* not just reflected the dandy but helped create the model for them—and strongly satirizes contemporary culture. (One of the criticisms of *Pelham*, which sold well—"probably the biggest long-term bestseller of the century," in the words of John Sutherland—but was indifferently received by critics, was that the novel was "contemptuous of English society." It was, but today we find that a positive.)

Unfortunately, *Pelham* contains numerous references to contemporary politics and culture and to the destinations and locales of the fashionable London clique, and has satires of contemporary figures. (For example, Glanville represents the scandalous poet Lord Byron [1788–1824], Pelham's mother Frances stands in for Bulwer-Lytton's own mother, and the dandy Russelton for the archetypal dandy Beau Brummel.) Like any work of popular culture that is thick with references to contemporary culture, *Pelham* is horribly dated in that regard. Too, the passages full of ideas and philosophy which are interspersed among the light, punchy dialogue tend to be a drag on the story (although they are far easier to read than similar passages in Bulwer-Lytton's occult work).

And plot was not Bulwer-Lytton's primary concern in writing *Pelham*; the story meanders.

So *Pelham*, while not the stylistic kidney stone that *The Last Days of Pompeii* is—at times *Pelham* can be quite amusing—nonetheless shows its age. As Hilary Schor puts it in Tucker's *Companion to Victorian Literature and Culture*, the literature of the 1820s and 1830s, like *Pelham*, doesn't offer

> smooth, seamless prose offering a coherent narrative point of view from which to observe a variety of characters possessing coherent (and sense-making) selves ... they lack what the Victorians made inevitable, omniscience in the external and internal world, and a cohesion of social and individual perception. The earlier novels are also difficult to read because they contain clunky, ill-fitting, and digressive novelistic apparatuses: glossaries; footnotes, chunks of text in foreign languages and technical argot.... Bulwer's habit of introducing untranslated passages of Latin, painstakingly detailed elaborations of dress and social manner, local custom and map-making, and "dropping" into poetry, make England as alien as Pompeii—and as "novelistic."

But *Pelham*, like *The Last Days of Pompeii*, deserves attention for its importance to 19th century literary history. (And fashion history: *Pelham* was responsible for the fashion of men dressing in black for dinner.)

Pelham changed the *Bildungsroman* from more serious productions to a genre in which humor and wit were allowed—there would have been no **Great Expectations** without *Pelham*—and anticipated the formal flourishing of the *Bildungsroman* in the 1830s and 1840s. Through the digressions and philosophical passages *Pelham* introduced to England the "intellectual novel," the novel of ideas (rather than a single, usually political idea), a departure from the novels of Sensibility and **Romanticism** and "philosophical" novels which appealed to "the more emotional and mystical faculties." As one critic wrote in 1915, "It was not till Lytton we had the forces of the intellect given a prominent place."

Most importantly, *Pelham* was the foremost of the "Silver Fork" novels, as well as the transitional novel between the Silver Forks and the "Newgate" novels. The Silver Fork, or "fashionable" novels—the original Regency romances—were in John Sutherland's phrase "works purported to be by an insider, privy to the intimate secrets of the aristocracy and willing to divulge all to a middle-class reading public." Their main characters were, in Winifred Hughes' words, "the dandies, rakes and women of the world who populated the town houses and the country estates." The Silver Fork, again in Hughes' words, "was appropriately mercurial, by turns supercilious or witty, disenchanted or exuberant." The Silver Fork novel was dominant among English literary forms from the mid–1820s to the mid–1840s—perhaps the first best-sellers—and acted as the transitional form between the Romantic novel and the novels of the upper classes and the Victorian domestic realism novel, between "Regency aesthetic frivolity" and the "moral seriousness and bourgeois democracy" of the Victorian domestic novel—although, again quoting Sutherland, "silver forkery was not extinguished by mid-century realism so much as driven underground only to resurface in the 1890s cult of (Oscar) Wildean dandyism." *Pelham* was by no means the first Silver Fork novel, but it was the best-selling of them all and the most influential of them all.

Moreover, *Pelham*, with its murder mystery plot and its use of thieves' slang, had within it the core elements of the Newgate novel. The Newgate novel, which was prevalent from 1830 to 1847, was named for the criminals of the *Newgate Calendar*, the Newgate novels were fictional biographies of criminals, and were the first genre of novel to have criminals as "prominent characters." Much English popular literature, from broadsheets to chapbooks to popular journalism to plays, had dealt with the lives of criminals, but the Newgate novelists were the first not only to romanticize the criminals but to portray them as the victims of a cruel and repressive legal system. In the Newgate novels the criminal became the hero, a rebel against an unjust and uncaring society. The Newgate novels privileged the skills of the criminal rather than those pursuing him or her. The attitude of the Newgate novels toward their criminal protagonists is usually sympathetic rather than condemnatory, which is the largest reason that the Newgate novels became so controversial (and in turn sold so well). After the death of the Newgate novel respectable English novelists did not write about murder until the **Sensation Novel** and then the detective novel of the 1880s.

Bulwer-Lytton began the Newgate novel genre with his *Paul Clifford* in 1830 and essentially ended it with the last major Newgate novel in 1846, *Lucretia*. Between those dates were published numerous novels, including Charles Dickens' *Oliver Twist*. But *Pelham* stands as the major transitional novel between the Silver Fork and the Newgate novel, as well as what Heather Worthington calls "a transgressive act in both a literary and a social sense, contravening the conventions of the genre by bringing crime into its elevated social world and into the lives of its socially elevated readers."

Pelham is overlong for its subject matter, and its arch tone becomes as affected as its main character's attitudes. But *Pelham* is worth reading to understand several of the vital literary currents of the 1820s and 1830s.

Recommended Edition

Bulwer-Lytton, Edward George. *Pelham* (CreateSpace, 2015).

For Further Research

Allingham, Philip V. "Bulwer Lytton's *Pelham; or, Adventures of a Gentlemen* (1828)—A Commentary." http://www.victorianweb.org/authors/bulwer/pelham.html.
Brackett, Virginia. "Pelham, or the Adventures of a Gentlemen." *Facts on File Companion to the British Novel: Beginnings through the 19th Century, vol. 1* (Facts on File, 2006).

Hughes, Winifred. "Silver Fork Writers and Readers: Social Contexts of a Best Seller." *NOVEL: A Forum on Fiction* v25n3 (Spring 1992).

Worthington, Heather. "Against the Law: Bulwer's Fictions of Crime." Christensen, Allan Conrad, ed. *The Subverting Vision of Bulwer Lytton: Bicentenary Reflections* (University of Delaware, 2004).

Père Goriot

Père Goriot was written by Honoré de Balzac and was published as a serial in 1834 and 1835 and as a novel in 1835. Balzac (1799–1850) was one of the giants of French letters. *Père Goriot* is one of his best-known novels, and although it is slow and overly dramatic it has a number of virtues.

Père Goriot is a *Bildungsroman* (a coming-of-age novel) about Eugène de Rastignac, a poor law student who lives at the Maison Vauquer, a cheap boarding house in Paris. The Maison Vauquer is full of a variety of boarders, from the cheerfully sinister Monsieur Vautrin to the mysterious Monsieur Goriot. As Eugène discovers, Goriot has two daughters, Anastasie de Restaud and Delphine de Nucingen, who he has sacrificed everything for and who responded by cutting him out of their lives. Eugène, new to Paris, intends to find love and become a social success, and he prevails upon his socially powerful aunt, Madame de Beauséant, to give him an entrance into society. She invites him to a ball, where he meets and is attracted to the beautiful Anastasie, but he makes the mistake of mentioning her father to her, thus alienating her. Eugène then decides to pay court to Delphine, who responds positively to Eugène's words. Unfortunately for Eugène, Delphine's money is tied up in her failing marriage, and Eugène knows that he will need a great deal of money to succeed in society.

Monsieur Vautrin, in the middle of trying to convince Eugène to see society as Vautrin does, makes a suggestion to Eugène: one of the other borders at the Maison Vauquer stands to inherit a huge amount of money if her brother dies. Since it is clear that Victorine likes Eugène, Vautrin suggests that for two hundred thousand francs he could have Victorine's brother murdered (Vautrin knows a man who could easily kill the brother). Eugène could then marry Victorine and get her money. Eugène is both appalled and tempted by this offer, but ultimately decides to pursue Delphine rather than Victorine. Vautrin is revealed to be the infamous crook "Cat O'Nine Tails" and is captured by the police. Eugène is preparing to move into an apartment with Delphine when he discovers that both Delphine and Anastasie are in bad financial straits—both of their marriages are unsatisfactory. Eugène, who has come to care for Goriot both emotionally and as a caretaker, sees that Goriot is dying, but both of his daughters are too busy with their own lives to see their father, who they believe is only mildly ill. Goriot at last understands what his daughters really are, and realizes that it was his own bad parenting—he spoiled them rotten, growing up—that made them what they are. He slips into a coma and dies. Neither Delphine nor Anastasie will contribute any money to his burial costs, so Goriot is put in a pauper's grave. Only Eugène and a fellow boarder, a medical student who had helped Eugène care for the dying Goriot, attend Goriot's funeral; Delphine and Anastasie send empty carriages to follow the coffin. After the funeral is over Eugène vows to conquer Paris on its own terms and goes to have dinner with Delphine.

Père Goriot, like a certain number of other novels described in this book—see, for example, **The Hunchback of Notre Dame** or *Jude the Obscure*—is more historically important than likely to be enjoyed by modern readers. The average discerning reader of *Père Goriot* will appreciate its virtues and will understand why the novel is an important one and deserves inclusion in the literary Canon, but at the same time will see that Balzac's style is an impediment to contemporary readers enjoying *Père Goriot*. The novel should be read, but there is little cause to reread it.

That said, *Père Goriot* is historically important. Considered Balzac's best and most essential novel, *Père Goriot* was enormously influential on both French and British literature.

Balzac is one of literature's true originals. Critics have traced the influences on him to writers like James Fenimore Cooper (**The Last of the Mohicans**) and Sir Walter Scott (**Waverley**)–the former in Balzac's use of barbarism in human form, the latter in Balzac's use of historical settings and detail—but Balzac's creation of the realist novel and his creation of the linked universe of the *Comédie Humaine* were so memorable as to create the adjective "Balzacian" to describe writing similar to Balzac's. Balzac, in other words, transcended his influences so greatly that his very name became an adjective.

As mentioned, Balzac did create the realist novel (and through Zola—see **Nana**—the Naturalist novel). In English literature, George Eliot's **Middlemarch** would be a milestone in realist literature, but *Middlemarch* post-dates Balzac by almost forty years. Realism was the literary movement in the United States, Europe, and England during the 19th century which was dedicated to portraying life accurately, as it "really" is, without the use of literary conventions or romanticization. (This is one of the major differences between Sir Walter Scott and Balzac; Scott romanticized history, while Balzac was a more truthful and accurate creator.) Typically realist fiction concentrates on middle and lower class characters, portraying their daily lives in a "warts and all" fashion. Balzac's realism was a break with the **Romanticism** which was dominant in French letters at this time, and was heavily influential on numerous other nineteenth century authors, from Mark Twain to (at a remove, as he didn't read Balzac) Theodore Dreiser (see *Sister Carrie*) to Thomas Hardy to the aforementioned Émile Zola.

Balzac's realism resulted in a fictional world of unmatched intricacy. Critics use the word "panoramic" to describe his portrayal of Parisian society from the top—the drawing room of Madame de Beauséant—to the bottom, in the Maison Vauquer—and from the Fauborg Saint-Germain of the old aristocracy to the gutters around the Maison Vauquer. Likewise, his realism resulted in a memorable and ground-breaking portrayal of greed, ambition, corruption, and despair, and of a world in which a devoted parent wastes away, heartbroken, and in which criminals and not the police are triumphant.

Balzac's particular realism includes not just his unblinking portrayal of Parisian society—something which scandalized French critics—but his unvarnished portrayal of human characters, tawdry flaws and all, from Eugène's social climbing to the greed of the Goriot daughters to the perversion of parental affection that is Goriot. Moreover, Balzac's realism included the portrayal of money as central to human existence, what might be called the socio-economic approach to literature, which was another new innovation in French letters. Lastly, as critic David Bellos wrote, "Balzac's novel abandons the love intrigue as the central plot element of its analysis of feelings; it incorporates a properly tragic element in the principal narrative of the death of Goriot; and it brings an entirely new seriousness to the description of the physical setting in which its characters live. In these ways, Old Goriot makes a major development of the novel as a form, and contributes significantly to its emergence from the limbo of popular entertainment as the dominant form of serious cultural expression in the nineteenth century."

Another of Balzac's firsts in *Père Goriot* is Monsieur Vautrin. As critic Graham Robb notes, Vautrin is the first three-dimensional gay character in modern literature who is not defined by his sexuality. Vautrin's sexuality is never made explicit—Balzac would never have been able to publish *Père Goriot* had he done so—but Vautrin's homosexuality is implicitly and repeatedly established, through both his attraction to Eugène and to other young men, and through certain of Vautrin's sayings, which were contemporary codes for homosexuality. Vautrin is hardly heroic—even Balzac would not have gone so far as to make a heroic gay figure the lead in his fiction—but he is tremendously charismatic, the equivalent of a **Gothic** Hero-Villain. Vautrin's role in *Père Goriot* is as tempter to Eugène, and the novel definitely picks up momentum and increases readerly interest when Balzac puts Vautrin front and center.

Père Goriot is indeed a *Bildungsroman*, but the lessons Eugène learns are quite different from those other Victorian characters learned in their *Bildungsromans*. What Eugène learns is that ruthlessness is the key to advancement in society, that in the words of Monsieur Vautrin, "you must either cut your way through these masses of men like a cannon ball, or steal among them like a plague." This lesson, and more broadly Balzac's portrayal of Parisian society as corrupt, amoral, and money-obsessed—Paris becomes a character in *Père Goriot* just as it did in **The Hunchback of Notre Dame** and as London becomes in Dickens' work (see, for example, **David Copperfield**) —and his theme of merciless social stratification were what led to *Père Goriot*'s mixed reception with critics, a number of whom decried his portrayal of society as amoral on Balzac's part. The thinking among these critics was that Balzac was too slanderous of French society and that he should have made *Père Goriot* didactic and moralistic, but Balzac was dedicated to realism as a writer and so reflected what he saw in his writing—wrote about life as it was, rather than as it should be.

Père Goriot is generally seen as the novel which inspired Balzac to write his *Comédie Humaine*, and as a microcosm of the whole. The *Comédie* is one of the great achievements of French letters; it is a linked cycle of over 90 novels with hundreds of recurring characters. In addition to being a monumental work, the first sustained effort to portray an entire society from top to bottom in detail, these novels are also the first systematic attempt to create an ongoing fictional universe in an organized and ambitious way. *Father Goriot* is the first novel of the *Comédie* to use characters from Balzac's previous works. Later writers, like Emile Gaboriau and Jules Verne (**Twenty Thousand Leagues Under the Sea**) would imitate the *Comédie*, and the trope of the crossover (in which two or more characters from discrete texts would meet in a third text) would become common in global popular culture based on their efforts, but the modern crossover truly began with Balzac's work and with *Père Goriot*.

Balzac would have a similarly influential (if less directly so) role in the history of detective fiction. Monsieur Vautrin would, in Balzac's *The Last Incarnation of Vautrin* (1895), become the head of the Sûreté, the Parisian police force. Balzac deliberately modeled Vautrin on Eugène François Vidocq (1775–1857), whose career followed an arc similar to Vautrin and who Balzac knew personally. Vidocq became well-known as a crime-fighter, not least through his own p.r. efforts, but the literary prominence and respectability of the *Comédie Humaine* established Vautrin as a character type, something that Vidocq, even with the success of his fictional autobiography, had not achieved. Vautrin is an early version of the Great Detective, the Sherlock Holmesian detective character, and was influential, at some remove, on both Jean Valjean and Inspector Javert in Victor Hugo's *Les Misérables* (1862) as well as on Holmes himself.

Balzac's realism is achieved through the abundant use of meticulous details, to the point that the plot suffers from it. Even the ideal novel has to choose what to sacrifice—no novel can have everything in it, and every author has to choose what to emphasize in writing his or her novel. Balzac's stylistic choice was to emphasize the small details of the lives of his characters at the expense of his plot, just as Jane Austen in *Emma* chooses dialogue and character interaction at the expense of her plot. The result is that *Père Goriot* has a relatively simple plot but a fictional world of such detail that it remains vivid to the reader even weeks after finishing the novel. Even the stench of the Maison Vauquer is limned. Similarly, Balzac's characters are fully three-dimensional, and even his minor characters are given space to become real.

However, this depth of detail and characterization comes at a cost. Balzac succeeds in his attempt to create a detailed, real setting, but this makes the novel a slow read. The dialogue is dramatic, even theatrical, with some long monologues, long-winded speeches, and some clichéd phrases. The characterization, while realistic, tends toward the theatrical and even hysterical—what Balzac's contemporaries read as heightened passion often reads for modern readers as turgid and excessive. The heavy handedness of the narration removes any subtlety from the novel; Balzac lays his themes out for the reader and then repeats them until the point is driven home. The level of detail is realistic, but the plot itself is pure melodrama.

The style, perhaps inevitably, has a dated and slow feel to it in many places—a product in part because of the novel's age and in part due to bad translations (although Burton Raffell's 1994 translation is acclaimed and Olivia McCannon's 2011 translation is quite readable). Too, there is the question of what might be called the French style of narration, which tends toward more intrusiveness by the narrator than is usual in English-language literature and toward tossed-off epigrams and casual ventures of wit which work better in the original French, and on French ears and eyes, than they do in translation and to American and English readers, to whom it can all sound labored and artificial. For some writers this works well; some writers are quite capable of being epigrammatic, even in an off-handed manner. But Balzac wrote at such a speed—the first draft was completed in only three weeks—and used editing as an excuse to expand (and expand and expand) that his epigrams fail at wit and often become mere padding. Balzac could not write like Jane Austen (see, for example, *Pride and Prejudice*), both because of his natural limitations as a writer and because of the furious speed at which he wrote—but unfortunately, he tried to, and failed.

The triumph of *Père Goriot* is its realism, both in terms of the novel's inner workings, its characters and its world-creation, and its influence on later writers and novels. The failure of *Père Goriot* is in its prose. Even with this failure, however, the novel is worth reading, as much for the reading experience as to understand its historical role. As critic Martin Kanes wrote, "Anyone interested in the novel must eventually come to Balzac; anyone who comes to Balzac must eventually encounter *Père Goriot*. In fact, to have read a nineteenth century novel is to have felt, knowingly or not, the influence of this extraordinary work."

Recommended Edition

Balzac, Honoré de. *Old Man Goriot* (Penguin Classics, 2011).

For Further Research

Bellos, David. *Old Goriot* (Cambridge University Press, 1987).
Bloom, Harold. "Bloom on Honoré de Balzac." *Novelists and Novels* (Checkmark Books, 2007).
Burt, Daniel S. "*Le Père Goriot*." *The Novel 100: A Ranking of the Most Influential Novels of All Time* (Checkmark Books, 2010).
James, Henry. "The Lesson of Balzac" (1905). https://archive.org/stream/questionourspee01jame-goog#page/n8/mode/2up.
Robb, Graham. "Introduction." *Old Man Goriot* (Penguin, 2011).

The Picture of Dorian Gray

The Picture of Dorian Gray was written by Oscar Wilde and was published in 1890 as a serial and 1891 as a novel. Oscar Fingal O'Flaherty Wills Wilde (1854–1900) is famous as the wittiest writer of the 19th century as well as its most prominent gay writer. He was also an articulate voice for social reform and wrote several surprisingly sweet children's stories. *The Picture of Dorian Gray* is one of those works more spoken of than read, which is a shame, since the novel is much more than just the story of a man and the painting which reflects his sins.

The Picture of Dorian Gray is about three men: Basil Hallward, Lord Henry "Harry" Wotton, and Dorian Gray. Basil Hallward is a famous painter. Lord Harry is a notorious wit and cynic (who may have been Wilde's "Me" character). And Dorian Gray, at the start of the novel, is a beautiful young man, naive but friendly, from a wealthy, aristocratic family. (All three men are part of London Society.) Dorian sits for Hallward. The resulting portrait is Hallward's best work, in large part because Hallward falls in love with Dorian and invests the painting with his adoration for Dorian, what he calls his "curious artistic idolatry." Just after the painting is finished Dorian utters a wish:

> "How sad it is!" murmured Dorian Gray, with his eyes still fixed upon his own portrait. "How sad it is! I shall grow old, and horrible, and dreadful. But this picture will remain always young. It will never be older than this particular day of June.... If it were only the other way! If it were I who was to be always young, and the picture that was to grow old! For that—for that—I would give everything! Yes, there is nothing in the whole world I would not give! I would give my soul for that!"

Dorian does not give up his soul, but the rest of his wish comes true, and the sins he commits are reproduced on Hallward's painting, rather than on Dorian's body. Dorian is Hallward's friend, but after Dorian is introduced to Lord Henry, Dorian falls under Lord Henry's spell and separates himself from Hallward. As the years pass Dorian grows jaded, cruelly ending a love affair with an actress and then engaging in increasingly depraved vices. As he does so the painting becomes increasingly grotesque, the vices making the image of Dorian bloated and corrupt. Dorian eventually shows Hallward the painting. Hallward's reaction is to implore Dorian to pray, which causes Dorian to feel an uncontrollable loathing for Hallward and then to stab him to death. Dorian has the corpse disposed of and continues on his way, but eventually he tires of his life of vice and sin and decides to destroy the painting. When he stabs it, he dies, and all of his sins rebound upon him, leaving his corpse "withered, wrinkled, and loathsome of visage" and the painting as exquisite as the day it was finished.

The Picture of Dorian Gray was initially poorly received, both by critics and by the public, and it took decades for the novel to be seen as the masterpiece that it is.

The Picture of Dorian Gray has a surfeit of aspects and themes available to be written about. There is the obvious retelling of the Faust story. There is the examination of the psychology of temptation and corruption and the charting of Gray's moral downfall, which, like Fitzgerald's money loss, comes gradually and then all at once. There is Wilde's attack on the upper classes and the emphasis placed by the middle classes on surface values. There is the airing of Wilde's artistic views through Lord Harry's epigrams, and an examination of the bearing of beautiful Aestheticism on depressing reality. There is an examination of the effect a life of absolute freedom would have on a person. There are the echoes of other works: Charles Maturin's **Gothic** masterpiece, *Melmoth the Wanderer* (1820); Balzac's *The Wild Ass's Skin*; and *Studies in the History of the Renaissance* by Walter Pater (**Marius the Epicurean**).

There is the use of Decadence. Wilde was much influenced by the critical writing of Pater and by Joris-Karl Huysmans' *À Rebours* (1884), one of the key works of French *fin de siècle* Decadent writing, and made substantial use of it in *Dorian Gray*. *À Rebours* is the "yellow book" which "poisoned" Gray and turns him into a Decadent. Gray imitates Des Esseintes, the protagonist of *À Rebours*, in his indulgence in color fetishism and general decadence. The passages in which Gray is most affected by *À Rebours* are even written in the overripe, piled-on-detail way of the Decadents.

And there is the theme of homosexuality. Of the three main characters only Hallward is solely gay. Lord Harry is married to a wife he is fond of; although, that does not stop his affairs. And Dorian gets involved with at least one woman along with all of his male conquests. But the men are primarily gay, and the novel implies they have been involved with each other to greater or lesser degrees. Hallward's tragedy is that he is in love with Dorian, an affection which Gray reciprocates only briefly. Dorian is heavily influenced by Lord Harry, but theirs is a mentor-pupil relationship rather than one of lovers.

Lastly, there is the question about what kind of story *Dorian Gray* is: moral, or immoral? The Victorians answered one way; Wilde himself differently, and modern critics quite another. Many modern critics claim that the question is inapt, that *Dorian Gray* is neither moral nor immoral, but a story without a moral, despite the eventual fate of Dorian himself. These critics claim that *Dorian Gray* is a modern novel—a *postmodern* novel, one in which there is no overseeing God and in which morality is only a series of decisions society has made over time. If this is the case, then Dorian is the perfect postmodern character.

The preceding may make *The Picture of the Dorian Gray* sound dully serious. It is not. The passages of philosophy are interestingly written, the wit and epigrams drip off the page, and the story is an absorbing one. The Gothic elements, from the *Doppelgänger* to the hidden secrets, entertainingly add to the novel without turning it into a Gothic novel. Despite having the same rough plot as Stevenson's **Doctor Jekyll and Mister Hyde** *Dorian Gray* is told much more richly and goes in much different directions, and in all is a much more mature and artistic work.

Recommended Edition

Wilde, Oscar. *The Picture of Dorian Gray* (Penguin Classics Deluxe Edition, 2010).

For Further Research

Callow, Simon. "Mirror, Mirror." http://www.theguardian.com/culture/2009/sep/19/oscar wilde picture dorian gray.
Dickson, Donald. "'In a Mirror That Mirrors the Soul:' Masks and Mirrors in Dorian Grey." *The Oscholars Library* http://www.oscholars.com/TO/Appendix/Library/Dickson.htm.

Gates, Barbara T. "Oscar Wilde's *The Picture of Dorian Gray*." http://www.victorianweb.org/books/suicide/06g.html.
McCrum, Robert. "The 100 Best Novels: No 27—The Picture of Dorian Gray by Oscar Wilde." http://www.theguardian.com/books/2014/mar/24/100 best novels picture dorian gray oscar wilde.
Ross, Alex. "Deceptive Picture." http://www.newyorker.com/arts/critics/atlarge/2011/08/08/110808crat_atlarge_ross?currentPage=all.
Sweets, Sparky. "The Picture of Dorian Gray—Book Summary and Analysis." https://www.youtube.com/watch?v=s8iAuBdQJUg

—·—

The Portrait of a Lady

The Portrait of a Lady was written by Henry James and was published as a serial in 1880 and 1881 and as a novel in 1881. James (1843–1916) was an American expatriate in England who was responsible for some of the finest novels in the English language. *The Portrait of a Lady* is usually seen as the best novel of James' middle period.

Isabel Archer, a young American, is taken to England by her aunt, Mrs. Touchett. While there she meets her uncle and her ailing cousin, Ralph, charming both of them. While at Gardencourt, the Touchett's home, Isabel is visited by her American journalist friend, Henrietta Stackpoole, and receives a letter from a disappointed suitor, Caspar Goodwood, asking to see her. (She declines.) Then she is proposed to by a wealthy English nobleman, Lord Warburton, which she turns down on the grounds that she wants to experience more of life and that marriage to him might be restrictive. While visiting London, she hears that Mr. Touchett is dying, and she returns to Gardencourt. While there she meets Madame Merle, Mrs. Touchett's old friend, and hits it off with her.

Mr. Touchett dies, leaving Isabel a great deal of money. This was at Ralph's request—he is in love with her (though he knows it is hopeless) and wants her to have the freedom that wealth can bring. Isabel visits Paris and then Florence with her aunt, and while in Florence they meet Gilbert Osmond, a friend of Madame Merle's. Unbeknownst to Isabel, Merle and Osmond have connived to have Isabel fall in love with Osmond, so he can get her money. Osmond turns on the charm and wins Isabel's heart, and despite the objection of her friends marries Osmond.

However, three years pass and Isabel begins to realize that she has married a monster of dispassionate malignity. She doesn't let her unhappiness show to anyone, however. When Ralph returns home to die Mrs. Touchett telegraphs Isabel to let her know of Ralph's declining health. Osmond flatly refuses to allow Isabel to see Ralph before he dies. After a discussion with Osmond's sister, in which she reveals Osmond's daughter is actually his by Merle instead of by his dead first wife, Isabel goes to England and sees Ralph before he dies. Caspar Goodwood finds her there and offers to rescue her from her marriage, but she refuses and returns to Rome to be with her husband.

The Portrait of a Lady is a *Bildungsroman* (coming-of-age novel) which is accounted as one of the great novels of the 19th century. Whether or not a student agrees with that has much to do with how the student takes to James' style.

James' style is the sticking point for a number of readers—traditionally as well as currently. It is a sophisticated, elliptical, mannered style, a world different from what modern readers are used to, or what Victorian readers would have been used to, and for some or many readers the style is off-putting or even boring:

> The Countess gave rise indeed to some discussion between the mistress of the house and the visitor from Rome, in which Madame Merle (who was not such a fool as to irritate people by always agreeing with them) availed herself felicitously enough of that large licence of dissent which her hostess permitted as freely as she practiced it. Mrs. Touchett had declared it a piece of audacity that this highly compromised character should have presented herself at such a time of day at the door of a house in which she was esteemed so little as she must long have known herself to be at Palazzo Crescentini.

These two sentences are good examples of the mid-period Jamesian style: the elaborate sentence structure, the wit, the prolixity, the indirect approach to subject, the sense that each sentence was individually crafted rather than written as part of a whole. (The Jamesian attention to detail and crafty use of metaphor do not appear, but are as much a part of his style as his wit and mannered narration.) It requires effort to read—the reader must pay attention to each sentence—and that effort can seem to be not worth it, to students. *The Portrait of a Lady*, for all its length, is not a novel in which much happens—James himself worried that there was too little incident in the novel—and students can feel that the ongoing psychological focus and slow development of the plot are boring.

Boredom is subjective and personal, obviously; one can't argue with it. But students bemused by James' almost rococo style and distressed by the lack of events are, in large part, missing the point of the novel. James' style and approach to his subject matter result in a leisurely, expansive, almost casually paced novel, one in which incident is traded for a depth of characterization and an exploration of moral and psychological development. The action of the novel takes place inside Isabel's head; the focus of the novel is on her moral and psychological maturation; the exciting or imaginative setting of the romance (action/adventure novels) is replaced with the realistic portrayal of upper-class English and European life; and the entertainment derived from the novel comes from James' wit and from his close observation of the lives of Isabel and those around her.

In other words, the point of *The Portrait of a Lady*, and a large part of what makes it such an exceptional read, is Isabel Archer's upper class life, her growth and heartbreak. The reader grows to know her, and to a lesser extent the rest of the characters, as one does a friend. It is ultimately a novel of personality rather than a novel of incident, and some readers—the same readers who find Hardy's *Jude the Obscure* tedious—prefer the excitement of incident over the excitement of getting to know someone.

Regardless of what students think of the novel, *The Portrait of a Lady*'s place in history is secure. Like James himself, the novel rebounded from isolation to be seen as achieving greatness. It is commonly credited by critics with introducing into the ranks of the great fictional characters the first American, Isabel Archer, as well being the first major American novel to, in the words of critic Daniel Burt, "to absorb and expand upon the lessons of social and psychological realism by such European practitioners as Stendhal (**The Charterhouse of Parma, The Red and the Black**), Balzac (**Père Goriot**), Flaubert (**Madame Bovary**), Turgenev, and George Eliot (**Middlemarch**)." And the novel's theme of America—in Burt's words "naive, headstrong, and deluded"—being exposed to experienced, clear-eyed Europe would become a recurring theme, not just in James' work but in 20th century literature as a whole.

Similarly, *The Portrait of a Lady* is a transitional novel between the 19th and the 20th century, not just in its use of sex—challenging the moral limitations placed on novels by the lending libraries—but also in its emphasis on Isabel's psychological self, becoming almost, as Roger Luckhurst points out, stream-of-consciousness. James began with realist models—Eliot's *Middlemarch* and to a lesser extent Jane Austen's **Pride and Prejudice** were obvious and openly acknowledged influences on James—but in his shift toward psychological exploration and the depiction of one character's perspective, as begun in *The Portrait of a Lady*, James anticipates the fracturing of narrative of 20th century modernist literature.

The Portrait of a Lady can be seen as a *Bildungsroman*, concerned as it is with Isabel's growth. But like **Jane Eyre**, *The Portrait of a Lady* is not a traditional "female *Bildungsroman*," a story about the quest for marriage and a stable place. *The Portrait of a Lady* is a *Bildungsroman* about Isabel Archer's quest for knowledge and maturity, but a quest that ends badly for Isabel, as the knowledge she gains—about herself, about real life and real marriage, about Europe (as opposed to Isabel's native America)—function as a kind of poisoned chalice. If as critic Daniel Burt says the culmination of the novel is a reversal of the traditional American "lighting out for the territory" (see **Huckleberry Finn**), with Isabel forsaking the freedom of uncivilized territory for the limitations of a real life and a real, bad marriage, then Europe stands in for those limitations.

This comparison—between America and Europe—is an ongoing theme in the book, and both Isabel and Henrietta Stackpole, Isabel's journalist friend, can be seen as representing America, in its pride, brashness, wilful flouting of convention, originality, and ignorance of the higher things in life. As noted, James spends a great deal of time exploring the psychology of Isabel, and to a lesser degree Henrietta, so that he cannot be accused of stereotyping either character, as women or as Americans, but he definitely sees Americans as having flaws as a culture compared to Europeans, and results to stereotypes to portray these flaws.

Truthfully, Henrietta Stackpole is not a particularly flattering portrayal of Americans, or of the new class of woman, the independent, professional woman in control of her own sexuality and her own life—not a **New Woman**, for that phrase was still a decade away from being coined, but a New Woman *avant la lettre*—who were arising in the 1870s and 1880s. One gets the sense that James didn't approve of these new women, or of the bad side of Americans, but that he reluctantly had to admit them into his proper English universe. James certainly makes a feminist argument on behalf of Isabel, arguing about the repression of sexuality and marriage, and he is undoubtedly interested in what Roger Luckhurst calls "the interiority of the feminine self," but James seems to have been uncomfortable—at least, in *The Portrait of a Lady*—with an actual feminist character.

This uncomfortableness with the new is a part of the same note of *fin de siècle* unease that novels as varied as **Jude the Obscure**, **New Grub Street**, and **The Invisible Man** portray. James is much more sanguine and contemplative about the end of the era than Hardy, Gissing, and Wells are, but James nonetheless has it, in statements like Mr. Touchett's.

> There's a considerable number like him, round in society; they're very fashionable just now. I don't know what they're trying to do—whether they're trying to get up a revolution ... you see they want to disestablish everything ... I thought England was a safe country. I call it a regular fraud if they are going to introduce any considerable changes....

Even more notable than the *fin de siècle* passages, and far and away the major theme of the book, is sex, and what James Wood calls its "strongly felt recoil from it." Those interpretations which stress how sexual Isabel is, and her repulsion from it, are, I think, correct. *The Portrait of a Lady* is largely about sex, and Isabel's actions largely boil down to her fear of giving in to its power, to a loss of control to it. This is reflected in how much of the novel is low key to the point of being muted, but James breaks out of this in the final scene with the fortuitously named Caspar Goodwood, in which Isabel, probably for the first time in her life, is aroused.

The Portrait of a Lady is one of the great novels of the 19th century. Students may need some adjustment in their expectations to enjoy it, but if they do, they will be rewarded with an outstanding read.

Recommended Edition
James, Henry. *The Portrait of a Lady* (Penguin Classics, 2011).

For Further Research
Bloom, Harold. "Bloom on *The Portrait of a Lady.*" *The Portrait of a Lady* (Bloom's Modern Critical Interpretations, 2004).
Burt, Daniel S. "*The Portrait of a Lady.*" *The Novel 100: A Ranking of the Most Influential Novels of All Time* (Checkmark Books, 2010).
Herron, Bonnie L. "Substantive Sexuality: Henry James Constructs Isabel Archer as a Complete Woman in His Revised Version of *The Portrait of a Lady.*" *The Henry James Review* v16n2 (1995).
Kincheloe, Henderson. "The Portrait of a Lady." *Masterplots* Fourth Edition (Dec. 2010).
Luckhurst, Roger. "Henry James: The Portrait of a Lady—An Audio Guide." http://global.oup.com/uk/academic/series/owc/audio/portrait/.
Wood, James. "Perfuming the Money Issue." *London Review of Books* v34n19 (11 Oct. 2012). http://www.lrb.co.uk/v34/n19/james wood/perfuming the money issue
Yu-cheng Lee. "*The Portrait of a Lady* as a Bildungsroman." *American Studies* v12n3 (Sept. 1982). http://www.ea.sinica.edu.tw/eu_file/12010594324.pdf

Pride and Prejudice

Pride and Prejudice was written by Jane Austen (***Emma***) and was published in 1813. Austen (1775–1817) is generally regarded as one of the greatest of English novelists. Her best novels, like *Pride and Prejudice*, are a part of the Canon of great literature, and she remains one of the most popular authors in the world.

Pride and Prejudice is a novel of manners (a novel about the manners and customs of a particular group of people in a particular time and place) about

Elizabeth Bennet, the daughter (one of five) of a country gentleman, Mr. Bennet. The Bennets face a difficulty: although they are currently of middle-class status, their estate is entailed—it can only legally pass to a male heir, which Mr. Bennet does not have—so that if he dies, the estate will pass out of the hands of the Bennets and into the hands of the pompous and clueless Mr. Collins, who will in all likelihood not support the surviving Bennets. This prospect, of financial ruin and homelessness, is a quite serious one for the Bennets, and to counter it the daughters must make good matches in their marriage—a difficulty, as there are few suitable men in Meryton, the town near which the Bennets live. (There are troops camped nearby, the officers of which the younger Bennet sisters flirt with, but those flirtations are not considered serious.)

Thus the news of the arrival of Mr. Bingley, a wealthy bachelor, into the neighborhood is a welcome one, not least to Mrs. Bennet, who is obsessed to an unpleasant degree with marrying her daughters off. Bingley's apparent attraction to Jane Bennet—an attraction equally felt by her—seems to hint that a marriage will soon be in the works. Unfortunately for Elizabeth Bennet, Mr. Bingley's best friend is Mr. Darcy, a proud, stiff, awkward and haughty man who initially treats Elizabeth in a rude manner, arousing her dislike for him. By contrast Elizabeth befriends George Wickham, a military officer who confesses to having been treated badly in the past by Mr. Darcy, and when Bingley abruptly returns to London without having proposed to Jane, and Elizabeth becomes convinced that Mr. Darcy was responsible for Bingley severing the budding relationship, her dislike for him deepens.

Mr. Collins proposes to Elizabeth, who declines him, and he marries Elizabeth's best friend, the homely and aging (but wealthy) Charlotte Lucas. Elizabeth then begins to find out more about Mr. Darcy, discovering that Wickham is a scoundrel (a discovery confirmed when Wickham runs away with Elizabeth's younger sister Lydia) and that he once tried to elope with Darcy's younger sister Georgiana when she was only fifteen. Darcy proposes to Elizabeth, who declines him, but after a letter from him explaining his actions, and after Darcy forces Wickham to marry Lydia, Elizabeth realizes that Darcy has a good soul and accepts his proposal. Bingley realizes that Jane loves him and marries her after all, and there is a happy ending for the Bennet sisters.

Pride and Prejudice's place in history is secure; it is the most popular of Austen's novels with readers, is highly rated by critics, and is arguably the most influential of her novels. In reader polls *Pride and Prejudice* is routinely rated as one of the two or three most popular in the world. The critical apparatus around the novel, as with *Emma*, continues to grow despite the novel's age, as critics continually find things to write about. As the mother of all romance novels—Germaine Greer wrote that "*Pride and Prejudice* is the matrix on which all

Harlequin romances are built. It's the best selling plot line in literature"—*Pride and Prejudice* can claim to have had as much influence as any other single novel in existence. And *Pride and Prejudice* is also one of the strongest early feminist novels.

Pride and Prejudice is usually described as a comedy. This is true, so far as it goes, but where *Emma* can be described as a serious novel with comic overtones, *Pride and Prejudice* is a comic novel with serious undertones. Austen meant the novel to be playful, "light and bright and sparkling" in her own words, and thought that it "lacks shade"—and indeed the novel is a bit of a fairy tale, between its stereotypically English setting and its happy endings and contrived resolutions to very real problems—but the final impression one gets from *Pride and Prejudice* is that the novel's comedy has bite and is accompanied by very serious and very real matters, matters more fitting to a drama than a comedy.

Too, despite being a comedy the novel is an outspokenly feminist novel. Despite her own words regarding *Pride and Prejudice*, and despite Austen's general political and social conservatism, Austen infused *Pride and Prejudice* with a significant amount of feminism. Charlotte Lucas' sadly wise words regarding her marriage to Mr. Collins—"I am not romantic you know. I never was. I ask only for a comfortable home; and considering Mr. Collins' character, connections, and situations in life, I am convinced that my chance of happiness with him is as fair, as most people can boast on entering the marriage state"—are a moving damning of the position of women and marriage in Austen's era. As well, in its criticism of the system of entailment (in which only male heirs can inherit ownership of an estate) *Pride and Prejudice* strikes a strong feminist note against a fundamentally sexist system. Similarly, Elizabeth's insistence that she is the equal of Mr. Darcy—"He is a gentleman; I am a gentleman's daughter; so far we are equal"—is feminism in its purest form.

Elizabeth's mother, Mrs. Bennet, is a part of the novel's comedy, and she is roughly analogous to Miss Bates, in *Emma*, but where Miss Bates succeeds in being a comic and irritating figure—albeit not without a pathos of her own, as Mr. Knightley famously points out to Emma—Mrs. Bennet is cringe-inducing—and, I think, deliberately so on Austen's part. There is comedy in Mrs. Bennet's grasping, marriage-obsessed character and her gauche behavior and lack of decorum, and she constantly verges on becoming a caricature, but she is also a constant reminder to Elizabeth about what a failure as a mother and as a wife looks like. *Pride and Prejudice*, in fact, is—despite its happy endings—deeply cynical about marriage, with a variety of bad marriages, real and potential, being visible throughout the novel, and the happy unions at the novel's ending being in their way as unconvincing as the ending of Dostoevsky's *Crime and Punishment*. Mr. and Mrs. Bennets' marriage is a deeply unhappy one, but it is rarely portrayed in comic terms, instead being shown in serious and realistic ones, in ways that most readers of any time and place can recognize as being deeply painful (rather than amusing) to Mr. Bennet, to Elizabeth, and even to Mrs. Bennet, self-deluded though she is.

Pride and Prejudice was Austen's second novel and is the first real "Jane Austen" novel, the first to successfully merge Austen's wit and comic sense with her trademark irony and serious concerns. *Sense and Sensibility*, Austen's first novel, has what one Austen biographer called a "wobble in its approach," an authorial indecision about whether sense or sensibility should triumph and a disappointing authorial choice about the marriage of Marianne Dashwood. There is no such wobble or disappointment to be found in *Pride and Prejudice*; Austen skillfully combines the comic and the serious to superlative effect. Too, *Pride and Prejudice*, unlike the later *Emma*, is located chronologically, in real time and in a relatively real place; the timeless idyll of Highbury, in *Emma*, is replaced with the backdrop of the Napoleonic War and the presence of the troops and their effect on Meryton, the nearest village to Elizabeth's home. And unlike *Sense and Sensibility* and the later *Northanger Abbey*, *Pride and Prejudice* is not a didactic novel; the moralism of *Pride and Prejudice*, the intended lessons to be learned—the preferred inscribed narrative—are much more skillfully and naturally woven into the weft of the novel.

Surprisingly, *Pride and Prejudice* has a stronger and more complicated plot than *Emma*, though plot is not Austen's strong suit, and is far more rereadable than *Emma*, thanks to Austen's epigrammatic style. *Pride and Prejudice* is in fact an interesting comparison to *Emma*, in that *Emma* is usually thought of as the better novel but *Pride and Prejudice* is far and away the more popular of the two. Critically there is little comparison between the two, as critics almost universally see *Emma* as the stronger of the two; but the average reader of Austen almost universally favors *Pride and Prejudice*—and always has, from when *Pride and Prejudice* was first published. (*Pride and Prejudice* was critically popular on its initial publication but was far more popular with the average reader—a case that still holds today.) Why readers prefer *Pride and Prejudice* is after all not a deep mystery, but the reasons deserve explication.

Pride and Prejudice has what passes for villains in an Austen novel: the odious George Wickham, the snobbish Miss Bingley, the pompous Mr. Collins, and the haughty Lady Catherine de Bourgh, who does what she can to foil the marriage between Mr. Darcy and Elizabeth. *Emma* has no villains. Novels are always more enjoyable when the heroes have proper villains to set themselves against, and the actions of the villains in *Pride and Prejudice* give the plot a great deal of its forward momentum.

Pride and Prejudice is a bitchier novel than *Emma*. There is far more of Austen's epigrammatic wit in *Pride and Prejudice* than in *Emma*, beginning with the novel's famous first line, "It is a truth universally acknowledged, that a single man in possession of a good fortune, must be in want of a wife." But the dialogue in *Pride and Prejudice* is generally spikier than *Emma*, reflecting the tendency of the era to put the action sequences in the dialogue itself. Just as *Pride and Prejudice* has villains where *Emma* has none, *Pride and Prejudice* has conflict, reflected in and generated by the dialogue, where *Emma* simply has plot complications.

Pride and Prejudice has the more likable characters of the two novels. Austen famously said of Emma Woodhouse that "I am going to take a heroine whom no one but myself will much like," which is perhaps a slight over-exaggeration, but not too much of one. There remains an ambiguity about Emma even by the end of the novel. But few readers dislike Elizabeth Bennett, whose main flaw is not Emma's vanity but a more identifiable quickness to judge—the "prejudice" of the novel's title. (Contrasted with the "pride" of Mr. Darcy—features both Elizabeth and Darcy set aside by novel's end.) Emma's father is a subject of comedy, while Elizabeth's father is ultimately a tragic figure, hiding his disappointment at a marriage-gone-wrong behind his ever-present wit. And Mr. Knightley, while an honorable man, lacks the three dimensions and the Gothic Hero-Villain appeal of Mr. Darcy. Similarly, where *Emma* has as secondary characters people like Miss Bates, *Pride and Prejudice* has Elizabeth's sisters.

Pride and Prejudice is the more relatable of the two novels. Emma has no problems, being young, beautiful, wealthy, and privileged; her main difficulty is having *too little to do*. The problems of Elizabeth, conversely, are quite recognizable: money problems, family problems, relationship problems. These are universal problems, recognizable by men and women across time and cultures, rather than the more limited problems—limited socioeconomically and chronologically—of Emma. The reader ends up liking Emma despite her elevated condition and her lack of real problems; the reader almost immediately recognizes Elizabeth and identifies with her.

The stakes are much higher in *Pride and Prejudice* than in *Emma*. Emma is after all wealthy and privileged in her position in Highbury, a situation which is not going to change if she fails to win the love of the right man. She will still have the friendship of Mr. Knightley, still be the social queen of Highbury, and still have her father's (quite heavy) love. But Elizabeth and her sisters are in a financially precarious situation, with only their father's life being between them and financial ruin. Elizabeth is still young, but in her friend Charlotte Lucas the reader gets a (shudder-inducing) glimpse at what life for a spinster (at only age 27!) would be like, and the sorts of loveless marriage Elizabeth might be forced in to if she wanted to avoid being a burden to her family. Emma only need fear being a spinster; Elizabeth has to worry about the family ultimately being homeless.

Lastly, *Emma* is a kind of idyll, with Highbury being a kind of pastoral paradise for its inhabitants. Real world considerations do not intrude upon it, nor do the characters face real world problems. The world of *Pride and Prejudice* is quite different, despite its fairy tale structure, and Austen even allows sex to appear—never explicitly stated, true, but the storyline about Lydia bringing social disrepute upon her family and being shamed is all about Lydia having sex before marriage, and the world knowing about it. Moreover, Lydia's reaction to her elopement with Mr. Wickham, and her blithe lack of understanding for the shame she has brought to the Bennets, indicates that Austen, despite being a virgin herself, had a clear understanding that woman can actually enjoy sex rather than seeing it as a mere onerous experience to be suffered through.

The appeal of *Pride and Prejudice* to readers is obvious: a pleasingly ironic narration, witty dialogue, likable characters, a romantic relationship that is realistic in its slow and steady attraction between the two characters, and real problems. It is no surprise that modern polls of readers show that *Pride and Prejudice* is regularly ranked in the top three best books ever written. In fact, it is a sign of Austen's strength as a writer that the novel is as popular as it is with readers despite its flaws. As mentioned, the dialogue is spiked, and bristling with sharp exchanges and ill-will buried beneath a veneer of *politesse*; this makes the novel an entertaining read but hardly a smooth one. Too, unlike *Emma*, there are a significant number of dated, antiquated, or obscure terms used in *Pride and Prejudice* and a reliance on a knowledge of contemporary social distinctions; the use of explanatory notes, annotations, and scholarly commentary is advised when reading *Pride and Prejudice*, unlike with *Emma*. Lastly, the characters of *Pride and Prejudice* are more carefully described than the ones in *Emma*, made more three-dimensional by Austen, but this consequently leads to their flaws and oddities being more pronounced. As critic Harold Bloom put it, *Pride and Prejudice* has a "social world that borders oddly on the bizarre, for everyone in it is rather more idiosyncratic than at first they appear to be"—a critical judgment that not all readers will share but which will strike some readers as forcefully accurate.

Part of the comic material of *Pride and Prejudice* can be seen as overstaying its welcome. Miss Bates, in *Emma*, is intended to be funny, but Austen overdid the degree to which the reader is exposed to Miss Bates and her blather, with the result that what was intended to be funny actually becomes irritating and skippable. Mrs. Bennet in *Pride and Prejudice* is similarly intended to be funny, but whether deliberately or by accident Austen reigned herself in and limited the amount of Mrs. Bennet's comic stylings. Mrs. Bennet actually makes the superior comic foil to Miss Bates, as the comedy in Mrs. Bennet is both more realistic—one can more easily imagine Mrs. Bennet existing and saying the things she does than Miss Bates—and less comic and more cringe-inducing—the difference, perhaps, between the American sense of humor and the British sense of humor.

Even with these flaws, however—flaws which are after all relatively small—*Pride and Prejudice* is quite understandably one of the most popular novels in the world, one read and reread both popularly and critically with pleasure.

Recommended Edition

Austen, Jane. *Pride and Prejudice* (Oxford World's Classics, 2004).

For Further Research

Bloom, Harold. "Bloom on *Pride and Prejudice*." *Pride and Prejudice* (Chelsea House, 2004).
Brower, Reuben. *Light and Bright and Sparkling: Irony and Fiction in Pride and Prejudice* (1963).
Jones, Darryl. "Pride and Prejudice." *Pride and Prejudice*, Updated Edition (Bloom's Modern Critical Editions, 2004).
Kordich, Catherine. "Pride and Prejudice." *Bloom's How to Write About Jane Austen* (Chelsea House, 2008).
Stafford, Fiona. "Introduction." *Pride and Prejudice* (Oxford World's Classics, 2004).
Sweets, Sparky. "Pride & Prejudice—Book Summary & Analysis." https://www.youtube.com/watch?v=5Nm61IoNdHg.

The Red and the Black

The Red and the Black was written by "Stendhal," the pen-name of Marie-Henri Beyle (***The Charterhouse of Parma***), and was published in 1830. Beyle (1783–1842) is best known as one of France's foremost writers of naturalism, and *The Red and the Black* is his masterwork.

Julian Sorel is the son of a coarse, brutal carpenter in the small town of Verrières in France. Because the age of Napoleon is gone, and the army (the red of the novel's title) is no longer a possible path to greatness and power,

Julian chooses the church (the black of the novel's title) as his life's mission. Because of his intelligence and supposed piety, he is chosen to be the tutor of the children of Monsieur de Renal, the mayor of Verrières. While with the de Renal family he begins an affair with Madame de Renal. Eventually Monsieur de Renal sends Julian to a seminary, an experience which Julian finds miserable. But he does befriend the Abbé Pirard, who sees to it that Julien is made the secretary of the Marquis de la Mole.

Julien's experience in the de la Mole household is eye-opening, for it exposes Julien first-hand to the aristocracy and the rich. It also introduces Julien to Mathilde, the Marquis' daughter, a proud and even haughty young woman. They spend much of their time together, both having a taste for Voltaire, and at length she falls in love with him and sleeps with him. However, she soon decides that loving a mere secretary is an insult to her noble lineage, which affronts Julien, who plans to gain power over her and over the entire de la Mole household. He does so by wooing another woman while treating Mathilde coldly, which leads to her falling more intensely in love with him.

But she gets pregnant, and when her father finds out he gives Julien money and a position in the army, so that Mathilde will not marry a mere carpenter's son. However, Madame de Renal sends a letter to the Marquis letting him know about her former relationship with Julien, which outrages the Marquis, who refuses to let Julien marry Mathilde. Enraged, Julien rides to Verrières and shoots Madame de Renal during church services. After being arrested Julien admits his guilt and refuses the help of his friends—he is ready to die. Madame de Renal visits him in jail, and the love between the two flares anew. But Julien is executed. Mathilde buries his head separately from his body, following a de la Mole family legend, and Madame de Renal dies three days after Julien.

The Red and the Black is an important novel. But it is a less than enthralling read.

Students are likely to be assigned to read *The Red and the Black* because of its place in literary history. Less well-known to English-language readers than Balzac (**Père Goriot**), Stendhal preceded Balzac by five years in writing a realistic novel. Stendhal was not appreciated for *The Red and the Black* during his lifetime, of course; he himself said it would take fifty years for the novel to be appreciated, and it took until the 1890s for Stendhal and *The Red and the Black* to get their just due. At that time, Leo Tolstoy said that he learned more from Stendhal than any other writers, Emile Zola (**L'Assomoir, Nana**) and the naturalists (see **New Grub Street**) claimed Stendhal as their forefather, and Andre Gide claimed that *The Red and the Black* was a novel of the 20th century, rather than the 19th.

So any discussion of *The Red and the Black* must take into account the fact that, important though the novel is, and of good quality, the book was not influential during or after Stendhal's lifetime. It was Balzac, not Stendhal, who created the realist novel, for it was Balzac who other writers looked to throughout most of the century, not Stendhal.

That said, Stendhal did write a revolutionary book. In the words of Daniel Burt, *The Red and the Black* was the first novel to "attempt to extend the range of the novel in two different directions simultaneously—outwardly to capture in depth a particular historical moment and inwardly to reveal the concealed recesses of the human heart and psyche." *The Red and the Black*—again, before Balzac and *Père Goriot*—created a new template for the novel, making previous approaches to novel-writing outdated and anticipating the realist and naturalist approaches to come.

The Red and the Black was like nothing audiences had seen before. A novel without a hero or happy ending, devoted to exposing the "hypocrisy, deviousness, and crass self-interest" of modern society, *The Red and the Black* was a savage indictment of modern French society in novel form, not something readers had previously encountered. *The Red and the Black* featured one of fiction's first major anti-heroes, and an existential hero a century before such a thing would be conceived of. It showed society as it was rather than as it wanted itself to be, something unprecedented in French fiction. It spent as much time focusing on Julien's psychology, thoughts and feelings, as it did on plot. Critic Irving Howe writes,

> The modern hero, the man who forces society to accept him as its agent—the hero by will rather than birth—now appears for the first time.... Before the revolution men had been concerned with privileges, not expectations; now they dream of success, that is, of a self-willed effort to lift oneself, through industry or chicanery, to a higher social level. Life becomes an experiment in strategy, an adventure in plan, ruse, and combat; the hero is not merely ambitious but sensitive to the point of paranoia, discovering and imagining a constant assault upon his dignity; and Stendhal carries this outlook to its extreme limit, perhaps even to caricature, by applying it to the affairs of love.

At the same time, *The Red and the Black* is a *Bildungsroman* (coming-of-age story) and Julien is a **Romantic** hero, caught between reason and passion. So the novel has a unique combination of Romanticism and realism, appearing as it does at the height of French Romanticism and with (through Julian) the cult "of the superior individual in revolt against society and ideology" and "the portrayal of sensitive, passionate souls on the quest for happiness." Like many Romantic writers, Stendhal made Julien into an idealized version of himself, but a version of himself that is confronting real society, not an idealized society, and in a novel that lacks the typical Romantic hyperbolity. We are not meant to enjoy or like Julien, but some critics—like Harold Bloom—admire him for his imagination and find him attractive despite his repellant treatment of the two women of the novel, or argue that his role is not to be the main character but to emphasize the heroism of the two women. In Bloom's words, "One could argue that Julien, like Lord Byron, has that cool passivity which provokes his women into a return to themselves, so that his function is to spur these remarkable (and very dissimilar) ladies on to the epiphanies of their own modes of heroism."

However, the importance of a novel and its inherent qualities do not necessarily make a novel a good read, and *The Red and the Black* fails at being that. The 2003 translation by Burton Raffel is certainly readable in ways that previous translations were not, or were less so, and Raffel heightens Stendhal's conversational style. Stendhal's women are unusually strong and three-dimensional. And for the first half of the novel the reader is, if not especially involved with the novel, then not bored by it, at least. But *The Red and the Black* is very much a novel of its time and place—"a chronicle of 1830," as the novel's subtitle has it—and, thanks to its level of references, not particularly comprehensible to modern readers without a good set of subtitles. Worse, the novel is overlong for the points it wants to make, and the Raffel translation cannot do away with certain of Stendhal's stylistic infelicities.

Recommended Edition
Stendhal. *The Red and the Black* (Modern Library Classics, 2004).

For Further Research
Bloom, Harold. "Stendhal: *The Red and the Black.*" *Novelists and Novels* (Chelsea House, 2005).
Burt, Daniel S. "*The Red and the Black.*" *The Novel 100: A Ranking of the Most Influential Novels of All Time* (Checkmark Books, 2010).
Howe, Irving. *Politics and the Novel* (Ivan Dee, 2002).
Taylor, Karen L. "*The Red and the Black.*" *Facts on File Companion to the French Novel* (Facts on File, 2007).

Salammbô

Salammbô (1862) was written by Gustave Flaubert (**Madame Bovary**). Flaubert (1821–1880) is one of the truly major writers of the 19th century.

Although he is best known for *Madame Bovary* he has a respectable body of work, from short stories to dramas. His work is generally placed in the realist genre, but his skill as a stylist and technician is far above most of the other realists. *Salammbô* is one of the greatest historical romances of the 19th century.

Salammbô is the story of Carthage in 237 B.C.E., during the mercenary rebellion described by the Greek historian Polybius in his *History*. The novel is not really about Salammbô, who is the priestess of Tanit, the moon, and is the daughter of the mighty general Hamilcar Barca. *Salammbô* is about the mercenary rebellion itself. Salammbô only appears as a subplot, albeit a compelling one and one which Flaubert himself saw as important to the novel. The mercenaries rebel against Carthage because the city elders refuse to give them their pay. The mercenaries are led by Mathô, a Libyan, and are opposed by first the Carthaginians and then by Hamilcar Barca himself. The war is lengthy, and there is a great deal of suffering and cruelty on and from both sides. The mercenaries win several temporary victories, only to suffer reversals. The mercenaries eventually lay siege to Carthage and destroy the city's aqueduct, which subjects the city to thirst as well as famine. But the Carthaginians sacrifice children to their god Moloch, which brings rains to the city. Eventually Hamilcar Barca defeats the mercenaries, trapping and killing most of their troops in a ravine in the mountains. Mathô is captured and forced to run a gauntlet through the city before he dies.

Salammbô is not central to the result of the rebellion, but she is influential on Mathô, who is desperately in love with her. Early in the siege Mathô breaks into Carthage to see Salammbô, but on the advice of his wily slave Spendius Mathô changes his mind and steals the zaïmph, the sacred veil of Tanit. The zaïmph is not to be touched by any mortal, and by stealing it Mathô hopes to destroy the morale of the Carthaginians. Soon afterward Mathô and Salammbô have a brief meeting. Mathô tells Salammbô his feelings for her and reveals that he stole the zaïmph. Infuriated, she calls down curses and imprecations on him for defiling the zaïmph. Mathô flees from her and escapes from the city. When the Carthaginians discover that the zaïmph has been stolen, their spirits are lowered, as Mathô planned. Eventually Salammbô steals into the rebels' camp and goes to Mathô's tent. He repeats his love for her and she submits to him. When he has fallen asleep she takes the zaïmph and returns with it to Carthage, thus rallying the Carthaginians. At the end of the novel, when Mathô runs the gauntlet, he falls dead at her feet. Remembering his words to her, she feels something for him, but then drops dead "for having touched the mantle of Tanit."

Salammbô has a lot in common, at least on a surface level, with Victor Hugo's **Notre Dame de Paris**. Like Hugo, Flaubert created a fictional world with a truly astonishing amount of detail. Flaubert spent over four years researching Carthage, and *Salammbô* is proof of his efforts. There is a wealth of architectural, military, and social detail on every page. Like Hugo, Flaubert makes his chosen subject come alive on the page. (Notably, however, Flaubert insisted that he was writing about an image of Carthage rather than an accurate historical recreation.) But *Salammbô* is a far more compelling read than *Notre Dame de Paris*, and an infinitely better historical novel. Flaubert's declamatory, faux-epic style—what he considered a lyrical, "Biblical" style—is smoother and more polished than Hugo's more conversational tone. Hugo's characterization is rather heavy-handed, while Flaubert's characterization, such as it is—*Salammbô* is not a novel of characterization, but of history-in-action—is, if not subtle, then less overt and clumsy. Flaubert's style has *impressionismus*, the quality in art of evoking emotions and impressions in the eyes and minds of the readers. And Flaubert has the advantage of describing romantic history, rather than gritty urban history.

There is, as mentioned, an enormous amount of historical detail in *Salammbô*. More than that, however, Flaubert devotes a great deal of space to describing, in detail, the sights, sounds, smells, tastes, and physical feelings. Flaubert's effort to create sensual impressions in the minds of the readers, to make the smells and sounds waft from the page, is not wasted; *Salammbô* is peculiarly vivid and atmospheric and sensual, and although the novel is ultimately exotic and alien to modern readers it is absorbing and feels real. Of course, Flaubert does sacrifice characterization, psychological depth, and an exploration of the love story between Matho and Salammbô for the space given to the descriptions and to the conflict between the Barbarians and the Carthaginians. But no novel is perfect (except perhaps **Middlemarch**).

The novel is a precursor to the Symbolist and Decadent movements of the late 19th and early 20th centuries, in the self-indulgent luxuriousness of its style, the *fin de siècle* tone of the story (which some critics have seen as Flaubert's commentary on French society of the time), and the colorful excess of the novel's content. Symbolist and Decadent artists like Gustave Moreau counted *Salammbô* among their favorite books, and Decadent and proto-Decadent writers like Theophile Gautier and Charles Baudelaire praised it highly. Flaubert takes a realist approach to the details of Carthaginian life, "by applying to antiquity the methods of the modern novel" in his words, and layers them on so thickly as to make reality a symbol and history a kind of epic. As in *Madame Bovary*, Flaubert in *Salammbô* takes the stuff of ordinary life and makes it into an epic, but here the facts he writes about are the stuff of historical romance, the genre of historical fiction which uses the conventional narratives of adventure fiction to tell a historical story. Historical romances are usually set in opposition by critics to mimetic, Naturalist stories, but in *Salammbô* Flaubert has the luxury of being both realistic *and* historical romantic.

Salammbô's success as a historical novel has been fiercely debated, with some 19th century critics calling it a failure because of its exotic locale and obscure subject matter or its failure to meet the contemporary criteria of a historical novel, and with some 20th century critics accusing it of being too modern in its psychology, and even going so far as to call the novel the end of the historical romance. Modern readers will disagree on both counts. Despite its difficult vocabulary and obscure subject matter, *Salammbô* is quite successful as a novel, and rather than being a failure as a historical novel should be seen as a rare link between historical romance and the Symbolists and Decadents, and a significant departure from the historical novel's later turn toward Naturalism.

Moreover, in its exoticism and excessive violence, *Salammbô* can be seen as a precursor to modern fantasy fiction, what is called "secondary world" fiction. Flaubert creates what is in essence a fantasy world (despite its historically accurate content) and makes the stuff of history into the fantastical. Critics have often objected to the excessive violence, and the amoral way in which it is described, but as an antecedent to modern fantasy fiction *Salammbô*—especially the more brutal and less romanticized fantasy novels—fits right in. In the words of critic Brian Stableford, "*Salammbô* relentlessly smashes the idols of romantic fiction: true love, honor, cunning, bravery in battle, and other such staples of public and individual mythology all are shown to be nonsense."

As in *Madame Bovary* the lead is an innocent young woman. Flaubert described Salammbô as "a maniac controlled by a fixed idea." She is obsessed with Tanith, the moon, and spends much of her time just looking at the stars and the moon. Salammbô is appalled when the zaïmph is stolen. But like Emma Bovary Salammbô is disillusioned when she at last touches the sacred veil/has sex. Salammbô is really just a young woman filled with inchoate urges and longings. She is chaste but curious, decadent in the way she revels in her clothes and makeup but ignorant of lust, and innocently oblivious to the reality of the war outside Carthage. She remains an innocent to the end, wise in the ways of the gods but ignorant about humanity.

Thematically *Salammbô* is about oppositions: the moon (Tanith, Salammbô herself) and the sun (Moloch, Matho), female and male, barbarity (the Barbarians and Mercenaries) and civilization (Carthage), speech and vision, chastity and eroticism, myth and history and religion, the profane and the sacred. Symbolically *Salammbô* has been seen as a commentary on the European and French experience of Napoleon I, and on the French colonial and military efforts in Africa.

Salammbô is worth reading for the power of its descriptions and for its place in the history of the historical romance.

Recommended Edition
Flaubert, Gustave. *Salammbô* (Penguin Classics, 1977).

For Further Research
Green, Anne. *Flaubert and the Historical Novel: 'Salammbo' Reassessed* (Cambridge University Press, 1982).
Hammett, Brian. *The Historical Novel in Nineteenth Century Europe: Representations of Reality in History and Fiction* (Oxford University Press, 2012).
O'Gorman, Ellen. "Decadence and Historical Understanding in Flaubert's *Salammbô*." *New Literary History* v35n4 (Autumn 2004).
Porter, Laurence M., ed. *A Gustave Flaubert Encyclopedia* (Greenwood, 2001).
Stableford, Brian. "*Salammbô*." *Masterplots* Fourth Edition (Nov. 2010).

The Scarlet Letter

The Scarlet Letter was written by Nathaniel Hawthorne and was published in 1850.

In the early days of the Massachusetts Colony a young woman, Hester Prynne, is condemned to wear on the breast of her gown the scarlet letter "A," for adulterer. She stands on the stocks for three hours, alone but for her infant daughter Pearl, for all of Boston to see her. No one knows who fathered Pearl, only that it was not Hester's husband, who is thought to be dead, and Hester will not give up his name. While Hester is standing there an old, nearly deformed man appears from out of the forest, and he later visits her in jail. Although he calls himself Roger Chillingworth, he is actually Hester's husband, but she refuses to tell him who fathered Pearl. He tells her not to divulge his true identity, and that he will spend the rest of his days trying to identify Pearl's father.

Hester takes a house on the outskirts of town and lives the life of a scandalous exile from society, patiently bearing the slights and gibes of the other Puritans. Chillingworth meanwhile moves in with Arthur Dimmesdale, the local reverend, and tends to Dimmesdale's health. Chillingworth perceives that there is some secret that Dimmesdale is hiding, but Dimmesdale, when he tells his parishioners that he is a sinner, is only the more highly thought of by them. Chillingworth begins to suspect that Dimmesdale is Pearl's father, and one night, when Dimmesdale joins Hester and Pearl on the pillory, Chillingworth sees them together. Hester begs Chillingworth to be merciful to Dimmesdale, but Chillingworth refuses. Hester and Dimmesdale meet in the forest and agree to leave America for Europe together after Dimmesdale preaches his sermon on Election Day. But on Election Day, when Dimmesdale publicly takes Hester and Pearl's hand, he is obviously extremely ill, and after confessing his guilt to the public he dies—but as he does, he exposes his breast, where witnesses say that a scarlet A was imprinted on the flesh there. Chillingworth, robbed of his vengeance, dies within the year, and Hester and Pearl leave the colony, although Hester eventually returns there to live out her days.

The Scarlet Letter is historically important. It is generally regarded as the first great American novel, and some critics describe it as one of the ten best American novels ever. Even if the latter is not so, it is true that *The Scarlet Letter* is a work of cumulative power.

The Scarlet Letter's place in history remains assured. It was the first American best-seller and the first American masterpiece, and creates, in Hester Prynne, what Harold Bloom calls "the American Eve":

> For Hester is, in many ways, the American Eve, the Emersonian vision that atones for our lack of any adequate representation of the American Adam. Like Milton's own Eve, Hester is far superior to her fate, and imaginatively preferable to Adam's (and Milton's) God. Hawthorne subtly conveys Hester's sexual power to us, with far less ambivalence than Milton manifests in celebrating Eve's sexual strength. Sensual and tragic, Hester is larger than her book and her world, because her greatness of spirit, like her heroic sexuality, is ill served by the terrible alternatives of the Satanic Chillingworth (Iago's understudy) and the timid Dimmesdale, an absurdly inadequate adulterous lover for the sublime Hester.

As critic Daniel S. Burt says, *The Scarlet Letter* anticipates the later quest for the Great American Novel, departing from the British and European realist mode to create something more mythic and American in nature. The novel's setting was not new—there were enough novels set in Puritan Massachusetts that there was a veritable sub-genre of them by the time *Scarlet Letter* was published—but Hawthorne brought a new depth of symbolism, historical detail, and a sophisticated portrayal of character psychology as well as a depth of understanding about the nature of sin and repentance. And its style was an advance on that of Hawthorne's contemporaries.

As with many Victorian novels, of course, the elements that make *The Scarlet Letter* great do not necessarily make it readable. Fortunately for students, *The Scarlet Letter* gains power as it goes, and if its style is not as smooth as, say, **Bleak House**—published only two years later—*The Scarlet Letter* is still quite readable.

The Scarlet Letter is by no means without flaws. The opening section, "The Custom-House," has only the slightest bearing on the central story, and practically can be skipped by students. Hawthorne's style in the novel is on the older side, thicker, more verbose and descriptive, in the mode of (though an infinity better than) James Fenimore Cooper in *The Last of the Mohicans*, and not necessarily the easiest to read. Hawthorne's dialogue, in its historical recreation of how the Puritans actually spoke to each other, is similarly tough sledding:

> "I pray you, good Sir," said he, "who is this woman?—and wherefore is she here set up to public shame?"
> "You must needs be a stranger in this region, friend."

But the plot does move relatively quickly. Hawthorne maintains a tight focus on the four main characters. And the mysteries of the novel mount as time progresses, lending the story forward momentum.

The symbolism of the novel is deep, from the A on Hester's breast to the dark forest around the colony, and as numerous critics have pointed out they all do "double duty" as symbols, from small to large. The themes are numerous and not particularly obscure: the attacks on Puritan hypocrisy and blind conformity, the effects of sin on the individual and on society, the "hidden recesses of human nature, the consequences of moral transgressions, the conflicts between authority and personal freedom and responsibility," "the ambiguity of sin, the conflict between head and heart, the corrosive power of guilt," all are worked out openly and skillfully.

And there are the **Gothic** elements, from the hunchbacked grotesque Chillingworth, a late period Hero-Villain, to Pearl, the elf-child out of the German *Kunstmärchen* (German literary fairy tales), to the mysterious yellow parchment mentioned in "The Custom-House," to the ominous meteor writing an "A" across the sky. The supernatural atmosphere in the novel begins early and is skillfully manipulated and increased, so that by novel's end *The Scarlet Letter* seems to be as much a supernatural thriller or horror story as a symbolic romance.

Recommended Edition

Hawthorne, Nathaniel. *The Scarlet Letter* (Oxford University Press, 1990).

For Further Research

Bloom, Harold. "Nathaniel Hawthorne: *The Scarlet Letter.*" *Novelists and Novels* (Chelsea House, 2005).
Buckner, Sally. "*The Scarlet Letter.*" *Masterplots* Fourth Edition (Dec. 2010).
Burt, Daniel S. "*The Scarlet Letter.*" *The Novel 100: A Ranking of the Most Influential Novels of All Time* (Checkmark Books, 2010).
Harding, Brian. "Introduction." *The Scarlet Letter* (Oxford University Press, 1990).
Sweets, Sparky. "The Scarlet Letter – Book Summary & Analysis." https://www.youtube.com/watch?v=3P3zh4S6RmI.

She

She was written by H. Rider Haggard and appeared was published in magazine form in 1886 and 1887 and as a novel in 1887. Haggard (1856–1925) was a prolific, popular, and influential novelist whose works are still read for pleasure today.

She: A History of Adventure is about Ayesha, She Who Must Be Obeyed, the Queen of the Amahagger people of Africa. Centuries ago Ayesha, then the "mighty Queen of a savage people," met and fell in love with Kallikrates, an Egyptian priest who had fled Egypt with his love, the Princess Amenartas. Kallikrates will not leave Amenartas, however, and the enraged Ayesha kills Kallikrates. The pregnant Amenartas flees, but the heartbroken Ayesha remains, mourning Kallikrates and waiting for him to return. Amenartas meanwhile charges her descendants with avenging Kallikrates' death. *She* takes place in the modern day as Cambridge don L. Horace Holly and his adopted son Leo Vincey discover that Leo is the descendant of Amenartas. Holly does not initially believe it, but Leo does, and the pair travel to Africa, accompanied by their servant Job, to find the truth behind the story. After some hardships—Haggard accurately portrays travel in Africa as difficult and dangerous—they discover the Amahagger, a cannibalistic group who try to kill and eat them, but Leo and Holly fight them off and are saved by Ayesha's powers. They are brought to Ayesha, who lives in the ruins of the great city of Kôr. Ayesha treats Holly in a friendly fashion, but he makes the mistake of asking to see her unveiled. She is breathtakingly beautiful and he is instantly entranced by her. She is not attracted to him (he is ugly and misogynistic), but remains friendly with him. But when she sees Leo, she is shocked, because he is the twin of Kallikrates, and is, she is sure, Kallikrates reincarnated. Leo, seeing the unveiled Ayesha, is smitten with her. Ayesha joins the trio and they venture to the Flame of Life, where Leo will be made immortal, like Ayesha. But Leo is afraid of the Flame, so Ayesha volunteers to bathe in it first, as she did once before (it is the source of her powers). The Flame kills her, and Leo and Holly, much shaken, return to civilization.

She is one of the landmark fantasy novels of the 19th century, not so much because of how it is written—though always entertaining, the novel has certain stylistic infelicities—but because of its influence and its still potent symbolism and imagery.

She was one of the most influential romances of the 19th century. The romance was the older form of the novel, a heroic adventure story, but in the 19th century it became something else. Norman Etherington describes "romance" as "a label applied in the nineteenth century to works in a literary line of descent from Walter Scott and the 'Gothic' novels of late eighteenth-century romanticism." Critic Patrick Brantlinger notes that the romance of the 19th century has a number of different aspects:

> Applied to empire, the romance form occludes the materialist, economic forces of expansion and exploitation ... it is also fundamentally nostalgic, harking back to an ahistorical, childlike realm of myths and daydreams. Although the romance form could be turned to utopian, radical and anti-imperialist ends ... it is more typically reactionary—a sort of holding out for an earlier, simpler model of experience untrammeled by the complications of the modern world and of mundane, material reality. And, insofar as romance simplifies the complexities of the real world, tending to reduce them to binary oppositions of light versus darkness, good versus evil, and civilization versus savagery, it is also inherently a regressive, childlike form.

She meets all of these qualifications, and, influential as it was on later writers, seems to not just embody them but to act as an archetypal form of them. The 1890s were the prime years of the "Age of Storytellers," the great flowering of high-quality popular fiction from the 1880s until 1914, and *She* was one of the most influential novels written during that period.

Ayesha's centuries-spanning obsession with Kallikrates verges on necrophilia; as she demonstrates to Holly and Leo, she has preserved the body of Kallikrates and "night by night have I slept in his cold company." The confrontation between the misogynists (Holly, Job, and to a lesser extent Leo) and the powerful, highly sexualized queen, and their willing submission to her, is a lightly veiled dominance/submission game. Ayesha herself is alternately coquettish and forbidding, kind and cruel, a dominatrix in down. Even more than that, however, she is a sexual fantasy of another kind, the powerful woman who becomes completely submissive and willing when she meets the right man. She is haughty and powerful, though friendly enough, to Holly, but for she is willing and almost eager to submit to Leo—and even Victorian readers understood that Ayesha is offering more than just emotional submission.

Sexuality pervades *She*, from the homosocial setting of the novel's early moments to the matrilineal and sexually permissive society of the Amahaggers, to the marriage between Leo and the native woman Ustane, to the almost lascivious description of Ayesha's appearance, to the sexually frustrating interaction between Ayesha and Holly and then the union between Leo and Ayesha. But accompanying this haze of sexuality is an ambience of cruelty, from the treatment of Holly (the constant insults he endures because of his looks and Ayesha's teasing of him) to Ayesha's vicious, jealousy-born actions toward Ustane to Haggard's treatment of Ayesha. This combination of cruelty and sexuality, along with the overwhelming presence of death (Ayesha dresses in a shroud and reminds Holly and Job of a corpse) and the dead in Kôr (a city of mummified corpses) and Ayesha's necrophilic obsession with Kallikrates, leaves *She* as, in the words of scholar E.F. Bleiler, "one of the clearest statements of death eroticism ever written."

But the presence of sexually aggressive women in a book is no guarantee of that book's respect for women, and unfortunately *She* is a statement of misogyny. Women are either good or evil in *She*, with nothing in-between: the two main female roles are the devoted and good Ustane and the powerful and wicked Ayesha. But though devoted and faithful to Leo, Ustane is sexually aggressive, and the fate reserved for her by Haggard is death. Ayesha, too, is killed, even after voicing her desire to submit to Leo and let him be her master. Powerful independent women are wicked, in Haggard's world. *She* is often seen as Haggard's most pointed attack on the **New Woman**, and the cumulative message of the novel is of a deep distrust and even hatred for modern women, whose recent social and sexual independence was apparently threatening to Haggard. In the words of critics Sandra Gilbert and Susan Gubar, *She* is a leading example of the misogynistic "fictive explorations of female authority" of late Victorian literature—Margaret Atwood lists some examples:

> The young-but-old supernatural women in George MacDonald's "Curdie" fantasies, but also various Victorian *femmes fatales*: Tennyson's Vivien in *The Idylls of the King*, bent on stealing Merlin's magic; the Pre-Raphaelite temptresses created in both poem and picture by Rossetti and William Morris; Swinburne's dominatrixes; Wagner's nasty pieces of female work, including the very old but still toothsome Kundry of *Parsifal*; and, most especially, the Mona Lisa of Water Pater's famous prose poem, older than the rocks upon which she sits, yet young and lovely, and mysterious, and filled to the brim with experiences of a distinctly suspect nature.

But to describe Haggard as just a misogynist in the line of other Victorian misogynists is to slight him. Haggard shared the *fin de siècle* pessimism of many of his contemporaries, a feeling that the Empire had passed its best days was in an irreversible decline—an unease that can be seen in works as varied as **New Grub Street**, *She*, and **The Invisible Man**. The *fin de siècle* unease was caused by a variety of sources, including a distrust of and unease with the lower classes, the changing role of women in society, and a perceived degeneration in the physical fitness of the English people and especially English men. This *fin de siècle* unease did not produce in Haggard a desire for a return to the days of the ever-expanding British Empire with its muscular Christianity and muscular

Christian men—Haggard, for all his faults, was never an advocate or propagandist for Empire—but rather, as can be seen in his best work, a hunger for a return to a simpler existence, a time in which exploration, not conquest, was the best work which men could do and modern ideas did not complicate traditional social structures and relationships.

There is also the question of race in *She*. In *She* Holly briefly describes Ayesha's plans to go to England, and he muses that she would likely take control of "the British dominions and probably over the whole earth." This is part of the psycho-sexual fantasy of the novel—Ayesha replacing Queen Victoria as a new, hypersexualized ruler of the British Empire—but also part of Haggard's views on race. (In a later novel about Ayesha Haggard talks of her plans to move to China and "flood the little Western nations" with the "unaccountable … multitudes" of Chinese). Many readers have only read about Haggard and not read him, and have misconceptions about him and his work. One charge often level against Haggard's work is that it is racist. This is a gross oversimplification of Haggard's more complex attitudes. By 21st century standards Haggard and his books are all racist. The attitude of Haggard toward native Africans is paternalistic, to say the least, not least in the assumption that white men know better than the natives what the natives really need. Haggard occasionally refers to African men as "boys" and describes those of African descent in uncomplimentary terms. Quatermain, like Haggard, is a believer in races having innate traits.

And yet Haggard is rather progressive relative to their contemporaries. It is all too easy to judge previous generations by current standards, and doing so often prevents an evaluation and appreciation of writers of those generations on their own terms. Haggard's attitudes were seen by his contemporaries as quite liberal, *because* he viewed races as having innate traits. For Haggard, each people, or "race," has different virtues, just as the "race" of Englishmen have virtues specific to themselves. Haggard does not portray of all Africans as the same, but rather as Kafirs (Xhosa), Zulus, Kakuanas, and so on. Haggard in fact shows much more respect for Zulus than for the white Boers. Nor is Haggard blind to the flaws of the English—he argues most effectively in other works that the distance between the natives and the English is much smaller than the English would like to think. In several ways Haggard is a later version of James Fenimore Cooper (**The Last of the Mohicans**), albeit a much better writer.

She is entertaining and never boring, and is full of tropes which appeared in later fantasy stories novels, especially quest fantasies, a subgenre upon which *She* was particularly influential. But *She* is not perfect. It lacks fluidity, and has long infodumps, descriptions, and lectures. The travel sequences in the beginning of the book cannot help but be less interesting to today's audience than to the less-traveled and less-aware audiences of Haggard's day. Although *She* is narrated in the colloquial, the dialogue with Ayesha is done in a mock archaic style:

> "Nay, nay," she answered in the same soft voice, "thou dost not understand—the time has come for thee to learn. *Thou* art my love, my Kallikrates, my Beautiful, my Strong! For two thousand years, Kallikrates, have I waited for *thee*, and now at length thou hast come back to me!"

This was undoubtedly intended to convey the immensity of Ayesha's age and her Otherness but may try the patience of the modern reader. Although the characterization of Ayesha is fine, Holly is less well-delineated and Leo mostly a cipher. Haggard is a dab hand at vivid imagery and powerful ideas and is a strong storyteller, but his literary ability and style are not the equal of his other skills.

Recommended Edition
Haggard, H. Rider. *She* (Penguin, 2001).

For Further Research
Brackett, Virginia. "She: A History of Adventure." *Facts on File Companion to the British Novel: Beginnings through the 19th Century, vol. 1* (Facts on File, 2006).
Brantlinger, Patrick. "Introduction." *She* (Penguin, 2001).
Etherington, Norman. "Critical Introduction." *The Annotated She* (Indiana University Press, 1991).
Gilbert, Sandra, and Susan Gubar. *No Man's Land: The Place of the Woman Writer in the Twentieth Century, Volume 2: Sexchanges* (Yale University Press, 1991).

Silas Marner

Silas Marner was written by George Eliot (**Middlemarch**) and was published in 1861. "George Eliot," the pseudonym of Mary Anne Evans (1819–1880), was regarded in her lifetime (especially after the death of Dickens and Thackeray) as perhaps the greatest living English novelist. *Silas Marner* is usually seen as the best of her early novels.

Silas Marner, a young weaver in the small English religious hamlet of Lantern Yard, is accused of theft. He is innocent of the crime, but his supposed best friend—who actually committed the crime—turns on him, and the lots chosen to determine crime and innocence choose him, and his fiancée abandons him, and Marner leaves Lantern Yard, now an atheist, and wanders south until he reaches the rustic village of Raveloe. There he settles, and for fifteen years works there as a weaver, accumulating money but being a desolate wasteland spiritually and emotionally, and misanthropic to the natives of Raveloe, who view him as an unwelcome outsider. This changes one day when Dunstan Cass, the evil son of the local squire, steals Marner's money, devastating him still further. Cass disappears, and Marner does not recover his money. Not long afterward Molly, the secret wife of Godfrey Cass, Dunstan's weak-willed brother, dies next to Marner's cottage, leaving an infant child behind—the daughter of Godfrey and his wife. The child totters into Marner's cottage, and Marner adopts her, naming her "Eppie" after his dead sister. As Eppie grows up Marner comes to love her, and her love for him changes him emotionally and spiritually, and through that change allows him to become part of the Raveloe community. When she is nineteen Dunstan Cass' body is found and Marner's money is returned to him, giving him closure on that issue; the revelation of Dunstan's theft forces Godfrey Cass to confess all to his wife and to Marner and Eppie, and to offer to adopt Eppie, who refuses; and when Marner eventually takes a trip to Lantern Yard, to see if the natives there ever found out that he was innocent, he finds that a growing city has swallowed up Lantern Yard and that its inhabitants are gone.

Silas Marner is in every way a lighter book than *Middlemarch*. It is lighter physically, obviously, coming in at roughly a quarter the length, but lighter aesthetically and thematically. Where *Middlemarch* was a panoramic, panoptical view of society and its inhabitants throughout an entire county, *Silas Marner* focuses on a handful of characters in one small village, and specifically on one person, as opposed to the six protagonists of *Middlemarch*. Thematically *Middlemarch* covered as much of English society of 1829–1832 as could be crammed into the novel; *Silas Marner* focuses on one main theme, that of wealth, both spiritual and material. In *Middlemarch* the narrator was a distinct character as ever-present as any of the protagonists; in *Silas Marner* the narrator is barely present. In *Middlemarch* Eliot performs deep dives on the character's emotions, thoughts, and psychologies; in *Silas Marner* Eliot's explorations of motive and feeling are comparatively small. *Middlemarch* is a novel, and arguably The Novel, of the Victorian century. *Silas Marner* is an agreeable trifle, a straightforward allegory in which the good are rewarded and the wicked receive their just desserts.

Certainly *Silas Marner* isn't *bad*. Eliot was too good a writer to create something bad, or substandard. Even her simpler works have levels of sophistication to them that lesser writers would never attempt, much less achieve—in the case of *Silas Marner*, the allegory of one soul's fall and redemption, what F.R. Leavis calls a "moral fable." The fairy tale atmosphere of the novel is never allowed to interfere with the essential realism of the milieu or with Eliot's usual deft touch with characterization, so that Silas, Godfrey, and the other main characters are rendered in three dimensions, despite living in an allegory. Nor does Eliot leave Raveloe described in simple terms; her familiarity with provincial life in England is displayed here in extensive detail, both good and bad. (Fairy tale locales are simplistic by their very nature; not so Raveloe and its natives, whose best and worst sides are both shown. Eliot loved rural England but was too good a writer to sentimentalize or romanticize it.) The novel has more forward momentum than *Middlemarch*, and its simpler structure makes it an easier read (if a less rewarding one).

Nonetheless, compared to *Middlemarch*, *Silas Marner* is a lightweight entry in Eliot's bibliography. It was her third book, and like her previous two was an immediate success, popularly and critically, and it continues to be well thought of. Critics play up the sophistication of the allegory and cite the influence of European thinkers on the novel. Critics talk about the mix of the social realism and the fairy tale, and describe *Silas Marner* as being "suprarealism." (This, despite the entertaining **Sensation Novel** elements in *Silas Marner*.) Critics see the portrayals of Godfrey and Dunstan Cass as a castigation of the squire class, and the portrayals of the poor as a lauding of the working class poor, something Eliot had already written about. Critic Frederick Karl sees the theft of Marner's gold as something springing from Eliot's own life:

> The theft does seem linked to Eliot's uncertainty about her work, her inability to listen to even the slightest criticism, her sense of her writing as falling beneath her highest achievement, and her more generalized fear that everything was precarious. The theft, to this extent, is connected to deep inner anxieties that it all might vanish, that something—destiny, circumstance, Nemesis—was waiting to dispossess her of her gifts, and it would all be swallowed up as rapidly as it appeared.

But the modern reader will be forgiven for seeing *Silas Marner* as a rather slim branch to bear all this weight.

Notwithstanding the preceding, readers are better advised to spend their time with *Middlemarch*.

Recommended Edition

Eliot, George. *Silas Marner* (Signet, 2007).

For Further Research

"George Eliot's *Silas Marner*: An Overview." http://victorianweb.org/authors/eliot/silasov.html.
Karl, Frederick R. "Introduction." *Silas Marner* (Signet, 2007).
"Silas Marner." *In Our Time*. http://www.bbc.co.uk/programmes/b00q4310.

Sister Carrie

Sister Carrie was written by Theodore Dreiser and was published in 1900. Dreiser (1871–1945) was an American Naturalist writer and journalist who is best known for *Sister Carrie*, which though not Dreiser's best novel was his first major novel.

Eighteen year old Caroline "Carrie" Meeber moves from her small hometown to Chicago, to live with her sister and brother in law. Carrie is pretty but hapless, and attempts to find work do not pan out. She takes one job, but then become sick and loses it. On the brink of returning home, immensely dissatisfied with life and what she believes she is entitled to, she runs into Charles Drouet, a traveling salesman, who she'd briefly met while traveling to Chicago. Drouet gives her money for clothing and then puts her up in an apartment. Soon they are living together.

Drouet invites his friend George Hurstwood, the manager of a prosperous saloon, to visit. Hurstwood, who is unhappy at home, is taken with Carrie, and she with him, and he begins to visit her while Drouet is out. He courts her, and when she takes part in an amateur theatrical production he sees to it that the production is well attended. (She is the best part of the production.) She agrees to leave Drouet if Hurstwood marries her (she is unaware that he is already married). When Hurstwood's wife finds out about Carrie, she threatens divorce. Hurstwood responds to this by stealing money from his saloon's safe and, through a deception, getting Carrie onto a train to Montreal with him.

In Montreal they marry, and then move to New York City, and three years pass, years in which Carrie realizes she does not love him and becomes discontented with her now diminished lifestyle. Then Hurstwood loses the lease on his business and becomes depressed and apathetic, then gambles away the last of their money. Carrie finds a job in the theater, and through a well placed ad lib gains some notoriety and then a new, better role and a new, better salary. Hurstwood eventually finds work as a scab driver on a trolley line, but is beaten by a mob and leaves that work. Carrie leaves him, his life goes into a permanent decline, and he commits suicide as she becomes a successful actress.

Sister Carrie is one of the foremost early works of American literary Naturalism. In practice this means that its style and effects will be so normal to students that they may not understand what an achievement the novel is.

American and English literature during the Victorian age went through three major phases: sentimental, influenced by the Cult of **Sensibility**; **Romanticism**; and Realism. Realism in fiction was a reaction to Romantic fiction, with Realistic authors like Balzac in *Père Goriot* emphasizing an accurate representation of reality in their novels, as opposed to a stylized reality full of artificial emotions, morals, and symbolism, as had been the case with Romantic literature. One reaction to Realism was Naturalism, which more or less began in France with the work of Emile Zola (*L'Assomoir*, *Nana*)—he was the one who coined the term—and spread to the United Kingdom and the United States. Like Realism, Naturalist novels reflected the reality which its authors observed, but unlike Realism Naturalism was written with an ideological, programmatic intent. Realistic novels simply reflected reality as an author saw it; Naturalist novels were written to promote a common point of view. Naturalist writers believed—a belief reflected in their work—that humanity was the product of circumstance and its environment, rather than being something that triumphed over both, as in Romantic literature. (As critic Andrew Delbanco says of *Sister Carrie*, the Naturalist novel is an "unrelenting assault on the notion that one's rise or fall has anything to do with a general economy of virtue and reward or vice and punishment.") The Naturalist novel, emphasizing the new industrialization, urbanization, mechanization, and immigration of urban life, was usually about the poor, the uneducated, the mundane—the rabble—in what one critic called "living in squalor and struggling to survive in an amoral and indifferent world." Naturalist writers focused on the power of money and sex and humanity's baser instincts and disdained conventional social taboos, and often—though not always, as was the case with Dreiser—wrote with an eye toward prompting reform of the ills they wrote about.

Students in the 21st century will have been exposed to literature and popular culture with Naturalist tendencies for all of their lives. Naturalism, though succeeded by Modernism and Postmodernism, remains a common impulse among creators of popular culture; the idea that people are controlled by circumstances rather than themselves is almost a cliché now. So most students will probably view that aspect of *Sister Carrie* with a blasé eye. But *Sister Carrie* was new when it appeared, as was Naturalism. Writers—respectable American writers above all—simply didn't write about protagonists prostituting themselves with nary a qualm and not suffering any consequences. The Victorian morals that forced Mary Elizabeth Braddon, in **Lady Audley's Secret**, to condemn Lady Audley to a madhouse (rather than getting away with child abandonment, bigamy, and attempted murder) were still in place. Writers didn't write about main characters—who were not villains—keeping women in apartments, or living with them in sin. Writers didn't portray deeply flawed characters without judgment but with empathy for their positions and circumstances. Writers didn't include swears and exclude God. It simply wasn't done.

All of this is why *Sister Carrie* was important when it was published. It was controversial—Dreiser's own publisher, Alfred Doubleday, hated it and did his best not to promote it, and some critics felt that the novel's sexual content (explicit for the era) made it unacceptable. The book did not sell well initially, despite generally positive reviews. But its content, its overall quality, and its importance to the Naturalist movement have guaranteed it longevity and a place in the literary canon.

Of course, *Sister Carrie* may be the worst written book in the canon. It was only Dreiser's first novel, and it displays many stylistic infelicities. His sentence structure can be awkward and ungainly; he overrelies on cliche; a number of his sentences grate; and his frequent philosophizing asides constantly interrupt the action. English was likely not Dreiser's first language, and it shows, as does it being his first novel. Dreiser aimed for an immersive experience, portraying—like Balzac, and like Dickens—an entire world. He succeeded, but at the cost of a book which might charitably be described as over-long and uncharitably described as bloated.

What Dreiser does do is layer on the detail to an astonishing degree. His world comes alive, although it is a world of squalor and poverty and want that many us will not enjoy reading about. Similarly, Dreiser's compassion for his characters leads to a depth of characterization which is unusual; we may grow frustrated with the inarticulate, shallow, un-introspective Carrie and Hurstwood, full of (in Clare Eby's phrase) "restless indecision," but we recognize them, and they step off the page, even if they are not people we would care to spend time with in real life.

Similarly, the dominant concerns of Carrie and Hurstwood—sex and the desire for material goods—are quite human, and the seductive, exhilarating, depressing environment of Chicago and New York are quite recognizable to any city-dweller. The novel's portrayal of class conflict, especially the clash between strikers and police, is nearly as apposite now as it was in Dreiser's day. And Dreiser's personal familiarity with the pains and struggles of being poor show; as critic Andrew Delbanco wrote, "Among post–Civil War writers, Theodore Dreiser was the first to write powerfully about the experience, rather than the spectacle, of poverty." The phrase "reportorial realism," originally applied to *Sister Carrie* in a rejection letter, is apt indeed.

Sister Carrie is a triumph of Naturalism. Students may find it over-long, but they will not forget its world or its protagonist.

Recommended Edition

Dreiser, Theodore. *Sister Carrie* (Random House, 1997).

For Further Research

Delbanco, Andrew. "Introduction." *Sister Carrie* (Random House, 1997).
Eby, Clare Virginia. "Cultural and Historical Contexts for *Sister Carrie*." http://www.academia.edu/995372/The_Problem_of_American_Literary_Naturalism_and_Theodore_Dreisers_Sister_Carrie_.
Kazin, Alfred. "Introduction: Theodore Dreiser and *Sister Carrie* Restored." *Sister Carrie* (Penguin, 1994).
McCrum, Robert. "The 100 Best Novels: No 33—*Sister Carrie* by Theodore Dreiser." http://www.theguardian.com/books/2014/may/05/100 best novels sister carrie theodore dreiser.

The Sorrows of Satan

The Sorrows of Satan was written by Marie Corelli and was published in 1895. Corelli (1855–1924) was one of Great Britain's top authors at her peak—John Sutherland calls her "the bestselling of all Victorian authors"—although she was critically scorned. *The Sorrows of Satan* is generally seen as her best and most typical work.

The Sorrows of Satan is about Geoffrey Temple, a starving, struggling novelist. At the very end of his resources, he receives a bequest of £5 million from a relative he didn't know he had, at the same time being introduced to Prince Lucio Rimanez. (SPOILER: Prince Rimanez is Satan.) Rimanez informally adopts Temple, giving him advice and loaning him money while also treating him to endless lectures about the nature of reality, the reality of society and human nature, and so on. Rimanez tells Temple how to get his book published (use his new wealth) and "boomed," or talked up by reviewers (essentially bribe the reviewers), and Rimanez introduces Temple to the cold society beauty Lady Sibyl Elton. Elton describes herself as corrupted by **New Woman** novels and by modern society, but she agrees to marry Temple anyhow. Secretly, Elton lusts after Rimanez and offers herself to him, but when this is revealed she poisons herself. Temple despairs, and then discovers that Rimanez is actually Satan, and that what has transpired is one long temptation. Temple is tempted to commit suicide, but ultimately decides not to, and his wealth then evaporates. Temple's salvation in all of this is the brilliant young author, Mavis Clare, who is loathed by the critics but enormously popular with readers of all rank and nationality. She is also the last, best hope for Western civilization, and the ultimate redemption of Rimanez.

Marie Corelli was a unique author—unique for the Victorians and for ours. A best-seller who was a critical punching bag, a successful woman who scorned her feminist contemporaries (and especially the New Woman), an author, popular with all classes, whose work is poisonous with class resentment, both up and down, a conservative whose work is actually reactionary, Corelli is an object lesson for readers and critics. But which lesson is to be learned?

The problem for both readers and critics is the impossibility of separating Corelli from her work. For some authors this is no bad thing; who among us would not prefer to think of Jane Austen as someone out of **Emma** or **Pride and Prejudice**, as someone with that sparkling wit and compassionate insight into humanity? For some authors this is a blatant mistake—what could we possibly assume about Emily Brontë based on **Wuthering Heights** that was not cruel and remote? And for some authors, an inability to separate them from their work hints at truths—some palatable, some not—about those authors; in all likelihood Ouida little knew how much she was saying about herself when she wrote **Under Two Flags**.

Marie Corelli falls into the latter category. Reading *The Sorrows of Satan*, it becomes impossible for readers not to see the real Marie Corelli in every resentful word, and to view the novel as a *cri de mauvais coeur* more than just a dispassionately created work. For those who are just readers, this is not an insuperable problem. They can just note this and carry on reading. But for critics, or those forced to write papers (or indeed book entries) or simply think in a critical and elevated fashion about Corelli and *The Sorrows of Satan*, it adds an additional and thorny complication.

The only choice, it would seem, is to treat them at the same time, and to note that in discussing the one you discuss the other. Corelli more than any other Victorian author *is* her work, and the flaws of her work correspond to the flaws in her personality.

The Sorrows of Satan is readable, and competent work. That must be admitted before all else. The tens of thousands who rabidly consumed Corelli's work would not have put up with anything else, nor could a successful writer—and she was quite successful—be a success without readability. There is a certain style in the fiction of the 1890s, to be found in stories in magazines as well as in novels, which hasn't aged badly or much, and which today can still be read with pleasure. Corelli partially partakes of that style, in *Satan*, so that the dialogue does not seem particularly dated and the descriptions are acceptable. So the reader who takes on *The Sorrows of Satan* will put forth less effort than, say, in reading Bulwer-Lytton's **The Last Days of Pompeii**. *The Sorrows of Satan* is the work of a professional.

And a woman of imagination. Even Corelli's harshest critics freely admit that her fantastikal work, her science fiction and her fantasies (like *Satan*), are exuberant in their free-wheeling deployment of fantastikal tropes. (Witness the ghastly fate of Lady Sibyl's mother and the glee with which Corelli describes it, or indeed the entire ascension scene at the end of *Satan*.) In another time Corelli might have been a writer of science fiction romance, although she could hardly have been more successful at that than she already was.

But competence and imagination only take a writer so far, and there is much about Corelli that a reader has to put up with, if they must read *The Sorrows of Satan*.

Like Bulwer-Lytton, Corelli has a fatal weakness for the long aside, and like Bulwer-Lytton (in his occult work, not *Pompeii* or **Pelham**) these asides too often contain over-written philosophical ramblings and religious lectures. Such screeds do date, and quickly, and today make for tedious reading—not at all what Corelli intended or how her audience considered them. Her dialogue often shades into monologues during which the veil between author and narrative grows very thin indeed.

It is a traditionally sexist criticism to complain that a woman's work is "over-emotional"—as if men do not fall prey to that and do not have their own surfeit of emotion. So say instead that *Satan* is full of highly-strung emotion and sentiment. The mood and pitch could not be higher, nor could the pathos be more melodramatically expressed. One critic aptly described her as possessing "an intense, emotive imagination almost totally uninhibited by considerations of style, taste, or factual reality."

Nor does the content of *The Sorrows of Satan* redeem it. The criticisms of *Satan* are numerous, and writing them down can resemble the writing of a grocery list. Nonetheless, any fair reading of *Satan* leads to making such a list.

Perhaps the largest flaw in *Satan*'s content is the person of Mavis Clare. Clare, a pure higher being than ordinary humans, perfect in every way, is Corelli's fictional stand-in (even the initials are the same), but beyond that, Clare is Corelli's "Mary Sue." In fiction written by amateurs or first time writers, whether published in fan magazines, vanity presses, or on the Internet as "fan fiction," stories written by fans featuring characters from their favorite books, television shows, or movies, a common phenomenon is the Mary Sue character. A Mary Sue character is an idealized stand-in for the author, and is tougher, smarter, cooler, nicer, sweeter, more charming, more capable, and more skilled than the established characters, and becomes worshiped by them. Although

Mary Sues appeared in 19th century magazine stories written by teenagers, as in stories where a teenaged girl saves a sleeping Indian chief from being mauled by a bear or is raised by Indians and becomes their leader, the traditional modern Mary Sue appears in *Star Trek* fan fiction, where a new ensign on the starship *Enterprise* is a better pilot than Captain Kirk, smarter than Spock, and makes both fall in love with her. Mavis Clare is Corelli's Mary Sue.

Satan was a score-keeping exercise on Corelli's part—the list of newspapers Mavis Clare has her dogs rip apart correspond to the newspapers which had reviewed her badly—but is a tightly-wound one, without a sense of humor (it's doubtful that Corelli herself had one) or an ability to look inside itself in any way. Corelli notably lacked not only any ability of introspection or self-awareness, but was prey to her own delusions, delusions of grandeur and genius. *Satan* is one long affirmation of both.

Satan is also a deeply, and unpleasantly, conservative work. The two are not synonymous, of course, but *Satan* displays Corelli's worst reactionary instincts. The novel is anti-feminist and anti–New Woman: "The self-degrading creatures who delineate their fictional heroines as wallowing in unchastity, and who write freely on subjects which men would hesitate to name, are unnatural hybrids of no-sex." Corelli's fetish for royalty is on display in *Satan*, but so is her poisonous sense of class grievance, her loathing of those below her and her hatred of those above her. Too, Corelli's distaste for all readers but her own shines through. Scorn and abuse are heaped upon publishers, critics, and readers while Corelli simultaneously congratulates herself and her readers on being too intelligent to fall for the lies of those publishers and critics and wiser than other readers. Lastly, accompanying the novel's strident moralism and nebulous, vague mysticism is an anti-intellectualism and an equation of the Decadent authors and readers (and the Naturalists, and the French) with moral and intellectual depravity.

The last word here on Corelli is left to two critics of hers. Louis James:

> Corelli saw herself as fulfilling a mission to assert "the underlying spiritual quality of life as it really is," and her work was widely quoted by both fashionable and popular preachers. Her success points to an undoubted thirst for religious literature. She also made it comfortable: the only evil was that willed by man, and every reader had the power for spiritual growth towards total goodness. She embodied this message in fiction that is vulgar in the fullest sense, clichéd, melodramatic, uninformed; yet with an imaginative flair, theatricality, and self conviction that ultimately defies criticism by literary conventions.

And Brian Stableford:

> Marie Corelli presumably owed her success to the fact that she was prepared to expose to the world the silly sophistry by which she tried to shore up her religious faith with borrowed jargon, supplemented by her narcissistic fantasies of being more suited for the company of angels than mere men. Unabashed by the savage derision of more sensible

folk, she heroically took this crusade into an imaginative terra incognita which no one else has ever dared explore. The astonishing, if temporary, success of her works demonstrates that her expression of her own delusions and aspirations were capable of soothing, at least in some small measure, the distress of millions of her contemporaries.

The Sorrows of Satan is not representative of anything but Corelli (she was never a joiner, instead insisting that others join her). It does, however, represent her exceptionally well—a representation that she would have regretted, had she but known.

Recommended Edition
Corelli, Marie. *The Sorrows of Satan* (Valancourt Books, 2007).

For Further Research
Casey, Janet Gallignani. "Mary Mackay." British Short Fiction Writers, 1880 1914: The Romantic Tradition. Ed. William F. Naufftus (Gale, 1995).
Gannon, Christine. "Marie Corelli's The Sorrows of Satan: Literary Professionalism and the Female Author as Priest." *English Literature in Transition 1880 1920* v56n3 (Summer 2013).
James, Louis. "Marie Corelli: Overview." *Twentieth Century Romance & Historical Writers.* Ed. Aruna Vasudevan. 3d ed. (St. James Press, 1994).
Loufbourow, Lili. "Gollum's Mother: On Marie Corelli." *Los Angeles Review of Books*, Feb. 13, 2013. https://lareviewofbooks.org/essay/gollums mother on marie corelli.
Salmonson, Jessica Amanda. "Marie Corelli & her Occult Tales." http://www.violetbooks.com/corelli.html.
Stableford, Brian. "Marie Corelli: Overview.[qm] *St. James Guide to Fantasy Writers.* Ed. David Pringle. (St. James Press, 1996).

Tess of the d'Urbervilles

Tess of the d'Urbervilles was written by Thomas Hardy (*Jude the Obscure*) and was published as a serial and later as a novel in 1891. Hardy (1840–1928) was an English novelist and poet regarded as one of the greatest of his generation. *Tess of the d'Urbervilles* is seen as his most characteristic work.

Tess Durbeyfield, a young Wessex maiden, finds out from her father that their family is descended from the very old D'Urberville line. Her father is a slacker who never works more than the bare minimum, and he sends Tess to visit the wealthy Stoke-D'Urbervilles and claim relationship with them, as a way to gain a good job and possibly a wealthy husband from one of them. Tess meets Alec D'Urberville, the suave, slick young son, who is immediately attracted to Tess and places Tess with the D'Urbervilles as a poultry maid while also making a series of inappropriate remarks to her. Tess tries to avoid him, but he manages to get her alone and rapes her.

Tess goes home and endures the slander of those who know her, and gives birth to a baby, which does not live long. Tess then goes to a dairy farm to the south, far from where she is not known. She makes friends at the dairy farm and enjoys herself, for once in her life, but she also meets Angel Clare, a pastor's son. She and Clare are attracted to each other, but he thinks her innocent and pure where she does believes she is not, and he continually courts her and asks her to be his wife, and she refuses. Eventually she is worn down by him and agrees to marry him. But she does not tell him about her past until the night of the wedding, and he reacts very badly to this information, telling her that she's not the woman he thought she was, and leaving her to move to Brazil to farm, though he leaves open the possibility of a reconciliation.

Tess goes from farm to farm, working enough to keep her family fed. But she meets Alec again. He had temporarily converted to an evangelical Christianity thanks to the efforts of Angel Clare's father, but Alec's attraction to Tess proves to be too much for his fragile faith, and he begins pursuing her. Angel never responds to Tess' letters to him, so at length Tess gives in to Alec's importunings and goes to live with him. Angel returns, now fully in love with Tess, but discovers Tess with Alec and turns away from her, very hurt. Tess quarrels with Alec and stabs him dead, then flees to be with Angel. They enjoy a few days of happiness before the police catch up with them, and Tess is hanged.

Tess is skillfully wrought, as is usual with Hardy's work. But readers are likely to differ with critics in their judgment of it.

Tess was a critical and popular success despite the controversy which Hardy's relatively explicit treatment of sexuality and frankness regarding money brought. Hardy is above all else a skilled writer, and he beautifully evokes rural west England and its people. His characters are three-dimensional. His symbolism is skillfully wrought and particularly deep, rewarding multiple interpretations. His style is the very readable one of the 1890s, which modern readers will find not very dated at all. *Tess* is in sum a very readable book, which feels short despite its length, and which reads quickly.

So there is that much to be said for it: it is very readable, and is symbol-heavy, and has numerous contrivances of the kind that critics adore writing about. But the very symbolism and contrivances that literary critics so adore is where readers and critics are likely to part company.

Certainly *Tess* is symbolism-heavy: Tess as earth mother, Tess as universal woman, Tess as universal redemptive sufferer, Tess as the country and Alec as the city, and so on. The symbolism is particularly deep in *Tess*, to the point where readers and critics can create multiple readings of the text based on the novel's symbolism. But the judgment of critic Daniel Burt, that *Tess* has a "penetration of surface reality to reveal a deeper significance of universal truth," and that it "elevates ordinary experience and raises the theatrical to the level of genuine mythic, tragic, and universal," seems to be a case of critical special pleading. There is certainly a depth of symbolism, and an adroit combination of deep symbolism with surface naturalism. As a work which relies heavily on imagery and symbolism, *Tess* argues its points through that imagery and symbolism rather than through logic and realism, and wins its arguments. Hardy makes his point, *contra* the Victorians' sexual mores and ideals of purity, that purity is a matter of will and intent rather than circumstance and behavior—the very subtitle of the book, "A Pure Woman Faithfully Presented," describes Hardy's argument.

But the contrived events of the novels, the use of coincidence and melodrama to achieve Hardy's ends, read to modern readers as authorial deck-stacking against Tess—the situations she endures are forced, and arise out of authorial contrivance rather than out of a more genuine and natural series of events. One cannot force a narrative to become mythical and universal, after all, and *Tess* is as much a product of Hardy's world—and limited because of it—as any of Hardy's other novels. Tess as redemptive-sufferer is a much a product of 19th century England as she is a universal figure. Too, there is a significant distance between a novel of effective sophisticated symbolism, which is what *Tess* is, and a novel of "universal truth" and the "genuine mythic," which is a grandiose claim even for *Tess*. In other words, these critical judgments are not made because of *Tess*' innate qualities—which are many—but instead because critics want the novel to be more than it is.

Tess is, after all, a novel with significant **Sensation** elements in it, including Tess' rape, her dead baby, and the climactic murder of Alec d'Urberville. Similarly, the **Gothic** elements, the omens and symbols and Biblical references, are a product of the late-19th century Gothic revival, done deliberately rather than innocently, as the original Gothic authors did. And *Tess* is a didactic novel more than a realist/Naturalist one: its arguments about the frailty of poor English workers' livelihoods, its rebuttal of the Victorian notion that the poor were to blame for their own poverty; its argument that machinery was destroying what was good about farming; and its attack on constrictive, hypocritical Victorian sexual mores and marriage laws and customs. *Tess* is a programmatic novel, deliberately written to describe what happens after a woman's fall/seduction, rather than before and during, as was the Victorian way. None of these things are conducive to creating that most pure and unselfconscious of creations, myth.

Tess has what critical Daniel Burt calls a "grandiosity of vision," not least in its depth of symbolism, but myth and universal truth are neither of *Tess*' qualities.

Readers are likely to find *Tess* a compelling picture of bleakness, if not quite on the level of *Jude the Obscure*; the following exchange is a memorable one:

> "Did you say the stars were worlds, Tess?"
> "Yes."
> "All like ours?"
> "I don't know; but I think so. They sometimes seem to be like the apples on our stubbard tree. Most of them splendid and sound—a few blighted."
> "Which do we live on—a splendid one or a blighted one?"
> "A blighted one."

Tess wonderfully portrays the rural world and the realities of farm work, comparable in its portrayal to **Lorna Doone**. *Tess* has some of *Jude the Obscure*'s *fin de siècle* unease, if not to the same degree. *Tess*, despite is heaping of miseries on poor Tess, is much more sympathetic to its female characters, and even feminist in its way, than several of Hardy's other novels. And *Tess* has the aforementioned symbolic depth. *Tess* is readable, well-plotted (in its contrived way), and well-told. *Tess* just doesn't have universal significance. But then, how few novels do?

Recommended Edition
Hardy, Thomas. *Tess of the d'Urbervilles* (Oxford University Press, 2005).

For Further Research
Boumelha, Penny. "Introduction." *Tess of the d'Urbervilles* (Oxford University Press, 2005).
Brackett, Virginia. "*Tess of the D'Urbervilles*." *Facts on File Companion to the British Novel: Beginnings through the 19th Century*, vol. 1 (Facts on File, 2006).
Burt, Daniel S. "*Tess of the D'Urbervilles*." *The Novel 100: A Ranking of the Most Influential Novels of All Time* (Checkmark Books, 2010).
Ghosh, Bishnupriya. "Tess of the d'Urbervilles." *Masterplots* Fourth Edition (Dec. 2010).

The Three Musketeers

The Three Musketeers was written by Alexandre Dumas *père* and was published as a serial in 1844 and later that year as a novel. Dumas *père* (1802–1870) was a giant of 19th century French letters. He wrote a vast number of novels, plays, and poems, and is considered the greatest of the French romantic novelists. *The Count of Monte Cristo* and *The Three Musketeers* are regarded as Dumas' masterpieces; it is the latter that Dumas considered his best, and it has traditionally been his most popular novel. It is a beloved classic, and those readers who have not read it in decades will find that, stylistic faults aside, the novel is rollicking good fun.

In 1625, during the reign of Louis XIII, a young Gascon, D'Artagnan, travels to Paris in the hopes of becoming a musketeer. Once there he meets and after an initial unpleasantness befriends three of the most prominent musketeers: Aramis (a would be priest), Porthos (a vain braggart and ladies' man), and Athos (a sorrowful man with a hidden aristocratic past). D'Artagnan finds himself enmeshed in a series of schemes, in support of the Queen's love affair with the English Duke of Buckingham and in opposition to the plots of Cardinal Richelieu. During one of these schemes D'Artagnan and the three other musketeers rides across France and into London, to retrieve some highly valuable diamond studs for the Queen. D'Artagnan finds love with the Madame Constance Bonacieux, the sweet wife of his landlord, and rescues her from prison. D'Artagnan finds an enemy in the venomous but beautiful Milady, the best agent of Cardinal Richelieu and the woman who was the wife of the Comte de la Fere, a.k.a. Athos. (He had her hung as a thief years before and assumed she was dead. For her part, she does not know that Athos is the Comte de la Fere.) D'Artagnan and the other Musketeers fight the English at the siege of La Rochelle. The four men uncover the identity of Milady and condemn her to death for her crimes. The four men find love, riches, and sorrow (Milady arranges to have Buckingham assassinated and poisons Constance before she is executed) before separating, and D'Artagnan, having gained the approval of Richelieu through his bravery, gains a high rank in the musketeers.

The Three Musketeers was originally published as a *roman feuilleton*, a serialized novel appearing in newspapers. The *roman feuilleton* was the dominant mode of 19th century French literature in terms of sales, stature, and influence, and eventually became a sort of genre and literary mode on its own: action adventure thrillers with a surfeit of incident and melodrama and an emphasis on plot complications over characterization or style. Typical themes are honor, love, and revenge.

The Three Musketeers is one of the most perfect examples of the *roman feuilleton*'s virtues—and its flaws. Dumas' style is, to put it politely, dated. (Less politely, Dumas is a shoddy stylist with a deplorable tendency toward inflated, stagey, and prolix dialogue.) Plot is all; there is no internal character growth or development. Dumas has little time for the interior life or backgrounds of the characters, much less textual revision. (The novel was, as mentioned, written as a serial, meaning Dumas had no time to go back and change the text once it was published.) The paid by the line nature of the text is reflected in the frequent cliffhangers and Dumas' occasional detour, in which he sometimes spends too long on a particular subplot or conversation. And where *The Count of Monte Cristo* was a novel of manners, *The Three Musketeers* is purely a thrill ride: action rather than emotion, characterization, social humanitarianism, or verisimilitude is Dumas' concern.

But on that level *The Three Musketeers* succeeds magnificently. To quote critic David Coward,

> *The Three Musketeers* is a stirring tale of adventure but it is also a historical saga, a macabre chiller, a thriller, a romance, and a kind of detective novel. It has, in other words, all the ingredients of classic story telling. Each page moves the action excitingly forward in a variety of moods which run from the drama of the chase through humour to the superreality of an allegorical quest. For what Dumas describes is a Homeric clash of Titans and his characters are gods: it is in this sense that he was, as Anthony Burgess has said, "one of the great myth makers."

The Three Musketeers is a grand spectacle of duels, sword fights, hell bent rides across the French countryside, resplendent musketeers, court politics, and love affairs. Dumas vividly creates a world of casual love affairs and even more casual duels, a world in which manners are supremely important and personal honor is worth fighting for. It is the world familiar to readers from dozens of movies, but done by Dumas with high spirits and good humor. The lives of the musketeers show elements of the picaresque, which adds to the spirit of the novel. Milady is a wonderfully devious villain and *femme fatale*. Dumas delivers regular doses of action and incident, and with the occasional, regrettable, exception he does not linger over events or people of no bearing to the main plot. Dumas does a good job of providing context for the historical events and personages in *The Three Musketeers*, so that even those readers with no knowledge of 17th century French history will not feel completely lost. And only a grouch would complain that these events and people have been unrealistically sanitized and romanticized.

The Three Musketeers is, as mentioned, a grand example of the *roman feuilleton*—as was *The Count of Monte Cristo*. But unlike *Monte Cristo* *The Three Musketeers* is influenced not only by Dumas' fellow *feuilletonist* Eugène Sue but also by the work of Sir Walter Scott (**Waverley**). *Monte Cristo* was a novel of manners, initially dealing with the Napoleonic era but later switching to only a decade behind the time in which it was published. *The Three Musketeers* is a historical novel, set two centuries before the time it was written and following Scott's **Romantic** example in bringing color, narrative speed, and vividly drawn historical characters to life.

Any reader willing to put up with the novel's minor stylistic flaws will be well rewarded in reading or rereading *The Three Musketeers*. As Terence Rafferty writes, Dumas' "historical novels always wind up saying that everything that matters — love, courage, pleasure and, especially, all for one and one for all friendship — exists most vividly not in the supposed centers of power, but elsewhere: in the margins of history, where the musketeers, immortally, live."

Recommended Edition
Dumas, Alexandre. *The Three Musketeers* (Modern Library Classics, 2001).

For Further Research
Rafferty, Terence. "All for One." *New York Times Book Review*, Aug. 20, 2006.

The Time Machine

The Time Machine was written by H.G. Wells and was published as a serial and as a novel in 1895. Although Wells (1866–1946) is known today primarily for his science fiction, during his lifetime he was one the most prolific, versatile, and popular writers in the English language. *The Time Machine* is a neat little classic, Wells' first great novel, the one that established him, and still a major work in the science fiction canon.

The Time Machine is about the unnamed Time Traveler, a scientist who invents a machine for traveling through time. His friends disagree with his theory that time travel is possible, but he ignores them and goes ahead with his planned trip. He travels ahead in time, to the year 802,701, and finds the Earth inhabited by two species, both descendants of *Homo sapiens*. The first species is the Eloi, a race of innocent naïfs. They are childlike in appearance, personality, and intellectual capabilities. The Eloi live above ground, are frugivorous and fear the dark. The second species is the Morlocks. They appear to be degenerate apes and live underground. They are cruel cannibals, feeding on the Eloi, but the Morlocks also operate the machinery which makes the Eloi's clothing and shoes. The Traveler stays with the Eloi for eight days, during which time he saves the life of Weena, one of the Eloi, who becomes devoted to him. Unfortunately, the seventh night is the dark of the moon. The Morlocks, who are sensitive to the light and avoid venturing above ground during the day and while the moon shines, attack the Eloi and the Traveler. Weena is among those captured by the Morlocks. The Traveler sadly goes forward in time after recovering the Time Machine; it had been taken by the Morlocks, but after he kills several they return it to him. The Traveler goes to a time many hundreds of thousands of years in the future, when all human life is gone and only creepy huge crab things remain. Then the Traveler leaps forward 30 million years, to an Earth on which life has almost completely died out. Sick with what he has seen, the Time Traveler returns home, tells his friends his story (they disbelieve him, but he has proof: the flowers which Weena gave him), then packs for a longer expedition and leaves. The story ends with the Traveler having been gone for three years.

As with all of Wells' best work, *The Time Machine* is a combination of great entertainment, interesting ideas, and ideology. As entertainment the novel works well, and if the Traveler's relationship with Weena is hardly the love story later movie versions of the book have made it, the novel has enough other interesting and enjoyable moments. Wells' ideas are quite satisfying. Although they are clichéd now, the concepts of traveling through time, of future humanity developing into separate species, and of traveling to the earth's final days are developed simply, clearly, and effectively in this, one of their first fictional renditions. Wells' style—straightforward narration coupled with apt description—grounds the novel well, so that the fantastic elements becomes easier for the reader to accept.

And Wells' ideology, while offensive to the conservative Victorians of Wells' day, who objected to his conclusions, is logical (if not agreeable) to the modern reader. Wells ignores Judeo-Christian ideology and portrays humanity not as the end result of evolution but as just another point on the evolutionary line. Wells shows an earth which is not just post–*Homo sapiens* (the 802,701 section), but which is post-life itself (30 million C.E.). Wells' essentially entropic message—things fall apart, the center cannot hold, life degenerates—is, like his evolutionary message, logical if not pleasant to our vanity. And Wells adroitly gives examples of three different kinds of time—historical (the absurdly specific date of 802,701), evolutionary (the date with the crab creatures), and astronomic (30 million C.E.)—without being clumsy about it.

Finally, there are the Eloi and the Morlocks. Certain aspects of the Eloi and the Morlocks are usually overlooked or not commented upon. Both the Eloi and the Morlocks are smaller than the Traveler himself. Although readers are conditioned by film and comic book versions of *The Time Machine* to think of the Morlocks as hulking brutes, the Traveler describes them in this way:

a queer little ape like figure, its head held down in a peculiar manner ... it was a dull white, and had strange large greyish red eyes; also that there was flaxen hair on its head and down its back. But, as I say, it went too fast for me to see distinctly. I cannot even say whether it ran on all fours, or only with its forearms held very low.

The diminished size of both the Eloi and the Morlocks is another sign of their degeneration, like the Eloi's lack of intellectual capacity and the Morlocks' cannibalism. As for the Eloi, while the usual description of them is "childlike," "animal-like" is perhaps closer to the mark. When Weena almost drowns, the Eloi do not react in a human way:

> It will give you an idea, therefore, of the strange deficiency in these creatures, when I tell you that none made the slightest attempt to rescue the weakly crying little thing which was drowning before their eyes.

That is not the behavior of children or the child-like. That is the behavior of animals, and not all animals, either, since there are a number of examples of animals of various species rescuing drowning members of their own species. The Eloi have a limited vocabulary and attention span and seem to have no conception of the past or future—they live perpetually in the present. Weena is pathetically devoted to the Traveler after he rescues her. These are the traits of animals as well as children, and "animal-like" is more apt than "childlike" when describing the Eloi.

The Time Machine being what it is, of course, the Eloi and the Morlocks represent more than just themselves. The general critical interpretation of them both is that they represent the final state of class warfare in a capitalist Britain, with the Eloi as the "leisured aristocracy" and the Morlocks as the "mass of downtrodden workers," but Wells' extrapolation of English society takes this division to the point of the Morlocks actually preying on the Eloi, rather than vice-versa. One can see in this arrangement Wells' feelings about how aristocratic employers had treated Wells' own mother in Sussex when she was working as a servant during Wells' childhood.

Too, *The Time Machine* makes a statement on Wells' part about the evolution of society. The standard travel narrative of the era had the traveler entering a distant land and observing the exotic people and culture of that land. In *The Time Machine* the Time Traveler journeys not in space but in time and observes the exotic Eloi and Morlocks. But Wells means for *The Time Machine* to be a symbolic travel narrative. When *The Time Machine* was being written the exploration of Africa was at its height, and European thinkers saw Africa as a "manifestation of the process of social evolution in its infancy." Wells' response to this line of thought was to portray the future, when civilization should have become highly advanced, as cannibalistic and brutal. For Wells evolution is not linear and progressive, but degenerative and harsh.

Recommended Edition
Wells, H.G. *The Time Machine* (Penguin Classics, 2005).

For Further Research
Caldwell, Tracy M. "H.G. Wells' 'The Time Machine.'" *Literary Contexts in Novels: H.G. Wells' 'The Time Machine'* (2006).
Slusser, George, Patrick Parrinder, and Daniele Chatelain, eds. *H.G. Wells's Perennial Time Machine* (University of Georgia Press, 2001).

Twenty Thousand Leagues Under the Sea

Twenty Thousand Leagues Under the Sea was written by Jules Verne and appeared as a serial in 1869 and 1870 and as a novel in two parts in 1869 and 1870. The French Verne (1828–1905) is, with H.G. Wells (*The Invisible Man, The Time Traveler*), the man responsible for modern science fiction. In some ways Verne's work was surprisingly accurate in its predictions, and his prose can still be read with pleasure.

Twenty Thousand Leagues Under the Sea begins with a series of sightings of a mysterious sea creature which is blamed for sinking several ships. An American warship is dispatched to hunt it down and kill it, and Pierre Aronnax, a noted professor at the Museum of Paris, is invited along. He is accompanied by his servant Conseil. The creature is found and fired upon, only to have it strike the ship, throwing Aronnax, Conseil, and the French Canadian whaler Ned Land overboard. The trio is rescued. They do not know their rescuer's name at first, but it quickly becomes clear that they have been rescued by Captain Nemo and are on the *Nautilus*, Nemo's wonderful submarine. Unfortunately, Nemo is a misanthrope who has foresworn human society, and the trio are not so much guests on the Nautilus as they are prisoners. Months pass as the trio are held on the sub. For Aronnax, this is not an imposition, but rather a pleasure, for Nemo is usually good company as well as a man who delights in showing Aronnax the splendors of the sea. Conseil is content to accompany Aronnax wherever he go. Land, however, is uninterested in fish except as things to be caught and eaten, and grows restive.

Nemo's pleasant side is more often on display, but occasionally his misanthropy comes to the fore. Nemo's idiosyncratic vendetta against the hated cachalots (sperm whales) does not appear particularly reprehensible to Aronnax, but Nemo is as merciless to his enemies as he is to the cachalot. When the *Nautilus* sinks a warship Aronnax is offended. Nemo, meanwhile, declines from his initially not-unfriendly mood into one of melancholy and despair. Over the course of the novel he loses two sailors and kills many men with his submarine, and eventually it is too much for him. The *Nautilus*, aimlessly drifting, makes its way into the Maelstrom off the coast of Norway, and Aronnax, Conseil, and Land barely escape. *Twenty Thousand Leagues* ends with Aronnax and the reader not knowing what the final fate of Nemo and the *Nautilus* was.

Twenty Thousand Leagues Under the Sea is typical Verne—although what "typical Verne" is varies from critic to critic. Per critic Martin Willis,

> To different critics, Verne is a modernist, the last optimistic nineteenth-century novelist, the father of science fiction, a forerunner of Wells or a complement to Poe, a Romantic, a realist, or a writer of didactic juvenile adventure stories. As far as his position in the literary and theoretical history of science fiction is concerned, Verne is variously a scientific pragmatist, a fantasist, or a utopianist.

Twenty Thousand Leagues has, as is typical for Verne's vehicular-utopian science fiction, the scrupulous attention to achievable, realizable science and a careful extrapolation from known science and scientific principles. Verne is concerned with the probable and the possible, as opposed to his rival Wells, who uses science as a tool for his message, as in, for example, *War of the Worlds*. So the *Nautilus* is as close to real as Verne could make it, with the exception of the source of its power, which Verne explains away with a hand-waving dismissal: "'Professor,' said Captain Nemo, 'my electricity is not everybody's and that is all that you will permit me to say about it.'"

There is the careful attention (or, less kindly, the pedantic obsession) with details and facts; Verne made sure that *Twenty Thousand Leagues* is full of accurate information about the sea. Unfortunately, Verne lets his obsession overwhelm his storytelling sense, so that what might have been a fluidly told story is constantly interrupted, sometimes for pages on end, with lists of animals and plants which Aronnax sees. Dialogue often is used for infodumps, so that Verne can unload great heaps of information on the reader. Characters lecture each other at length, and while the information therein establishes verisimilitude and shows that Verne did his homework it is often uninteresting to the reader as well as damaging to the pace of the novel.

There are Verne's favored themes of travel and the sea. Verne had long been interested in the sea—a Verne family story, possibly apocryphal, had him trying to run away as an eleven year old and enlist as a cabin boy on a ship bound for the Indies, but being caught at the last moment—and he returns to it in a number of his novels. World travel, something much more exotic and interesting and unusual to readers of his day than to ours, is similarly an interest and it is one indulged here, with Nemo taking the *Nautilus* around the world.

And then there is Nemo's misanthropy. The general critical consensus is that the darkening of Verne's personal outlook—he underwent a series of personal tragedies in 1886, including an attempt on his life by a nephew, the deaths of his mother and his good friend and publisher Pierre Jules Hetzel, and the crippling of his leg, all of which left him cynical and depressed—is reflected in the increased misanthropy of his protagonists. But Nemo's misanthropy (much more pronounced in *Twenty Thousand Leagues* than in the novel's sequel, *Mysterious Island*) is not the result of Verne's personal misanthropy—*Twenty Thousand Leagues* was after all written years before Verne's life went sour—but instead comes from the **Romantic** tradition. Verne intended Nemo to be a Romantic great man and genius, a type of updated **Gothic** Hero-Villain. The Romantics saw the defiance of society as indication of genius, of a man unrestrained by the degrading shackles of society. The ostracized Romantic genius is unappreciated, his talent unvalued, and his intellectual and spiritual values rejected by the soulless materialistic society which does not appreciate his naturally superior talents. Nemo is a conscious successor to this tradition.

But the modern reader is likely to notice, and dislike, the hypocrisy which accompanies Nemo's Romantic pose. Nemo is critical of Aronnax and those who have pursued him, but Nemo has been sinking civilian ships—hardly the act of a man who truly wants to be left alone. Nemo proudly claims that "I am not what you call a civilized man! I have broken with society entirely, for reasons which I alone have the right to assess. I therefore do not obey its laws, and I advise you never to allude to them before me again!" Nemo seems to think that this and this alone renders him immune to the judgment of society, despite his sinking ships and funding revolutions. To modern readers, the flaws in his thinking are obvious, and not particularly salutary. Likewise, his desire to "live—live in the bosom of the waters! Only there can one have independence! There I recognize no masters! There I am free!" is at odds with his interaction with the surface world and with his stated desire to help oppressed peoples. He can't be, in essence, a patron to rebels and remain free from the world.

This hypocrisy extends to Nemo's respect for nature. He does, indeed, value the world beneath the sea and sees it as superior to the world above the sea, but he is no pacifist, and he is happy to slaughter every cachalot he finds. Like the Romantic heroes, he sees his values and judgment as superior to all others' and takes actions based on them without thinking about consequences. The cachalots are a part of the natural food chain. Killing them seriously imbalances the population of the sea. To Nemo this point does not occur; all he sees are the defenseless whales and the predatory cachalots.

Nemo is so far gone in his rejection of the surface world that he will not even eat food produced on it: "For a long time I have renounced the food of the earth, and I am never ill now.... I never use the meat of land animals." This extends even to the clothing he and his crew wear.

Nemo is a hypocrite, and his sinking of the warship betrays a streak of viciousness. But Aronnax does mention his "kindness" on several occasions. It is all part of the Romantic Great Man syndrome. Nemo is capable of conscienceless killing (which, admittedly, he feels remorse for afterward) but he weeps for his dying sailor.

In some ways *Twenty Thousand Leagues* is typical Verne taken to extremes: the lists of facts are longer, the lectures (intended to instruct as much as to entertain) are more detailed, the central character more interesting, and the science as grounded but more extrapolated than in his other works. The novel lags until Nemo appears, and although he is the clear center of the novel Verne spends a great deal of time on Aronnax, Ned Land, and the flora and fauna of the sea, so that the personality of Nemo, that which is truly compelling about the novel, appears much more briefly than, for example, lectures on the science of the Nautilus. This is unfortunate, as it dilutes the power of the novel. Verne's interests are not likely to be the same as the modern reader's, which makes the novel less interesting than it should be. Too, the style of the dialogue is formal and stiff, which lessens the power of Verne's ideas for the modern reader. There are numerous exchanges like this:

> "Professor," said Captain Nemo, "my electricity is not everybody's and that is all that you will permit me to say about it."
> "I shall not insist, sir, and I shall be satisfied with being astonished by such a result. I have only one question, which, nonetheless, you will not answer if it is indiscreet. The elements which you use to produce this marvelous agent must be depleted quickly. Zinc, for example, how do you replace it, as you no longer have any communication with land?"
> "Your question will be answered," replied the captain. "First I shall tell you that in the depths of the sea there exist zinc, iron, silver, and gold mines whose exploitation would certainly be practicable. But I have borrowed nothing from these earthly metals, for I wished to find the means of producing my electricity only in the sea itself."

There are marvelous ideas in the dialogue, but they are delivered in a stilted and even wooden manner—wooden despite the best efforts of modern translators. This is unfortunate, since what Verne wrote about was impressive to his contemporary audience. Similarly, the speed of the *Nautilus* (20 miles per hour) and the sheer distance the *Nautilus* covers in the course of the novel (20,000 leagues or roughly 60,000 miles) are less interesting to modern audiences who are jaded by the ease and speed of air flight.

One thing not usually remembered about Nemo is that, much as he is a scientist and engineer, he is also a passionate artist. (This is, again, part of the Romantic genius.) Nemo is a skilled and emotional organ player, to the point where he loses himself, "plunged in a musical ecstasy." As an artist he is concerned with the aesthetics of the *Nautilus* as much as its engines and technical aspects.

As a side note, for decades Jules Verne was victimized by bad translators, particularly English and Americans. In the early translations of Verne's books, especially *Twenty Thousand Leagues*, many passages were deleted and altered, and as much as a quarter of the novel is omitted. It was only in the 1990s that accurate and readable translations of *Twenty Thousand Leagues* began appearing, and interested readers should seek out those rather than the hack jobs available in earlier decades.

Recommended Edition
Verne, Jules. *Twenty Thousand Leagues Under the Sea* (Oxford University Press, 1998).

For Further Research
Butcher, William. "Introduction." *Twenty Thousand Leagues Under the Sea* (Oxford University Press, 1998).
Dirda, Michael. *The Classics for Pleasure* (Mariner Books, 2008).
Willis, Martin. *Mesmerists, Monsters, and Machines: Science Fiction and the Cultures of Science in the Nineteenth Century* (Kent State University, 2006).

Under Two Flags

Under Two Flags was written by Ouida and published in 1867. Ouida, née Marie Louise Ramée (1839–1908), was for three decades one of the most successful and effective popular writers in Britain. She wrote forty-four novels and collections of stories and drew praise from the likes of Edward Bulwer-Lytton and even Henry James, but by the 1890s the vogue for her work had passed and she died penniless. (She lives on as the model for Lucia in E.F. Benson's "Mapp and Lucia" novels.) *Under Two Flags* is her best-known work.

Under Two Flags is about Bertie Cecil, a young British noble who is a member of the First Life Guards, a cavalry unit. Bertie's life is ever so tiresome. His languid personality is just so strained by the sheer effort of being Bertie, or

"Beauty," as his friends and admirers call him. The horse races, the hunting, being the darling of the fast and first sets, it is all such a bother. Bertie is popular and handsome, admired by his male friends and the object of universal female admiration. His life is nearly perfect except for two difficulties: he has next to no money, and to live properly, that is, with the best of everything, and to gamble as a man should merely worsens his debts; and his younger brother Berkeley has a bad gambling problem and worse debts. Bertie eventually loses all he has on a horse race—he staked everything on his beloved horse Forest King, but one of Bertie's enemies, a welsher who Bertie humiliated, drugged Forest King so that he ran badly—and almost simultaneously discovers that Berkeley forged Bertie's name on a bill. Bertie could reveal that he did not sign the bill, but he could only do so by revealing that at the time the bill was forged he was with the Countess Guenevere, a married woman. Bertie won't allow himself to ruin the good name of Guenevere as well as that of his brother, and so Bertie flees, accepting disgrace for himself in the place of Guenevere and Berkeley. Bertie goes to Algeria and joins the *Chasseurs d'Afrique*. Twelve years pass in which he establishes himself as one of the *Chasseurs'* best soldiers. Then he meets the delightful gamine Cigarette, the darling of the *Chasseurs*. He endures deprivation, hardship, wounds, the combat deaths of friends, the death of his father while he himself is far away from his family, and the brutality of his commander, Châteauroy, until Cigarette sacrifices herself for Bertie—she has fallen in love with Bertie, although he does not reciprocate—and Berkeley, who has encountered Cigarette in the streets, is shamed by her into revealing that it was he, not Bertie, who signed the bill. Bertie is restored to his title, he marries the Princess Venetia Corona, who he fell in love with while in Africa, and Bertie and Venetia live happily ever after.

Under Two Flags is the archetypal "French Foreign Legion Novel." P.C. Wren's *Beau Geste* (1924) is the best known Foreign Legion novel and the one most often filmed and parodied, but *Under Two Flags* preceded it by over fifty years and was enormously popular and influential, both at the time and for years afterwards. Although Wren never admitted being influenced by Ouida, *Under Two Flags* was still being read by schoolboys when Wren was a child, and virtually all of the important aspects of *Beau Geste* are to be found in *Under Two Flags*. (It must be said that *Under Two Flags* is not about the French Foreign Legion, but rather about the *Chasseurs d'Afrique*, a light cavalry troop founded in 1831 to hunt and kill mounted Algerian Arab insurgents. The Legion were the scum of Europe; the *Chasseurs* were noble gentlemen.)

Under Two Flags is not well written. Strictly speaking, it is not even a good book. It is too long by about a third. Ouida repeats herself; too many of her descriptions are long lists of items, sensations, or names, designed to let the reader know how well acquainted Ouida is with the fashionable things of the fast set. Ouida seems to think that if one example or sentence clause is good, four or five will automatically be better. Everyone talks too much, in great rambling monologues and speeches; Cigarette's dying farewell stretches across five pages. Ouida's characters are in many ways cartoons, so that Bertie is unrealistically noble, the Princess Venetia is the epitome of aristocratic breeding and kindness, Bertie's servant Rake is the perfect example of a slavishly devoted underling, and Cigarette is the very definition of brio.

Ouida's father, who she worshiped, abandoned her, and so Ouida seems to be using *Under Two Flags* to work out her daddy issues. Everyone in the novel worships Bertie, as Ouida clearly does. Cigarette proves her great love to Bertie just as Ouida wanted to but never could to her own father. In fiction written by amateurs or first time writers, whether published in fan magazines, vanity presses, or on the Internet as "fan fiction," stories written by fans featuring characters from their favorite books, television shows, or movies, a common phenomenon is the "Mary Sue" character. A Mary Sue character is an idealized stand-in for the author, and is tougher, smarter, cooler, nicer, sweeter, more charming, more capable, and more skilled than the established characters, and becomes worshiped by them. Although Mary Sues appeared in 19th century magazine stories written by teenagers, as in stories where a teenaged girl saves a sleeping Indian chief from being mauled by a bear or is raised by Indians and becomes their leader, the traditional modern Mary Sue appears in *Star Trek* fan fiction, where a new ensign on the starship *Enterprise* is a better pilot than Captain Kirk, smarter than Spock, and makes both fall in love with her. Cigarette is Ouida's Mary Sue.

Bertie's affected languor is genuine, a reflection of the behavior of upper-class young British men, especially military officers, of the early and mid–19th century, but it comes off as a pose, and an extremely annoying one. In addition, a strain of anti–Semitism runs through *Under Two Flags*. Ouida's class biases are overt; Bertie, and those of his class, are innately superior, so that not only do the lower classes worship them simply for being themselves, and are happy to do so, but the mere presence of Bertie begins to reform even the most brutish and criminal of the *Chasseurs*.

The list goes on. And yet in a very real sense these flaws not only do not matter but are beside the point. *Under Two Flags* is an immensely successful bad novel. It was successful financially, for it was a bestseller many times over and remains in print today. It was successful historically, for the genre of French Foreign Legion stories begins with *Under Two Flags*. And it is successful as a reading experience. *Under Two Flags* can and will annoy the modern reader. Ouida's stylistic failings will be irritating. Readers will react negatively to Bertie simply because he is so much the subject of Ouida's hero worship. But readers will be affected by *Under Two Flags*, and if they let themselves be drawn into it, accept that the book is not well-written, set aside their critical faculties and simply enjoy the novel as an overwrought melodramatic romance, they will be rewarded with a compelling and sometimes moving experience. The emotion evoked in *Under Two Flags* is not of the exquisite, refined variety; Ouida could not write in the Henry James (**The Portrait of a Lady**) mode, and didn't try. But Ouida succeeds at the over-the-top moments and the melodramatic emotion, premier among them the moments leading up to Cigarette's death. Bertie faces death by the firing squad for a crime he did not commit, and Cigarette has acquired his pardon, and so she rides all night at breakneck speed across the desert to rescue him. Her horse spent, she surrenders herself to her enemies, the Arabs, telling them that they can torture her to death if only they deliver Bertie's pardon in time. The Arabs, touched by her willing martyrdom, send her on her way, complete with a fresh horse. Cigarette arrives in time to save Bertie by throwing herself in front of his firing squad and taking the musket balls meant for him. The sequence is melodramatic and purple and splendid. The cumulative weight of the characterization of Bertie and Cigarette—and for all her other faults Ouida vividly draws her characters (they may be irritating, but they are memorable)—almost irresistibly leads the reader to sympathize with them. The reader comes to identify with Bertie and Cigarette, and, even with their unrealities and more annoying traits, comes to see their goodness and even nobility of spirit, and to wish them well, and so will be moved by Bertie's sacrifice and the miseries and sorrows he must endure.

Viewed critically, *Under Two Flags* has a number of elements of interest. There are elements of the **Sensation Novel**, especially Ouida's dedication to writing a page-turner, the threat to Bertie's freedom, money, and status, and the crime which drives Bertie to exile, but the class insecurity of the Sensation Novels is absent: class, for Ouida, is as essential a part of the human body as blood, and can no more be subtracted from human beings than blood can. Too, it is not a young professional who saves Bertie's family name, but aristocrats themselves, the true heroes of *Under Two Flags*.

Under Two Flags has elements of the Silver Fork or "fashionable" novel. (Indeed, it might be argued that Ouida's entire approach to *Under Two Flags* was to write a fashionable novel.) The Silver Fork, or "fashionable" novels—the original Regency romances—were in John Sutherland's phrase "works purported to be by an insider, privy to the intimate secrets of the aristocracy and willing to divulge all to a middle-class reading public." Their main characters were, in Winifred Hughes' words, "the dandies, rakes and women of the world who populated the town houses and the country estates." The Silver Fork novel was dominant among English literary forms from the mid–1820s to the mid–1840s—perhaps the first best-sellers, like *Pelham*, which was written by Ouida's friend Bulwer-Lytton—and acted as the transitional form between the Romantic novel and the novels of the upper classes and the Victorian domestic realism novel, between "Regency aesthetic frivolity" and the "moral seriousness and bourgeois democracy" of the Victorian domestic novel—although, again quoting Sutherland, "silver forkery was not extinguished by mid-century realism so much as driven underground only to resurface in the 1890s cult of (Oscar) Wildean dandyism." The only aspect of the Silver Fork novel missing from *Under Two Flags* is the Silver Fork's supercilious wit and exuberance; much of *Under Two Flags* is essentially melancholy, with Bertie's moral languor and ennui being real rather than a pose. Bertie fails at being a dandy because of his lack of seriousness about being fashionable—it is simply a part of him—and because of his sorrow and poor opinion of himself.

There is also the notion of Cigarette as a **New Woman** *avant la lettre*. Ouida herself ended up being opposed to the New Woman and to late-Victorian feminism, labeling the New Woman an "unmitigated" bore. But as Pamela Gilbert demonstrates, Ouida's own conservatism is "formulated through a radical rhetoric," taking some of the tenets of Victorian feminism and simply drawing different conclusions from them. Gilbert further writes that "many of her [Ouida's] women reject traditional gender roles, being active, heroic, able to fight men and win. Although these characters succumb to the fate prescribed by mid-Victorian narrative—they die—they retain the sympathy of the reader and in so doing, sustain a critique of the conditions that necessitate their elimination," an apt description of Cigarette.

As Jane Jordan notes, *Under Two Flags* is part of Ouida's tendency to "rewrite the male romance in order to examine the function of the romantic heroine within the homosocial power structure and to analyze erotic borderlines of homosocial desire; women are positioned in the text solely in relation to the bond between male friends." Bertie is repeatedly described as "effeminate," albeit never as less than manly, and the ties between Bertie and other men, even the sadistic Chateauroy, are of far more import to him than the ties between Bertie and other women, and the language of the novel—Bertie's "forbidden longing" for Seraph, "the friend whose love he feared," is rife with homosexual underpinnings.

Under Two Flags is not Art. It has many faults. But it is wonderful reading nonetheless.

Recommended Edition

Ouida. *Under Two Flags* (Oxford University Press, 1995).

For Further Research

Addcox, J.S. "Inoculation and Empire: Cigarette's Healing Power in Ouida's Under Two Flags." *VN: Victorian Network* v1n1 (Summer 2009). http://victoriannetwork.org/index.php/vn/article/view/5.

Embry, Kristi. "Toward an Entente Cordiale: The Cultivation of Cosmopolitan Sympathies in Ouida's Under Two Flags." *Studies in the Novel* v42n3 (Fall 2010).

Gale, Robert L. "Under Two Flags." *Masterplots* Fourth Edition (Dec. 2010).

Gilbert, Pamela. "Ouida and the Other New Woman." *Victorian Women Writers and the Woman Question* (Cambridge University Press, 1999).

Jordan, Jane. "'Between Men': Romantic Friendship in Ouida's Early Novels." *Ouida and Victorian Popular Culture* (Ashgate, 2013).

Marucci, Franco. "Ouida: the Fascination of Moral Laxity." *LISA* v7n3 (2009). http://lisa.revues.org/149.

Schroeder, Natalie, and Shari Hodges Holt. *Ouida the Phenomenon: Evolving Social, Political, and Gender Concerns in Her Fiction* (Rosemont Publishing Corp, 2008).

Sutherland, John. "Introduction." *Under Two Flags* (Oxford University Press, 1995).

Vanity Fair

Vanity Fair was written by William Makepeace Thackeray (**Barry Lyndon**) and was published in 1847 and 1848 as a serial and in 1848 as a novel. Thackeray (1811 1863) was an English novelist who in his lifetime was ranked behind only Charles Dickens (*Bleak House, Great Expectations*) and George Eliot (*Middlemarch*) but whose stock has fallen considerably and who is now known primarily for *Vanity Fair*.

Rebecca "Becky" Sharp and Amelia Sedley are friends as schoolgirls, despite being very different—Becky sharp and cynical, Amelia nice and soft. When the pair leave school Amelia takes Becky into her home, where Becky schemes to capture the heart of Amelia's fat brother Jos. But fortune plays Becky false, and Jos. returns to India instead of marrying her. Becky leaves for the Crawley household as a governess, where she wins over the head of the household, Sir Pitt Crawley, and ensnares Pitt's son Rawdon as a spouse—thereby outraging Pitt's sister Miss Crawley, who sees Rawdon as having married below himself, and who cuts off Rawdon and Becky from any money in her will.

Amelia's husband (who Becky was carrying on a flirtation with) dies at Waterloo, while Rawdon does not. Rawdon and Becky live together in penniless extravagance, first in Paris and then in London. Becky gains a rich, elderly admirer, Lord Steyne, and climbs the social ladder, eventually even being presented in court. Becky has a son (who she ignores and treats shabbily) and carries on the social life, but when Rawdon is imprisoned for debt Becky refuses to pawn her jewelry and has Lord Steyne pay off Rawdon's debts—but when Rawdon returns home he finds Lord Steyne in a compromising situation with Becky, and Rawdon thrashes Lord Steyne, thereby leading to Becky's social downfall. Rawdon leaves his wife, and Lord Steyne and Becky's other enemies spread stories (mostly true) about her scandalous conduct. Becky falls lower and lower on the social scales, and is found by Amelia and Jos. at a very low point. Becky ensnares Jos., and when Jos. dies under ambiguous, mysterious circumstances Becky is the recipient of his life insurance policy. Becky spends the rest of her days on the Continent.

On the short list of the great Victorian novels, *Vanity Fair* is a comic satire which is panoramic in its scope and scale. It has an over sizedness which can be intimidating to students, who may view not only its size with alarm but the critical terms used to describe it. Daniel Burt's "*Vanity Fair* expanded the novel's usual focus on a few central characters to chronicle the full range of society itself," while true, may be off putting to students, who might be daunted at the thought of starting a fictional edifice like *Vanity Fair*. That would be a shame, because *Vanity Fair* is in its way as delightful a reading companion as Eliot's *Middlemarch*, and as deserving of claims of greatness.

There are two different planks for analysis of any book: is it worth reading, and is it worthy reading? Which is to say, is it readable, and is it any good? *Vanity Fair*, more than nearly any work covered in this book, is both of those, in abundance (one might even say excess).

To understand Thackeray's achievement one must understand the state of British fiction itself when he wrote *Vanity Fair*. Silver Fork fiction (see **Pelham**) had reigned supreme in the marketplace for twenty years, with the Newgate Novel (see *Pelham*) a close second. Dickens, though popular, was still in his early phase, having only published (of his major works) *The Pickwick Papers*, *Oliver Twist*, and *A Christmas Carol*. The novel was still bound and limited in the genres in which it could acceptably appear.

Thackeray, and *Vanity Fair*, changed all of that. As a critic, Thackeray quarreled with Bulwer Lytton (***The Last Days of Pompeii***, *Pelham*) and satirized the Newgate Novel genre in the pages of *Punch* in 1846 as part of the critical storm that ended the genre. And Thackeray, via the satires of his *Dukes and Dejeuners* (1847) and *Vanity Fair*, helped to put paid to the Silver Fork genre. (In the words of critic Ellen Miller Casey, *Vanity Fair* is "both a repudiation of the silver fork genre and its apex.") What replaced them both was the domestic novel, of which *Vanity Fair* was the principal work before *Middlemarch*. (Bulwer

Lytton's *The Caxtons* (1849) was immensely popular but not was not the first domestic novel; Bulwer Lytton merely capitalized on the current trend.)

The domestic novel was in John Sutherland's words "scarcely a 'school,'" being more of a "well defined anti type." It was a novel about real life, a novel without heroism and without villainy, but instead ordinary people doing ordinary things—domestic by name and domestic by deed. It gave the reader ordinary stories, akin to what Balzac (***Père Goriot***) and Stendhal (***The Charterhouse of Parma, The Red and the Black***) were doing with French literature, but without the (to Victorian readers) distasteful aspects of sex and sin. Domestic fiction gave readers stories of the everyday, stories and characters to which they could relate. Readers, and writers, loved this. *Vanity Fair* was a runaway best seller as a serial, even before it was finished, and single handedly established the domestic novel and realism as a dominant novelistic mode—a mode which the **Sensation** novelists reacted against (as Sutherland puts it, the domestic novel "gave the sensation novelists of the 1860s a sense of their identity") but which outlasted them and became accepted as the primary (or sole) mode in which fiction should work, an acceptance which still holds true today. *Vanity Fair* did that.

If that was all *Vanity Fair* had done, it would be celebrated. But Thackeray accomplished so much more in *Vanity Fair*. There is its incisive satire of British society, from small to large, from the poor to the aristocracy—Thackeray wields his literary knife with force and with acuity. There is the comedy which accompanies the satire, which may not make modern readers laugh out loud but will make them smile, whether from rueful recognition or from appreciation of Becky Sharp's wit. There is the overwhelming sense that Thackeray has let the characters take the reins of the novel and live out their lives according to their wills rather than manipulating them for the ends of the story. If as Daniel Burt says we regard "elaborately structured works" with a "tighter dramatic focus" as the superior approach, Thackeray stands as a rebuttal to that approach—his freewheeling approach is jazz to everyone else's classical music.

There is the narrator, what Burt calls "intrusive, garrulous, and guiding." The narrator, omnipresent, omniscient, heavy handed (even over bearing), fourth wall breaking, and at all times accompanying the reader through the text, is far more present than in most Victorian novels, and modern readers may find it an acquired taste, though the ultimate effect of the narrator is contemplative charm. Thackeray's use of the narrator (inherited from 18th century novelists like Henry Fielding) as a tool with which to tell the story is a writerly reveling in the "possibilities of the novel" and a way in which to show us how Thackeray, the master puppeteer, pulls his puppet's strings—how the fiction sausage is made in the fiction factory—while making the reader enjoy it.

There is the amount of time spent on not just society, large and small, but various characters, from the protagonists down to minor characters, so that the cumulative effect is truly panoramic, and Thackeray creates an entire world, a world as real in its way as Jane Austen's Highbury (see *Emma*); the other great panoramic novel of the century, Tolstoy's *War and Peace*, was overtly influenced by *Vanity Fair*, an influence that Tolstoy freely acknowledged.

Vanity Fair is a novel that defies categorization. It is a historical novel—it treats of events thirty years before the writing of the novel—but it disregards the traditional construction of the historical novel. This is part of the novel's revolutionary status—that accepted conventions are ignored and even exploded. *Vanity Fair* is a historical novel which largely ignores history. It is a picaresque novel in which the "settled conclusion" of picaresques, the resolution of the novel with the hero's fortunes settled, is ignored. It is a novel in which the traditional hero is replaced with a most untraditional (but modern, for the time) *femme fatale*, but also with no hero—as the title says, *Vanity Fair: A Novel Without a Hero*—a stroke of realism unprecedented in English novels, to create a novel in which there are no overt heroes or sentimentalized caricatures, simply ordinary people. It is a comic satire without a reforming motive—for Thackeray society and human nature cannot be reformed. It is a novel in which there is no poetic justice—just us.

Vanity Fair is not without faults, of course. The novel's approach to race is unfortunate, to say the least—Thackeray was an out and out racist, and his racism appears throughout *Vanity Fair*. This isn't a case of an author's bigotries not affecting the text; the text itself is racist and anti Semitic, much more so than other contemporary works. *Vanity Fair*'s style is a little dated—unsurprisingly, considering how long ago it was written. And as mentioned the narrator is an acquired taste.

But generally the novel makes for splendid reading. Once the taste for the narrator is acquired by the reader, the reader comes to welcome the narrator's musings and asides. *Vanity Fair* is bracingly cynical—appropriate, for a satire—and blasts everyone and everything (not coincidentally including the upper class groups which had wronged Thackeray in real life). The novel has great vitality. The plot is appropriately complex while never being confusing. The characters are appealing while also being appropriately flawed, and Becky Sharp is an all time great character.

Vanity Fair is one of the great fictional achievements of the era.

Recommended Edition
Thackeray, William Makepeace. *Vanity Fair* (Penguin Classics, 2003).

For Further Research
Brier, Peter. "Vanity Fair." *Masterplots* Fourth Edition (Dec. 2010).

Catalan, Zelma. "Irony in Vanity Fair." http://victorianweb.org/authors/wmt/catalan.html.
McCrum, Robert. "The 100 Best Novels: No 14—Vanity Fair by William Thackeray (1848)." http://www.theguardian.com/books/2013/dec/23/william thackeray vanity fair 100 best novels.
Sutherland, John. "William Makepeace Thackeray: Racist?" http://blog.oup.com/2011/07/thackeray/.

Waverley

Waverley was written by Sir Walter Scott and was published in 1814. Scott (1771–1832) has fallen considerably in stature since the 19th century. Seldom read today, Scott was phenomenally popular during his lifetime and was acclaimed as a poet, novelist, and critic of brilliance. *Waverley* is the first of Scott's Waverley sequence of historical novels. Waverley is significant in literary history, but it is more familiar to modern readers than it is actually read. This is as it should be.

Waverley is about the maturation and education of Edward Waverley, the son of a noble English family in the year 1745. Edward is raised by both his father and his uncle. Both love Edward, but hte pair are otherwise estranged because to politics: Edward's father is loyal to the king, and Edward's uncle is a Jacobite. Once Edward is old enough his father gets him a commission in the army. Edward goes north with the army to Scotland. While there he visits an old family friend, Sir Cosmo Comyne Bradwardine, and befriends Sir Bradwardine's daughter Rose. Edward is also taken with the Baron's servant, Davie Gellatley, and his stories about the wild Highlanders. While Edward is staying with the Baron they are visited by one of the men in the service of Fergus Mac Ivor Vich Ian Vohr, one of the great clan chiefs. Curious about the Highlanders, Edard travels north to meet Fergus. After a brief interlude with a notorious bandit, Edward meets Fergus and Fergus' sister, Flora Mac Ivor. Edward falls in love with Flora, but Flora turns him down; she has only one goal in life, to see Bonnie Prince Charlie on the throne of England, and she feels that Edward deserves complete love from a wife rather than acquiescence and tolerance, which is all she will be able to give a husband until Prince Charlie becomes king. While with the Mac Ivors Edward is relieved of his command in the army by his Colonel because of Edward's association with traitors (i.e., the Mac Ivors). Angered at this disgrace, Edward tries to go home but is caught and arrested. He is freed by some Highlanders who help him return north and join with the Mac Ivors. Edward enlists with the forces of Prince Charles, who Edward meets and befriends. They march south and defeat an English army in battle, but a later advance to the South ends badly. The Highlanders lose and Prince Charles eventually orders a retreat. At the battle of Culloden many of the Highlanders are killed, and Edward is separated from his friends. He leaves the battlefield and returns to Scotland and thence to England. Edward's name is eventually cleared, thanks in large part to the largesse of an English colonel whose life Edward had saved, and Edward marries Rose, who he decides is preferable to Flora. Fergus is executed as a traitor, the Jacobite cause is ended, Flora packs herself off to a Catholic convent, and Edward and Rose live happily ever after.

Waverley was one of the first best-selling novels and made Scott a phenomenon, to the point where his contemporaries and successors in the historical novel genre were inevitably compared with him and competed with him. *Waverley* is a historically important novel; it essentially created the modern historical novel. Before *Waverley* **Gothic** novels were the vogue, and while they made use of historical trappings their settings or details were not accurate. *Waverley* changed that, so that the reader came to expect novels to have a specific, identifiable time and place, and one that went beyond living memory. Scott also exchanged the generic character types and idealized situations of the prose romance for more realistic (if still idealized) characters and settings, and included some (though not many) homely details, of the kind his predecessors never included in their novels. Scott included dialect and regional variations in speech to a far greater degree than previous novelists had. Scott included protagonists who, like Edward, were ordinary people, not heroes out of romances. Via *Waverley* and the twenty-seven Waverley novels Scott transformed the prose novel from the preserve of women, as it was seen at the time, into a masculine one, and in doing so gave the prose novel a respectability it had not previously possessed. Before Scott prose romances were written in large part by women for women. Scott, via *Waverley* and the Waverley novels, changed that, and showed that it was possible not only for men to write novels, but for *gentlemen* to write novels.

Waverley is not horrible. The nearly unintelligible dialect which ruined *Rob Roy* is much more tolerable here. After the first, long and uninvolving, section, in which the Waverley family and Edward's childhood and education are given entirely too much space and attention, the novel slightly picks up the pace, so that the reader at last meets some partially interesting characters and sees the plot begin to move forward. The portrayal of the Scottish culture and language and customs is certainly convincing, even if the amount of detail too often overwhelms what little momentum the novel has. There are moments of bracing harshness, as with the fate of Flora and Edward's father Richard. And as a sentimental, romanticized look into an interesting historical period, *Waverley* could be worse.

But it certainly could be a lot better. As historical fiction *Waverley* is important, but it is only marginally interesting now. Mark Twain put it harshly but well in one of his letters:

> 1. Are there in Sir Walter's novels passages done in good English—English which is neither slovenly or involved?
> 2. Are there passages whose English is not poor and thin and commonplace, but is of a quality above that?
> 3. Are there passages which burn with real fire—not punk, fox fire, make believe?
> 4. Has he heroes and heroines who are not cads and cadesses?
> 5. Has he personages whose acts and talk correspond with their characters as described by him?
> 6. Has he heroes and heroines whom the reader admires, admires, and knows why?
> 7. Has he funny characters that are funny, and humorous passages that are humorous?
> 8. Does he ever chain the reader's interest, and make him reluctant to lay the book down?
> 9. Are there pages where he ceases from posing, ceases from admiring the placid flood and flow of his own dilutions, ceases from being artificial, and is for a time, long or short, recognizably sincere and in earnest?
> 10. Did he know how to write English, and didn't do it because he didn't want to?
> 11. Did he use the right word only when he couldn't think of another one, or did he run so much to wrong because he didn't know the right one when he saw it?
> 12. Can you read him? and keep your respect for him? Of course a person could in his day—an era of sentimentality and sloppy romantics—but land! can a body do it today? Brander, I lie here dying, slowly dying, under the blight of Sir Walter. I have read the first volume of *Rob Roy*, and as far as chapter XIX of *Guy Mannering*, and I can no longer hold my head up nor take my nourishment. Lord, it's all so juvenile! so artificial, so shoddy; and such wax figures and skeletons and spectres. Interest? Why, it is impossible to feel an interest in these bloodless shams, these milk and water humbugs. And oh, the poverty of the invention! Not poverty in inventing situations, but poverty in furnishing reasons for them. Sir Walter usually gives himself away when he arranges for a Situation elaborates, and elaborates, and elaborates, till if you live to get to it you don't believe in it when it happens.
>
> I can't find the rest of *Rob Roy*, I can't stand any more *Mannering*.... I do not know just what to do, but I will reflect, and not quit this great study rashly. He was great, in his day, and to his proper audience; and so was God in Jewish times, for that matter, but why should either of them rank high now? And do they? honest, now, do they? Dam'd if I believe it.

Twain was letting his own spleen flow a bit, as usual, but also as usual he scores some direct hits. The vast forests of verbiage which Scott poured into *Waverley* do not add to the reader's enjoyment of the novel. Scott is not a particularly good stylist, and the old-fashioned narrative style is a massive drag on the novel's pace and the modern reader's interest. Despite the immense length of the novel, colorful and memorable descriptions, whether of scenery or clothing or battles, are lacking. The dialogue is almost obscenely formal and long-winded and the humor is lumbering and faux-jocular. The people and culture of Scotland are too sentimentalized; the dirt and fear and poverty of that time and place are missing, and the reader too often gets the feeling that life as a poor Scotsman was a lark. While the awful dialect of *Rob Roy* is missing, there are more than enough difficult or obscure words, either Scottish or English, to require the modern reader to have a dictionary ready while reading *Waverley*. (Few modern readers are likely to know, without consulting the *Oxford English Dictionary*, what "beevor" or "pibroch" or "land louper" mean.) The novel builds up to the battles, but Scott describes the battles too quickly and anti-climactically. When Fergus and Waverley quarrel their argument feels forced and unnatural, as if Scott decided that there needed to be conflict between them and manufactured some. And while Flora seems to have been intended as the ideal woman, and many critics have taken her as such, her treatment of Edward is so cold and unfeeling that she is ultimately unlikable. Rose may be childlike and naive, but she is much more appealing than Flora.

Only Scott completists and those acutely interested in reading the roots of the historical romance need read *Waverley*.

Recommended Edition

Scott, Sir Walter. *Waverley* (Penguin Classics, 2012).

For Further Research

Burt, Daniel S. "Waverley." *The Novel 100: A Ranking of the Most Influential Novels of All Time* (Checkmark Books, 2010).
Lukacs, Georg. *The Historical Novel* (Merlin Press, 1962).
Phillpott, Matthew J. "A Novel Approaches prelude: A Brief History of Historical Fiction." http://ihrconference.files.wordpress.com/2011/11/mphillpott history of historical fiction.pdf.

— · —

The Way We Live Now

The Way We Live Now was written by Anthony Trollope (**Barchester Towers**) and was published as a serial in 1874 and 1875 and as a novel in 1875. Trollope (1815–1882) was one of the most successful and prolific of all Victorian authors. *The Way We Live Now*, the last major Victorian triple-decker, was not initially well-received due to its perceived misanthropy but has come to be regarded as the best of Trollope's individual (non-series) novels.

The Way We Live Now is a set of interlocking storylines involving various upper class characters in London. There is Lady Carbury, who works as a novelist to support herself, her daughter Hetta, and her spendthrift, wastrel, caddish no-damn-good son Sir Felix. Country nobleman Roger Carbury (a cousin to Lady Carbury) is in love with Hetta, but she loves Roger's best friend Paul Montague.

Sir Felix's heedless lifestyle and gambling are a drain on his mother's finances, but she eventually persuades him to use his facile charm to convince Marie Melmotte, the only child of financier Augustus Melmotte, to marry him, so that the Melmotte money will be his and their financial problems will be solved. Marie loves Felix. However, Augustus is opposed to the marriage and wants Marie to marry Lord Nidderdale, whose money problems are no better than the Carburys' but whose name is nobler.

Augustus Melmotte is at heart a swindler and fraud, but one on a gigantic scale, and he gulls many members of the British upper classes into his financial schemes, primary of which is a projected railroad from Utah to Mexico. Melmotte organizes a board of directors for the railroad which includes Sir Felix Carbury and Adolphus "Dolly" Longstaffe, the son of a Suffolk squire. The Longstaffe family's financial straits—no one in The Way We Live Now has money except Roger Carbury—lead them to sell Pickering, their house, to Melmotte, but foolishly they give him the title deeds before receiving the money from him. Melmotte forges Dolly's signature on a piece of paper giving Melmotte ownership of Pickering, something which eventually leads to his downfall. Melmotte successfully runs for Parliament, but it becomes known to all of London that Melmotte is a forger and fraud, and when the police get too close to Melmotte he commits suicide.

Happily-ever-afters occur to a measured degree. Hetta Carbury marries Paul Montague, Lady Carbury marries her best friend, Marie Melmotte marries an American financier, and Felix is sent abroad.

The Way We Live Now is generally seen as Trollope's most successful satire on modern life. The novel is indeed scathing in its view of British society. Trollope had spent eighteen months abroad and returned to find Britain venal, commercial, coarse, and shallow, and gripped with what he called the "commercial profligacy of the age," and "a certain class of dishonesty, dishonesty magnificent in its proportions, and climbing into high places ... so rampant and so splendid that there seems to be reason for fearing that men and women will be taught to feel that dishonesty, if it can become splendid, will cease to be abominable." He wrote The Way We Live Now to excoriate society and those who prospered in it. In the words of critic John Sutherland, "With this novel the aged Trollope raised his lash and let it fall on a society gone decadent, as he thought." That is both the novel's greatest virtue and its most critical flaw.

The Way We Live Now is not subtle in its satire, and indeed barely qualifies as a satire at all. Rather, it's an outright *attack* on British society. No one is spared: not the aristocracy, not the upper class, not the middle class, not financiers, not the literary establishment, not the religious, not even upper class women—no one. Gambling and speculation, corruption in publishing and the Church of England and upper class society, all come under attack from Trollope, in a portrayal of dishonesty and corruption on a systemic level. Of all the varied characters in *The Way We Live Now*—and the preceding summary left out a number of storylines and characters—only three are more good than bad: Roger Carbury, Ezekiel Brehgert, a Jewish banker, and John Crumb, a country grain dealer. All the rest are contemptible to various degrees. Trollope is too good a writer to cast his characters as entirely black or white, so that even the worst of the cast, Sir Felix, has some redeeming qualities, and even the best, Roger Carbury, comes off as an interfering prig. But the negative qualities of the bad characters are outsized, just as the world of *The Way We Live Now* is almost grotesquely exaggerated in its venality, its greed, its general amorality, and its blithe abandonment of all that is good about England's past and traditions. *The Way We Live Now* is one long bracing savaging of modern Britain, delivered with a blunderbuss' vigor and impact and lack of subtlety.

That's the good part of the novel. Trollope has good reason to find English society the way that he did, and his attack is effective because it is an accurate one. (Indeed, as George Packer points out, *The Way We Live Now* is as acute an attack on modern society today, with our ruthless, gross, rapid accumulation of wealth, as it was in Trollope's day.) From Lady Carbury's willingness to do *anything* to get a good review for her books to the husband- and heiress-hunting young men and women to Augustus Melmotte's forging his own daughter's name on a document, anything goes in the London of *The Way We Live Now*, and Trollope condemns it all equally, and viciously.

It's also the novel's flaw. 800 pages of unrelenting attack on unlikable characters can be an awful chore to read, even when the writer is as talented as Trollope is. (For all its flaws *The Way We Live Now* is never less than readable and entertaining.) Trollope knew this, which is why, as in *Barchester Towers*, Trollope shifts gears roughly halfway through the novel, turning it from an attack into a drama. As mentioned Trollope lends his characters complexity and three dimensions—he's so very good at sketching character quickly and precisely—so that in the latter half of the novel the reader understands the very real-seeming dilemmas that the characters face. (Who among us has not felt the pressure of financial stress, as Trollope's characters do?) Unfortunately for *The Way We Live Now*, Trollope spent the first half of the novel showing us (and telling us) how bad his characters are, so that when the time comes in the second half of the novel for their dire straits to make us feel sympathy for them and to wish them well, we don't.

Academics often compare Trollope negatively to Dickens, in large part because Trollope produced his work on a clockwork daily basis, viewing writing as just another profession rather than as Art. But Trollope, in *The Way We Live Now*, does things that Dickens wouldn't or couldn't. Trollope keeps as many plots moving forward, constantly forward, as Dickens ever did, but Dickens does not create characters as real as Trollope does. Dickens' villains are often grotesques and his heroes sentimental and even wooden. Trollope's villains are recognizably human, though all the worse because of that. Too, Dickens' worlds are often exaggerated; the only thing exaggerated or unrealistic about Trollope's world in *The Way We Live Now* is the greed and corruption gripping everyone. As Henry James—not particularly a fan of Trollope's—wrote, "there are two kinds of taste in the appreciation of imaginative literature: the taste for emotions of surprise and the taste for emotions of recognition. It is the latter that Trollope gratifies."

Finally, there is the tangled question of antisemitism in *The Way We Live Now*. Trollope is generally seen as an antisemite—based on *The Way We Live Now*—and some of the Jews in the novel are portrayed according to various traditional antisemitic stereotypes. But at the same time Trollope spends time letting characters condemn themselves out of their own mouths with antisemitic statements about one of the sole good characters in the novel, the Jewish banker Ezekiel Brehgert. Trollope's views about the Jews are debatable, but Anna Peak argues convincingly that *The Way We Live Now* "satirizes anti–Semitism and deconstructs 'the Jew' as a male racial Other in order to argue for greater tolerance of both religious conviction and female independence."

The Way We Live Now is flawed, but never less than readable, and at times is exhilarating in its venom.

Recommended Edition

Trollope, Anthony. *The Way We Live Now* (Modern Library, 1984).

For Further Research

Dodd, Marion E. "Introduction." *The Way We Live Now* (Modern Library, 1984).
McCrum, Robert. "The 100 Best Novels: No 22—The Way We Live Now by Anthony Trollope (1875)." http://www.theguardian.com/books/2014/feb/17/110 best novels way we live now trollope.
Mullen, Richard. *The Penguin Companion to Trollope* (Penguin, 1996).
Ozick, Cynthia. "Our Kinsman, Mr. Trollope." *Fame & Folly: Essays* (Vintage, 1997).

Packer, George. "When the Money Gets Too Big." *The New Yorker* (Mar. 20, 2013).
Peak, Anna. "Re-thinking Trollope and Anti-Semitism: Gender, Religion, and 'the Jew' in *The Way We Live Now.*" *The Ashgate Research Companion to Anthony Trollope* (Ashgate, 2015).

The Woman in White

The Woman in White was written by Wilkie Collins (***The Moonstone***) and was published in serial form from 1859 to 1860 and then as a novel in 1860. Collins (1824–1889), an English novelist and opium addict, wrote both mysteries and Gothic novels, including his most famous work, *The Woman in White*. Unlike most mid-level novelists of his era, Collins is still well thought of today; although, most readers are only familiar with *The Moonstone* and *The Woman in White*. His good reputation is well-deserved, because both are enjoyable novels.

In *The Woman in White* Walter Hartright, a drawing master, gains a job teaching drawing to Marian Halcombe and Laura Fairlie, the nieces of the wealthy but difficult Frederick Fairlie. On his way to Limmeridge House, the home of the Fairlies, Walter encounters a woman, dressed in white, wandering around the countryside and talking peculiarly. While at Limmeridge House Walter falls in love with Laura—who is the double of the woman in white—and she with him, but she is already betrothed to Sir Percival Glyde, so Walter leaves Limmeridge House. Sir Percival arrives, and despite Marian's dislike of him he marries Laura. Six months later, after the honeymoon, Marian moves in with Sir Percival and Laura. They are joined by Count Fosco, a huge, self-assured Italian who is Sir Percival's friend, and the Count's wife, who is Laura's aunt. Marian distrusts the Foscos and deeply distrusts and dislikes Percival, and she discovers that Count Fosco and Sir Percival are plotting to take Laura's money away from her.

Anne Catherick appears and tries to warn Laura Percival. But Fosco chases Anne away before she can say what it is, and Percival begins plotting with Fosco about killing Laura and taking her money. Marian overhears them plotting, but she exposes herself to the rain in doing so and catches a fever. Laura is lured to London, where she is given drugs, declared insane, dressed in Anne Catherick's old clothes, and put into the same asylum from which Anne Catherick had escaped. Sir Percival finds Anne Catherick and plans to kill her, because she is the physical double of Laura and can be buried under Laura's name. Anne is ill anyhow and dies of natural causes; when she dies it is announced that Laura has died. Marian, who was not moved to London but only to another room in the house, recovers from her long illness and is told that Laura is dead.

From that point forward Marian, Laura, and Walter have a long and difficult struggle to find each other, survive the machinations of Count Fosco, and prove that Laura is not dead and is entitled to her money. Eventually good triumphs over evil, and Walter and Laura marry and have a child, and Marian stays with them as their dear friend.

The Woman in White is the novel which began the **Sensation Novel** genre. If *The Woman in White* lacks the importance of *The Moonstone*, it was nonetheless one of the most popular novels written in England in the 19th century and remains a thrilling read—what critic Mary Ellen Snodgrass calls "the touchstone gaslight thriller," and the source of a huge amount of subsidiary material, such as perfumes, at the height of its popularity.

The first thirty pages of *The Woman in White* are admittedly tedious and long-winded. The appearance of the titular character is melodramatic rather than dramatic, and reveals contemporary concerns that will strike the modern reader as extremely dated. (The idea that the Woman in White has escaped from an asylum does not fill the modern reader with nearly the horror that it would have Wilkie's contemporary readers.) The modern reader could not be blamed for giving up the novel during these opening pages, as the prose seems to be in wordy High Victorian style—not unreadable and neither turgid nor torpid, but long-winded and somewhat aimless, as if Collins was still finding his way.

But once Marian Halcombe is introduced, the pace of the novel picks up, and once the plot of Walter's frustrated love for Laura begins in earnest, the novel reaches a high pitch of entertainment and readability. Walter and Laura are not particularly interesting as the hero and heroine; Walter is well meaning but ordinary, and Laura is a depressingly colorless milquetoast of a character. (Collins may have meant Walter and Laura to be satires of the traditional romantic leads; if so, he played up the uninteresting aspects of such characters without making his satires particularly biting or amusing.) But Collins does succeed in giving their dilemma some emotional weight.

One critical dismissal of Collins is that he could not create the "higher reaches" of criticism, and that his people are plot-dominated (and indeed, there are no subplots to allow them to flourish) and two-dimensional. But in *The Woman in White* Collins succeeds in making his secondary characters as vivid and interesting as Walter and Laura are dull and uninteresting. Walter's dwarf friend Professor Pesca is amusing, Mr. Fairlie is memorably crotchety, self-centered, and neurasthenic, Count Fosco is hugely amusing, and Marian Halcombe is extremely appealing. Marian is a good woman and has all the vitality, personality, and charm which Laura lacks. (It is not ridiculous, in fact, to say that Marian is far too alive for *The Woman in White* and deserves better than to remain a spinster aunt to Walter and Laura's children.) But many of the other characters are as alive as Marian, and it is clear that Collins' real affection was for Marian and for Fosco, and that Walter and Laura were the hero and heroine because the form demanded they be. By the novel's end the reader can only echo Fosco's admiration for Marian's capabilities, and regret that Marian was Fosco's opponent rather than his partner.

Collins has a great skill at establishing characterization through dialogue and monologue. His physical descriptions are equally as vivid, and while little of the dialogue and descriptions in *The Woman in White* are quotable, they work marvelously in the context of the novel. The plot is suitably complex, even if some of the mysteries (why Laura looks so much like Anne Catherick, for example) are not difficult to solve. Fosco's plotting is suitably devious—the critical comment that his greatest skill was dramatic rather than narrative seems to be apt—and the modern reader is likely to be struck by the Victorian manners at play in Walter's early interactions with Laura and Marian. Some Victorian novels have characters who could, with little adjustment, appear in a modern novel. Collins' characters read as if they were created 150 years ago—which they were. Collins uses a variety of narrations, from Marian's diary entries to Walter's accounts to the testimony of Count Fosco's cook, which hearkens back to the **Gothic** novel and anticipates the shifting perspectives in modern mystery stories. Collins also provides a brilliant and even unnerving violation when Marian's narration, in her diary, ends, and Count Fosco writes his own entry in Marian's diary. The reader has become so used to reading Marian's private thoughts that the appearance of Count Fosco's words in Marian's diary is almost as shocking to the reader as they were to Marian herself when she later read Fosco's words.

The Woman in White has also been described as "the greatest mystery novel of the 19th century." The accuracy of this assessment depends on the definition of "mystery novel." Purely as a mystery, *The Woman in White* is good but not excellent. Collins' presentation of the crime and exploration of how and why the crime is solved is inferior to work by, among others, Edgar Allan Poe's "C. Auguste Dupin" stories and and Arthur Conan Doyle's "Sherlock Holmes" stories. But as a novel with a mystery inside it *The Woman in White* is excellent, behind only *The Moonstone* as the best of the 19th century. (Dickens' **Bleak House** is not a mystery.) Nonetheless, *The Woman in White* was influential on later detective novels, not least because of its narrative device of including what John Sutherland calls the "pseudo-documentary form of written testimony, diary entries, sworn evidence; a device which creates a striking effect of authenticity," and a form which numerous later mysteries would make use of.

In the 19th century, in the long years between the last of Edgar Allan Poe's "C. Auguste Dupin" stories in 1845 and the first of Arthur Conan Doyle's "Sherlock Holmes" stories in 1887, there were a number of detective and mystery novels: proto-mysteries, which had some or many of the elements of mystery fiction without being actual mysteries, through the century; Newgate novels (see *Pelham*) in the 1840s; casebook mysteries, the precursors to modern police procedurals, in the 1850s; Sensation Novels in the 1860s; and pre–Holmesian detective novels in the 1870s and 1880s. But of all these works, there were two novels which were influential on later detective writers: Charles Dickens' *Bleak House*, thanks to Sergeant Cuff, the first major post–C. Auguste Dupin detective; and *The Woman in White*, thanks to intricacy of plot, general level of suspense, and characterization.

Most mysteries written in the 19th century sacrifice depth of characterization for exploration of the circumstances of the crime, and sacrifice the author's take on contemporary (and non-mystery) issues for a concentration on the criminal, the detective/crime solver, and the victims of the crime. And those who attempt to make their mysteries into proper novels usually lack the ambition to address contemporary issues and lack the talent to carry it off in good fashion. Collins managed both characterization and the addressing of contemporary issues, and had the talent to make it all extremely readable. As no less than T.S. Eliot wrote, "*The Woman in White* is the novel in which Collins most closely approaches Dickens.... [Collins] was a master of plot and situation, of those elements of drama which are most essential to melodrama."

Collins' concerns in *The Woman in White* are clearly greater than the mere writing of a mystery. He effectively demonstrates how helpless Laura is, once she has married the scoundrel Percival, and equally effectively shows how much of an impediment the law could be to those seeking justice. *The Woman in White* is as much a criticism of the strictures of marriage and the law as it is a mystery. And the gay subtext is pronounced; whether Collins intended to or not, many readers, both popular and critical, have seen Marian's affection for Laura as going beyond mere sisterhood into the realm of "intense friendship" which was for Victorian women an outlet for same-sex desire.

Fosco's identity as an Italian is due to Collins' thought that "the crime is too ingenious for an English villain." Collins was also, consciously or not, making use of the tradition in English popular culture, often seen in the Gothics, to make villains into extra-cultural Others, often Italian. Fosco's Italianness is not the only Gothic element in *The Woman in White*. The novel has a number of Gothic attributes, from the confinement of women in a country house to male marital tyranny to the multiple narrators to the threatened woman to the family secrets haunting the present to the resourceful heroine. In many ways *The Woman in White* is an updated and much better written Gothic.

Alongside the tremendously appealing Marian, Fosco is the best part of *The Woman in White*. A marvelously wicked character, Fosco is a kind of parody of the **Romantic** character, embodying his major traits while also being a fat bad guy. His incisive criticisms of Victorian society are likely Collins' own, conveyed via Fosco. Fosco is the first major obese villain in suspense/crime fiction, a body type later to become common, and is arguably the first super-villain/master criminal in English and American crime fiction. Poe's C. Auguste Dupin had no rival; Dickens' Inspector Bucket had no master criminal to pursue; and the two archetypal master criminals of the 19th century, Frederic Van Rensselaer Dey's Doctor Quartz and Arthur Conan Doyle's Professor Moriarty, both followed Fosco by decades.

The Woman in White is tremendously readable, exciting for much of its length, and features two characters who are too vital for the constraints of just one novel. It's well worth reading.

Recommended Edition
Collins, Wilkie. *The Woman in White* (Penguin Classics, 2003).

For Further Research
Ashley, Jr., Robert P. "Wilkie Collins Reconsidered." *Nineteenth-Century Fiction*, v4n4 (Mar. 1950).
Burt, Daniel S. "*The Woman in White.*" *The Novel 100: A Ranking of the Most Influential Novels of All Time* (Checkmark Books, 2010).
Eliot, T.S. "Wilkie Collins and Dickens." *The Victorian Novel*. Bloom, Harold, ed. (Chelsea House, 2004).
Miller, D.A. "Cage aux folles: Sensation and Gender in Wilkie Collins' The Woman in White." *Representations* n14 (Spring 1986).

Wuthering Heights

Wuthering Heights was written by Emily Brontë and was published in 1847. Brontë (1818–1848), the sister of Charlotte Brontë (*Jane Eyre*), only published one novel in her lifetime, *Wuthering Heights*. It was regarded as a failure for many years, but is now one of the most popular and critically acclaimed novels in the world.

The frame story of *Wuthering Heights* is about Mr. Lockwood, the novel's first narrator, renting a mansion in the north of England; he meets his surly neighbor, Mr. Heathcliff, and then learns Heathcliff's story from his former servant, Nelly Dean, who becomes the novel's second and main narrator. Heathcliff, a dark man with a "gipsy" cast to his features, was a foundling adopted by Mr. Earnshaw, taken to Earnshaw's mansion, "Wuthering Heights," and raised by Earnshaw alongside his two children, Hindley and Catherine. Hindley loathed Heathcliff from the first and always treated him badly. Catherine loved Heathcliff with a great passion, though she eventually, as a teenager, rejected the notion of marrying him because they were too similar. When Heathcliff—who detested Hindley and loved Catherine—discovered this rejection, he fled Wuthering Heights for three years.

When Heathcliff returned to Wuthering Heights, he found that Catherine had married Edgar Linton, who lived in the neighboring house of "Thrushcross Grange." Catherine feels for Edgar only a pale shadow of what she feels for Heathcliff, but when he returns they quarrel—their passion for each other manifests itself in emotions too strong to be controlled. Catherine and Edgar have a daughter, Cathy. Heathcliff marries Edgar's sister Isabella. But the marriage is a part of Heathcliff's implacable revenge against everyone who mistreated him growing up, a list which includes Edgar Linton. Heathcliff and Isabella have a son, although Isabella flees Thrushcross Grange before Heathcliff discovers that he is a father, to Linton Heathcliff. Hindley Earnshaw and his wife Frances have a son, Hareton. Catherine dies, driving Heathcliff to a kind of moral and emotional insanity, and the thought of her torments him daily, but he does not relent from his revenge scheme, and before he dies he has tortured, emotionally and physically, the entire cast except Lockwood and Nelly Dean. After his death Hareton Earnshaw and Cathy Linton become lovers, and Wuthering Heights and Thrushcross Grange are united.

Wuthering Heights was not successful during Brontë's lifetime. Victorian readers and critics had never read anything like it—indeed, there hadn't been anything like it before Brontë, and even *Jane Eyre*, written by Brontë's sister, looks conventional next to it—and (perhaps understandably) were not prepared to understand it or treat it as it deserved. It was only decades later that critics began to comprehend what a masterpiece *Wuthering Heights* is. To complain of the main characters is to cavil.

Wuthering Heights is one of those works whose technical mastery is so paramount that ordinary readerly objections must be waved aside. Modern readers—at least, those above the age of seventeen—might complain that Heathcliff and Catherine are unlikable, to say the least, that the extremity of their passions and their inability to control their emotions renders them both hateful, that their behavior toward each other and toward everyone else, before and after Catherine's death, makes one want to wash one's hands of them and wish them to the Devil. Modern readers might object that the grand romance between Catherine and Heathcliff is not a true romance at all, but a *folie à deux*, a mental illness occurring simultaneously in two people who know each other—that the "love" they share is not recognizable as love to anyone in the 21st century or over the age of seventeen—that it is an image of love created by someone who knew of romance and the softer emotions only from **Romantic** poetry and novels and not from life experience. (Emily Brontë was a recluse whose only friends were her sisters.)

(In fairness to Brontë, some literary critics *do* view *Wuthering Heights* as a kind of romance. The venerable critic Harold Bloom writes that the Catherine-Heathcliff pairing is Gnostic, deriving from the ancient beliefs in shunning the material world and embracing the spiritual:

> These extraordinary vitalists, Catherine and Heathcliff, do not desire in one another that which each does not possess, do not lean themselves against one another, and do not even find and thus augment their own selves. They *are* one another, which is neither sane nor possible, and which does not support any doctrine of liberation whatsoever. Only that most extreme of visions, Gnosticism, could accommodate them, for, like the Gnostic adepts, Catherine and Heathcliff can only enter the *pleroma* or fullness together, as presumably they have done after Heathcliff's self-induced death by starvation.

To this I say: yeah, right.)

The story isn't so much a great romance as a parable about domestic abuse. And the Scottish dialect is often nigh-unreadable.

But modern readers must wave those objections aside—as critic Daniel Burt writes, the novel "resists conventional moral judgment"—and bow to *Wuthering Heights*, which is simply one of the technically best novels ever written.

It's no surprise, in retrospect, that the early Victorians were unable to treat *Wuthering Heights* as the masterpiece it is. They had no experience with novels with such a complex narrative structure. The novel is not told in a linear fashion, but is broken up into segments, some of which are flashbacks and some of which are flash-forwards, and some of which are stories-told-within-stories—an arrangement utterly foreign to the Victorian readerly and critical mindset, and one which they objected strenuously to, and felt was one of the novel's weaknesses. (We know better now, of course, and properly see it as one of the novel's strengths, and the product of a singularly talented writer.)

The Victorians were used to novels with large casts of characters, but Brontë created a cast of moderate size which was nonetheless complexly interrelated, enough to bring confusion to the reader. Even modern readers lose track of who is related to who, and how—*Wuthering Heights*' Wikipedia entry has a useful "relationship map" which charts characters' relationship to each other.

Neither did the Victorians have any experience with the idea of the unreliable narrator—the concept that the person who narrates a story is not the omniscient, infallible, always truthful being of third-person narration, but a person like any other, with blind spots, opinions, prejudices, and limits to his or her intelligence, and who makes mistakes. *Wuthering Heights* has two unreliable narrators, Lockwood, whose early perception of Heathcliff and Cathy Linton are later proven to be grossly in error, and Nelly Dean, who is the main narrator for most of the novel and who provides her perspective on events, some of which she did not see and only heard about.

The unreliability of the narrators ties in to another aspect of *Wuthering Heights* which the Victorians were not prepared for: its radical incompleteness. There are gaps in the novel, elisions, and puzzles which were undoubtedly deliberately placed there by Brontë, and which have led readers and critics to seek closure where there is none to be had: who is Heathcliff's father? Where did Heathcliff disappear to for three years? Did Heathcliff and Catherine consummate their relationship? And so on. This narrative strategy, something common in the 21st century and used in popular culture to draw readers and viewers in to a fictional universe—part of the attraction of the original *Star Trek* to viewers was that it had similar gaps and elisions—was wholly new to the Victorians.

These aspects in turn lead to another quality of *Wuthering Heights* which the Victorians were not prepared for: its genre-busting. *Wuthering Heights* appeared the year after *Jane Eyre*, which revived interest in the **Gothic** genre, but *Wuthering Heights*, despite having numerous Gothic elements, including Heathcliff as an archetypal Gothic Hero-Villain, is far too complex to be classified as merely a Gothic novel. Nor is *Wuthering Heights* a domestic novel— the most dominant fictional type of the first half of the 19th century, domestic fiction is about the story of a young women winning her way in the world, and was associated with civilization, cultivation, and the feminine. As critic Emily Rena-Dozier puts it, "*Wuthering Heights* … carefully breaks down (the) opposition between gothic and domestic modes by illustrating the ways in which the domestic is predicated on acts of violence." *Wuthering Heights* was *sui generis*, as radically surpassing the limits of genre as Charles Maturin's Gothic masterpiece *Melmoth the Wanderer* (1820) and Herman Melville's **Moby Dick** (1851) did.

The sheer intensity of *Wuthering Heights* was also, in its way, a radical departure from English letters. The domestic novel has emotion in it, as does the Gothic and the historical novel, but the primal emotions and the depth of the passions of Heathcliff and Catherine instead recall the heights of Romantic poetry and novels of Sensibility. Emotions run rampant and uncontrolled, and uncontrollable, in *Wuthering Heights*—so much so that the landscape and the heavens themselves reflect them, in what was called by T.S. Eliot the "objective correlative." The symbolism of nature and weather is heavy and strong in the novel.

Modern readers are of course curious about the novel's sexuality and that of its characters. Brontë could not include or even adequately express sexuality in the novel, at least not in terms that her contemporaries would accept, so she expressed it through nature, the weather, and through the symbolic behavior of her characters—behavior, like Heathcliff's violence, which shocked Brontë's readers. (But although Brontë could not express Heathcliff's and Catherine's carnality, there are nonetheless references to sex in the novel, something remarkable given the period in which *Wuthering Heights* was published.)

Brontë's readers were appalled as well at Brontë's dark view of human nature, at the novel's attacks on religion and the religious, at her willingness to flout genre conventions (like the idea of a happy romantic ending for a protagonist), at the novel having been written by a woman (something which many Victorians refused to believe), at the novel's supernatural elements—at the novel's *everything*. Victorian readers entered the novel apparently expecting something both realistic and conventional, and instead got a novel whose realness lies in elements the Victorians didn't welcome: in the novel's language (so much more direct, unfeigned, and full of curses than a Victorian novel had been, but which were close to what Victorians actually experienced in real life), in the physical and emotional violence of the characters, in the focus on id over super-ego (much like the work of Brontë's sister Charlotte).

The prose is lyrical. The characterization is strong (albeit it is characterization of characters we are well glad to be rid of, once the novel is over). The novel's vision is unique. The drama is, in Joyce Carol Oates' phrasing, "operatic." The story allows for numerous interpretations, from feminist to Marxist (Heathcliff as the working class revenging itself on the oppressor bourgeois). The competing voices and perspectives are acutely drawn. Influenced by the Romantics and the Gothics, but rising high above its influences, *Wuthering Heights* is a masterpiece.

Recommended Edition

Brontë, Emily. *Wuthering Heights* (Oxford University Press, 1995).

For Further Research

Burt, Daniel S. "Wuthering Heights." *The Novel 100: A Ranking of the Most Influential Novels of All Time* (Checkmark Books, 2010)

"Emily Brontë." http://www.victorianweb.org/authors/bronte/ebronte/index.html.

Oates, Joyce Carol. "Introduction." *Wuthering Heights* (Oxford University Press, 1999).
McCrum, Robert. "The 100 Best Novels: No. 13—*Wuthering Heights*." http://www.theguardian.com/books/2013/dec/16/emily bronte wuthering heights 100 best.
Rena-Dozier, Emily. "Gothic Criticisms: *Wuthering Heights* and Nineteenth-Century Literary History." *ELH* v77n3 (Fall 2010).
Stoneman, Patsy. "Introduction." *Wuthering Heights* (Oxford University Press, 1995).
Sweets, Sparky. "Wuthering Heights—Book Summary & Analysis." https://www.youtube.com/watch?v=2mt3sIWwUSw.

Appendix: Concepts

Victorian literature, like Victorian culture itself, is full of underpinning concepts and tropes and motifs—ideas and trends which provide a foundation for the literature. Entire books can and have been written explicating these concepts, and I don't propose to attempt to duplicate those books' efforts here. However, there are four concepts—the Gothic, the New Woman, Romanticism, and the Sensation Novel—which were so common in the Victorian era, or so influential upon it, that some sort of definition of them was demanded here. As with the novel entries, the following concept entries are not intended to be the last word on the subject, but instead to be enough of an introduction to each that the reader of this book will understand why they are relevant to Victorian literature and the novels included in this book.

The Gothic. The use of the word "Gothic" to describe the literature of terror and horror of the late 18th and early 19th century is a modern innovation. For the writers of the Gothic novels the word "Gothic" meant something medieval, something obsolete and outdated, and did not refer to literature at all. The term was rarely used by writers during the genre's heyday, but because Horace Walpole had given his novel the full title of *The Castle of Otranto. A Gothic Story* the term was eventually attached to the genre as a whole.

The history of the Gothic genre begins with Walpole's novel, in 1764. A few novels written in the 1750s have substantial Gothic elements, but *Otranto* is the first true Gothic novel, and it provided a blueprint for the genre. But although there were a number of imitations, especially in women's periodicals, the reading audience's appreciation for the genre did not become a craze for it until the 1794 publication of Ann Radcliffe's *The Mysteries of Udolpho*. The publication two years later of M.G. Lewis' *The Monk* provided writers with the second of two models which would dominate the genre for decades: the Radcliffean, female-centered, rational Gothic, and the Lewisian, male-centered, supernatural Gothic. The Gothic novel was the dominant genre of the late 1790s and early 1800s, which were, in the words of David Punter, "were chaotic years in which domestic unrest and fears of invasion from abroad shaped political and cultural life, and the literary market was flooded with a mass of fiction which rejected direct engagement with the activities of contemporary life in favour of geographically and historically remote actions."

Production of the Gothic novel peaked around 1810. What followed were a decline in production, the occasional pointed satire (particularly in Jane Austen's 1818 *Northanger Abbey*), and a final late efflorescence in 1820, Charles Maturin's *Melmoth the Wanderer*. By 1830 the Gothic novel, as created by Horace Walpole, was dead, killed by the historical novel and changing literary tastes. The motifs and themes of the genre diffused through mainstream literature, in novels like **Wuthering Heights** and *Jane Eyre*, and appeared overtly in the **Sensation** novel, but novels specifically in the Gothic mode were few. There was a temporary revival in the 1830s following Harrison Ainsworth's imitation Gothic *Rookwood*, and a smaller one in the penny bloods of the 1840s, but it was not until the final decades of the century that the Gothic returned, reinterpreted for the *fin de siècle* by authors like Robert Louis Stevenson (in **Doctor Jekyll and Mr. Hyde**), Bram Stoker (**Dracula**), and Oscar Wilde (**The Picture of Dorian Grey**).

Many different elements fed into the creation of the Gothic: a rise in scholarly and popular interest in antiquity; an increasing awareness of Middle and Far Eastern cultures (leading to Arabesque Gothics) resulting from the rise in colonial trade; 18th century horror poetry; the rise in Jacobinism, the philosophy of the rights of the individual; the influence of the Burkean aesthetic of the sublime and the picturesque; sentimental literature and the Cult of Sensibility; a conservative Protestantism and nationalism reacting to developments on the Continent, including secret societies (real and rumored), Catholicism, and the movement for Catholic emancipation in England; the propaganda of the French Revolution; **Romanticism**, especially its defiance of authority (in the case of the Gothic, defiance of literary authority and convention), its reaction to neoclassic (1660–1798) rationalism and logic and what critic Mary Ellen Snodgrass calls "its unspeakable subtext, the avoidance of death and decay through an artificial aura of control of the unexpected"; and the German *Sturm und Drang*.

The influence of the Cult of Sensibility was particularly strong. The best example of the Sensibility and the sentimental genre is Henry Mackenzie's *The Man of Feeling* (1779), a novel of lachrymose excess whose titular character, Harley, is controlled by his emotions to the point that he is overwhelmed by the sufferings of other human beings and appears to die from joy alone. Harley's

Sensibility is benevolence, compassion, and crying at the slightest opportunity taken to extremes. The heroes of Sensibility live in a society of injustice and evil and embody the feelings which others lack, but the heroes of Sensibility do not allow their emotions to be governed by self-interest. While *The Man of Feeling* contains an implicit critique of Sensibility—Harley's uncontrollable emotions lead him to defeats, unnecessary self-denial, and an early death—the English who adopted Sensibility overlooked or ignored this criticism and stressed the superiority of emotions and emotional responses to logic and rational thought. Those who easily blushed, cried, and fainted in response to sad or happy art or situations were therefore thought to be particularly virtuous. Sensibility was common in the Gothics, both in the heroine's personality and in the inability or unwillingness of the Gothic's primary villain, the Hero-Villain, to resist his passions.

The German influence on the Gothics is also notable. The three dominant literary genres in Germany in the 18th century were the *Ritterroman*, the *Räuberroman*, and the *Schauerroman*. The *Ritterroman* ("knight novel") told stories of chivalry, the Middle Ages, and knights in armor, and gave the Gothic feudal settings, Catholic conspiracy, and encounters with the supernatural. The *Räuberroman* gave the Gothic the figure of the bandit lurking on the fringes of society.

But it was the *Schauerroman* ("shudder novel") which had the most influence on the English Gothic. The *Schauerroman*, which predated the English Gothic (though first translated into English in 1794) was a direct influence on the Gothics of supernatural excess and gore. The *Schauerromans* were Grand Guignol, a century earlier, in their plunge into bloodbaths and horrors; Thomas Carlyle called them "bowl and dagger" novels. Recurring motifs in the *schauerroman* included walking corpses, the appearance of Satan, Satanist secret societies, ghostly nuns, and bandits engaging in human sacrifice.

The German Gothic, especially the *colporteur* novels (a French word: those sold by wandering peddlers), is comparable to the *Kriminalgeschichte*; it preceded its English counterpart, developed apart from it, was popular in its homeland, and, in the case of the German Gothic, survived for decades longer. *Colporteur* Gothic novels remained popular until the end of the century, and stories about hangmen were particularly popular. The best-selling German novel of the 19th century was Victor von Falk's *Der Scharfrichter von Berlin*, a 3,000-page colporteur novel which fictionalized the life of Julius Krautz, the official executioner of Berlin. Among its many other Gothic-influenced Grand Guignol pleasures *Der Scharfrichter von Berlin* had insane asylums, parricides innocent women hanged, orgies, poisonings, grave robberies, espionage, child kidnaping, child murder, train crashes, the fall of a trapeze acrobat, and living people buried alive. *Der Scharfrichter* sold over one million copies from 1890–1892.

The Gothic quickly developed a set of stock devices, motifs, and settings which authors repeatedly drew upon. These included: ancient architecture, usually a castle, usually supposed to be haunted; inside the castle were trap-doors, deserted wings, darkened staircases, and paintings of great significance to the central mystery of the story; beneath the castle were dungeons and claustrophobic tunnels; weather operated either as omen or as the objective correlative of the protagonist or villain; messages were delivered in dreams; high-pitched emotions abounded, including swoons and fits. The supernatural terrifying was an accepted part of life; the clergy, nearly always Catholic, was corrupt; patriarchal figures were revealed to be tyrants; a device, from birthmark to miniature, was crucial in the resolution of the plot; and scenes take place in tombs and crypts. Innocent heroines were pursued by evil men intent on rape and/or murder, action took place at night and in remote, archaic locations, the past returns to haunt the present. Stereotypes from a limited range of characters were common. The common tone of the novel was of suspense, emotional, intellectual, and physical. Confrontation with the taboo, a form of the Romantic sublime. An opposition to realism. The pathetic fallacy, chiaroscuoro, and foreign exoticism. Hidden passageways, sliding panels, and trapdoors. Ominous sense impressions. Wild mysterious landscapes such as bleak moors and mountainous locales, all allegories of the main male protagonist. Enclosed, confined, claustrophobic spaces, such as tunnels and crypts. Men: inherited powers or status; were solitary and egocentric; were flawed with deep psychological problems; were obsessive; were the anti-hero who appeals yet repulses. Motifs transcended boundaries (barbaric/civilized, mortality/immortality, order/disorder, pleasure/pain); fear, foreboding, and tension to evoke pleasurable terror in reader; multiple narratives; Faust motif—forbidden knowledge or power; tension between scientific and supernatural; secrets; dreams, nightmares revealing unconscious mind; omens. Within the antiquated space are hidden some secrets from the past that haunt the characters. As Patrick Brantlinger writes, the Gothic "scattered its ingredients into various modes, among them aspects of the more realistic Victorian novel. Yet it also reasserted itself across the nineteenth century in flamboyant plays and scattered operas, short stories or fantastic tales for magazines and newspapers, 'sensation' novels for women and the literate working class, portions of poetry and painting, and substantial resurgences of full-fledged Gothic novels—all of which were satirized for their excesses." Gothic works to confound the distinctions between inside and outside, between dream and reality. Obsessive doubling between characters, scenarios, milieus and events. Containment often of women.

The Gothic story has provided fruitful ground for critics, who have traditionally attempted to divide it into binary/oppositional categories. The most common interpretation of the Gothic is that stories in the genre can be divided into "male" or female." (Though this judgment is often based on the sex of the writer, it is no postmodern critical gimmick: even during the 18th century the Gothic was thought of in sexual, gendered terms.) Many of the Gothics' writers were women, and the genre had a large female readership. During the mid–18th century the novel was thought of as the province of men, but the Gothic changed this perception, so that before the rise of the historical novel the novel was thought to have been feminized. But for many decades Gothics were classified as male or female, usually depending on the sex of the story's author. The female Gothic is a *Bildungsroman*, a coming-of-age story for the female protagonist, with Sensibility as a dominant concern and with a male authority figure as the story's villain. Conversely the male Gothic puts a male figure at the center of a story of social, sexual, and/or religious transgression and usually reduces the heroine to the status of object, to be sexually and physically threatened, rescued, and married. In the words of critic Mary Ellen Snodgrass, the male Gothic "often victimizes and graphically brutalizes heroines as a source of titilation and voyeuristic fascination. In contrast to the male preference for wantonness, the female Gothic reflects concern for the powerlessness and male domination of heroines within the rigid gender restrictions of society and church." Radcliffe's *The Mysteries of Udolpho* was one of the earliest and was the most influential of the female Gothics. Lewis' *The Monk* was a powerful response to *Udolpho* and is the quintessential male Gothic.

However, a simplistic classification of the Gothic into male-vs-female based on the sex of the author quickly breaks down. Radcliffe, responding to Lewis, wrote a male Gothic, *The Italian*, with Vincentio, the novel's protagonist, the subject of the coming-of-age. Other female writer wrote male Gothics while male writers wrote female Gothics. Although most female Gothics were written by women and most male Gothics were written by men, this was by no means a constant.

Another way of categorizing the Gothic was provided by Ann Radcliffe. The "terror" Gothic, usually the female Gothic, provides an elevating sensation ("expands the soul, and awakens the faculties to a high degree of life") and is based on physical fear, from physical threats to psychological terror. The "horror" Gothic (usually the male Gothic) provides dread, "contracts, freezes, and nearly annihilates" the intellect. The horror Gothic stresses motivations and the devastating consequences of acting on them.

A third categorizing scheme is the "external," socially-oriented Gothic versus the "internal," psychologically-oriented Gothic. The external Gothic is concerned with the home: the lineage and patrimony of the hero, his disinheritance by the villain, and the revelation of the hero's true identity and the restoration of his estate. In the external Gothic the home is defined by the male's possession of it (or the lack of same). External Gothics with female protagonists are love stories in which the lovers are separated and the home is damaged, and the resolution of the plot enables the lovers to come together in marriage and the home to be healed. The internal Gothic is about the male hero's rebellion and exile or flight from home, which assumes a negative (ruled by a patriarchal figure who cannot be unseated) or unreachable status.

For Further Research
"Conventions of the Gothic Genre." http://www.heckgrammar.co.uk/index.php?p=10727.
Nevins, Jess. *The Encyclopedia of Fantastic Victoriana* (Monkeybrain, 2004).
Punter, David. *A Companion to the Gothic* (Wiley-Blackwell, 2001). https://archive.org/details/a_companion_to_the_gothic.
The Literature of Terror (Longman, 1996).
Snodgrass, Mary Ellen. *Encyclopedia of Gothic Literature* (Facts on File, 2005).

The New Woman. While the term "feminism," in the sense of advocacy of the rights of women, did not come into use in Britain until the mid–1890s, feminism and "The Woman Question," the question of the nature of women and their role in society, had been debated in Britain since at least the end of the 18th century. Mary Wollstonecraft's *Vindication of the Rights of Woman* (1792) gained significant attention for its arguments on behalf of the rights of women to education, employment, and full citizenship. The first half of the 19th century saw an increasing amount of discussion about the need for radical changes in women's position in British society. In the 1820s and 1830s socialists, following the writings of the utopian socialist Robert Owen (1771–1858), argued that the only way to end the treatment of women as property in English society was to abolish private property. The 1832 Reform Act confirmed the disenfranchisement of women but also helped organize feminists, who began campaigning for female emancipation. By the early 1850s there was an organized feminist movement in England, thanks to the actions of middle-class female philanthropists and the writers for women's magazines, whose work stimulated a desire for change. In 1866 a petition of almost 1500 women's signatures was presented to Parliament demanding that suffrage reform be extended to women. By the late 1880s English feminists were focused primarily on women's suffrage, although activists worked on a number of other issues, and women's issues were an accepted if unwelcome part of the political landscape.

A number of factors aided English feminists. The social and economic position of women changed greatly in the 19th century, particularly in the latter half of the century. Huge numbers of women entered the workforce; in 1851 approximately 2.8 million women worked, a number that had risen to 4.75 million by 1901. Feminist campaigns for education reforms in the 1860s led to the establishment of girls' schools, mostly for middle- and upper-class girls, and the establishment of state-controlled primary schools, with attendance made compulsory in 1880. Women were first admitted to King's College, London, in 1847, with Bedford College for Women established in 1849, Girton College of Cambridge University enrolling women in 1869, and Owens College allowing women in 1871. Marriage law increasingly gave women rights which they had previously lacked; the Married Women's Property Acts of 1870 and 1882 gave married women the right to own their own property, and in 1884 the Matrimonial Causes Act widened the classification of male desertion of a wife and allowed for men who refused to return to their wives to be ordered to pay alimony.

All of these developments led to the creation of the "New Woman," a social and literary type who emerged in the 1880s. The term, coined by the writers Ouida (***Under Two Flags***) and Sarah Grand (***The Heavenly Twins***) in a pair of articles in the *North American Review* in 1894, entered common parlance in the mid-1890s and referred to a group of women who took many of the theoretical ideas of feminism and put them into practice as a lifestyle. The New Woman was usually (though not always) middle class and worked for a living, often at a job that until recently had been limited to men. She advocated self-fulfilment rather than self-sacrifice, and chose education and a career over marriage. (The phrase "Girton girl," which has thankfully fallen out of usage, was derisively used in the late Victorian and Edwardian years to refer to women who had completed their university courses.) She spoke directly and was forthright about her political views, arguing publicly for the destruction of class distinctions and for economic independence for women. She smoked and drank openly. She decried restrictive fashions, rejecting petticoats and corsets and instead wearing "rational" (usually men's) clothing. She exercised and played sports, especially bicycling, which moved from an eccentricity to a fashionable activity in the space of three months in 1895. And, most alarming to the critics of the New Woman, she was sexually active, or at least advocated sexual freedom, and avoided marriage, seeing it as a trap designed to rob women of their independence.

This goes against the popular stereotype of the Victorians as sexually and emotionally repressed, but the truth is that at the end of the 19th century women in England were presented with a variety of role models to emulate. Clerical, medical, sociological, literary and political spokesmen, all the mouthpieces of high culture, stressed the sanctity of marriage, family, duty, chastity, feminine modesty, and other attributes that we today think of as stereotypically Victorian. But there were a varied number and type of female figures, from writers to journalists to activists to explorers, on which women could and did model themselves, and some of these women were notable New Women. There were, of course, the Mrs. Grundys, the morally upright, prudish figures of the popular imagination, of whom Queen Victoria might be seen as the exemplar. But there were others who were not so confined to the morality of the upper classes and who not only acted independently but flaunted their unconventional lifestyle and were praised for it rather than scorned. These women, whether or not they were open advocates for the ideas of the New Woman, lived their lives as if they were one.

The New Woman appeared in literature as well: over one hundred New Women novels were written between 1883 and 1900. Most of these novels were domestic dramas, like Olive Schreiner's *Story of an African Farm* (1883), Sarah Grand's *Heavenly Twins* (1893), Mona Caird's *Daughters of Danaus* (1894), and Grant Allen's *The Woman Who Did* (1895), the latter being the most notorious of the New Woman novels. But some New Women, or female characters with the attributes of New Women, appeared in positive roles in adventure and detective fiction, either as the heroines of the stories or as female love interests who were more independent and less subservient than was the norm. In this they differed from the heroines of the **Gothic** novels, who were for the most part helpless and dependent on others. The Gothic heroines appeared before organized feminism in Britain, while the female detectives and adventuresses had the benefit of a coherent feminist philosophy and movement.

New Woman fiction was often overtly didactic, determined to confront the reader with the problems of modern women. The aggressive nature of much New Woman literature brought about an inevitable backlash from the press, which used it to create an easy stereotype with which to criticize the New Woman, and from conservative critics, who saw New Woman literature as socially and sexually irresponsible. Although the heroines of many New Woman novels were socially above reproach and were more concerned with sexual autonomy and a freedom from male sexual predation, critics seized on and generalized about the New Woman as a group based a few examples of New Woman protagonists who were hostile to men, in favor of free love, or were opposed to motherhood.

One popular genre for the New Woman was the mystery. The figure of the detective in mystery literature in the 1890s was particularly well suited to the New Woman. By the mid–1890s the influence of Sherlock Holmes had grown to the point where nearly all mystery writers were creating characters based on him. The Great Detective character is financially and socially independent, extremely intelligent, and unconcerned with romantic relationships. The protagonists of New Woman novels generally shared those attributes, although the ideology of the New Woman writers (and the assumptions of the reading audience) often required that the New Woman protagonist become involved in some form of relationship. Like New Women, Great Detectives were products of the 1890s, modern men whose characters and habits would not have been possible in previous decades. The first of the New Woman Great Detectives was C.L. Pirkis' Loveday Brooke, and by the end of the century there were several more just like her.

The reaction in literature to the New Woman was mostly negative. For many middle and upper-class Victorian men, women were the guardians of civilization and English culture's higher values. For the New Woman to strive for more than a role as wife and mother was deeply threatening to conservative moralists. Most troubling was the New Woman's efforts to replace the conservative conception of sexuality, as something only men enjoyed, with newer one which allowed women to not only initiate sex but also to enjoy it. Victorian men of all classes knew that women did enjoy sex—the diaries and letters of Victorian men and women are often revelatory on this subject—but literature which espoused this view shocked moralists. That most New Woman literature was more concerned with the social and legal power structure of Victorian society, and used sex as a microcosm for it, and further portrayed the New Woman as the opposite of the Fatal Woman, was ignored by the moralists, who saw New Woman writers as aligning themselves with the forces of anarchy and as a danger to society. These moralists, both male and female, responded to New Woman fiction with stories and novels opposing the New Woman and portraying her as coming to bad ends. The New Woman was aligned with other troubling developments of the 1890s—see the *fin de siècle* unease passage in the **Pelham** entry below—and seen as the greatest danger to the English status quo.

For Further Research

Diniejko, Dr. Andrzej. "The New Woman Fiction." http://www.victorianweb.org/gender/diniejko1.html.

Ledger, Sally. *The New Woman: Fiction and Feminism at the Fin de Siècle* (Manchester University Press, 1997).

Nielsen, Danielle. "The Dangerous New Woman in the Victorian Press: 'blind alike to maiden modesty and maternal dignity.'" http://www.oscholars.com/Latchkey/Latchkey4/essay/Nielsen.htm.

Richardson, Angelique, and Chris Willis, eds. *The New Woman in Fiction and Fact; Fin-de-Siècle Feminisms* (Palgrave, 2002).

Romanticism. Historically Romanticism was an artistic and philosophical movement of the mid-to-late 18th century and the early 19th century. The years vary from country to country. In Great Britain, the period is usually defined as running from 1760 to 1832, the year of the passing of the Reform Act, which greatly extended the democratic rights of men to vote. In France, the Romantic period is 1802–1856, while in Germany the period is only 1801–1822. But by the 1850s Romanticism was dead in all places, although individual elements continued to live on.

Romanticism was a reaction to Classicism and the Enlightenment, but as a movement it was nebulous. There was no school of romanticism, no coordinated international movement, no figurehead. Romanticism was considerably more amorphous than well-defined. So in speaking of its background, its elements, and what it was reacting to, I'm perforce trying to be specific about things that were neither specific nor aligned to begin with. Indeed, as Marilyn Butler noted, it's doubtful whether writers of the time would have felt they belonged to the same movement: "some Romantic writers were fired by opposition to the rationalism of the Enlightenment, some by the ideals of the French Revolution, others by admiration for 'sublime' natural phenomena—mountains, rivers, storms—and still others by the mysteries of Orientalism and the East."

The movement preceding Romanticism was Classicism, a movement in which ancient Greece and Rome were held up as models to be emulated, being the supposed incarnations of humanism and reason and the wellsprings of civilization. As Harltey S. Spatt writes in Dabundo's *Encyclopedia of Romanticism*,

> the influence of Greek and Roman models on Romantic writers was paradoxical. Classicism was linked to the heavy hand of 18th-century prescriptivism; its appeal to absolute, rational judgment and its claims to be the universal and the permanent were antithetical to Romantic relativism and intuition. Yet, at the same time, the purity of its forms served as the perfect backdrop for Romantic investigations of impure, unpredictable human emotion. Thus, even as they rejected the spirit of Classicism, the Romantics embraced its incarnation....

To Classicists and intellectuals of the 18th century, Greece "symbolized purity and tranquility, an ideal Arcadian state of existence which had been lost to successive occupations," a civilization based upon humanism and reason above all else.

Romanticism was a reaction against this. It called into question the basic principles of Classicism and became, in Francis Claudon's words, the "driving force of spiritual life, philosophy, the arts, society and mores, and the social and political revolutions of the time." This book is most interested in literary Romanticism, so it is that that I will be spending most of my attention on.

The critic M.H. Abrams noted five critical principles of Romantic poetry, which is a good place to start: poetry is a representation of the inner feelings of the author, not an imitation of life; poetry should be spontaneous, free from traditional poetic rules and effects; a reverence for nature, especially nature "unsullied" by man; the elevation of the humble and rustic life; the sense of a supernatural dimension, the land of dreams.

Romanticism was intimately involved in the past. Called "romanticism" because it took its freedoms—freedom from rules, freedom to act—from the old romances, Romanticism was tied up with a sense of time's passing, in the love of (and the finding of poetic inspiration in) ruins and antiquity, especially inspired by the discovery in 1755 of Pompeii and Herculaneum.

Paradoxically, however, Romanticism was seen as the movement of the present. The established political systems were seen as corrupt and fading—revolution was what was called for, metaphysically as well as socially and politically, of themes, sentiments, and of national liberation. Romanticism was tied in with the revolutionary movements of the era, the French Revolution and the Industrial Revolution, with the dissatisfaction of the individual with "established power structures" and the individual's yearning for change. These revolutions were wholly new, and did not have classical examples which they could be compared to or which could be looked to for inspirations or judgment. In politics as well as in literature, the revolution of freedom versus authority and freedom and individualism versus tradition took place.

This desire for revolution was also a desire for a new place, an ideal place, untouched by the past and free from tyranny—in painting, landscape paintings of notable melancholy, but in literature and politics, a desire for the new, the exotic (Spain, Greece, the Orient), and the unexplored (the Americas). This desire for the exotic was attached to a desire for revolt, so that Hellenism and other national struggles became identified with and a part of Romanticism, as well as national literatures like folklore.

The Romantic not only yearned for new places, but wanted himself to be new and pristine, untouched by previous tyrannies. He—and it was usually he, women were objects rather than subjects to the Romantic—refused to be a successor to tradition, something unlike his Classical or Renaissance predecessors. The outsider became the Romantic, and vice-versa, and outsiders of previous eras were adopted by Romantics as predecessors to the movement.

The feeling that the times the Romantic were living in was revolutionary was widespread, as was the notion that these times would be seen by later generations as new and out of the ordinary. Democratism was new. So, too, was what the novel became, suddenly seen as a political form with which to attack the affects of aristocratic literature. Before 1814, when **Waverley** was published, the novel was seen as the lowest literary form, one read by women rather than men, with the female *Bildungsroman* (a coming-of-age novel in which the quest for marriage and stability is foremost) with the predominant plot. But thanks to Sir Walter Scott and *Waverley*—as well as to changes in book publishing and the huge expansion in the reading public during the Romantic era—the novel became seen not just as something not everyone could write (unlike during the 18th century), but as a particularly male form of literature, one with a heightened social and literary status, a role to play (in the form of moral instruction of young men), and a new origin and history. The novel was no longer a part of aristocratic literature, it was now about ordinary humans and their day-to-day lives, as well as the state of society.

The writer of novels, too, became something special. He (and rarely she) became a political partisan, unlike the a-political or conservative writers of the previous century. He was supposed to be an isolated genius, a poet at odds with coarse, materialistic society and belonging to two worlds, the material world and the world of the soul and dreams. The latter world had to be evoked by poetry and myths and by manipulating the unconscious. The world of dreams was a magical world, a secondary world that art made reference to and which became a place for Romantics to escape to. Dreams became vitally important, with unconsciousness being the necessity for the revelations of art.

This unreal world was a feminine one, and women became worshiped and praised above everything else. A mythology of Woman developed, and their passions and suffering were explored through art. Love became a major theme, and the rights of lovers, rather than the duties of lovers, also became a major theme. Women became thought of as angels, and love as something which trumped logic.

But Woman became seen as the cause of pain—the concept of the *femme fatale* first began during the Romantic age. There were other negative aspects of the Romantic era. Personal revolution and the desire for the new became the French *mal du siècle* and the German *Weltschmertz* and English dandyism, disenchantment, and world weariness. The fall of Rome and the death of what was beautiful in Classicism engendered an almost hatred of life itself and an obsession with the unspeakable. What Mario Praz called "Black Romanticism," a fascination with the abominable, manifested itself in the confusion of pleasure and pain and beauty and horror. Satan, monsters, demons and witches appear. For some critics of Romanticism, what was Classical was healthy and clean, and what was Romantic was unhealthy and soiled.

For Further Research:

Claudon, Francis. *The Concise Encyclopedia of Romanticism* (Chartwell Books, 1980).
Maunder, Andrew. *Encyclopedia of Literary Romanticism* (Facts on File, 2010).
McCalman, Iain, ed. *An Oxford Companion to the Romantic Age: British Culture 1776–1832* (Oxford University Press, 1999).
"Romanticism: an Overview" http://www.victorianweb.org/previctorian/misc/romanticov.html.

The Sensation Novel. Sensation fiction was a popular genre of English fiction during the 1850s and 1860s. The 1850s has been seen as the "age of equipoise," the decade of rapid economic growth and gradual calming of labor relations. This changed in the 1860s, beginning with the "cotton famine" (1861–

1864), a drastic rise in the price of cotton due to the Union embargo of the Confederacy during the American Civil War. The cotton famine hit the English textile industry particularly hard, and the depression spread to the general economy in mid decade, with bad harvests in 1865 and 1866 and the bankruptcies of Overend and Gurney, two of London's most powerful financial houses. There were outbreaks of cholera and the bubonic plague in Bristol, London, and Liverpool in 1866 and an increase in activity by the Fenian anarchists. Divorce cases became big, salacious news following the new divorce courts, the result of the Matrimonial Causes Act of 1857.

This was the historical backdrop for the rise of the sensation genre, which began in the 1850s but reached its peak popularity in the 1860s. (The roots of the sensation genre have been traced as far back as the late 1830s, with Charles Dickens' *Oliver Twist* [1838]). The calm of the previous decade had been replaced with economic uncertainty, and while parts of the middle and upper classes were benefitting from booming portions of the economy, other members of the middle and upper classes faced anxiety about their future. One of the most popular literary genres of the 1850s had been the domestic novel, but as sensation novel writer Charles Reade noted, "domestic is Latin for tame," and readers displayed an appetite for wilder fare. Finally, the 1860s were a time when the literary marketplace grew hugely commercialized and magazines were serializing novel, creating a new demand for fast, exciting writing.

Sensation novels were the reaction of writers to their times. The economic uncertainty of the middle and upper classes was transformed into stories focusing on the security of the bourgeois family. Mid century debates about feminism and the role of women became women written stories about women departing from traditional female roles. Concerns about class, race, and empire became fodder for both radical and conservative commentary. The sensation novelists reacted against the resolute placidity of the domestic novel by writing novels of crime and passion. And the novelists took advantage of the new market for popular (that is, not "serious") fiction by writing novels for that market.

The basic plot of the sensation novel is a threat posed to a middle class family. The threat is a secret, usually from the family's past, and what is threatened is the family's legal freedom, money, and ultimately its status as members of the middle class. This was the central theme of the sensation novel: class anxiety and insecurity, whether about the sanctity of the family or the stability of marriage and individual identity. The family's ancestors or older members are gentry or aristocrats, but they are immoral or incompetent and no longer have any social power. The specific threats to the family include murder, violence, bigamy, adultery, the loss of a family fortune or legacy, impersonators, adventuresses set on using marriage for financial gain, and social humiliation and rejection—the sensational elements which gave the genre its name. What saves the family is the appearance of young professionals, usually lawyers and doctors, who foil the threats, defeat the villains, and prove themselves as the replacement for the old aristocracy.

Influenced by the rise in yellow journalism and in melodramatic theater, the earliest sensation novels appear in the early 1850s, particularly the early work of Wilkie Collins (*Basil*, 1852), but the genre became fantastically popular early in the 1860s, with Collins' **The Woman in White** generally accounted as the first best selling sensation novel. (Notably, however, the term "sensation fiction" was already in critical use by the time *The Woman in White* was published.) Other popular sensation novels include Mrs. Henry Wood's **East Lynne** (1860 1861), M.E. Braddon's **Lady Audley's Secret** (1861) and *Aurora Floyd* (1863), Charles Reade's *Hard Cash* (1863), and Wilkie Collins' *Armadale* (1864 1866) and **The Moonstone** (1868).

The sensation novels were popular, but they were critically scorned and condemned. Sensation novels were alleged to be immoral, badly written, inherently scandalous, and socially dangerous. Critics were dismayed that the public's appetite was not for elevating or purifying fiction, but instead for something base and immoral. Critics charged that they appealed to the emotions rather than to the mind and so corrupted rather than elevated; the question was asked in 1863 whether "the pleasure of a nervous shock is worth the cost of so much morbid anatomy."

This charge was a repeat of the criticism leveled at the "male" **Gothic** novel, and in several ways the sensation novel was the modern Gothic. (Although of course the sensation novel took elements from other genres, including melodrama, romance, and realist fiction.) The sensation novelists used several aspects and motifs of the Gothic in their novels, including melodramatic plots, heightened emotion, characters faking their own deaths, false endings, and an emphasis on scandalous material. But the Gothic novel was set in a nebulous past and in remote cultures, while the sensation novel was set in the present and its characters modern. Above all, the sensation novel was topical, the writers seizing on contemporary scandals and controversies and incorporating them into their novels' plots.

Critics were not pleased at the use of the journalist sensations *du jour*. The more literary minded critics objected to sensation novels' plot driven stories, rather than the character driven stories of realist and domestic fiction. But what particularly appalled the critics and reviewers was the sensation novelists' subject matter. Wilkie Collins' second novel, *Basil* (1852), is an early version of the sensation novel, and includes a scene in which a husband hears through a hotel wall his fiancée having sex with another man. *East Lynne* features an adulteress as the main character. The protagonists of *Lady Audley's Secret* and *Armadale* are bigamists and would be murderers. Other sensation novels included sexual assaults and scenes in insane asylums and thinly veiled homoerotic relationships (of both sexes).

That this material should appear in popular fiction was bad enough. That women should often be not only the villains of sensation fiction but the protagonists, performing the acts traditionally left to men and operating in the spheres of men—compared especially to the weak, confused, and vacillating male characters of sensation novels—added to the critics' horror. (So did the prominence of women writers of sensation fiction, and what essentially was a recurring theme of women objecting to their traditional roles as daughters, wives, and mothers.) The moral ambiguity of the sensation novels and their knowingness, compared to the relative innocence of melodrama, was seen as appalling. Middle class women were thought to be the main readers of the sensation novel, adding to critics' horror—"making the literature of the kitchen the favorite reading of the drawing room." (The reality of course was that sensation fiction was popular across classes.) Completing the revulsion of the critics and reviewers, and thrilling the reader, was the presence of these crimes in middle class settings.

Gothic novels were remote in time and space. Newgate novels (see **Pelham**) were urban and focused on lower class criminals. The sensation novel happened in ordinary cities and towns, to ordinary middle class men and women. The most popular crime genre of the previous decade, the casebook genre, had portrayed crime as a working class affair, its criminals and its victims the poor and the working classes. The sensation novel, made crime a middle class affair, which the critics and reviewers (though not the audience) found objectionable both morally and on class grounds.

Throughout the 1850s and into 1860 the domestic novel was the most popular form, and realism seemed to be the novel's future, but following *The Woman in White* authors like George Eliot (**Middlemarch**), and Mrs. Gaskell (**Mary Barton, North and South**), leaders in domestic and realist fiction, were suddenly seen as past their prime, and throughout the 1860s the sensation novel battled the realist novel for dominance. But the decline in Wilkie Collins' health, the refusal of the major lending libraries to carry scandalous novels, and the reading audience's desire for less sensationalist and subversive material led to the practical end of the sensation genre in the early 1870s, although the genre can be said to have lingered on in various forms into the 1890s. Its conventions reappeared in the work of authors like Thomas Hardy (**Jude the Obscure, Tess of the d'Urbervilles**), while the crime elements would appear in both mainstream fiction and in mystery novels.

For Further Research

Brantlinger, Patrick. "What Is 'Sensational' about the 'Sensation Novel'?" *Nineteenth-Century Fiction* v37n1 (June 1982).

Gilbert, Pamela. *A Companion to Sensation Fiction* (Wiley-Blackwell, 2011).

Harrison, Kimberly, and Richard Fantina. *Victorian Sensations: Essays on a Scandalous Genre* (Ohio State University Press, 2006).

Pykett, Lynn. *The Sensation Novel* (Northcote House, 1994).

"Sensation." *In Our Time*. http://www.bbc.co.uk/programmes/p005492t.

Index

Adam Bede 130
Aesthetic movement 124, 169
Ainsworth, Harrison 81, 246
Alcott, Louisa May 70, 108–114
Allen, Grant 252
Anarchy novel 76
The Ancient Mariner 60
Anti-Semitism 78, 220, 226, 233
À Rebours 170
Armadale 258, 259
L'Assommoir 5–9, 11, 149, 150
Aurora Floyd 258
Austen, Jane 10, 51–57, 82, 101, 109, 138, 139, 158, 167, 173, 175–181, 202, 226, 246

Balzac, Honoré de *see* de Balzac, Honore
Barchester Towers 9–12, 232
Barnaby Rudge 25
Barry Lyndon 10, 13–15
Basil 258
Baudelaire, Charles 134, 186
Beau Geste 219
Beerbohm, Max 49
Belloc, Hillaire 78
Ben Hur 101
Beyle, Marie-Henri *see* Stendhal
Bildungsroman 22, 26, 27, 51, 55, 61, 64, 87, 109, 124, 157, 161, 166, 172, 173, 249; female *Bildungsoman* 80, 173, 255; male *Bildungsroman* 22, 124
Blackmore, R.D. 114–119
Bleak House 15–20, 26, 62, 67, 82, 99, 126, 141, 145, 189, 236, 237
Bluebeard 83
Braddon, Mary Elizabeth 96–99, 199, 258
Brodie, William 36

Brontë, Charlotte 78–84, 202, 239
Brontë, Emily 238–243
Brooke, Loveday 253
Brummel, Beau 160
Bucket, Inspector 99, 145, 238
Bulwer-Lytton, Lord 23, 49, 100–103, 159–163, 203, 218, 222, 224, 225
Bunyan, John 83, 109
Byron, Lord 57, 160

Caird, Mona 252
Carlyle, Thomas 12, 16, 156
Casebook mysteries 20, 99, 145, 237
Castle of Otranto 245
Catechism of a Revolutionary 76
The Caxtons 225
The Charterhouse of Parma 21–24
Chartist movement 126
Chesterton, G.K. 78
Childers, Erskine 95
Christie, Agatha 78
A Christmas Carol 224
Cinderella 83
Class and classism 46–47, 64, 74, 77, 81, 82, 87, 213, 220
Collins, Wilkie 20, 41, 97, 117, 143–148, 234–238, 258
Colporteur novels 247
The Coming Race 160
Conan Doyle, Arthur 20, 145, 236, 237, 238
"Condition of England" novel 12, 16–17, 26, 76–77, 126–127, 156
Conduct novel 110
Coningsby 12, 16, 23, 24–27, 126
Cooper, James Fenimore 93, 103–108, 164
Corelli, Marie 201–205
Count of Monte Cristo 28–32, 40, 73, 210

Crime and Punishment 178
Crossovers 166
Cuff, Sergeant 20, 237
Cult of Sensibility 6, 54, 110, 149, 153, 161, 199, 241–242, 246–247, 249
Cupid and Psyche 83, 124

Daniel Deronda 130
Darwin, Charles 37, 50, 149
Daughters of Danaus 252
David Copperfield 166
de Balzac, Honoré 6, 20, 22, 23, 109, 130, 131, 149, 153, 163–168, 169, 173, 181, 199, 200, 225
de Beauvoir, Simone 22
Decadent movement 124, 170, 186
Defoe, Daniel 14
de Sade, Marquis 77
de Staël, Madame 131
Detective novels and mysteries 20, 99, 136, 144–146, 160, 162, 166–167, 236–237, 252–253
Diana of the Crossways 32–34, 76
Dickens, Charles 11, 12, 13, 15–20, 25, 26, 49, 61–65, 67, 82, 126, 130, 131, 145, 156, 162, 166, 200, 223, 224, 233, 237, 238, 257
Disraeli, Benjamin 12, 16, 23, 24–27, 49, 76, 126, 156
Dr. Jekyll and Mr. Hyde 35–38, 87, 90, 170
Domestic fiction 110, 160, 161, 224–225, 240, 257, 259
Doppelgänger 38, 60
Dos Passos, John 41
Dostoevsky, Fyodor 177
Doubleday, Alfred 200
Dracula 39–43, 87
Dreiser, Theodore 165, 198–201
Dukes and Dejueners 224
Dumas, Alexandre, père 28–32, 208–211
Du Maurier, Daphne 81
Dupin, C. Auguste 20, 99, 145, 236, 237, 238

Eco, Umberto 30, 31
East Lynne 43–47, 258
The Egoist 33, 47–50
Eliot, George 33, 86, 120, 128–133, 138, 139, 173, 195–197, 223, 259
Eliot, T.S. 41, 78, 83, 145, 147, 164, 237, 241–242
Emma 10, 11, 51–57, 81, 109, 167, 178, 202
Evolution and natural selection 37–38, 50, 149, 212–213

Fantasy fiction 187, 191–192
Felix Holt 130

Feminism 49–50, 66–67, 80, 87, 112, 138, 177, 204, 222, 250–253
Fielding, Henry 11, 14, 225
Fin de siècle unease 8, 34, 42, 76, 88, 94, 151, 154, 174, 193, 253
Flaubert, Gustave 6, 92, 119–122, 123, 134, 149, 173, 184–188
Ford, John 95, 116
Fowles, John 36
Frankenstein 37, 40, 57–61
Frankenstein, Victor 38
Fraser, George MacDonald 14
French Foreign Legion novels 219
Frontier fiction 95, 104–105, 116

Gaboriau, Emile 166
Gaskell, Mrs. 12, 16, 26, 67, 76, 125–128, 155–159, 259
Gauthier, Theophile 41, 186
Georgian era 52
Gide, Andre 182
Gissing, George 6
Gnosticism 240
Godwin, William 57
Gothic 20, 27, 38, 40, 54, 55, 59, 60–61, 64, 73, 81–82, 87–88, 99, 102, 105, 142, 146, 169, 170, 189, 207, 228, 236, 237–238, 240, 245–250, 252, 258
Gothic hero-villain 31, 73, 82, 83, 102, 166, 190, 216, 240
Grand, Sarah 65–68, 251, 252
Great Expectations 61–65, 161
Gulliver's Travels 77
Guy Mannering 229

Haggard, H. Rider 35, 89, 191–195
Hard Cash 258
Hardy, Thomas 84–88, 165, 173, 205–208, 259
Hawthorne, Nathaniel 10, 61, 77, 188–190
Heavenly Twins 65–68, 252
Hemingway, Ernest 23, 70
Hetzel, Pierre Jules 216
Historical romances and novels 54, 64, 81, 101, 115–118, 124, 186–187, 228, 236
The History of the Life of the Late Mr. Jonathan Wild the Great 14
Holmes, Sherlock 20, 145, 167, 236, 237, 252
Homoerotics and homosexuality 27, 37, 42, 98, 111, 142, 165–166, 170, 222, 237
Huckleberry Finn 69–72, 93, 143, 174
Hugo, Victor 6, 7, 30, 72–75, 93, 123, 133–136, 167, 185–186
Hunchback of Notre Dame 72–75, 123, 135, 164, 166

Huxley, Aldous 18
Huysmans, Joris-Karl 170

Imperialism 14, 50, 83, 94, 147
Inspector Bucket 20
The Invisible Man 8, 34, 42, 75–78, 88, 151, 154, 174, 193
The Island of Doctor Moreau 77

James, Henry 10, 22, 33, 35, 45, 49, 89, 93, 123, 132, 133, 145, 150, 171–175, 218, 221
Jane Eyre 78–84, 97, 239, 240, 246
Jude the Obscure 84–88, 164, 173, 174, 208

Kidnapped 35, 89–91, 109, 117
Kim 92–96, 142
Kingsley, Charles 110
Kipling, Rudyard 92–96
Kunstmärchen 190

Lady Audley's Secret 44, 45, 96–99, 199, 258, 259
The Last Days of Pompeii 100–103, 160, 203
The Last Incarnation of Vautrin 166
The Last of the Mohicans 103–108
Lawrence, D.H. 86
Leaves of Grass 143
Les Misérables 6, 133–136, 142, 167
Lewis, M.G. 245, 249
Little Women 108–114
Lorna Doone 83, 95, 114–119, 208
Lovecraft, H.P. 87
Lucretia 162

Mackenzie, Henry 54
Madame Bovary 6, 119–122, 187
Mad scientist 60, 77
The Man of Feeling 54, 247
The Man Who Shot Liberty Valence 95, 116
Mansfield Park 52
Marius the Epicurean 101, 122–125
Mary Barton 12, 16, 26, 67, 125–128, 157
Mary Sue characters 26–27, 203–204, 220
Matrimonial Causes Act 46, 251, 257
Maturin, Charles 169, 241, 246
Melmoth the Wanderer 169, 241, 246
Melville, Herman 140–143, 241
Meredith, George 32–34, 44, 47–50
Middlemarch 8, 10, 120, 128–133, 141, 164, 173, 196, 224
The Mill on the Floss 130
Milton, John 60
Les Misérables 6, 133–136, 142, 167
Miss Marjoribanks 137–140
Moby Dick 140–143, 241
Modernism 41, 50, 124, 130, 173, 199

The Monk 245, 249
The Moonstone 20, 142, 143–148, 236, 258
Moriarty, Professor 238
"La Morte Amoureuse" 41
The Mysteries of Paris 29, 30, 136
The Mysteries of Udolpho 245, 249

Nabokov, Vladimir 18, 19
Nana 11, 16, 148–152
Naturalism 6–7, 11, 86, 120, 136, 149, 153, 164, 181, 198–200, 207
Nechaev, Sergei 76
Neo-classicism 52
New Grub Street 6, 8, 34, 42, 76, 88, 149, 151, 152–155, 174, 193
New Woman 34, 41, 65, 66, 87, 139, 174, 193, 204, 222, 250–253
Newgate novel 64, 99, 162, 224, 237, 259
North and South 12, 16, 26, 155–159
Northanger Abbey 55, 178, 246
Norton, Lady Caroline 33–34
Notre Dame de Paris 30, 185–186
La Nouvelle Justine 77
Novel of Manners 31

The Old Curiosity Shop 18
Oliphant, Mrs. 80, 97, 137–140
Oliver Twist 162, 224, 257
Orwell, George 154
Ouida 49, 65, 202, 218–223, 251
Owen, Robert 250

Pater, Walter 101, 122–125, 169–170
Paul Clifford 101
Pelham 23, 48, 159–163
Père Goriot 6, 20, 22, 64, 109, 130, 149, 153, 163–168, 173, 182, 183, 199, 225
Picaresque 14, 27, 70, 71, 95, 141, 225
The Pickwick Papers 224
The Picture of Dorian Grey 18, 168–171
Pilgrim's Progress 83, 109
Pirkis, C.L. 253
Poe, Edgar Allan 20, 99, 146, 236, 237, 238
Polidori, John 57
Political novel 25
The Portrait of a Lady 22, 93, 123, 171–175
Postmodernism 141, 170, 199
Pride and Prejudice 10, 31, 52, 53, 56, 79, 81, 101, 158, 173, 175–181, 202

Quartz, Doctor 238

Race and racism 27, 70, 83–84, 94, 105, 106, 107, 147, 194, 226
Radcliffe, Ann 245, 249
Räuberroman 247

Reade, Charles 258
Realism 6, 42, 120, 149, 153, 164–165, 199, 207, 259
Rebecca 81
The Red and the Black 21, 22, 23, 64, 181–184
Reform Act of 1832 130, 250, 256
The Regency 52, 161
Revenge tragedy 30–31
Revolution 50, 84
The Riddle of the Sands 94
Ritterroman 247
Robinson Crusoe 146
Rob Roy 228, 229, 230
Roman feuilleton 29, 73, 136, 209
Romanticism 6, 52, 59–60, 73, 81, 105, 116, 136, 145, 149, 153, 161, 165, 183, 199, 210, 216, 238, 240, 241–242, 246, 253–256
Rookwood 81, 246
Rosicrucians and Theosophists 102
Rymer, James Malcom 81

Salammbô 92, 120, 123, 184–188
Samson 83
Satan 60
Scarlet Letter 10, 188–190
Der Scharfrichter von Berlin 247
Schauerroman 247
School of Catastrophe 101
Schopenhauer, Arthur 87
Schreiner, Olive 252
Science fiction 58–59, 61, 77, 160, 215
Scott, Walter 74, 90, 101, 115, 164, 165, 210, 227–230, 255
The Searchers 95, 116
Sensation novel 20, 44, 45, 49, 62, 63, 97, 98, 99, 130, 144, 162, 197, 207, 221, 225, 235, 237, 246, 256–260
Sense and Sensibility 52, 178
Sentimental novel 110, 149, 153, 199
Sex 46, 66, 86, 87, 111–112, 147, 150–151, 173, 174, 175, 192–193, 242, 251–252, 253
Sexism and misogyny 41, 193
Shakespeare, William 83
She 8, 34, 42, 76, 88, 151, 154, 191–195
Shelley, Mary 37, 57–61
Shelley, Percy Bysshe 57
Silas Marner 130, 195–197
Silver Fork novel 34, 48, 101, 161–162, 221–222, 224
Sister Carrie 165, 198–201
Smart, Christopher 77
Smollett, Tobias 14
Sorrows of Satan 201–205
Star Trek 26, 203–204, 220, 240
Stendhal 21–24, 173, 181–184, 225

Stevenson, Robert Louis 35–38, 49, 89–91, 118, 170, 246
Stoker, Bram 39–43, 246
Story of an African Farm 252
A Strange Story 102
Studies in the History of the Renaissance 169
Sue, Eugène 29, 136, 210
Swift, Jonathan 77
Sybil 25
Symbolist movement 186

Tancred 25
"The Temple of Dulness" 77
Tess of the D'Urbervilles 87, 205–208
Thackeray, William Makepeace 10, 12, 13, 49, 130, 131, 223–227
The Three Musketeers 90, 208–211
The Time Machine 211–214
Tolstoy, Leo 23, 130, 133, 181, 226
Treasure Island 35, 89
Trollope, Anthony 9–12, 138, 230–234
Turgenev, Ivan 173
Twain, Mark 67, 69–72, 93, 105–106, 165, 229
Twenty Thousand Leagues Under the Sea 214–218

Under Two Flags 45, 202, 218–223
U.S.A. Trilogy 41

Vanity Fair 11, 13, 14, 83, 223–227
Van Rensselaer Dey, Frederic 238
Varney the Vampyre 81
Vautrin, Monsieur 20
Verne, Jules 166, 214–218
Vidocq, Eugène François 136, 166
Vindication of the Rights of Women 250
von Falk, Victor 247

Wallace, Lewis 101
Walpole, Horace 245, 246
The Wandering Jew 60
The Wandering Jew 29
War and Peace 130, 133, 226
War of the Worlds 215
"The Wasteland" 41
The Water Babies 110
Waverley 45, 101, 115, 227–230, 255
The Way We Live Now 230–234
Wells, H.G. 75–78, 211–214
The Wild Ass's Skin 169
Wilde, Oscar 18, 49, 124, 151, 168–170, 222, 246
Wollstonecraft, Mary 57, 250
The Woman in White 44, 45, 97, 145, 234–238, 258

The Woman Who Did 252
Wood, Ellen 43–47, 258
Wren, P.C. 219
Wuthering Heights 102, 202, 238–243, 246

Yellow Peril 41, 59, 194
Young England Movement 10, 25
Young England trilogy 25

Zanoni 102
Zola, Émile 5–9, 23, 120, 148–152, 153, 165, 181, 199

www.ingramcontent.com/pod-product-compliance
Ingram Content Group UK Ltd.
Pitfield, Milton Keynes, MK11 3LW, UK
UKHW041931140426
5217IPUK00014B/429